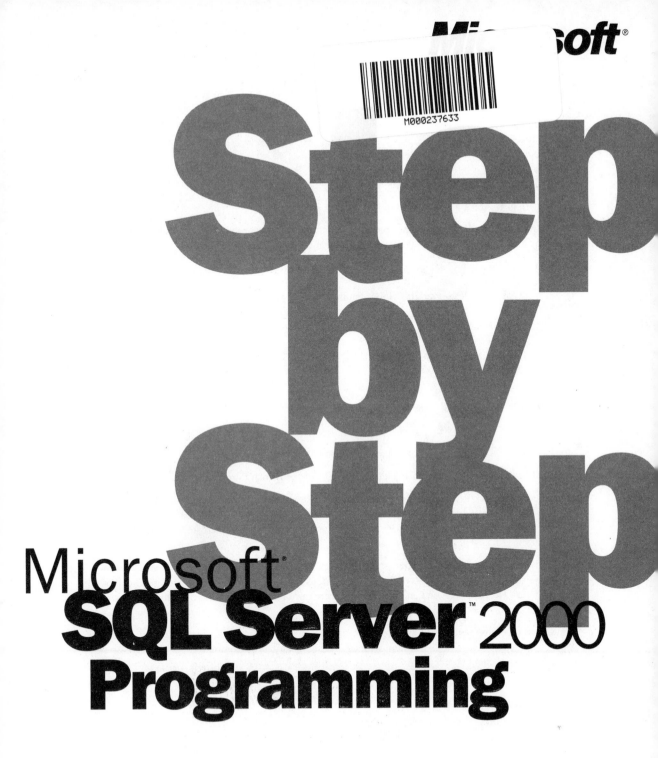

Microsoft®

M000237633

Step by Step

Microsoft® SQL Server™ 2000 Programming

Rebecca M. Riordan

PUBLISHED BY
Microsoft Press
A Division of Microsoft Corporation
One Microsoft Way
Redmond, Washington 98052-6399

Library of Congress Cataloging-in-Publication Data
Riordan, Rebecca.
    Microsoft SQL Server 2000 Programming Step by Step / Rebecca Riordan.
       p. cm.
    Includes index.
    ISBN 0-7356-1142-4
    1. Client/server computing. 2. SQL server. 3. Relational databases. I. Title.
QA76.9.C55 R57   2000
005.75'85--dc21   00-064748

Printed and bound in the United States of America.

1 2 3 4 5 6 7 8 9   QWE   8 7 6 5 4

Distributed in Canada by H.B. Fenn and Company Ltd.

A CIP catalogue record for this book is available from the British Library.

Microsoft Press books are available through booksellers and distributors worldwide. For further information about international editions, contact your local Microsoft Corporation office or contact Microsoft Press International directly at fax (425) 936-7329. Visit our Web site at www.microsoft.com/mspress. Send comments to *mspinput@microsoft.com.*

ActiveX, FoxPro, Microsoft, Microsoft Press, Visual Basic, Visual C++, Windows, and Windows NT are either registered trademarks or trademarks of Microsoft Corporation in the United States and/or other countries. Other product and company names mentioned herein may be the trademarks of their respective owners.

Unless otherwise noted, the example companies, organizations, products, people, and events depicted herein are fictitious. No association with any real company, organization, product, person, or event is intended or should be inferred.

Acquisitions Editor: David Clark
Project Editors: Alice Turner and Rebecca McKay
Manuscript Editors: Alice Turner and Denise Bankaitis
Technical Editors: Julie Xiao and Dail Magee, Jr.

To Alice Turner

TABLE OF CONTENTS

Introduction   xvii

PART **1**   **Getting Started with SQL Server**

Lesson **1**   **The SQL Server 2000 Environment**   **3**

Understanding the Enterprise Manager   4

    Starting the Enterprise Manager   5

Controlling SQL Server   6

    Registering a Server   7

    Starting and Stopping a Server   12

The Enterprise Manager Console Tree   13

The System Databases   14

Connecting to and Exiting a Database   16

    Database Objects   16

    Exiting the Enterprise Manager   17

Lesson **2**   **Administering SQL Server**   **19**

Backing Up and Restoring Databases   20

    Backing Up a Database   20

    Restoring a Database   29

    Using the Database Maintenance Plan Wizard   30

Lesson **3**   **SQL Server 2000 Security**   **41**

Understanding Security Modes   42

    Windows Authentication   42

    SQL Server Authentication   42

User Logins   43

    Creating User Logins   43

    Managing Logins   56

Database-Level Security   60

    Database Users   60

    Database Roles   63

PART 2   Creating Databases

Lesson 4	**Creating a Database**	**77**
	Creating Databases	77
	Creating a New Database	78
	Setting Database Properties	85
	Managing Databases	88
	Deleting a Database	88
Lesson 5	**Creating Tables**	**91**
	Creating Tables	92
	Understanding Data Types	93
	Creating a New Table	95
	Adding Columns to a Table	97
	Managing Tables	107
	Altering Columns	107
	Altering Tables	110
Lesson 6	**Creating Indexes**	**115**
	Understanding Indexes	116
	Creating Indexes	116
	Maintaining Indexes	131
	Altering Indexes	131
	Removing Indexes	135
Lesson 7	**Creating Relationships**	**139**
	Understanding Relationships	139
	Creating Relationships	142
	Managing Relationships	146
	Altering Relationships	146
	Maintaining Relationships	149

Lesson **8**   **Creating Check Constraints**   **157**

Understanding Check Constraints   157

    Creating Check Constraints   158

Managing Check Constraints   161

    Altering Check Constraints   161

    Maintaining Check Constraints   163

Lesson **9**   **Creating Table Objects**   **169**

Understanding Defaults   170

    Creating Defaults   170

Understanding Rules   176

    Creating Rules   176

Understanding User-Defined Data Types   181

    Creating User-Defined Data Types   182

Lesson **10**   **Creating Database Diagrams**   **187**

Understanding Database Diagrams   187

    Creating a Database Diagram from an Existing Schema   188

Using Database Diagrams to Maintain the Database   196

    Changing the Database Schema   196

    Creating Database Objects   198

PART **3**   **Retrieving Data**

Lesson **11**   **Retrieving Rows**   **207**

Using the Query Designer   208

    Viewing Rows in a Table   208

    Updating Rows in a Table   210

Understanding the SQL Server Query Designer   213

    The Diagram Pane   213

    The Grid Pane   214

    The SQL Pane   214

Lesson 12   **The SELECT Statement**   **217**

Understanding the SELECT Statement   218

     Selecting All Columns   218

     Selecting a Subset of Columns   220

     Creating Column Aliases   223

     Creating Calculated Columns   226

     Using the TOP *n* Clause   231

Lesson 13   **Sorting and Selecting Rows**   **235**

The ORDER BY Clause   236

     Sorting Rows   236

     Sorting by Multiple Columns   240

The WHERE Clause   245

     The Basic WHERE Clause   245

     Using Special Operators   248

     Combining Selection Criteria   252

Lesson 14   **Joining Tables**   **257**

Understanding the FROM Clause   258

Creating Joins   259

     Inner Joins   260

     Outer Joins   269

     Unions   277

Lesson 15   **Summarizing Data**   **281**

Understanding SELECT DISTINCT   282

     Using SELECT DISTINCT   282

Understanding GROUP BY   289

     Using GROUP BY   289

     Using the HAVING Clause   293

Lesson **16**	**Views**	**299**
	Understanding Views	299
	Creating Views	300
	Using Views	310
	Managing Views	317
	Altering Views	317
	Removing Views	320
PART **4**	**Working with Data**	
Lesson **17**	**Adding Rows**	**325**
	Understanding the INSERT Statement	326
	Using the INSERT statement	326
	Inserting Rows Using the Grid Pane	326
	Inserting Rows Using the SQL Pane	330
	Inserting Multiple Rows	335
Lesson **18**	**Updating Rows**	**345**
	Understanding the UPDATE Statement	345
	Using the UPDATE Statement	346
	Updating Rows Using the Grid Pane	346
	Updating Rows Using the SQL Pane	352
	Updating Rows Using the FROM Clause	355
Lesson **19**	**Deleting Rows**	**359**
	Understanding the DELETE Statement	360
	Using the DELETE Statement	361
	Deleting Rows Using the Grid and Diagram Panes	361
	Deleting Rows Using the SQL Pane	365
	Using the TRUNCATE TABLE Statement	372
	Deleting All Rows Using the TRUNCATE TABLE Statement	373

Lesson **20**	**Copying and Moving Data**	**377**
	The Data Transformation Services Wizards	377
	Using the DTS Import Wizard	378
	Using the DTS Export Wizard	388
	Attaching and Detaching Databases	396
	Detaching a Database	396
	Attaching a Database	397
	The Copy Database Wizard	399
	Using the Copy Database Wizard	399

PART **5**	**Transact-SQL**	
Lesson **21**	**The Query Analyzer**	**409**
	Understanding the Query Analyzer	410
	Starting the Query Analyzer	410
	Selecting a Database	413
	Using the Query Window	415
	Entering Transact-SQL Statements	416
	Using SQL Scripts	420
	Using the Object Browser	425
	Opening Objects	427
	Adding Objects to the Editor Pane	430
	Scripting Objects	434
Lesson **22**	**Data Definition Language**	**441**
	Understanding DDL	441
	Creating Objects	442
	Altering Objects	451
	Dropping Objects	459
	Using the Object Browser for Data Definition	463
	Scripting DDL	463
	Using Templates	465

Lesson **23**	**Analyzing Queries**	**471**
	Using the Query Analyzer to Optimize Performance	472
	Execution Plans	472
	Server Traces	479
	Client Statistics	480
	The Index Tuning Wizard	482
	Using the Index Tuning Wizard	482
Lesson **24**	**Transact-SQL Language Components**	**491**
	Transact-SQL Commands	492
	Data Manipulation Commands	494
	Data Definition Commands	494
	Database Administration Commands	495
	Other Commands	496
	Transact-SQL Operators	496
	Operator Precedence	496
	Comment Operators	497
	Arithmetic Operators	498
	Comparison Operators	501
	Logical Operators	503
	Bitwise Operators	505
	Other Operators	507
	Transact-SQL Functions	509
	Using Functions	510
	Date and Time Functions	510
	Mathematical Functions	513
	Aggregate Functions	516
	Metadata Functions	519
	Security Functions	521
	String Functions	523
	System Functions	526

Lesson **25**	**Programming Objects**	**529**
	Temporary Tables	530
	Understanding Temporary Tables	530
	Using Temporary Tables	531
	Variables	542
	Understanding Variables	542
	Using Variables	546
Lesson **26**	**Controlling Execution**	**553**
	Conditional Processing	554
	IF...ELSE	554
	CASE	557
	The GOTO Command	562
	Looping	564
	Simple WHILE loop	564
	Complex WHILE Loops	566
Lesson **27**	**Transact-SQL Cursors**	**571**
	Understanding Cursors	572
	Cursor Characteristics	573
	Cursor Types	574
	Using Cursors	576
	Creating Cursors	576
	Manipulating Rows with a Cursor	580
	Updating and Deleting Rows with a Cursor	590
	Monitoring Transact-SQL Cursors	592
Lesson **28**	**Stored Procedures**	**597**
	Understanding Stored Procedures	598
	Exchanging Data with Stored Procedures	598
	System Procedures	599
	User-Defined Stored Procedures	600

Using and Creating Stored Procedures 600

   Using Stored Procedures 600

   Creating Stored Procedures 609

Lesson **29** **Triggers** **623**

Understanding Triggers 623

   AFTER Triggers 624

   INSTEAD OF Triggers 625

Creating Triggers 626

   Using the CREATE TRIGGER Command 626

   Using the UPDATE Function 632

   Using the Inserted and Deleted Tables 634

Lesson **30** **User-Defined Functions** **639**

Understanding User-Defined Functions 639

   Scalar Functions 640

   Table-Valued Functions 640

Creating User-Defined Functions 641

   Creating Scalar Functions 642

   Creating Table-Valued Functions 644

Using User-Defined Functions 648

   Using User-Defined Functions in Transact-SQL Statements 649

   Using User-Defined Functions in Table Definitions 652

Glossary **659**

Index **665**

Acknowledgements

Once again, I am in debt to the outstanding editorial team at Microsoft Press for their support, their expertise, and most of all, their unfailing senses of humor. In roughly chronological order, my thanks go to: Ben Ryan, David Clark, Alice Turner, Julie Xiao, Denise Bankaitis, Dail Magee, Jr., and Becka McKay.

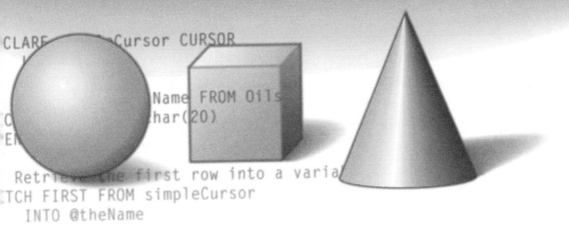

Introduction

Welcome to *Microsoft SQL Server 2000 Programming Step by Step*. The lessons in this book will first teach you how to use the SQL Server 2000 Enterprise Manager for creating and administering databases and database objects. You'll then move on to the Query Analyzer, learning how to automate functionality by using scripts, triggers, functions, and stored procedures.

SQL Server 2000 is a sophisticated, feature-rich relational database engine. To keep this book a manageable size, I've had to make some assumptions and limitations. I've assumed that you have some idea of what a relational database is and how to design one. You don't need any experience in implementing databases to follow the lessons in this book, but if the words "third normal form" strike fear in your heart, you might want to stop now and go buy my first book, *Designing Relational Database Systems* (Microsoft Press, 1999).

It's the nature of writing a book like this that whenever a functional area has to be cut, you lay awake nights worrying that it's precisely that area that your readers desperately need to understand. (Well, maybe that's just me.) Unfortunately, given a product with the functional scope of SQL Server 2000, it simply isn't possible to cover everything in an introductory text.

If I've done my job adequately, the lessons included in this book should give you a sense of what it is possible to achieve with the product. Certainly, you need to understand the functionality covered in this book *before* you move on to study more advanced areas, such as OLAP or e-commerce applications.

Finding Your Best Starting Point

Microsoft SQL Server 2000 is a client/server relational database management system (RDBMS) designed for high-performance online transaction processing (OLTP), data warehousing, and e-commerce applications. *Microsoft SQL Server 2000 Programming Step by Step* will help you quickly get up to speed with creating and maintaining databases using the interactive tools provided with the SQL Server 2000 Personal, Standard, and Enterprise Editions.

> **IMPORTANT** This book is designed for use with SQL Server 2000, which is not included on the companion CD. You must purchase and install SQL Server 2000 separately before you can complete the lessons.

This book is designed for beginners to relational databases, as well as individuals who have experience with other database management systems such as Microsoft Access and are upgrading to SQL Server 2000. Use the following tables to find your best starting point in this book.

If you are	Follow these steps
New to relational database systems	1. Install the practice files as described later in this introduction. 2. Get to know the SQL Server environment by working through Lessons 1 through 5. 3. Complete the lessons in Parts 2 through 4. 4. Complete the lessons in Part 5 as your interest and experience dictate.

If you are	Follow these steps
Switching from another database product	1. Install the practice files as described later in this introduction. 2. Get to know the SQL Server environment by working through Lessons 1 through 5. 3. Complete the remaining lessons as your interest and experience dictate.

If you are	Follow these steps
Upgrading from an earlier version of Microsoft SQL Server	1. Learn about the new features of SQL Server 2000 that are covered in this book by reading the following section, "New Features in SQL Server 2000." 2. Install the practice files as described later in this introduction. 3. Complete the lessons that cover the topics you need. The table of contents will help you locate lessons about general topics. The index will help you find information about specific topics.

If you are	Follow these steps
Referencing this book after working through the lessons	1. Use the index to locate information about specific topics; use the table of contents to locate information about general topics. 2. Read the Quick Reference at the end of each lesson for a brief review of the lesson's major tasks. The Quick Reference topics are listed in the order that they are presented in the lesson.

New Features in SQL Server 2000

The following table lists the major new features of Microsoft SQL Server 2000 that are covered in this book and also lists which lessons explain how to use each feature. You can also use the index to find specific information about a feature or a task that you want to perform.

To learn how to	See
Add a description to a column in the Enterprise Manager	Lesson 5
Cascade changes to the primary key table	Lesson 7
Create an index on a view	Lesson 16
Implement cascade deletes in the relationship	Lesson 19
Declare variables with a table data type	Lesson 25
Create INSTEAD OF triggers	Lesson 29
Create user-defined functions	Lesson 30

Using the Microsoft SQL Server 2000 Programming Step by Step Companion CD

The companion CD inside the back cover contains practice files that you'll use as you complete the exercises in the book. By using the files, you won't need to waste time creating databases and entering sample data. Instead, you can concentrate on how to use Microsoft SQL Server 2000. With the files and the step-by-step instructions in the lessons, you'll also learn by doing, which is an easy and effective way to acquire and remember new skills.

IMPORTANT Before you break the seal on the *Microsoft SQL Server 2000 Programming Step by Step* CD-ROM package, be sure that this book matches your version of the software. This book is designed for use with Microsoft SQL Server 2000 for the Microsoft Windows NT and Microsoft Windows 2000 operating systems.

System Requirements

To install and run Microsoft SQL Server 2000, your computer must have:

- Intel (or compatible) Pentium processor running at least 166 MHz (megahertz)

- Minimum 64 MB RAM, with 128 MB recommended for the Enterprise Edition

- Minimum 95 MB free disk space, with 250 MB required for the typical installation of SQL Server database components

- Minimum 50 MB free disk space, with 130 MB required for the typical installation of SQL Server Analysis Services

- 80 MB free disk space for English Query

- 44 MB free disk space for Desktop Engine only

- Minimum 800 x 600 resolution monitor

- Microsoft Mouse or compatible, and CD-ROM drive

- Microsoft Internet Explorer 5.0 or later

Installing the Practice Files

Installing the practice files requires approximately 6.21 MB of disk space. Follow these steps to install the practice files on your computer's hard disk so that you can use them with the exercises in this book:

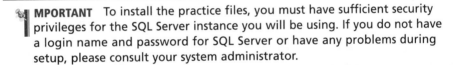 **MPORTANT**   To install the practice files, you must have sufficient security privileges for the SQL Server instance you will be using. If you do not have a login name and password for SQL Server or have any problems during setup, please consult your system administrator.

---

1. Insert the CD in your CD-ROM drive. (If a menu screen does not appear, double-click StartCD.exe in the root of the CD-ROM.)

2. Click the Install Practice Files option, and follow the prompts that appear on the screen.

3. When the files have been installed, remove the CD from your CD-ROM drive and replace it in the package inside the back cover of the book. A folder called SQL 2000 Step by Step has been created on your hard disk, and the practice files have been placed in that folder.

4. Start the SQL Server Enterprise Manager.

5. Expand the Microsoft SQL Servers group in the left-hand pane, and then expand the server group containing the server you will be using for these lessons.

MPORTANT Check with your system administrator to determine the server group and server you should use.

---

6. Right-click the Databases folder of the server you're using for the exercises, point to All Tasks, and select Attach Database.

   SQL Server displays the Attach Database dialog box.

7. Click the Browse button.

   SQL Server displays the Browse for Existing File dialog box.

8. Navigate to the SQL 2000 Step by Step folder, select Aromatherapy.mdf, and then click OK.

   SQL Server fills in the file locations for the data and transaction log files.

9. Click OK.

   SQL Server displays a message confirming that the database has been successfully attached.

MPORTANT In addition to installing the practice files, the Setup program creates a shortcut to the Microsoft Press World Wide Web site on your desktop. If your computer is set up to connect to the Internet, you can double-click the shortcut to visit the Microsoft Press Website. You can also connect to the World Wide Web site directly at *http://mspress.microsoft.com/*.

Using the Practice Files

The sample database files are used for all of the lessons in Parts 1 through 4. The lessons in Part 5 each have their own practice files. Each lesson explains when and how to use the files for that lesson. The lessons are built around a sample database that simulates a real work environment so that you can easily apply the lessons to your own work.

Uninstalling the Practice Files

Use the following steps to delete the practice files added to your hard drive by the *Microsoft SQL Server 2000 Programming Step by Step* installation program. Please note that you need to detach the Aromatherapy database in SQL Server in order to uninstall the practice files completely.

1. On the Windows taskbar, click Start, point to Settings, and then click Control Panel.

IMPORTANT Windows 2000 provides an option to display the Control Panel contents directly from the taskbar Start menu. If your computer has been configured in this way, the Control Panel items will be displayed as a submenu from the Settings menu.

---

2. Double-click the Add/Remove Programs icon.

3. Select SQL 2000 Step by Step from the list, and then click Add/Remove. (On Windows 2000, click Change/Remove.)

   A confirmation message appears.

4. Click Yes.

   The practice files are uninstalled.

5. Click OK to close the Add/Remove Programs Properties dialog box.

6. Close the Control Panel window, if necessary.

Corrections, Comments, and Help

Every effort has been made to ensure the accuracy of this book and the contents of the *Microsoft SQL Server Programming 2000 Step by Step* CD. Microsoft Press provides corrections and additional content for its books through the World Wide Web at:

http://mspress.microsoft.com/support

If you have comments, questions or ideas regarding this book or the CD, please send them to us.

Send e-mail to:

mspinput@microsoft.com

Or send postal mail to:

Microsoft Press
Attn: Step by Step Editor
One Microsoft Way
Redmond, WA 98052-6399

Please note that support for the SQL Server 2000 software product itself is not offered through the above addresses. For help using SQL Server 2000, you can call SQL Server 2000 Technical Support at 1-800-936-4900 on weekdays between 6 A.M. and 6 P.M. Pacific Time.

Visit the Microsoft Press World Wide Web Site

We invite you to visit the Microsoft Press World Wide Web site at the following location:

http://mspress.microsoft.com

You'll find descriptions of all our books, information about ordering titles, notices of special features and events, additional content for Microsoft Press books, and much more.

You can also find out the latest in software development and news from Microsoft Corporation by visiting the following World Wide Web site:

http://www.microsoft.com/

We look forward to your visit on the Web!

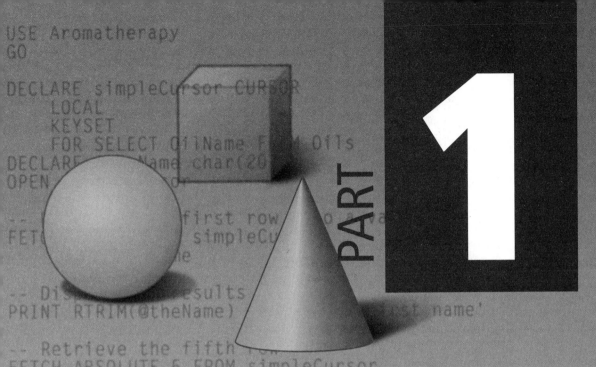

Getting Started with SQL Server

Lesson

1 The SQL Server 2000 Environment   3

2 Administering SQL Server   19

3 SQL Server 2000 Security   41

```
USE Aromatherapy
GO

DECLARE simpleCursor CURSOR
    LOCAL
    KEYSET
    FOR SELECT OilName FROM Oils
DECLARE @theName char(20)
OPEN

-- first row to a variable
FETCH        simpleCu

-- Dis       esults
PRINT RTRIM(@theName)              first name'

-- Retrieve the fifth
FETCH ABSOLUTE 5 FROM simpleCursor
    INTO @theName

-- Display the results
PRINT RTRIM(@theName) + ' is the fifth name'

CLOSE simpleCursor
DEALLOCATE simpleCursor
```
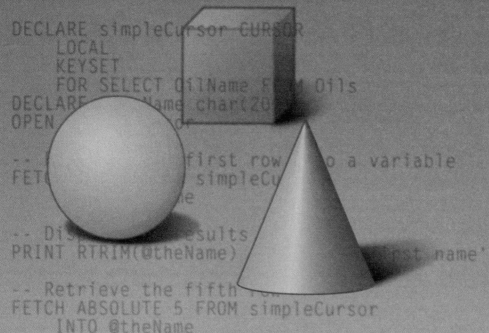

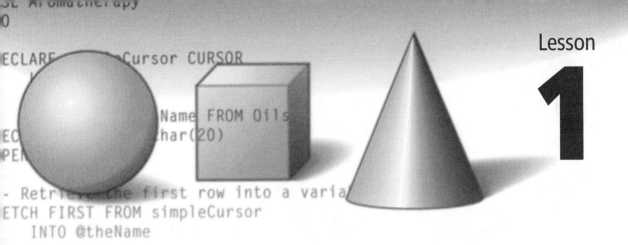

The SQL Server 2000 Environment

> **In this lesson you will learn how to:**
>
> - Start the Enterprise Manager.
> - Register a server.
> - Start and stop a server.
> - Display objects in the Enterprise Manager Console Tree.
> - Exit Enterprise Manager.

Microsoft SQL Server 2000 has been designed to support high-volume, mission-critical databases in a number of different application areas, including online transaction processing (OLTP), data warehousing, and e-commerce. To support these functions, SQL Server provides a number of tools, including command prompt utilities—such as bcp.exe, which copies data between SQL Server and an operating system file—and the Enterprise Manager, a sophisticated graphical tool for administering multiple databases and SQL Server itself.

Most of the lessons in this book will use the graphical tools provided by the Enterprise Manager, and in this first lesson you'll learn the fundamentals of working in this environment.

Understanding the Enterprise Manager

SQL Server Enterprise Manager is the primary tool used to administer SQL Server 2000. Using the Enterprise Manager's graphical interface, you can:

- Define groups of SQL Server instances and register individual servers within a group.

- Configure all SQL Server options for each registered server.

- Create and administer all SQL Server databases, objects, logins, users, and permissions in each registered server.

- Define and execute all SQL Server administrative tasks on each registered server.

- View the contents of tables and views using the Query Designer.

- Design and test SQL statements, batches, and scripts interactively by invoking the SQL Server Query Analyzer.

- Invoke the various SQL Server wizards.

Microsoft Management Console

Microsoft Windows includes a utility called the Microsoft Management Console (MMC), which provides a standard framework for managing server applications. The set of MMC tools you use to manage a specific server is called a "console." The most common type of server console is a "snap-in," and the SQL Server Enterprise Manager is the snap-in you use to administer SQL Server 2000. For more information on MMC, you can check Windows Help by clicking the Start button, choosing Help, and then entering "Microsoft Management Console" in the Search tab.

Starting the Enterprise Manager

You must start the SQL Server Enterprise Manager before you can begin performing administrative tasks. The Enterprise Manager is started and controlled like any other Windows program.

Start the Enterprise Manager

1. On the Microsoft Windows taskbar, click the Start button.

2. Point to Programs, and then to the Microsoft SQL Server folder.

   The icons in the Microsoft SQL Server folder appear in a list.

3. Click the Enterprise Manager program icon.

   The Enterprise Manager window appears, as shown in Figure 1-1.

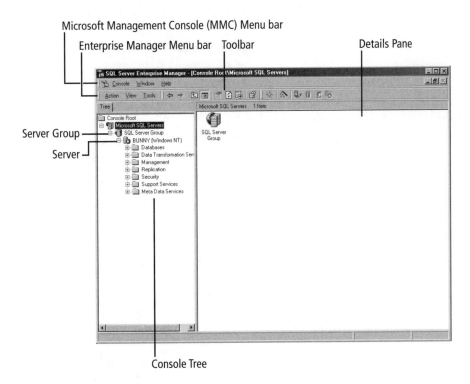

Figure 1-1. *The Enterprise Manager window.*

The Enterprise Manager provides the tools you need to administer SQL Server and to create and maintain databases. The Enterprise Manager window is divided into two *panes*: the Console Tree on the left, and the Details Pane on the right. The items in the Console Tree are arranged in a hierarchy, like the folders list in Microsoft Windows Explorer. You can expand subitems in the hierarchy by clicking the expand icon, or collapse them by clicking the collapse icon.

Expand icon   ⊞

Collapse icon   ⊟

IMPORTANT The objects displayed in the Console Tree when you start the Enterprise Manager probably won't exactly match the examples in this book. For example, the name of my server is BUNNY. Yours will be named something else.

Don't worry about that, it just means that your system administrator has configured SQL Server somewhat differently.

Controlling SQL Server

Before you can use the SQL Server Enterprise Manager to create new databases or access the data in existing databases, you must first identify the server instance to the Enterprise Manager, make sure that the server is running, and connect to the database with which you want to work.

SQL Server Security Modes

SQL Server supports two different *login security modes* for ensuring that only authorized individuals have access to sensitive data—*Windows Authentication* and *SQL Server Authentication*. The Windows Authentication model, which Microsoft recommends, allows users of Microsoft Windows 2000 and Microsoft Windows NT to log in transparently using their operating system user name and password. When you use the SQL Server Authentication model, the server itself handles user authentication and users must supply a login name and password when they connect to a database.

This book assumes that your server is using Windows Authentication, the recommended configuration. If your server uses SQL Server Authentication, you will be prompted for your login name and password when you register a server or connect to a database. If this happens, type in the login name and password provided by your system administrator, and then click OK.

We'll be examining SQL Server 2000 security in detail in Lesson 3.

Registering a Server

The first time you run the Enterprise Manager, it will automatically register all the instances of SQL Server running locally. If you install new instances of SQL Server or if you want to connect to an instance of SQL Server located across a network, you must explicitly register it.

MPORTANT Before you can register an instance of SQL Server, you'll need the name of the server, the type of security used to log into the server, your login name and password, if necessary, and the name of the group where you want the server to be listed after it is registered. If you don't know this information, consult your system administrator for assistance.

Register a server

MPORTANT If the name of the server is displayed in the Console Tree, it is already registered with the Enterprise Manager and you should *not* perform the following steps. Skip to the next topic, "Starting and Stopping a Server."

---

1. Right-click a server group in the Console Tree.

    The context menu appears.

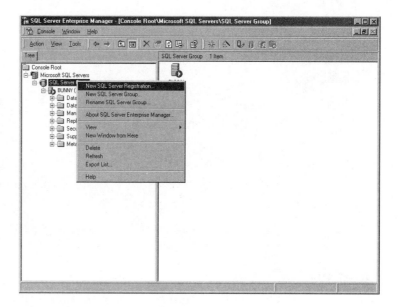

2. Click New SQL Server Registration in the context menu.

   The Register SQL Server Wizard welcome screen appears.

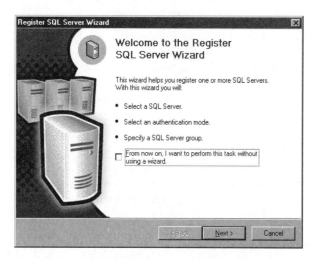

TIP You can also select New SQL Server Registration from the context menu displayed when you right-click a server in the Console Tree.

---

3. Click Next.

The first page of the Register SQL Server Wizard appears, listing the names of servers known to the system.

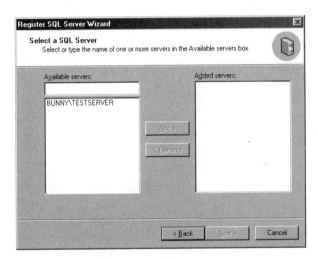

4. If the server you want to register is listed, select it in the list box, and click Add. If the server name does not appear, type it into the text box, and then click Add.

The wizard will display the server in the Added Servers list box.

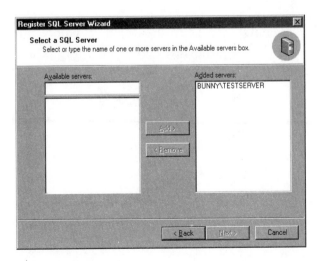

5. Click Next.

   The wizard will display a screen asking you to choose an authentication mode.

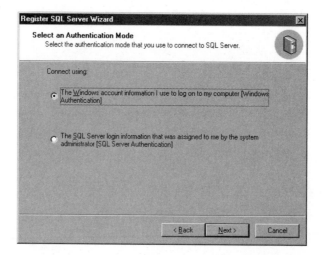

6. If your system administrator has told you to use SQL Server Authentication, click the option button labeled The SQL Server Login Information That Was Assigned To Me By The System Administrator [SQL Server Authentication].

7. Click Next.

   If you chose SQL Server Authentication, you will be prompted for your login ID and password. Enter this information, and then click Next.

   The wizard will display a screen asking you to choose the group to which the new server should be added.

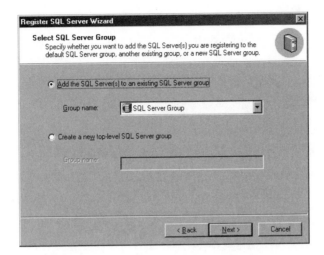

8. Click Next to add the server to the default group.

   The wizard will display a screen confirming the server to be added.

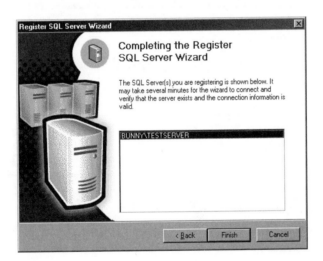

9. Click Finish.

The wizard will complete the tasks necessary to register the server, and then display a confirmation screen.

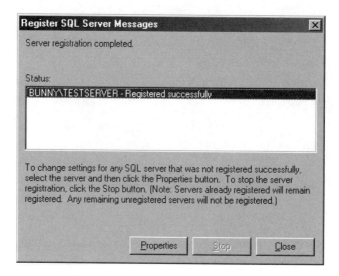

10. Click Close.

    The Register SQL Server Wizard will close, and the new server will be displayed in the Console Tree.

 IP You need to register an instance of SQL Server only once. The Enterprise Manager will remember the registered servers the next time you start the program.

Starting and Stopping a Server

Before you can connect to an instance of SQL Server, the service must be started. You can tell whether a service is running by looking at the server icon in the Console Tree of the Enterprise Manager. Table 1-1 shows each icon and its meaning.

Icon	Meaning
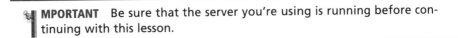	The server is running.
	The server is paused.
	The server is stopped.

Table 1-1.   *The server icon indicates whether the SQL Server instance is currently running.*

Start a server

- Right-click the server. Click Start in the context menu.

Pause a server

- Right-click the server. Click Pause in the context menu.

Stop a server

- Right-click the server. Click Stop in the context menu.

MPORTANT   Be sure that the server you're using is running before continuing with this lesson.

The Enterprise Manager Console Tree

The Console Tree of the Enterprise Manager window displays all the SQL Server objects known to the Enterprise Manager in a list.

MPORTANT   The objects displayed in the Console Tree of the Enterprise Manager on your system probably won't match the examples in this book exactly. Don't worry about that, it just means that your system administrator has configured SQL Server somewhat differently.

As you go through the lessons in this book, you'll be working with most of the items in the Console Tree. To get you started, Table 1-2 contains a brief description of each folder that contains the main objects in the tree.

Icon	Folder	Description
	Server Group	One or more servers grouped together to make administration more convenient.
	Server	An instance of SQL Server registered with the Enterprise Manager.
	Database	A collection of tables and other objects that stores a specific set of structured data.
	Data Transformation Services	A set of graphical tools and programmable objects that allow data to be extracted, transformed, and consolidated.
	Management	A set of graphical tools and programmable objects for managing SQL Server.
	Replication	A set of graphical tools and programmable objects that allow data and database objects to be copied and distributed from one database to another.
	Security	A set of graphical tools and programmable objects for controlling access to SQL Server.
	Support Services	Miscellaneous utilities for managing SQL Server.
	Meta Data Services	Utilities for maintaining meta data (data *about* the data) about databases.

Table 1-2. *Primary objects in the Enterprise Manager Console Tree.*

The System Databases

The Enterprise Manager Console Tree always contains four databases that are used by SQL Server itself. These databases are referred to as the *system databases*. Their role within SQL Server is described in Table 1-3.

IMPORTANT Because the integrity of the system databases is critical to the successful operation of SQL Server, you should always use the administrative tools provided by the Enterprise Manager or the programming interface (SQL-DMO) to modify the contents of the master and msdb databases.

Remember: Look but don't touch!

System Database	Purpose
master	The master database records all the information required to manage a SQL Server system, including the user accounts, the databases defined within the system, and the server's processes. Collectively, the tables stored in the master database are called the *system catalog*.
model	The model database is used as a template when creating new user databases.
	By default, the model database contains the tables making up the *database catalog*, the tables that are used by SQL Server to define the other objects within the user database.
msdb	The msdb database is used by SQL Server Agent for scheduling maintenance tasks such as *alerts* and *jobs* and recording backup histories. Alerts are user-defined responses to SQL Server events. Jobs are series of actions performed by SQL Server Agent.
tempdb	Tempdb is used as a temporary storage area. Its contents are dropped automatically when SQL Server is shut down. In fact, any temporary objects created by a user are dropped when that user logs out of the system.

Table 1-3.   *The SQL Server system databases.*

TIP Any objects you add to the model database will automatically be added to any new databases you create. This can be useful if there are, for example, certain users or database configuration options that you will want in all new databases.

Remember, however, that any objects you add to the model database will be added to *new* databases only, not to existing databases.

Connecting to and Exiting a Database

Once the server is registered with the Enterprise Manager and has been started, you can create a new database or connect to an existing database.

MPORTANT If you have not yet installed this book's practice files, work through "Installing and Using the Practice Files" in the Introduction, and then return to this lesson.

Database Objects

SQL Server databases exist as part of the SQL Server Console Tree, as shown in Figure 1-2. These databases contain various objects that define the data stored in the database and the ways in which that data can be accessed.

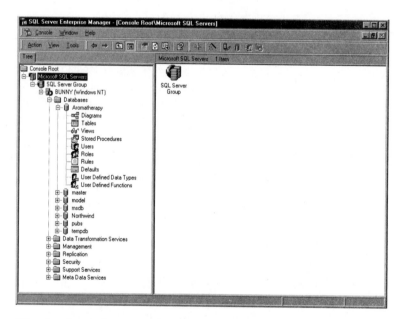

Figure 1-2. *The database objects in the SQL Server Console Tree.*

We'll be looking at most of these objects in detail in later lessons, but they're briefly described in Table 1-4.

Icon	Object	Description
	Diagram	A graphic representation of tables in the database.
	Table	A set of information organized into rows and columns.
	View	A virtual table that provides an alternative method of viewing the information in the database.
	Stored Procedure	A set of Transact SQL commands that are executed as a batch.
	User	An individual identified to the system for security purposes.
	Role	A group of permissions used for security purposes.
	Rule	A database object bound to a column or user-defined data type that specifies what data can be entered in that column.
	Default	A value assigned automatically by the system if the user does not provide it.
	User Defined Data Type	A data type defined for the user for custom data storage.
	User Defined Function	A set of Transact SQL commands that accept parameters and return a result.

Table 1-4. *Objects contained within a SQL Server database.*

Exiting the Enterprise Manager

When you've finished using the Enterprise Manager for the day, be sure to exit the program before shutting down your computer.

Exit Enterprise Manager

■ On the Console menu, click the Exit command. If you see a Save dialog box, click Yes.

The Enterprise Manager closes.

If you want to continue to the next lesson

■ Start the Enterprise Manager again and turn to Lesson 2.

If you want to stop using Enterprise Manager for now

■ If you've exited the Enterprise Manager, you're ready to stop.

Lesson 1 Quick Reference

To	Do this	Button or icon
Start the Enterprise Manager	Click the Start button on the taskbar. Point to Programs, Microsoft SQL Server, and click Enterprise Manager.	Start
Register a server	Right-click a server group or server in the Console Tree. Click New SQL Server Registration in the context menu.	
Start a server	Right-click the server. Click Start in the context menu.	
Pause a server	Right-click the server. Click Pause in the context menu.	
Stop a server	Right-click the server. Click Stop in the context menu.	
Expand an item in the object tree	Double-click the expand icon to the left of the item.	+
Collapse an item in the object tree	Double-click the collapse icon to the left of the object.	−
Quit the Enterprise Manager	On the Console menu, click Exit.	

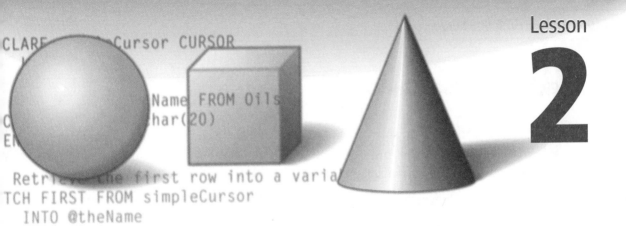

Administering SQL Server

> **In this lesson you will learn how to:**
>
> - Back up a database.
> - Restore a database.
> - Create a maintenance plan using the Database Maintenance Plan Wizard.

Just like your car needs regular tune-ups, Microsoft SQL Server will perform better and more reliably if you perform regular maintenance tasks. Fortunately, these tasks are generally a lot easier and less messy than changing car oil.

Administering a large-scale mission-critical database application can still be a complex task, but the tools provided by the Enterprise Manager go a long way toward simplifying the process. In this lesson, you'll learn how simple it is to protect your database by making backups, and how to make this task even easier by using the Database Maintenance Plan Wizard to tell SQL Server to do it for you.

Backing Up and Restoring Databases

No matter how reliable an underlying technology, stuff happens: computer hardware fails, software gets itself confused and dies, and users make mistakes. Your best protection is to take regular copies of your data and store them somewhere safe. This is called "taking a backup." If anything happens (and it will), you can use the backup to restore the database to the state it was in prior to the problem.

Backing Up a Database

SQL Server 2000 provides several different ways of backing up a database. The simplest of these is to take a *full backup*—an exact copy of the database at a specific point in time.

 TIP SQL Server allows backups to be taken while the database is in use; there's no need to close the system down for maintenance. However, certain types of operations can't be performed during backup. These include operations that change the structure of the database—such as creating or deleting files or creating indexes—and performing nonlogged operations.

SQL Server also provides a second kind of backup, known as a *differential backup*. A differential backup records only the information that has changed since the last full backup. The advantages of this are that in most environments a differential backup will be much smaller than a full backup, and that the process of taking the backup will be much faster.

 TIP Differential backups make sense if only a small percentage of data is changed. You might, for example, make a differential backup every day, and a full backup once a week.

The third type of backup operation provided by SQL Server is a *transaction log backup*. The transaction log is a record of all the transactions that have been performed against the database since the transaction log was last backed up.

TIP Transaction log backups also allow you to restore a database to a specific point in time. This can be useful if, for example, an operator error has caused incorrect information to be entered into a database; you can use a transaction log to restore the database to the state it was in prior to the addition of the erroneous information.

SQL Server uses the transaction log to restore the database automatically if the server fails, and you can use it to back up your data in combination with a full backup, or full and differential backups. The advantage of a transaction log backup is that under most circumstances the resulting backup file will be smaller than a full or differential backup.

 IP In some cases, a transaction log backup might be bigger than a database backup. This will be the case, for example, if a small group of records is being changed relatively frequently. In these cases, you can either do a full backup or take the transaction log backups more frequently.

Back up a database using the Create Database Backup Wizard

 MPORTANT If you haven't yet installed this book's Aromatherapy sample database, see the Introduction before returning to this lesson.

1. Select the Aromatherapy database in the Console Tree.

   SQL Server displays a list of database objects in the Details Pane.

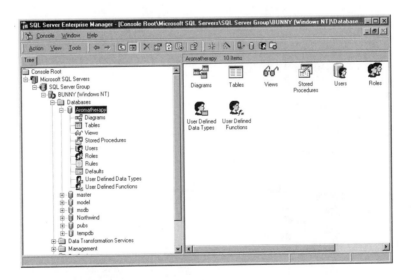

2. Click the Wizard button on the Enterprise Manager toolbar.

   SQL Server displays the Select Wizard dialog box.

Wizard button

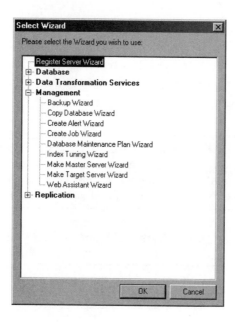

3. Click Backup Wizard in the Management section.

   SQL Server displays the first page of the Create Database Backup Wizard.

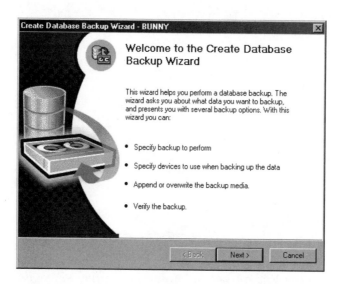

4. Click Next.

The wizard displays a page asking you to choose the database to back up.

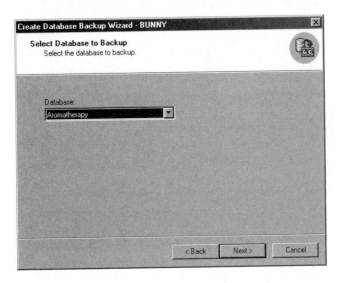

5. Make sure Aromatherapy is selected in the combo box, and then click Next.

   The wizard displays a page asking you to name and describe the backup.

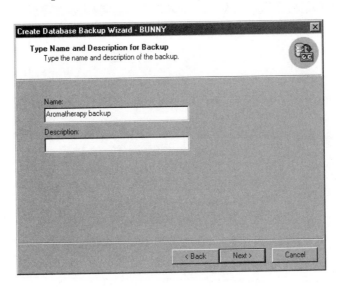

6. Type *Lesson 2 backup* in the description box.

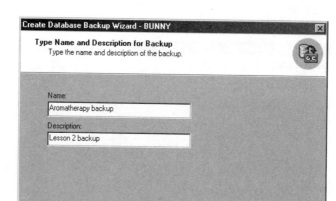

7. Click Next.

   The wizard displays a page asking you which type of backup you want to perform: a full backup, a differential backup, or a transaction log backup.

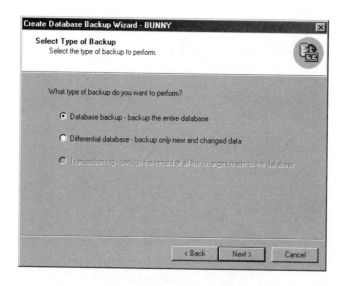

8. In this exercise we'll perform a full backup, so just click Next.

The wizard displays a page asking you to choose a backup destination.

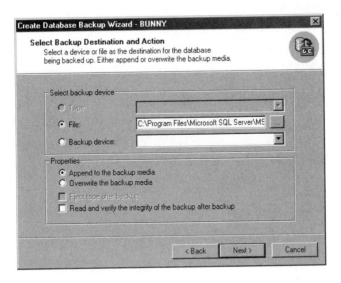

Browse button

9. Click the Browse button.

   The wizard displays the Backup Device Location dialog box.

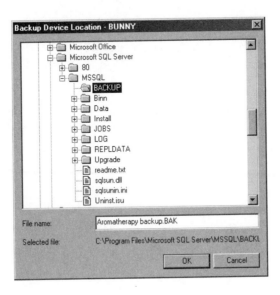

10. Navigate to the folder where you've installed the practice files.

IMPORTANT In a production environment, you should never store backups on the same physical device as the live database. Always store them in a safe place, preferably in a different location.

---

11. Click OK to return to the wizard. In the Properties section, you can choose to append to or overwrite the backup media. For this exercise, choose Append To The Backup Media.

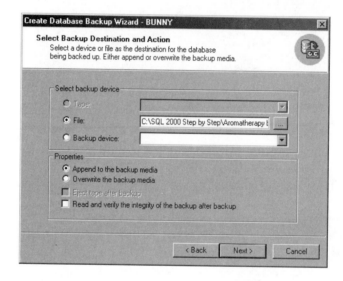

12. Click Next.

The wizard displays a page asking you for verification and scheduling details.

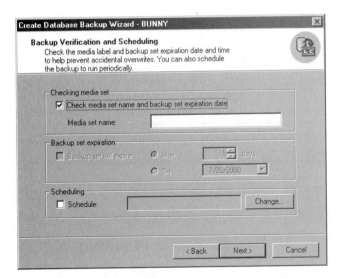

13. In this example, we don't need SQL Server to verify the backup, so uncheck the check box labeled Check Media Set Name And Backup Set Expiration Date.

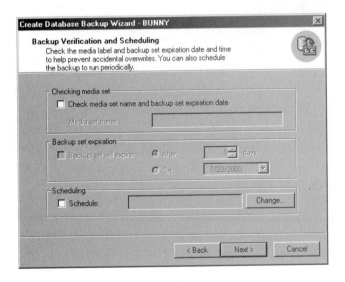

14. Click Next.

The wizard displays a page verifying the choices you have made.

TIP SQL Server organizes backup media in a *media set*. A media set could be a single disk file, or a set of twenty or more backup tapes.

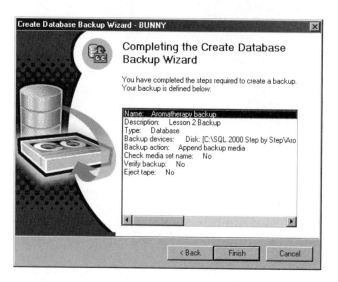

15. Click Finish.

The Create Database Backup Wizard displays a progress dialog box while it's performing the backup, and then a message indicating the backup has been completed successfully.

TIP You can also back up a database by selecting Backup Database on the database context menu. This option displays a single dialog box rather than using the Create Database Backup Wizard, but all the options are the same.

Restoring a Database

Obviously, making backups of your data isn't much use unless you have some way of getting that data back into your production system in the event of failure. This is called *restoring* the database, and the Enterprise Manager makes it just as easy to restore the database as it is to back it up.

Restore a database

1. Right-click the Aromatherapy database in the Console Tree, point to All Tasks, and then click Restore Database.

   SQL Server displays the Restore Database dialog box.

2. Click OK.

   SQL Server displays a progress dialog box while it's performing the restore, and then shows a message indicating the restore has been completed successfully.

   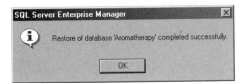

Using the Database Maintenance Plan Wizard

So far in this lesson you've learned how to back up and restore a database whenever you choose to. But backups should be performed regularly, and it's easy to forget to do them. SQL Server provides a mechanism for you to have backups performed automatically at regularly scheduled times. There are several ways to do this, but the easiest is to use the Database Maintenance Plan Wizard.

The Database Maintenance Plan Wizard also allows you to schedule several other maintenance tasks that should be performed regularly. The most important of these is updating the database statistics.

SQL Server maintains information about the statistical distribution of data in tables. This information is used by SQL Server to determine the most efficient method of retrieving information. However, over time this data becomes obsolete as data is changed and new data is added. SQL Server automatically updates the statistical information periodically, but you can force it to update this information at specified times using the Database Maintenance Plan Wizard.

In addition, you can use the Database Maintenance Plan Wizard to schedule SQL Server to perform regular *integrity checks*. These are low-level checks of the physical integrity of the user and system tables. Finally, you can use the Database Maintenance Plan Wizard to set up *log shipping,* which is a method of automatically maintaining a backup server by constantly copying the transaction logs to the server.

A single database maintenance plan can perform these tasks in any combination. Additionally, you can have SQL Server create a report on the results of the tasks it performs. This report can be stored to a specified directory as a text file or HTML document, or it can be e-mailed to an operator. In the exercise below, we'll simply set up a regular backup.

Create a maintenance plan to back up a database every month

1. Select the Aromatherapy database in the Console Tree.

    SQL Server displays a list of database objects in the Details Pane.

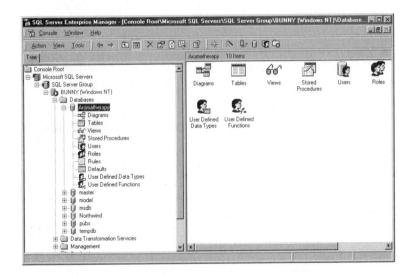

Wizard button

2. Click the Wizard button on the Enterprise Manager toolbar.

   SQL Server displays the Select Wizard dialog box.

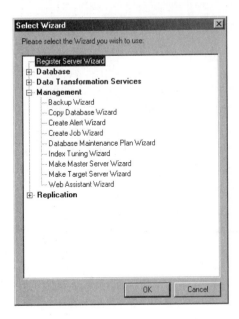

3. Select the Database Maintenance Plan Wizard in the Management section.

   SQL Server displays the first page of the Database Maintenance Plan Wizard.

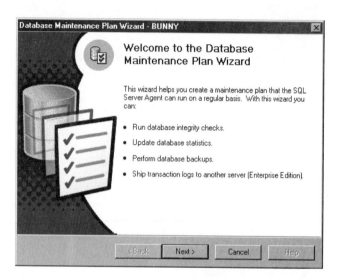

4. Click Next.

   The wizard displays a page asking you to choose the databases for which you are creating a maintenance plan. Since Aromatherapy was selected in the Console Tree when you started the wizard it will be selected by default, but you can change the selection by checking the appropriate options in this dialog box.

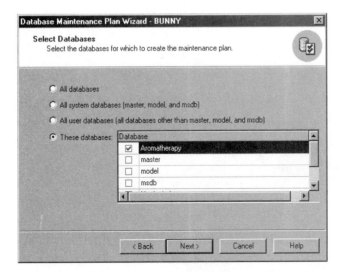

5. Click Next.

   The wizard displays a page asking you to select the optimization
   information to be updated.

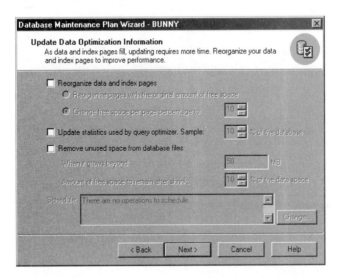

6. Click Next.

The wizard displays a page asking whether to perform integrity checks.

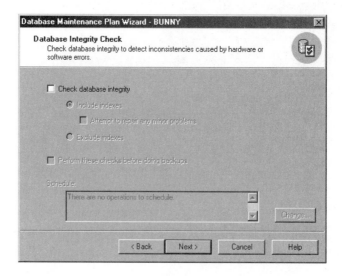

7. Click Next.

The wizard displays a page asking you to specify the database backup plan. For this exercise, we'll accept all the default settings and make changes only to the backup schedule.

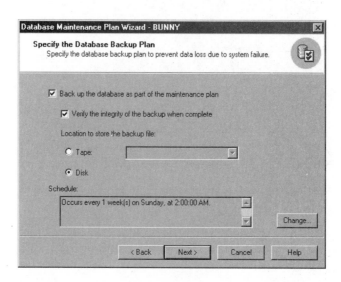

8. Click Change to change the backup schedule.

   The wizard displays the Edit Recurring Job Schedule dialog box.

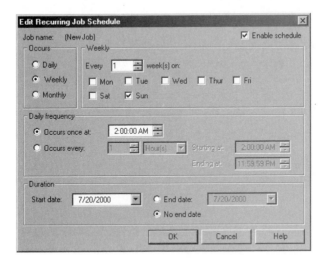

9. Select Monthly in the Occurs group.

   The wizard changes the dialog box to reflect the options for monthly backups.

10. Choose the option button to schedule the backup on the first Sunday of every month.

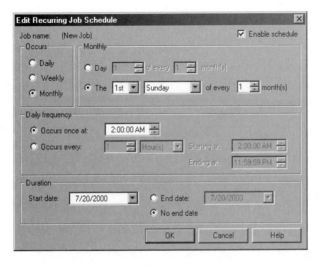

11. Click OK to return to the Database Maintenance Plan Wizard.

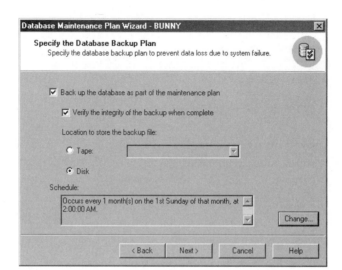

12. Click Next.

The wizard displays a page asking for the backup directory.

IP   If you're using the Database Maintenance Plan Wizard to schedule other maintenance jobs, and don't select the backup option, this page will not display.

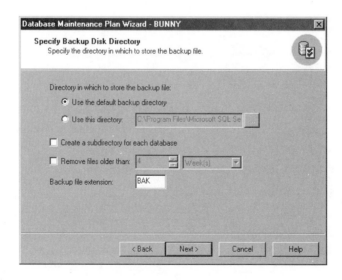

Browse button

13. Select the Use This Directory option button, and then click the Browse button.

   The wizard displays the File Backup Directory dialog box.

14. Navigate to the directory where the sample files are installed, and then click OK.

   The File Backup Directory dialog box closes.

15. Click Next.

   The wizard displays a page asking whether to include the transaction log in the backup plan.

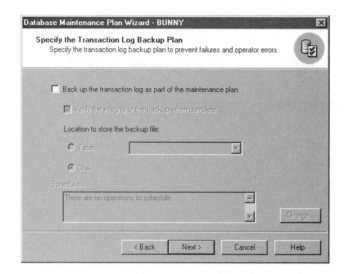

TIP You would use this page, rather than the page asking you to include the database in the maintenance plan, if you wanted to perform only a transaction log (rather than a full database) backup.

16. Click Next.

The wizard displays a page asking whether to generate a report when the plan is carried out.

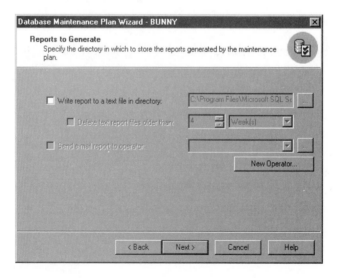

17. Click Next.

The wizard displays a page asking whether to store the maintenance history on the local server. For this example, accept the
default settings.

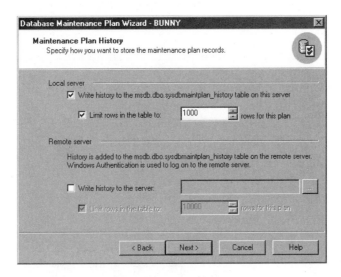

18. Click Next.

The Database Maintenance Plan Wizard displays a page confirming
the selections you've made.

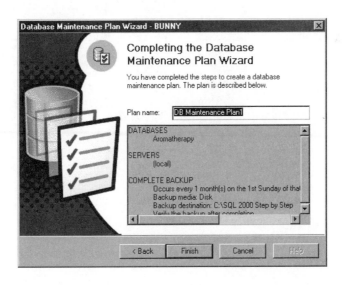

19. Click Cancel.

 MPORTANT Ordinarily you would click Finish to implement the maintenance plan, but we won't do that now since these are only practice databases.

 IP Maintenance plans are visible in the Management folder of the Console
Tree. You can view and edit the maintenance plan by double-clicking it in
the Details Pane.

Lesson 2 Quick Reference

To	Do this	Button
Back up a database	Select the database in the Console Tree, click the Wizard button on the Enterprise Manager toolbar to display the Select Wizard dialog box. Click Backup Wizard in the Management section and follow the wizard instructions.	
Restore a database	Right-click the database in the Console Tree, point to All Tasks, and then click Restore Database.	
Create a maintenance plan	Select the database in the Console Tree, click the Wizard button on the Enterprise Manager toolbar to display the Select Wizard dialog box. Click Database Maintenance Plan Wizard in the Management section and follow the wizard instructions.	

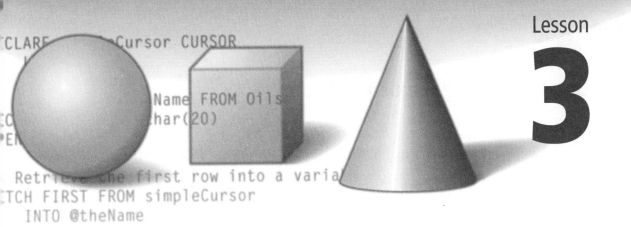

SQL Server 2000 Security

In this lesson you will learn how to:

- Create a Microsoft SQL Server login.
- Create a Microsoft Windows login.
- Remove a login.
- Create a database user.
- Remove a database user.
- Create a database role.
- Assign a user to a database role.
- Remove a user from a database role.
- Remove a database role.

One of the most important aspects of managing a database is ensuring the security of the data. You must ensure that everyone who legitimately needs access to the data can get it, but that no one has inappropriate access. In this lesson, we'll examine how SQL Server 2000 handles security, and learn how to create and assign security privileges.

Understanding Security Modes

When an instance of SQL Server receives a request for a connection, it is passed a *login ID*. The login ID is the account identifier that controls access to SQL Server 2000. SQL Server checks that the login ID it has been given is valid, and then determines whether the login ID has been granted sufficient security privileges to perform the requested operation. This process is known as *authentication*.

SQL Server 2000 can support authentication in either of two ways: it can rely on Microsoft Windows NT or Windows 2000 security to validate the ID, or it can perform the validation itself.

Windows Authentication

When using Windows Authentication (known as *integrated security* in previous versions of SQL Server), the system administrator grants security privileges to Windows NT and Windows 2000 accounts and groups. Windows client software requests a *trusted connection* to the server. Since a trusted connection will be granted only if Windows NT or Windows 2000 has already authenticated a user, SQL Server 2000 needs to ensure only that the login ID it has been provided has access to the server and the database.

> **IMPORTANT** Since Windows 98 does not support trusted connections, instances of SQL Server 2000 running on Windows 98 cannot use Windows Authentication Mode. Client software running on Windows 98 can, however, use Windows Authentication provided the server itself is running on Windows NT or Windows 2000.

SQL Server Authentication

In addition to being able to delegate login authentication to the Windows security system when it uses Windows Authentication Mode, SQL Server 2000 also implements its own security, called, not surprisingly, SQL

Server Authentication (known as *standard security* in previous versions of SQL Server). When a connection request is made using SQL Server Authentication, SQL Server 2000 receives both a login ID and a password, which it validates against the list of logins identified to it by the system administrator.

 MPORTANT Microsoft recommends that you use Windows Authentication wherever possible.

User Logins

Security within SQL Server 2000 is managed via several security objects. At the top-most level are the logins, which identify a SQL Server 2000 user, a Windows user, or a Windows group to the server.

 MPORTANT To complete the following exercises, you must have been assigned to either the Security Administrators or System Administrators roles within SQL Server. Please refer to your database administrator if you are in doubt about your privileges within the system.

Creating User Logins

Logins can be created manually by navigating to the Logins icon of the Security folder of a server and selecting New Login from the context menu, but the easiest way is to use the Create Login Wizard.

Create a SQL Server login

1. Select the server in the Console Tree.

   SQL Server displays a list of server objects in the Details Pane.

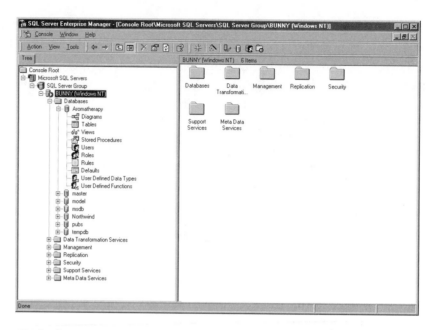

Wizard button

2. Click the Wizard button on the Enterprise Manager toolbar.

   SQL Server displays the Select Wizard dialog box.

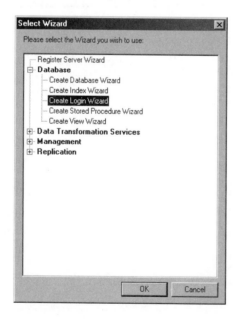

3. Select Create Login Wizard in the Database section, and then click OK.

   SQL Server displays the first page of the Create Login Wizard.

4. Click Next.

   The wizard displays a page asking for the server authentication mode for the login.

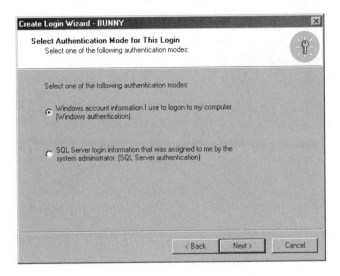

5. Select the option button labeled SQL Server Login Information That Was Assigned To Me By The System Administrator (SQL Server Authentication).

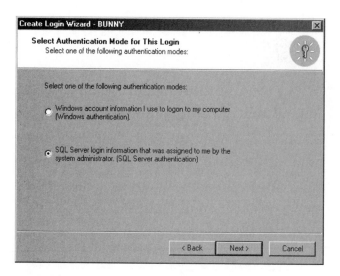

6. Click Next.

The wizard displays a page requesting the login ID and password.

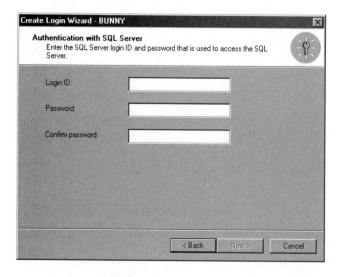

7. Enter *TestID* as the name and a password you like.

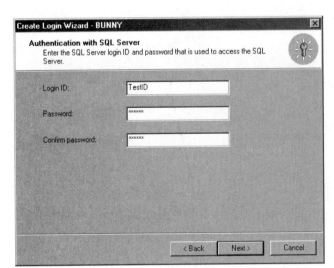

8. Click Next.

   The wizard displays a page requesting the security roles to which this login should be assigned.

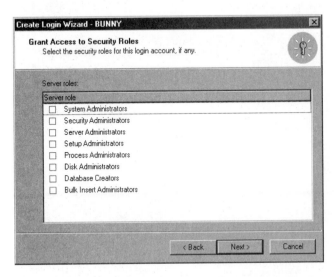

9. Add the login to the System Administrators role.

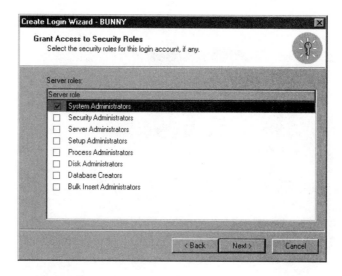

10. Click Next.

The wizard displays a page requesting the databases to which this login should be granted access.

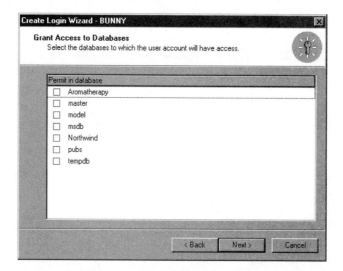

Server Roles

The server roles to which a login is assigned determine what security privileges the login has at the server level. Table 3-1 describes the privileges assigned to each role.

Full name	Name	Description
Bulk Insert Administrators	bulkadmin	Can perform bulk insert operations.
Database Creators	dbcreator	Can create, alter, and drop databases.
Disk Administrators	diskadmin	Can manage disk files.
Process Administrators	processadmin	Can manage processes running in SQL Server.
Security Administrators	securityadmin	Can manage logins and CREATE DATABASE permissions, and also read error logs.
Server Administrators	serveradmin	Can set server-wide configuration options and shut down the server.
Setup Administrators	setupadmin	Can manage linked servers, startup procedures, and extended stored procedures.
System Administrators	sysadmin	Can perform any activity in SQL Server.

Table 3-1.

11. Add the login to the Aromatherapy database.

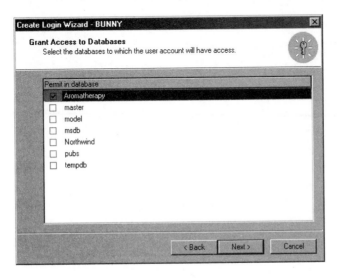

12. Click Next.

The wizard displays a page confirming the choices you have made.

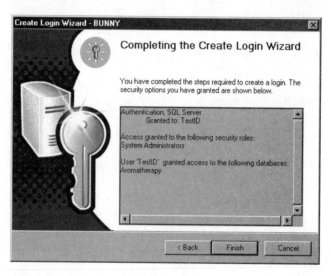

> **IMPORTANT** Logins that belong to specific server roles—in particular the System Administrators role—will have privileges on all databases, whether they have been specifically granted to the login or not.

13. Click Finish.

The Create Login Wizard displays a message confirming that the login has been added.

Create a Windows login

1. Select the server in the Console Tree.

SQL Server displays a list of object folders in the Details Pane.

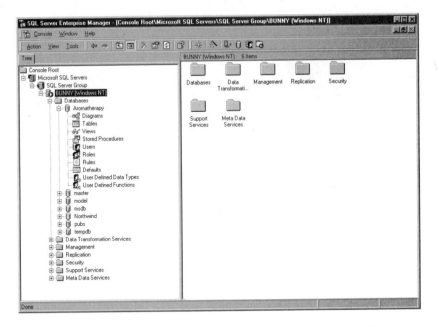

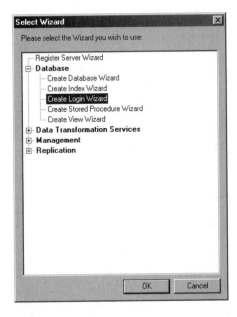

Wizard button

2. Click the Wizards button on the Enterprise Manager toolbar.

   SQL Server displays the Select Wizard dialog box.

3. Select Create Login Wizard in the Database section, and then click OK.

SQL Server displays the first page of the Create Login Wizard.

4. Click Next.

The wizard displays a page asking for the server authentication mode for the login. Accept the default setting.

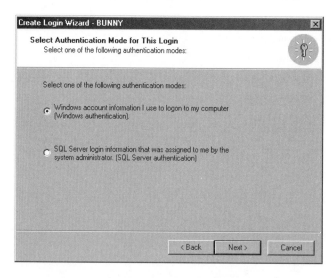

5. Click Next.

The wizard displays a page requesting the Windows account ID.

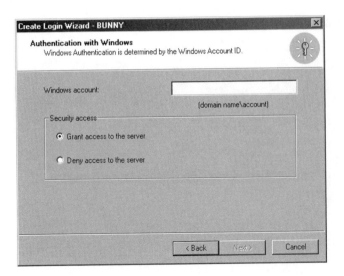

6. Enter a Windows ID in this form: domain name\account name (the account name can be a user or a group). Click Next.

The wizard displays a page requesting the security roles to which this login should be assigned.

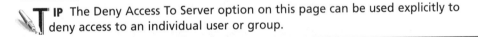

TIP The Deny Access To Server option on this page can be used explicitly to deny access to an individual user or group.

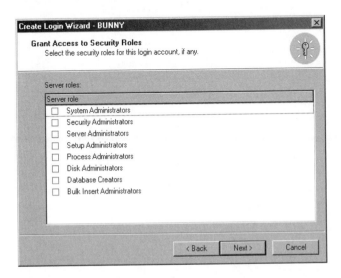

7. Add the login to the Database Creators role.

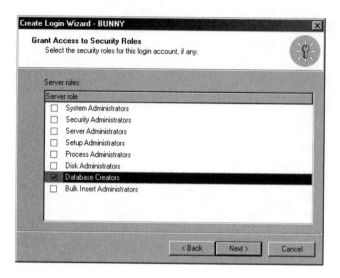

8. Click Next.

   The wizard displays a page requesting the databases to which this login should be granted access.

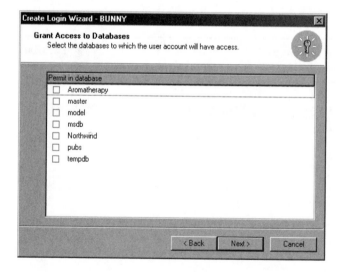

9. Add the login to the Aromatherapy database.

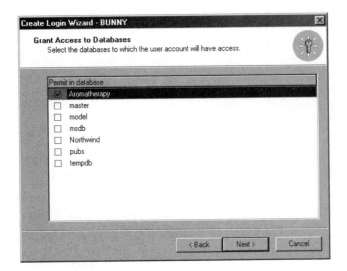

10. Click Next.

    The wizard displays a page confirming the choices you have made.

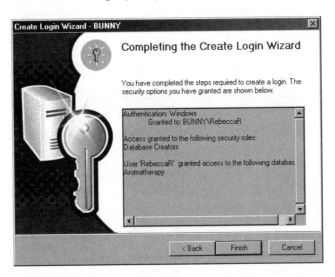

MPORTANT Logins that belong to specific server roles—in particular the System Administrators role—will have privileges on all databases whether they have been specifically granted to the login or not.

---

11. Click Finish.

The Create Login Wizard displays a message confirming that the login has been added.

Managing Logins

In the same way that other database objects need occasional maintenance, you might need to change the properties of a user login—for example, you might need to change the security role to which the login is assigned, or the databases to which it has access. And, of course, you will sometimes need to remove a login completely. All of these operations are easy using the Enterprise Manager.

Change login properties

1. Navigate to the Logins icon in the Security folder in the Console Tree.

   SQL Server displays a list of logins in the Details Pane.

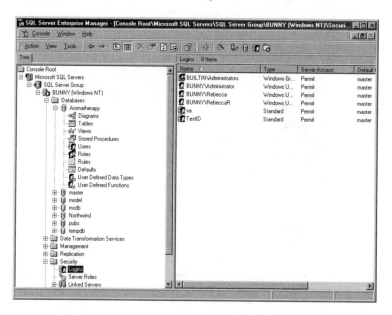

2. Double-click the TestID login in the Details Pane.

SQL Server displays the SQL Server Login Properties dialog box.

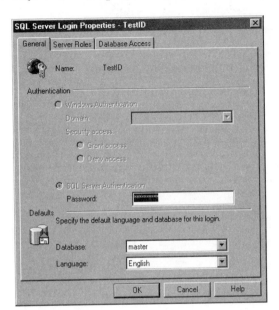

3. Select the Server Roles tab.

   SQL Server displays the server roles to which the login is assigned.

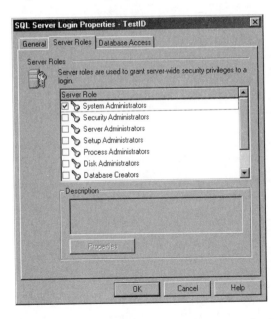

4. Remove the login from the System Administrators role.

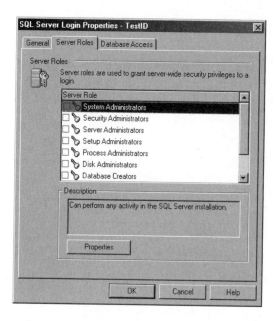

5. Select the Database Access tab.

   SQL Server displays the databases to which the login has been assigned access.

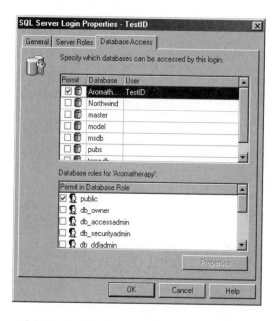

6. Add Northwind to the list of databases.

7. Click OK to close the SQL Server Login Properties dialog box.

SQL Server changes the login properties.

Remove a login

1. Navigate to the Logins icon in the Security folder in the Console Tree.

SQL Server displays a list of logins in the Details Pane.

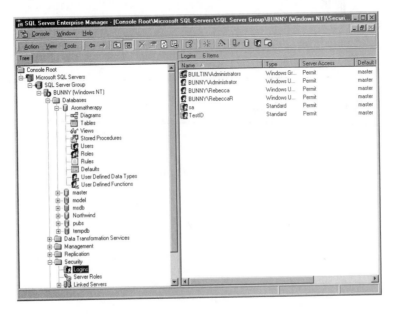

2. Select the TestID login in the Details Pane, and then press the Delete key.

SQL Server displays a message asking you to confirm the deletion.

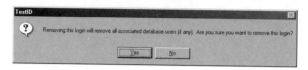

3. Click Yes.

SQL Server deletes the login.

Database-Level Security

At the database level, each user's Windows account or SQL Server login is mapped to a user account in a database. Even though an individual has been granted access to a SQL Server instance by being assigned a login, the individual will not necessarily have access to a specific database unless he or she has been made a user of that database.

Just as logins can be assigned to server roles that grant them specific privileges, users can be assigned to roles at the database level that grant them specific privileges.

IP Although security privileges can be assigned at the individual level, this isn't generally recommended, since it complicates managing the security. It's far easier to add or remove people to predefined groups that have a specific set of security privileges than it is to assign and re-assign privileges for individuals.

Database Users

When you create a new login using the Create Login Wizard, and assign it database access, the login will automatically be added to the users list of the database. However, when you create a new database, you'll probably want to add existing logins to it as users.

Create a database user

1. Navigate to the Users icon in the Aromatherapy database.

SQL Server displays a list of users in the Details Pane.

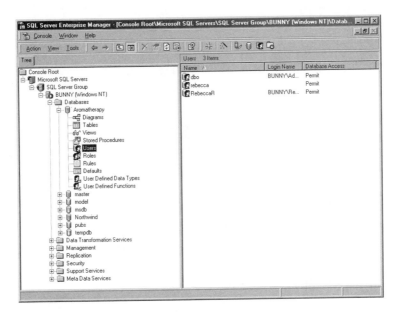

New button

2. Click the New button on the Enterprise Manager toolbar.

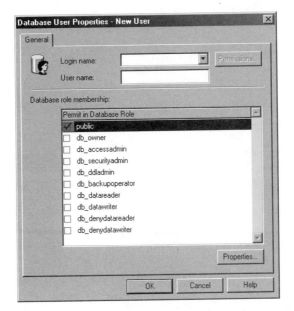

TIP You can also open the Database User Properties dialog box by right-clicking the Users icon in the Console Tree, and selecting New Database User from the context menu.

---

3. Select your login name in the combo box.

   SQL Server will propose the login name as the default user name, but you can change it if you want to.

4. Add db_owner to the roles assigned to the new user.

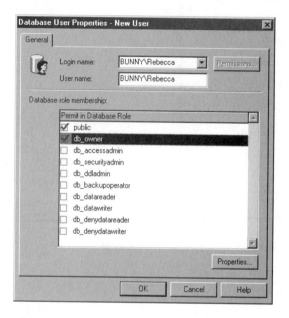

5. Click OK.

   SQL Server adds the user to the database.

IP The roles to which a database user is assigned determine what security privileges the user has for that database. See the following section, "Database Roles," for more details.

Remove a database user

1. Navigate to the Users icon for the Aromatherapy database in the Console Tree.

   SQL Server displays a list of users in the Details Pane.

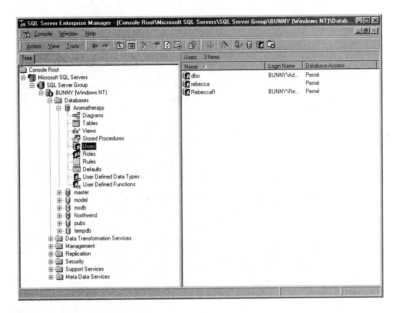

2. Select the user you created in the last exercise in the list, and then press the Delete key.

   SQL Server displays a message asking you to confirm the deletion.

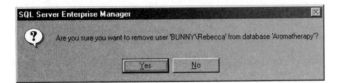

3. Click Yes.

   SQL Server deletes the user from the database.

Database Roles

A *database role* is like a virtual user that you create to manage database access. Any number of database users can be assigned to a role, and any given user can be assigned to multiple roles. When you assign privileges to a database role, and then assign a user to that role, the user inherits all the privileges of the role. This is far simpler than maintaining privileges for individual users. SQL Server 2000 provides a number of pre-defined roles, as shown in Table 3-2. You can also create custom roles that will be unique for your database.

> **TIP** Database roles that you create in the master database will be added to any new databases you create for that server.

Full name	Name	Description
Access Administrator	db_accessadmin	Can add or remove user IDs.
Backup Operator	db_backupoperator	Can issue DBCC, CHECKPOINT, and BACKUP statements.
Data Reader	db_datareader	Can select all data from any user table in the database.
Data Writer	db_datawriter	Can modify any data in any user table in the database.
Data Definition Administrator	db_ddladmin	Can perform Data Definition Language (DDL) statements, but cannot issue GRANT, REVOKE, or DENY statement.
Deny Data Reader	db_denydatareader	Can deny or revoke SELECT permissions on any object in the database.
Deny Data Writer	db_denydatawriter	Can deny or revoke INSERT, UPDATE, and DELETE permissions on any object in the database.
Database Owner	db_owner	Has all permissions in the database.
Security Administrator	db_securityadmin	Can manage all permissions, object ownerships, roles, and role memberships.
Public		The default role to which every database user belongs.

Table 3-2.

Create a database role

1. Click the Roles icon for the Aromatherapy database in the Console Tree.

SQL Server displays a list of existing database roles.

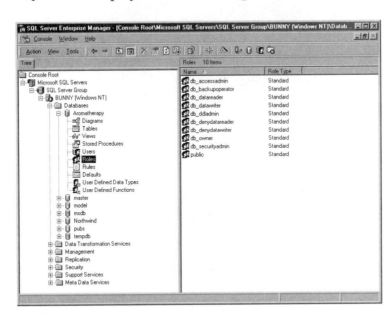

New button

2. Click the New button on the Enterprise Manager toolbar.

   SQL Server displays the Database Role Properties dialog box.

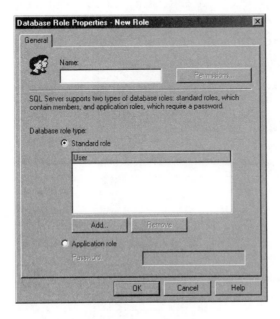

3. Enter *Lesson 3* as the role name.

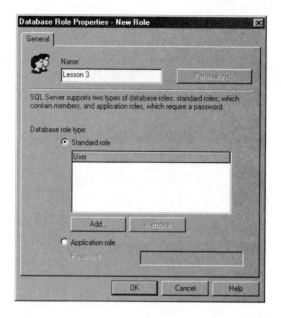

4. Click OK.

   SQL Server closes the Database Role Properties dialog box.

5. Double-click the Lesson 3 role in the Details Pane.

   SQL Server reopens the Database Role Properties dialog box.

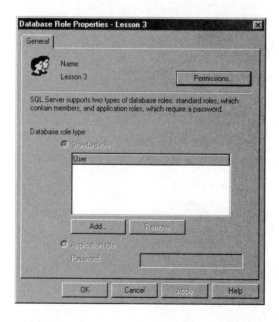

MPORTANT   You must close and reopen the Database Role Properties dialog box in order to enable the Permissions button.

---

6. Click the Permissions button.

   SQL Server displays the Permissions dialog box.

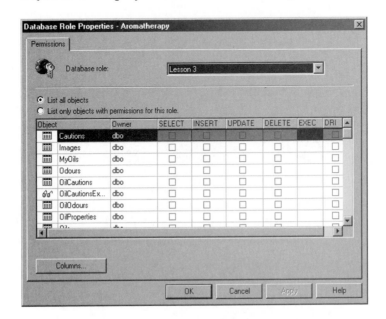

IP   The Database Role Properties dialog box supports two kinds of roles: *standard roles* and *application roles*. The roles discussed in this lesson are all standard roles. An application role is a special function that supports the needs of complex applications. See "Establishing Application Security and Application Roles" in SQL Server Books Online for details about application roles.

---

7. Give the role Select permission on the Oils table.

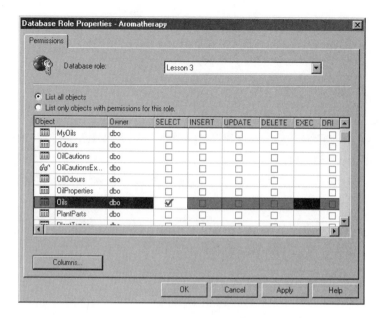

8. Click OK.

   SQL Server closes the Permissions dialog box.

9. Click OK.

   SQL Server adds the new role.

Assign a user to a database role

1. Navigate to the Users icon for the Aromatherapy database in the Console Tree.

   SQL Server displays a list of users in the Details Pane.

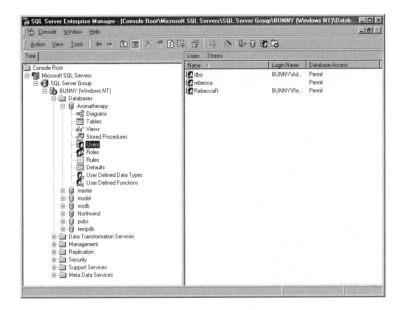

2. Double-click your user name in the users list.

   SQL Server displays the Database User Properties dialog box.

3. Add the user to the Lesson 3 role by clicking it in the Database Role Membership list box.

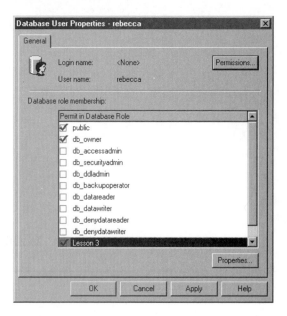

4. Click OK.

   SQL Server adds the user to the role and closes the Database User Properties dialog box.

Remove a user from a database role

1. Navigate to the Users icon for the Aromatherapy database in the Console Tree.

   SQL Server displays a list of users in the Details Pane.

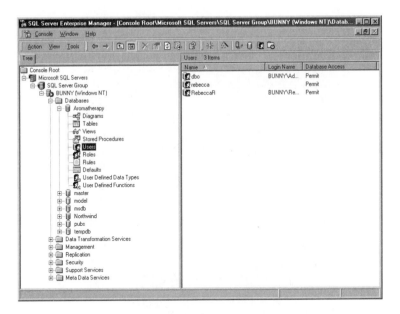

2. Double-click your user name in the list.

SQL Server displays the Database User Properties dialog box.

3. Uncheck the Lesson 3 role in the Database Role Membership list.

4. Click OK.

SQL Server removes the user's membership in the role and closes the dialog box.

Remove a database role

1. Navigate to the Roles icon for the Aromatherapy database in the Console Tree.

SQL Server displays a list of roles in the Details Pane.

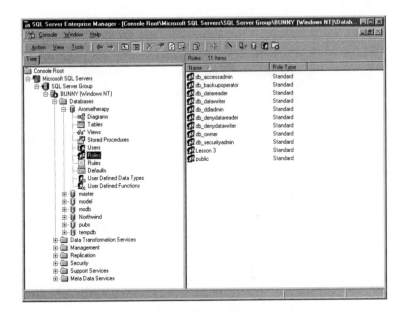

2. Select the Lesson 3 role in the Details Pane, and press the Delete key.

   SQL Server displays a message asking you to confirm the deletion.

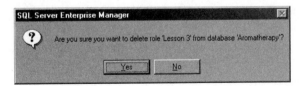

3. Click Yes.

   SQL Server deletes the role from the database.

Lesson 3 Quick Reference

To	Do this
Create a SQL Server login	Select the server in the Console Tree, and then click the Wizard button on the Enterprise Manager toolbar to display the Select Wizard dialog box. Select the Create Login Wizard in the Database section. Specify SQL Server Login Information That Was Assigned To Me By The System Administrator (SQL Server Authentication) on the page requesting an authentication method.
Create a Windows login	Select the server in the Console Tree, and then click the Wizard button on the Enterprise Manager toolbar to display the Select Wizard dialog box. Select the Create Login Wizard in the Database section. Select Windows Account Information I Use To Logon To My Computer (Windows Authentication) on the page requesting an authentication mode.
Remove a login	Select the Logins icon in the Security folder in the Console Tree. Select the login you wish to remove, and press the Delete key.
Create a database user	Right-click the Users icon for the database in the Console Tree, and then click New Database User. Select the login name in the combo box, change the user name if desired, select the desired roles, and then click OK.
Remove a database user	Navigate to the Users icon for the database in the Console Tree. Select the user in the list displayed in the Details Pane, and press the Delete key.
Create a database role	Right-click the Roles icon for the database in the Console Tree, and then click New Database Role. Enter the role name in the dialog box, and then click Permissions to specify permissions for the role.
Assign a user to a database role	Navigate to the Users icon for the database in the Console Tree. Double-click the user in the list in the Details Pane. Add the user to the role by clicking it in the resulting dialog box.
Remove a user from a database role	Navigate to the Users icon for the database in the Console Tree. Double-click the user in the list Details Pane. Remove the user from the role by unchecking it in the Database Role Membership list.
Remove a database role	Navigate to the Roles icon for the database in the Console Tree. Select the role in the list in the Details Pane, and press the Delete key.

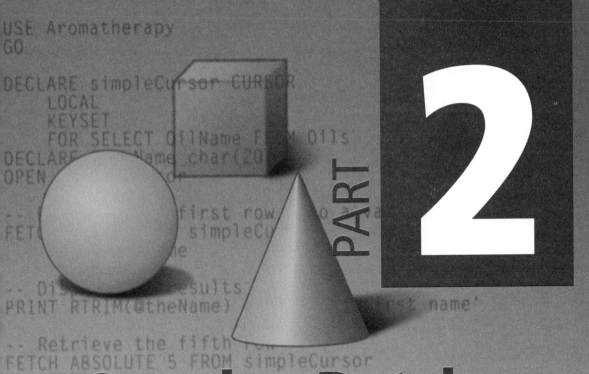

PART **2**

Creating Databases

Lesson

4	Creating a Database	77
5	Creating Tables	91
6	Creating Indexes	115
7	Creating Relationships	139
8	Creating Check Constraints	157
9	Creating Table Objects	169
10	Creating Database Diagrams	187

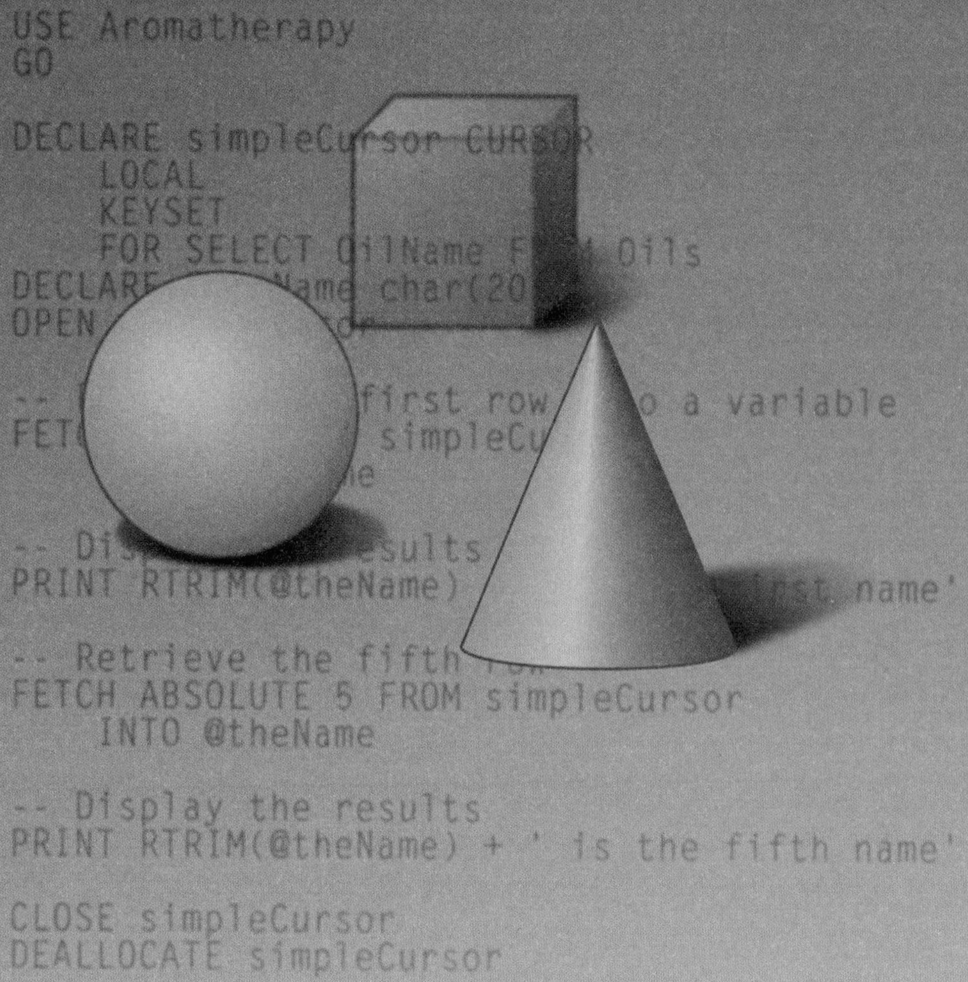

```sql
USE Aromatherapy
GO

DECLARE simpleCursor CURSOR
    LOCAL
    KEYSET
    FOR SELECT OilName FROM Oils
DECLARE @theName char(20)
OPEN simpleCursor

-- Retrieve the first row into a variable
FETCH FIRST FROM simpleCursor
    INTO @theName

-- Display the results
PRINT RTRIM(@theName) + ' is the first name'

-- Retrieve the fifth row
FETCH ABSOLUTE 5 FROM simpleCursor
    INTO @theName

-- Display the results
PRINT RTRIM(@theName) + ' is the fifth name'

CLOSE simpleCursor
DEALLOCATE simpleCursor
```

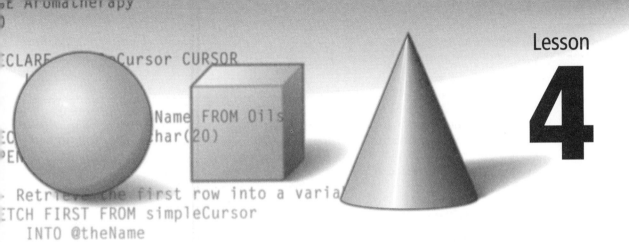

Creating a Database

E Aromacherapy

ECLARE   Cursor CURSOR

        Name FROM Oils
        har(20)

- Retri the first row into a varia
TCH FIRST FROM simpleCursor
    INTO @theName

- Display the results
RINT RTRIM(@theName) + ' is the first name'

In this lesson you will learn how to:

- Create a new database.
- Change database properties.
- Delete a database.

In the Microsoft SQL Server environment, you store tables, views, and other objects related to a particular set of information in a *database,* so the first step in implementing a database application is, obviously, to create the database, and in this lesson we'll learn how to do just that.

Creating Databases

For each logical database, SQL Server creates two physical files: one for the objects and one for the transaction log.

IP Although by default SQL Server suggests the same location for both the database file and the transaction log, in a production system you should always store the transaction log in a different location, preferably on a different machine. This makes it possible to restore the database in case of a hardware failure that prevents the disk from being read.

Creating a New Database

Although it's possible to create a new database by selecting the New Database command on the Database folder's context menu, the easiest way is to use the Create Database Wizard.

Create a new database

1. Navigate to the Databases folder of the server you're using for these lessons.

   SQL Server displays a list of databases in the Details Pane.

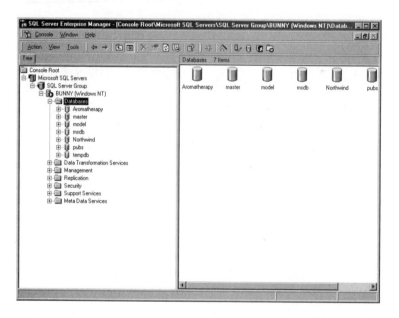

Wizard button

2. Click the Wizard button on the Enterprise Manager toolbar.

   SQL Server displays the Select Wizard dialog box.

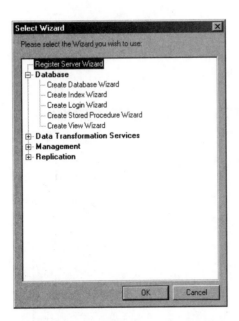

3. Select Create Database Wizard from the Database section, and click OK.

   SQL Server displays the first page of the wizard.

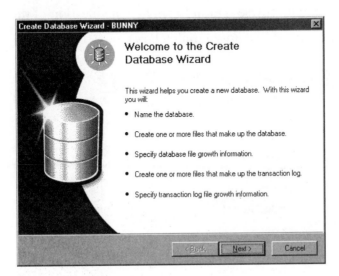

4. Click Next.

The Create Database Wizard displays a page requesting the name and location for the new database.

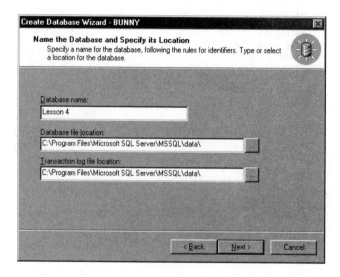

5. Type *Lesson 4* in the Database Name field.

Browse button

6. Click the Browse button to change the location of the database file.

The wizard displays a dialog box requesting the new location.

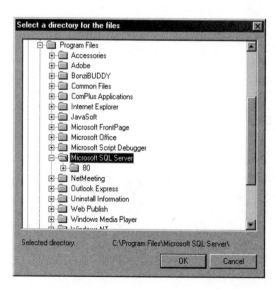

Database File Locations

When SQL Server is first installed, it sets the default location for new database files to MSSQL\data in the folder where the server is installed. This default is supplied in the Create Database Wizard. To permanently change the default, you can set a new location on the Database Settings tab of the SQL Server Properties dialog box, accessed by right-clicking the server in the Console Tree, choosing Properties, and then choosing the Database Settings tab.

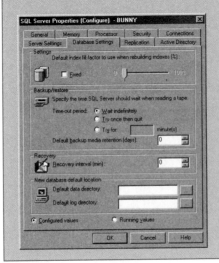

7. Navigate to the SQL 2000 Step by Step folder in the root directory, and then click OK.

   The wizard sets the database file location to the selected directory.

Browse button

8. Click the Browse button to change the location of the transaction log.

   The wizard displays a dialog box requesting the new location.

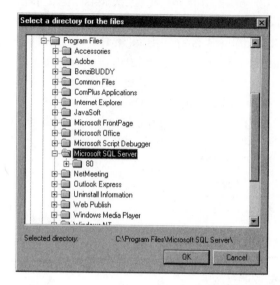

9. Navigate to the SQL 2000 Step by Step folder in the root directory, and then click OK.

   The wizard sets the transaction log file location to the selected directory.

10. Click Next.

    The wizard displays a page requesting a name and initial size for the database file.

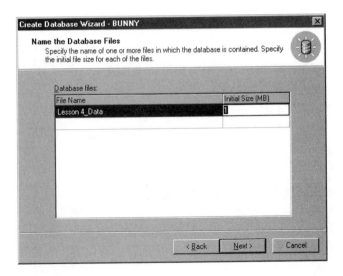

11. Click Next.

The wizard displays a page letting you choose whether the database files will grow automatically or grow only when you enlarge them. For this exercise, accept the default settings.

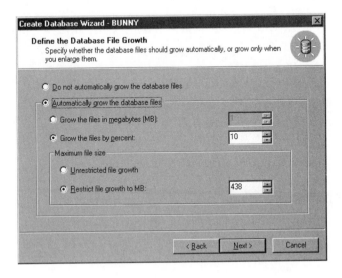

12. Click Next.

The wizard displays a page requesting a name and initial size for the transaction log. Accept the default value.

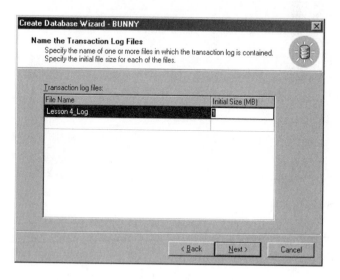

13. Click Next.

The wizard displays a page letting you choose whether the transaction log file should be grown automatically. Accept the default settings.

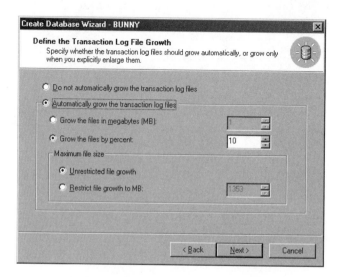

14. Click Next.

The wizard displays a page confirming the choices you have made.

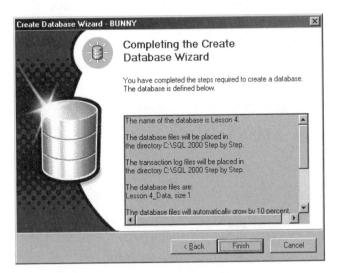

15. Click Finish.

The wizard creates the database and transaction log files, and then asks whether you would like to create a maintenance plan for the new database.

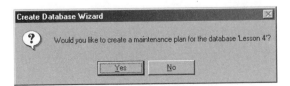

16. Click No.

The wizard closes.

Setting Database Properties

When you create a database using the Create Database Wizard, you specify certain characteristics, or *properties,* of the database, such as the name of the database and the file locations. After the database is created, you can change these properties by changing the appropriate settings in the database's Properties dialog box.

For example, enlarging the size of the physical data file ("growing the file" in SQL Server parlance) is a fairly expensive operation that slows down server response time. If you find that SQL Server has to enlarge the file too often, you might consider changing the file growth percentage setting in the Properties dialog box so that the server will expand the file by more than the default value of 10 percent.

Change the database file growth percentage

1. Select the Lesson 4 database in the Console Tree.

Properties button

2. Click the Properties button on the toolbar.

   SQL Server displays the database's Properties dialog box.

3. Click the Data Files tab.

   SQL Server displays the properties of the database's data files.

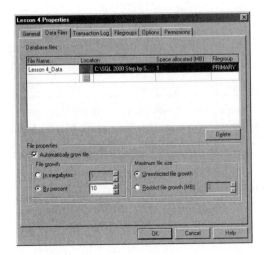

4. Set the growth percentage to 20 percent.

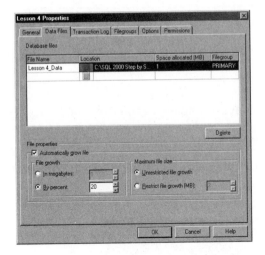

5. Click OK.

   SQL Server sets the new property and closes the Properties
   dialog box.

Managing Databases

In addition to changing the properties of a database, you will occasionally need to delete it altogether. The Enterprise Manager makes that very easy.

 OTE   Another management task you might want to perform, renaming a database, can't be done within the Enterprise Manager. We'll learn how to rename a database in Lesson 28.

Deleting a Database

When a database you have created is no longer needed, you can delete it from the server. Deleting a database removes both the physical files associated with the database and all references to the database in the system tables.

 IP   It's a good idea to make a backup of the system databases after a database is deleted.

Delete a database

1. Select the Lesson 4 database in the Console Tree.

2. Press the Delete key.

   SQL Server displays a message requesting you to confirm the deletion.

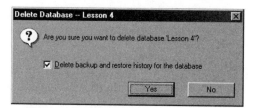

3. Click Yes.

   SQL Server removes the database and all associated references from the server.

Lesson 4 Quick Reference

To	Do this	Button
Create a new database	Click the Wizard button, select Create Database Wizard in the Database section, and then follow the instructions.	
Set database properties	Right-click the database in the Console Tree and choose Properties.	
Delete a database	Select the database in the Console Tree and press the Delete key.	

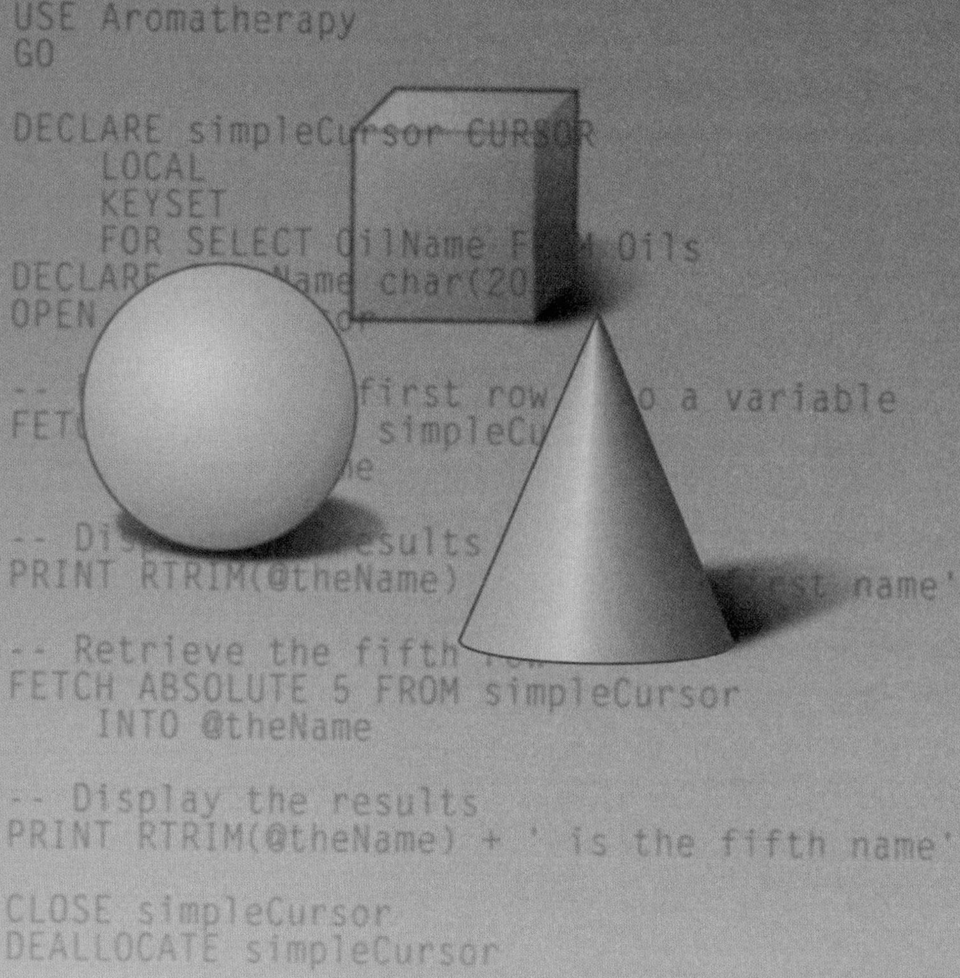

```sql
USE Aromatherapy
GO

DECLARE simpleCursor CURSOR
    LOCAL
    KEYSET
    FOR SELECT OilName FROM Oils
DECLARE @theName char(20)
OPEN simpleCursor

-- Retrieve the first row into a variable
FETCH NEXT FROM simpleCursor
    INTO @theName

-- Display the results
PRINT RTRIM(@theName) + ' is the first name'

-- Retrieve the fifth row
FETCH ABSOLUTE 5 FROM simpleCursor
    INTO @theName

-- Display the results
PRINT RTRIM(@theName) + ' is the fifth name'

CLOSE simpleCursor
DEALLOCATE simpleCursor
```

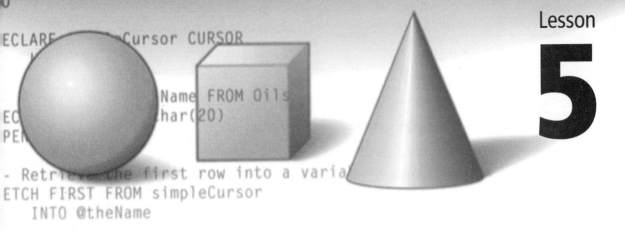

Creating Tables

In this lesson you will learn how to:

- Create a new table.
- Add columns to a table.
- Save and close a table.
- Rename a column.
- Remove a column.
- Rename a table.
- Remove a table.

In the Microsoft SQL Server environment, as in any relational database, information is organized into tables, orderly arrangements of rows and columns that store data for single objects.

In this lesson, you'll learn how to create a new table and specify the columns that comprise it.

 IP It's convenient to think of the contents of a table as a grid, like a spreadsheet. But it's important to realize that the records in a table have no intrinsic order. The idea of "previous" and "next" doesn't apply to records in a table.

If you need to perform sequential operations, you can do so by creating something called a *cursor*, an entity that points to a specific row in a set of records. We'll discuss cursors in Lesson 27.

Creating Tables

Tables are a fundamental unit of data storage in a relational database. As a general rule, each type of entity, such as an essential oil in our sample database, is represented by a table, whereas each instance of that entity, such as Clary Sage or German Chamomile, is represented by a row in the table.

> ## Database Design
>
> The most common method of defining databases uses the concepts of *entities* and *attributes*. When you move from the logical design to the physical implementation, the entities are (usually) implemented as tables, and the attributes are implemented as columns (also known as fields).

Understanding Data Types

Every column in a table has certain properties that define it to SQL Server. The most important of these properties is the column's *data type*, which is a definition of the type of information that will be stored in the column. SQL Server provides a wide range of data types, shown in Table 5-1.

In addition to the data types provided by SQL Server, you can also define your own. You'll learn how to do this in Lesson 9.

Data type	Acceptable values
Numeric values	
bigint	Integer values from -2^{63} through $2^{63} -1$.
int	Integer values from -2^{31} through $2^{31}-1$.
smallint	Integer values from -2^{15} through $2^{15} -1$.
tinyint	Integer values from 0 through 255.
bit	Integer values with a value of either 1 or 0.
decimal	Fixed precision and scale values from $-10^{38}+1$ through $10^{38}-1$. (*Decimal* values can also be defined as "numeric"; the range of values is the same.)
money	Monetary values from -2^{63} through $2^{63}-1$. (*Money* values are accurate to one ten-thousandth (.0001) of a unit.)
smallmoney	Monetary values from $-214,748.3648$ through $214,748.3647$. (*Smallmoney* values are accurate to one ten-thousandth (.0001) of a unit.)
float	Floating precision values from $-1.79E + 308$ through $1.79E + 308$. (*Float* values are only approximate.)
real	Floating precision values from $-3.40E +38$ through $3.40E + 38$. (*Float* values are only approximate.)

Table 5-1. *SQL Server Data Types* *(continued)*

Table 5-1. *continued*

Data type	Acceptable values
Date and time values	
datetime	Date and time values from January 1, 1753, through December 31, 9999. (*Datetime* values are accurate to three hundredths of a second, or 3.33 milliseconds.)
smalldatetime	Date and time values from January 1, 1900, through June 6, 2079. (*Smalldatetime* values are accurate to one minute.)
Character values	
char	Fixed-length non-Unicode character values with a maximum length of 8000 characters.
varchar	Variable-length non-Unicode character values with a maximum length of 8000 characters.
Text	Variable-length non-Unicode data with a maximum length of $2^{31}-1$ (2,147,483,647) characters.
Nchar	Fixed-length Unicode data with a maximum length of 4000 characters.
nvarchar	Variable-length Unicode data with a maximum length of 4000 characters.
ntext	Variable-length Unicode data with a maximum length of $2^{30}-1$ (1,073,741,823) characters.
Binary values	
binary	Fixed-length binary data with a maximum length of 8000 bytes.
Varbinary	Variable-length binary data with a maximum length of 8000 bytes.
image	Variable-length binary data with a maximum length of $2^{31}-1$ (2,147,483,647) bytes.
Other values	
cursor	A reference to a cursor. (A *cursor* is an entity that establishes a reference to a specific row in a result set.)
rowversion	A database-wide unique number that gets updated every time a row gets updated. (The *rowversion* data type was called a *timestamp* in previous versions of SQL Server.)
sql_variant	Values of any type except *text*, *ntext*, *rowversion* (*timestamp*) and *sql_variant*.
uniqueidentifier	A globally unique identifier (GUID).

Creating a New Table

Tables are created and maintained using the Enterprise Manager's Table Designer. The first step is to create and name the table itself by opening a Table Designer for a new table.

Create a new table

1. Navigate to the Tables folder of the Aromatherapy database.

   SQL Server displays a list of existing tables.

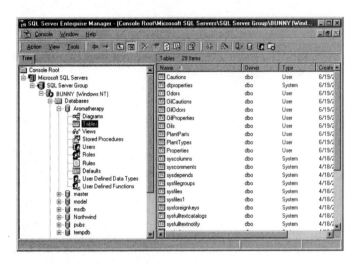

New button

2. Click the New button on the Toolbar.

   SQL Server opens the Table Designer.

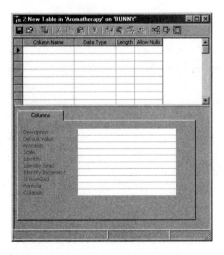

Properties button

3. Click the Properties button on the Toolbar.

SQL Server opens the table's Properties dialog box.

4. Change the Table Name to *Lesson 5*.

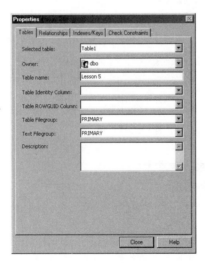

5. Click Close.

SQL Server closes the Properties dialog box.

Adding Columns to a Table

Although a table does have certain properties of its own, such as the name that we supplied in the last exercise, a table is primarily defined by the columns that comprise it.

Add a numeric column to the table

1. Type *MyNumber* in the Column Name cell, and then press Tab.

   SQL Server proposes *char* as the data type.

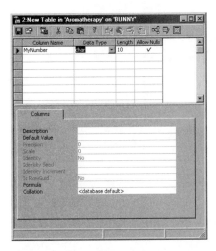

2. Change the data type to *decimal*.

   SQL Server changes the column length to 9 and enables the Precision, Scale, and Identity fields.

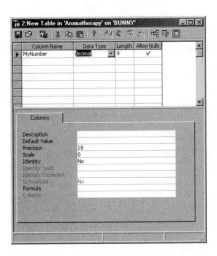

3. Type *Sample Numeric Column* in the Description cell.

4. Change the precision of the column to *5* and the scale to *2*.

   SQL Server changes the column length to 5, to reflect the new precision.

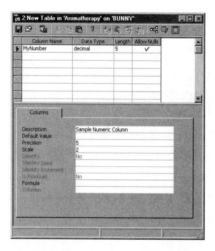

Column Descriptions

The ability to add a description to a column in the Enterprise Manager is new in SQL Server 2000. It's part of the new functionality known as *extended properties*. Microsoft has created some extended properties, such as the column description, as part of the standard server installation, and you can create additional extended properties to store application-specific or site-specific information about database objects.

Each extended property has a user-defined name and a value. The value of an extended property is a *sql_variant* value that can contain up to 7500 bytes of data. You can define multiple extended properties for any object using stored procedures. For more on stored procedures, see Lesson 28.

Precision and Scale

The *precision* of a numeric value is the maximum number of decimal digits that represent the value, to both the left and the right of the decimal point. The *scale* of the value is the number of digits to the right of the decimal point. For example, the value 3647.311 has a precision of 7 (total number of digits) and a scale of 3 (digits to the right of the decimal point).

It's important to understand that the precision and scale of a numeric value do not affect the column's length. The data type determines the length of a column. The precision and scale determine how SQL Server will interpret the data stored in the column.

Add an identity column to the table

1. Click in an empty cell in the Column Name column, type *MyIdentity*, and then press Tab.

   SQL Server proposes *char* as the data type.

2. Change the data type to *decimal.*

   SQL Server changes the column length to 9 and enables the Precision, Scale, and Identity fields.

3. Clear the Allow Nulls checkbox.

Nulls

A *Null value* is a special kind of value in relational technology that is used to indicate that a value is either missing or nonexistent. The use of Nulls is somewhat problematic, and definitely contentious.

---

4. Type *Sample Identity Column* in the Description cell.

5. Change the Identity field to *Yes (Not For Replication).*

   SQL Server proposes both the Identity Seed field and the Identity Increment field a value of 1.

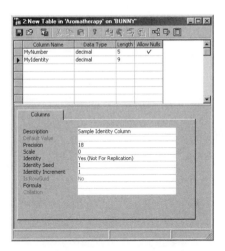

Identity Values

When you set the *Identity* property of a column, you're telling SQL Server to insert a value into the column that uniquely identifies each row. The data type selected determines the precise nature of the column. Identity columns can have the data type of *int*, *smallint*, *tinyint*, or *decimal.*

When SQL Server inserts a row into a table that has an identity column, it automatically generates the value for the column based on the last used value (beginning with the identity seed) and the identity increment that was specified when the table was created.

For example, if an identity column is defined as a *smallint* with an identity seed of 50 and an identity increment of 5, the first row inserted would be assigned the value 50, the second would be assigned the value 55, the third 60, and so forth.

Only one column in a table can have the *Identity* property set.

Add a GUID column to the table

1. Click in an empty cell in the Column Name column, type *MyGUID*, and then press Tab.

   SQL Server proposes *char* as the data type.

2. Change the data type to *uniqueidentifier.*

   SQL Server changes the column length to 16 and enables the Is RowGuid field.

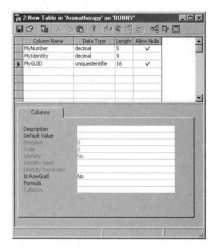

3. Type *Sample GUID* in the Description cell.

4. Change the Is RowGuid field to *Yes*.

   SQL Server sets the default value to *(Newid())*

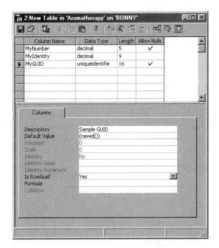

GUIDs

GUID, which stands for Globally Unique Identifier, is a 16-byte unique binary value—no other computer in the world will generate that value. The *uniqueidentifier* data type is used to store GUIDs.

SQL Server doesn't automatically generate GUID values in the same way it does identity values because a table can contain multiple GUIDs, but only a single identity. However, the NEWID function, which SQL Server proposes as the default value when the *Is RowGUID* property is set to *Yes*, will return a new GUID when the row is inserted.

Add a date column to the table

1. Click in an empty cell in the Column Name column, type *MyDate*, and then press Tab.

   SQL Server proposes *char* as the data type.

2. Change the data type to *datetime.*

SQL Server changes the column length to 8.

3. Type *Sample Date Column* in the Description cell.

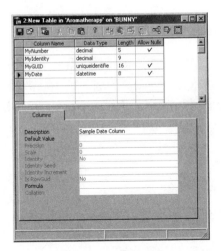

Add a character column to the table

1. Click in an empty cell in the Column Name column, type *MyChar*, and then press Tab.

   SQL Server proposes *char* as the data type.

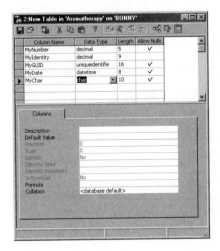

Character Data Types

SQL Server supports two different kinds of character columns: fixed-length and variable-length, each of which comes in two different "flavors," Unicode and non-Unicode, and three different lengths. Unicode is a method of character encoding that supports double-byte character sets.

If a column is declared as variable-length (for example, *varchar* or *text* for non-Unicode data and *nvarchar* and *ntext* for Unicode data), SQL Server will store only the actual data characters entered. If, on the other hand, the column is declared as fixed-length (*char* for non-Unicode data and *nchar* for Unicode data), SQL Server will pad the values entered with spaces.

For example, if a column is declared as a *char* with a length of 10, and the actual value is "hello," SQL Server will store the value as "hello ," with five spaces following the five actual characters.

2. Change the column length to *25*.

3. Type *Sample Character Column* in the Description cell.

4. Type '*Unknown*' in the Default Value cell. (Be sure to include the single quotes around the word.)

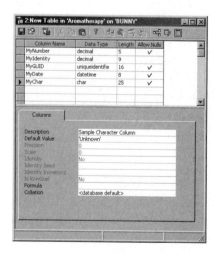

Default Values

A *default value* is a value that will be inserted into a column if the user doesn't explicitly provide one.

We've already seen two special kinds of default values: the identity value provided by SQL Server when you set the *Identity* property, and the NEWID function provided by SQL Server when you set the *Is RowGuid* property. In fact, you can specify default values for any column. Default values can be constants such as 'Unknown' or 123, functions such as NEWID or GETDATE, or mathematical expressions such as 3 + 5.

Save and close the table

Save button

1. Click the Save button on the Table Designer toolbar.

   SQL Server saves the table definition.

2. Close the window.

Managing Tables

Although "best practice" dictates that your database design should be stable before you begin implementation, in the real world things change. Fortunately, SQL Server makes it easy to perform maintenance tasks.

Altering Columns

You can re-open the Table Designer for a table by right-clicking the table name in the Details Pane and selecting Design Table from the context menu. Once the Table Designer is open, you can change the properties of existing columns, delete them, or add new ones.

Rename a column

1. Select the Tables folder for the Aromatherapy database in the Console Tree.

   SQL Server displays a list of tables in the Details Pane.

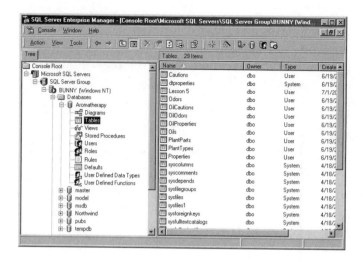

2. Right-click the Lesson 5 table in the Details Pane and select Design Table. SQL Server opens the Table Designer.

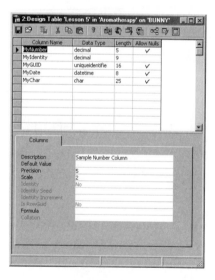

3. Select MyChar in the Column Name cell and type *MyCharacter*.

   SQL Server changes the column name.

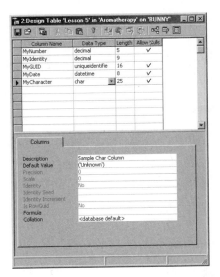

4. Click the Save button on the Table Designer toolbar to save the change.

Remove a column

1. Select the MyDate column by clicking on the gray box to the left of the column name.

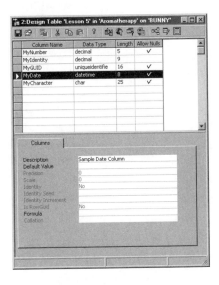

2. Press the Delete key.

SQL Server removes the column.

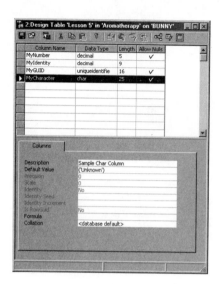

3. Click the Save button to save the change.

4. Close the Table Designer window.

Altering Tables

In addition to changing the column definitions of a table, the Enterprise Manager makes it easy to rename tables and delete tables from the database.

Rename a table

1. Navigate to the Tables folder for the Aromatherapy database in the Console Tree.

   SQL Server displays a list of tables in the Details Pane.

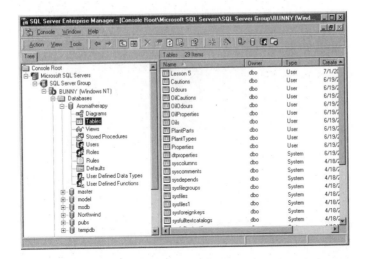

2. Right-click the Lesson 5 table in the Details Pane and select Rename.

3. Type *New Lesson 5* and press Enter.

   SQL Server displays the Rename dialog box warning you that changing the table's name will invalidate any references to it in other objects.

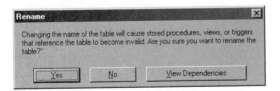

4. Click View Dependencies to display any objects that might be affected by the change.

   SQL Server opens the Dependencies dialog box.

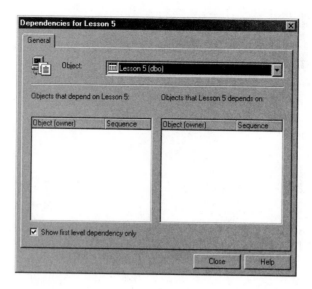

5. Click Close to dismiss the dialog box.

6. Click Yes in the Rename dialog box to confirm the name change.

   SQL Server displays a message confirming the successful completion of the name change.

Remove a table

1. Select the table New Lesson 5 in the Details Pane.

2. Press the Delete key.

   SQL Server displays the Drop Objects dialog box.

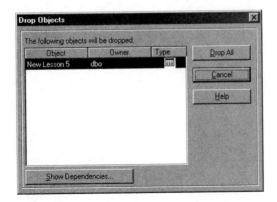

 IP You can click the Show Dependencies button to show any objects that would be affected by deleting the table.

3. Click Drop All.

   SQL Server removes the table from the database.

 MPORTANT When you delete a table, the table and all its data will be *permanently* removed from the database. The only way to restore it is from a database backup.

Lesson 5 Quick Reference

To	Do this	Button
Create a new table	Select the Tables folder of the database in the Console Tree, and then click the New button.	⚞
Add columns to a table	Specify the column properties in the Table Designer.	
Rename a column	Open the Table Designer, select the column name, and then type the new name.	
Remove a column	Select the column in the Table Designer and press the Delete key.	
Rename a table	Right-click the table in the Details Pane, and then select Rename. Type the new name, and click Yes on the confirming dialog box.	
Remove a table	Select the table in the Details Pane and press the Delete key.	

```
USE Aromatherapy
GO

DECLARE simpleCursor CURSOR
    LOCAL
    KEYSET
    FOR SELECT OilName FROM Oils
DECLARE @theName char(20)
OPEN simpleCursor

-- Retrieve the first row into a variable
FETCH FIRST FROM simpleCursor
    INTO @theName

-- Display the results
PRINT RTRIM(@theName) + ' is the first name'

-- Retrieve the fifth row
FETCH ABSOLUTE 5 FROM simpleCursor
    INTO @theName

-- Display the results
PRINT RTRIM(@theName) + ' is the fifth name'

CLOSE simpleCursor
DEALLOCATE simpleCursor
```

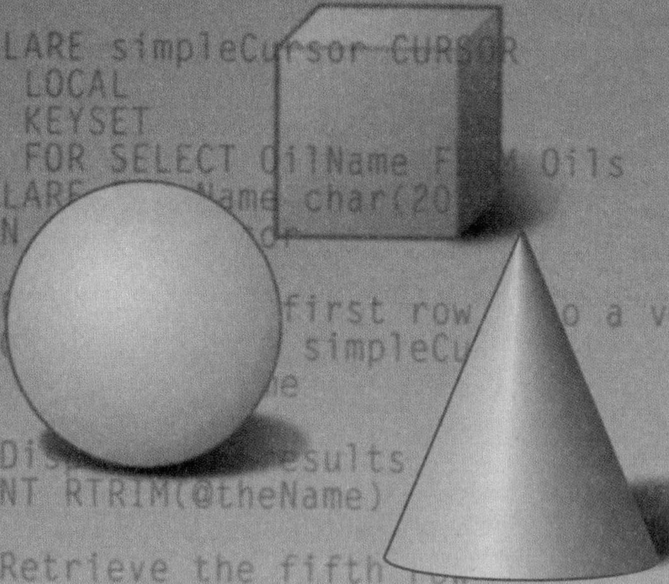

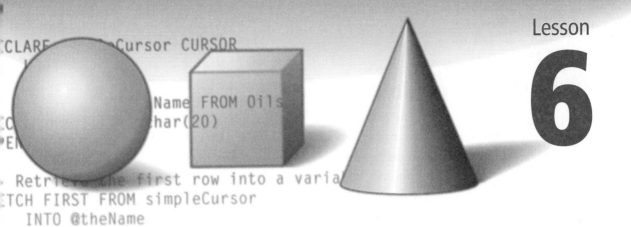

Creating Indexes

In this lesson you will learn how to:

- Create an index using the Create Index Wizard.
- Create a primary key index.
- Create a simple index.
- Create a composite index.
- Rename an index.
- Change the columns in an index.
- Drop an index.

Understanding Indexes

In a relational database, an *index* is a special object that allows the database to quickly access rows in a table based on the values of one or more columns in much the same way as the index of a book provides quick access to its contents based on specific keywords.

Microsoft SQL Server provides two different types of indexes: clustered and nonclustered. A *clustered index* determines the order in which the rows of the table are physically stored. A *nonclustered index*, on the other hand, is a separate object within the database that points to specific rows within a table but does not determine how the rows are stored.

An index can reference one or more columns in a table. An index that references only a single column is called a *simple index*, whereas an index that references multiple columns is a *composite index*.

In addition to the indexes you define yourself, SQL Server will automatically create a clustered index called a *primary key index* when you define a *primary key* for a table. A primary key is the column or columns that will be used to uniquely identify each row.

Creating Indexes

In the Enterprise Manager, indexes can be created using the Create Index Wizard or through the Table Designer either by setting the *Primary Key* property or by defining the index in the table's Properties dialog box.

Create an index using the Create Index Wizard

1. Navigate to the Aromatherapy database in the Console Tree.

   SQL Server displays a list of database objects in the Details Pane.

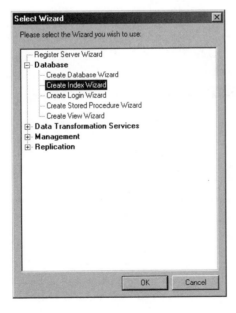

2. Click the Wizard button on the Enterprise Manager toolbar.

Wizard button

SQL Server displays the Select Wizard dialog box.

3. Select Create Index Wizard in the Database section, and then click OK.

   SQL Server displays the first page of the Create Index Wizard.

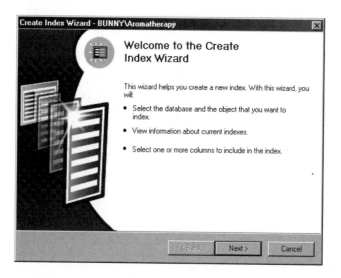

4. Click Next.

   The wizard displays a page requesting the database and table for which the index will be created.

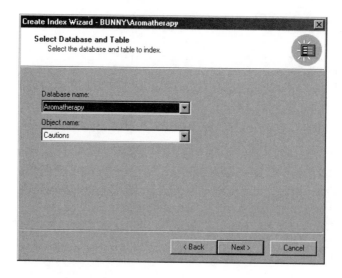

5. Make sure Aromatherapy is the selected database name and select Oils as the table name.

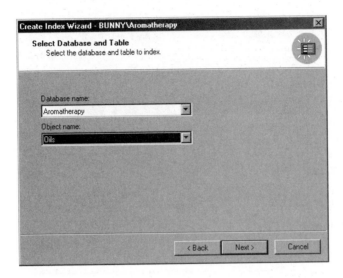

6. Click Next.

The wizard displays the existing indexes for the table. (The indexes with funny names are created by SQL Server to enforce relationships. We'll talk about relationships in the next lesson.)

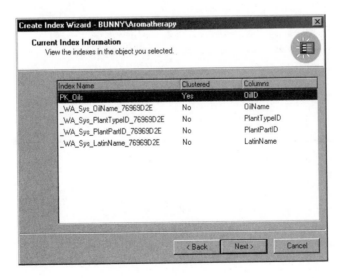

7. Click Next.

The wizard displays the columns in the table.

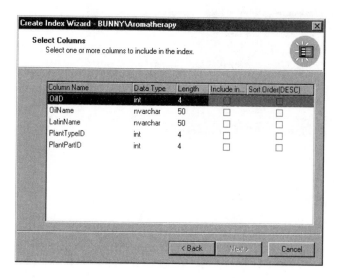

8. Click the Include In Index cell of the OilName and LatinName columns to include them in the index.

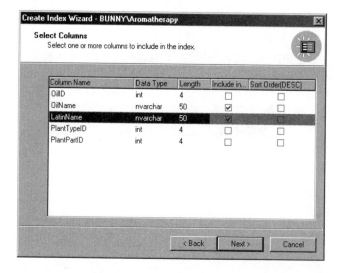

9. Click Next.

The wizard displays a page requesting the index properties.

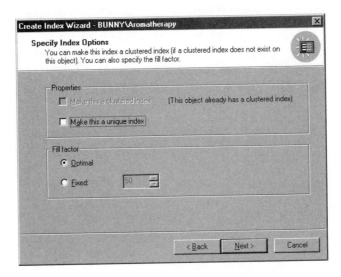

10. Accept the default values by clicking Next.

The wizard displays a page confirming your selections and requesting a name for the index. Accept the default name.

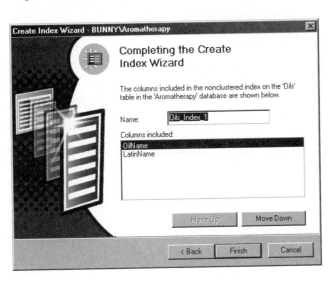

11. Select the LatinName field and click the Move Up button to change the order of the fields in the index.

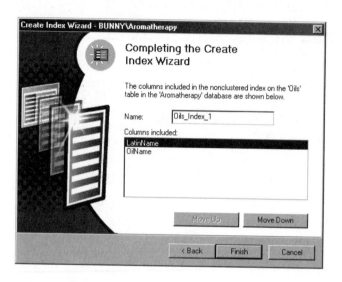

12. Click Finish.

    The wizard displays a message confirming that the index has been created.

Create a primary key index

1. Navigate to the Tables folder of the Aromatherapy database in the Console Tree.

    SQL Server displays a list of tables in the database.

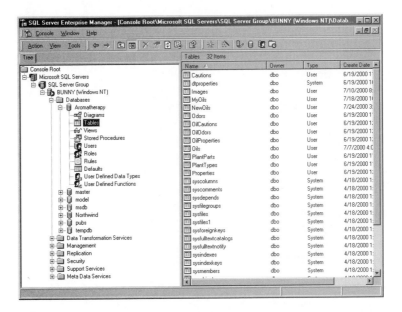

2. Open the Table Designer for the PlantTypes table by right-clicking the table name in the Details Pane and selecting Design Table.

SQL Server opens the Table Designer.

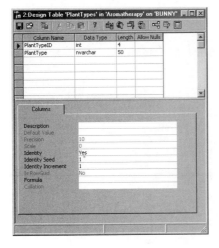

3. Select the PlantTypeID column in the grid by clicking to the left of the column name.

SQL Server selects the column.

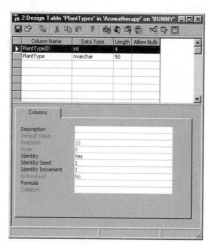

Primary Key button

4. Click the Primary Key button on the Table Designer toolbar.

SQL Server sets the selected column as the primary key.

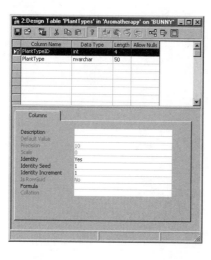

5. Click the Save button to save the change and close the window.

Create a simple index

1. Open the Table Designer for the Oils table by right-clicking the table name in the Details Pane and selecting Design Table.

   SQL Server opens the Table Designer.

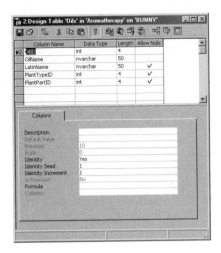

Indexes/Keys button

2. Click the Indexes/Keys button.

   SQL Server opens the table's Properties dialog box with the Indexes/Keys property page displayed.

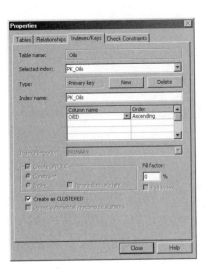

Properties button

TIP You can also open the table's Properties dialog box by clicking the Properties button and then clicking the Indexes/Keys tab.

3. Click New.

SQL Server proposes IX_Oils as the index name and OilID as the indexed column.

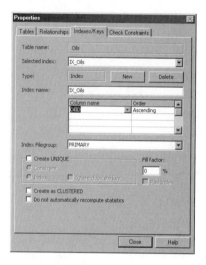

4. Change the name of the index to *IX_OilName*.

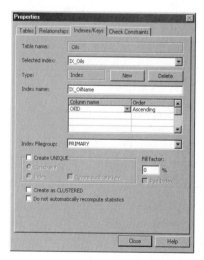

5. Change the index column name to *OilName* by selecting the column from the combo box.

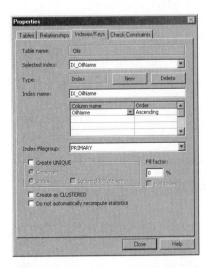

6. Check the Create UNIQUE check box to create a unique index.

   SQL Server enables the Create UNIQUE group box.

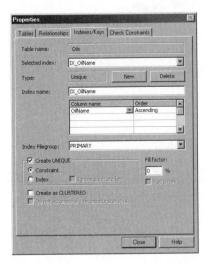

7. Select the Index option.

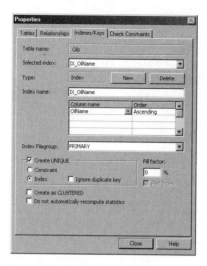

Unique Indexes

A *unique index* ensures that no two rows in a table can contain duplicate data for the column or columns specified in the index. Primary key indexes are always unique, but you can add additional unique indexes if you wish.

Be careful about creating unique indexes on columns that allow Null values, however. SQL Server will accept a single row with a Null value, but will reject subsequent rows as duplicate values.

8. Click Close.

   SQL Server closes the dialog box.

9. Click the Save button on the Table Designer toolbar to save the change, and then close the Table Designer window.

Create a composite index

1. Open the Table Designer for the OilOdors table by right-clicking the table name in the Details Pane and selecting Design Table.

   SQL Server opens the Table Designer.

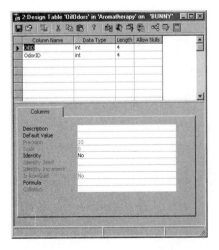

Indexes/Keys button

2. Click the Indexes/Keys button.

   SQL Server opens the table's Properties dialog box with the
   Indexes/Keys property page displayed.

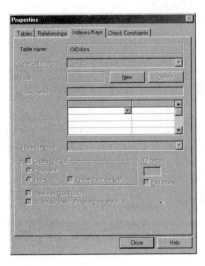

3. Click New.

   SQL Server proposes IX_OilOdors as the index name and OilID as
   the indexed column.

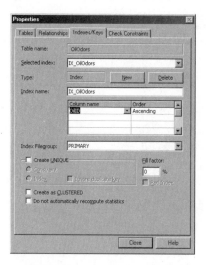

4. Add the OdorID column to the index by clicking in the Column Name cell and selecting it from the combo box.

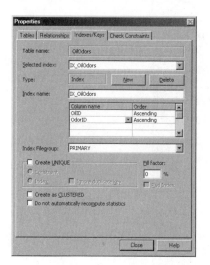

5. Click Close.

   SQL Server closes the dialog box.

6. Click the Save button on the Table Designer toolbar to save the change, and then close the Table Designer window.

Maintaining Indexes

Like any other object in the database, you will sometimes need to change the indexes that you create. Indexes and their properties are maintained in the Table Designer's Properties dialog box.

Altering Indexes

Just as you can alter column properties by opening the Table Designer and displaying the table's Properties dialog box, you can alter the properties of an index in the same way.

Rename an index

1. Open the Table Designer for the Oils table by right-clicking the table name in the Details Pane and selecting Design Table.

   SQL Server opens the Table Designer.

Indexes/Keys button

2. Click the Indexes/Keys button.

   SQL Server opens the Properties dialog box with the Indexes/Keys property page displayed.

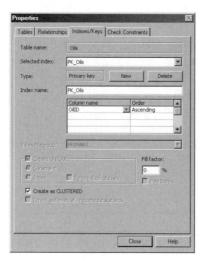

3. Select *IX_OilName* in the Selected Index combo box.

   SQL Server displays the index details.

4. Change the index name to *IX_Name*.

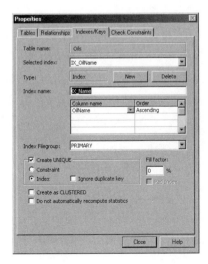

5. Click Close.

   SQL Server closes the dialog box.

6. Click the Save button on the Table Designer toolbar to save the change.

Change the columns in an index

1. If the Table Designer for the Oils table is not open, open it by right-clicking the table name in the Details Pane and selecting Design Table.

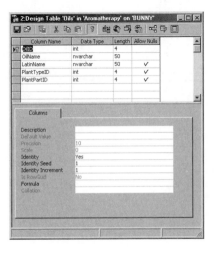

Indexes/Keys button

2. Click the Indexes/Keys button.

   SQL Server opens the Properties dialog box with the Indexes/Keys tab selected.

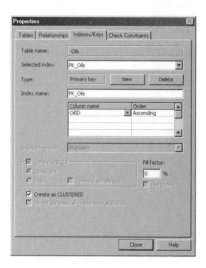

3. Select Oils_Index_1 in the Selected Index combo box.

   SQL Server displays the properties of the index.

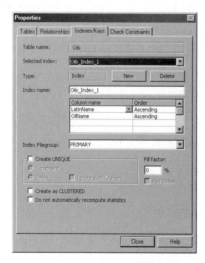

4. Select the LatinName cell in the Column Name field, and change the indexed column to PlantTypeID.

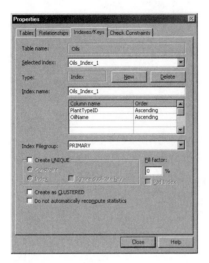

5. Click Close.

   SQL Server closes the dialog box.

6. Click the Save button on the Table Designer toolbar to save the change.

Removing Indexes

Sometimes you will need to remove an index from a table, either because it is no longer needed or because the improved data retrieval performance that the index provides is outweighed by the extra time required to maintain the index when the underlying data is updated. Like all other index maintenance tasks, deleting an index is accomplished by using the Indexes/Keys tab of the Table Designer's Properties dialog box.

Drop an index

1. If the Table Designer for the Oils table is not open, open it by right-clicking the table name in the Details Pane and selecting Design Table.

SQL Server opens the Table Designer.

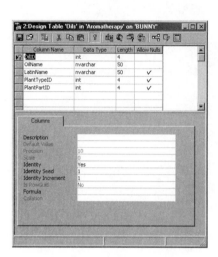

Indexes/Keys button

2. Click the Indexes/Keys button.

SQL Server opens the table's Properties dialog box with the Indexes/ Keys property page displayed.

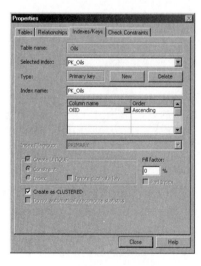

3. Select IX_Name in the Selected Index combo box.

   SQL Server displays the index details.

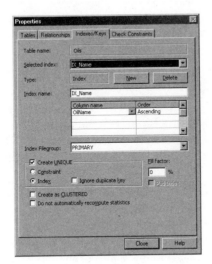

4. Click the Delete button.

   SQL Server deletes the index.

5. Click Close.

   SQL Server closes the dialog box.

6. Click the Save button on the Table Designer toolbar to save the change, and then close the Table Designer window.

Lesson 6 Quick Reference

To	Do this	Button
Create a primary key index	Open the Table Designer for the table, select the column or columns that make up the primary key, and then click the Primary Key button.	
Create an index	Open the Table Designer for the table, click the Indexes/Keys button to open the table's Properties dialog box with the Indexes/Keys property page displayed, click New, and then set the index properties.	
Alter an index	Open the Table Designer for the table, click the Indexes/Keys button to open the Properties dialog box with the Indexes/Keys property page displayed, and set the index properties.	
Remove an index	Open the Table Designer for the table, click the Indexes/Keys button to open the Properties dialog box with the Indexes/Keys property page displayed, select the index, and then click Delete.	

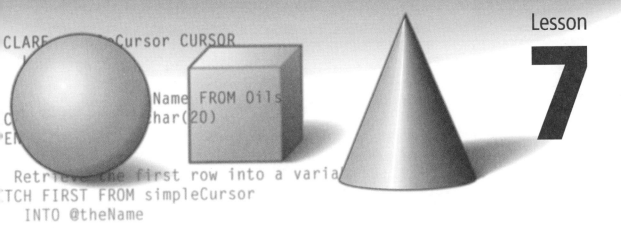

Creating Relationships

In this lesson you will learn how to:
■ Create a relationship.
■ Change a relationship.
■ Rename a relationship.
■ Delete a relationship.

Understanding Relationships

Most databases are intended to model some part of the real world, known as the *problem space*. At the logical level, the objects in the problem space are *entities* and the associations between them are *relationships*. At the physical level, Microsoft SQL Server represents entities as tables and relationships as *foreign key constraints*, which define foreign keys.

The Relational Model

Many people believe that relational databases are called "relational" because relationships are established between tables. In fact, the description comes from the term relation, which Dr. E. F. Codd (who originally developed the relational model in the late 1960s) chose to describe the object that is implemented in SQL Server as a table.

Logically, there are three types of relationships: *one-to-one*, in which each row of a table is related to zero or one row in another table; *one-to-many*, in which each row of a table is related to zero, one, or more rows in another table; and *many-to-many*, in which each row in the first table is related to zero, one, or more rows in the second table, and each row in the second table can be related to zero, one, or more rows in the first table.

One-to-one relationships are relatively rare. They're used most often when a set of attributes applies to only a few of the instances of the entity. For example, only a small subset of employees would play on the company softball team. A database designer might put all the attributes of the softball team in a separate table and then create a one-to-one relationship between it and the employee table.

One-to-many relationships are, on the other hand, quite common. In our sample database, a one-to-many relationship exists between the PlantParts table and the Oils table—any given row in the PlantParts table can be related to zero, one, or many rows in the Oils table.

Many-to-many relationships are also quite common. In the sample, a many-to-many relationship exists between the Properties table and the Oils table—any given oil can have multiple properties, and any property can be assigned to multiple oils.

SQL Server, like other relational database engines, models one-to-one and one-to-many relationships directly, but it uses a special kind of table known as a *junction table* to resolve many-to-many tables. A junction table consists of the primary keys of the tables on either side of the relationship. A one-to-many relationship is established between the junction table and each of the original tables, as shown in Figure 7-1.

Figure 7-1. *Many-to-many relationships are resolved using a junction table.*

Reflexive Relationships

Most relationships in a database are established between two different tables. However, it is possible to relate a table to itself, in either a one-to-one or one-to-many relationship. Such relationships are known as *reflexive relationships*.

Reflexive relationships are frequently used to model hierarchies. A common example is the hierarchy of employees in an organization. An employee has a manager, and the manager is an employee who might in turn also have a manager. This relationship is modeled by including the primary key of the employee table as a column in the table and establishing a reflexive one-to-many relationship.

At the table level, a relationship is modeled by including a unique identifier, usually the primary key, from the table on the one side (called the *primary key table*) in the table on the many side (called the *foreign key table*). The identifier is known as the *foreign key*.

 IP   The unique identifier that is used as a foreign key is usually the primary key of the primary key table, but it can be any column or set of columns that has been declared unique.

SQL Server can enforce the relationships you establish in the database. This is called *maintaining referential integrity*. By default, SQL Server will reject any changes to the primary key of a row in the primary key table that has related rows in a foreign key table.

New in Microsoft SQL Server 2000 is the ability to cascade changes to the primary key table. If you tell SQL Server to cascade deletes for the relationship, deleting a row in the primary key table will cause SQL Server to delete all related rows in the foreign key table. Similarly, if you tell SQL Server to cascade updates, changing the primary key of the primary key table will cause the related columns in the foreign key table to be updated.

 MPORTANT   Some database schemas can be quite complex. Using cascade deletes and updates can simplify maintenance of complex data structures, but SQL Server requires that the cascades not be circular. For example, deleting a row in Table A can cause a row in Table B to be deleted, which in turn causes a row in Table C to be deleted. However, a cascade cannot be established that would cause the (cascaded) delete of the row in Table C to cause a row to be deleted in Table A.

Creating Relationships

In SQL Server, relationships are created via the Relationships tab of the Table Designer's Properties dialog box. Both one-to-one and one-to-many relationships are created in exactly the same way. SQL Server will determine the type of relationship based on the columns specified in the foreign key table: if there is a unique index on the foreign key columns, the relationship will be one-to-one; otherwise, it will be one-to-many.

Create a relationship

1. Open the Table Designer for the Oils table by right-clicking the table name in the Details Pane and selecting Design Table.

   SQL Server opens the Table Designer.

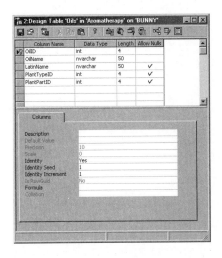

Relationships button

2. Click the Relationships button on the Table Designer toolbar.

   SQL Server opens the Table Designer's Properties dialog box with the Relationships property page displayed.

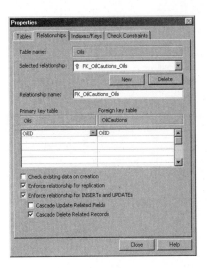

3. Click New.

   SQL Server proposes the first table in the table list for the new relationship.

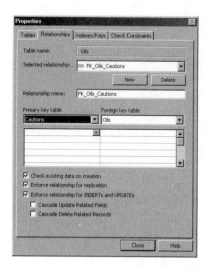

4. Select PlantTypes as the primary key table.

   SQL Server proposes FK_Oils_PlantTypes as the name of the relationship.

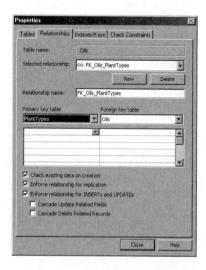

5. Select PlantTypeID as the primary key field.

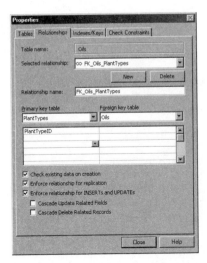

6. Select PlantTypeID as the foreign key field.

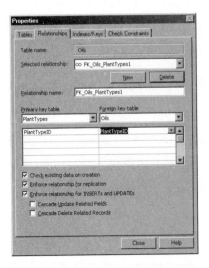

> **TIP** If you want to set cascading updates or deletions for the relationship, do so by selecting the check boxes on this property page.

7. Click Close.

   SQL Server closes the Properties dialog box.

8. Click the Save button on the Table Designer toolbar.

Save button

SQL Server displays a dialog box asking you to confirm that changes to the two tables will be saved to your database.

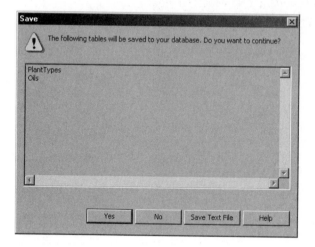

9. Click Yes.

   SQL Server creates the relationship.

10. Close the Table Designer window.

Managing Relationships

The relationships between tables tend to be fairly stable, but like any other part of the database schema, they can change from time to time. The Enterprise Manager makes managing these changes easy.

Altering Relationships

It's extremely uncommon to change a relationship, but sometimes a change in the structure of one of the underlying tables will require it. You can change the columns involved in the relationship by simply changing the specification on the Relationships property page of the table's Properties dialog box.

Change a relationship

1. Open the Table Designer for the Oils table by right-clicking the table name in the Details Pane and selecting Design Table.

SQL Server opens the Table Designer.

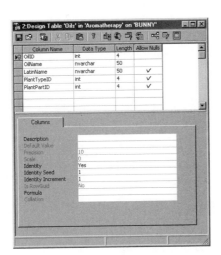

Relationships button

2. Click the Relationships button on the Table Designer toolbar.

   SQL Server opens the Table Designer's Properties dialog box with the Relationships property page displayed.

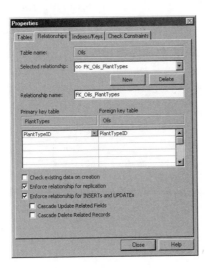

3. Make sure FK_Oils_PlantTypes is selected in the Selected Relationship combo box.

   SQL Server displays the properties of the relationship.

4. Select PlantPartID as the foreign key field.

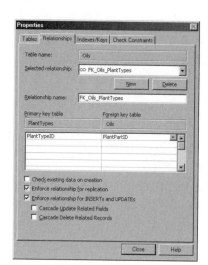

5. Click Close.

   SQL Server closes the Properties dialog box.

6. Click the Save button on the Table Designer toolbar.

   SQL Server displays a dialog box asking you to confirm that changes to the two tables will be saved to your database.

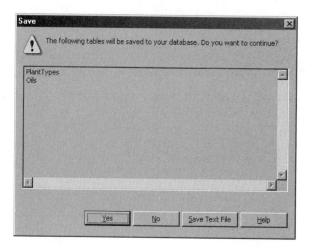

7. Click Yes.

   SQL Server changes the relationship.

8. Close the Table Designer window.

Maintaining Relationships

As you've probably come to expect by now, relationships are maintained using the same Properties dialog box that you use to create them.

Rename a relationship

1. Open the Table Designer for the Oils table by right-clicking the table name in the Details Pane and selecting Design Table.

   SQL Server opens the Table Designer.

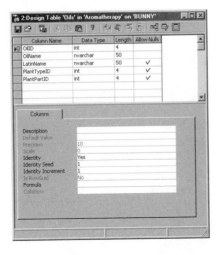

Relationships button

2. Click the Relationships button.

   SQL Server opens the Table Designer's Properties dialog box with the Relationships property page displayed.

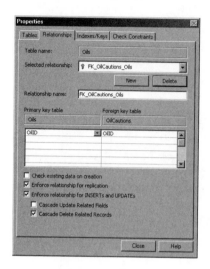

3. Select FK_Oils_PlantTypes in the Selected Relationship combo box. SQL Server displays the properties of the relationship.

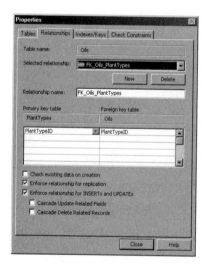

4. Select the text in the Relationship Name field, and type *DeleteMe.*

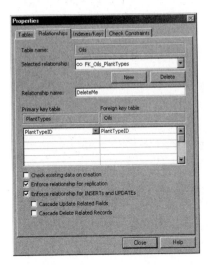

5. Click Close.

   SQL Server closes the Properties dialog box.

6. Click the Save button.

   SQL Server displays a dialog box asking you to confirm that changes to the two tables will be saved to your database.

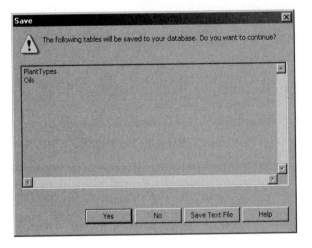

7. Click Yes.

   SQL Server changes the name of the relationship.

8. Close the Table Designer window.

Delete a relationship

1. Open the Table Designer for the Oils table by right-clicking the table name in the Details Pane and selecting Design Table.

   SQL Server opens the Table Designer.

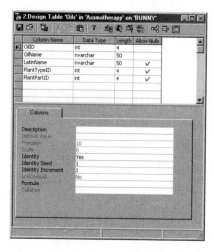

Relationships button

2. Click the Relationships button.

   SQL Server opens the Table Designer's Properties dialog box with the Relationships property page displayed.

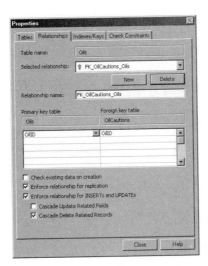

3. Select DeleteMe in the Selected Relationship combo box.

    SQL Server displays the relationship properties.

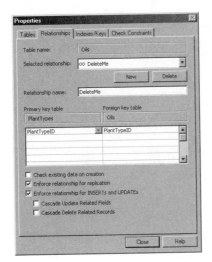

4. Click Delete.

SQL Server displays a message asking you to confirm the deletion.

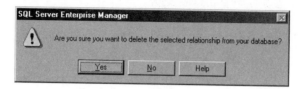

5. Click Yes.

6. Click Close.

SQL Server closes the Properties dialog box.

7. Click the Save button.

SQL Server displays a dialog box asking you to confirm that changes to the two tables will be saved to your database.

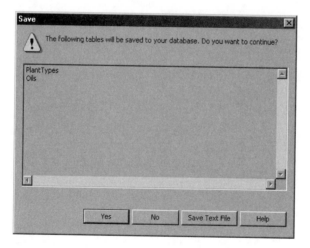

8. Click Yes.

SQL Server deletes the relationship.

9. Close the Table Designer window.

Lesson 7 Quick Reference

To	Do This	Button
Create a relationship	Open the Table Designer for the table, click the Relationships button to open the Table Designer's Properties dialog box, click New, and set the relationship properties.	
Change a relationship	Open the Table Designer for the table, click the Relationships button to open the Table Designer's Properties dialog box, select the relationship in the Selected Relationship combo box, and then select a different table column as the foreign key field.	
Rename a relationship	Open the Table Designer for the table, click the Relationships button to open the Table Designer's Properties dialog box, select the relationship in the Selected Relationship combo box, and change the Relationship Name property.	
Delete a relationship	Open the Table Designer for the table, click the Relationships button to open the Table Designer's Properties dialog box, select the relationship in the Selected Relationships combo box, and then click the Delete button.	

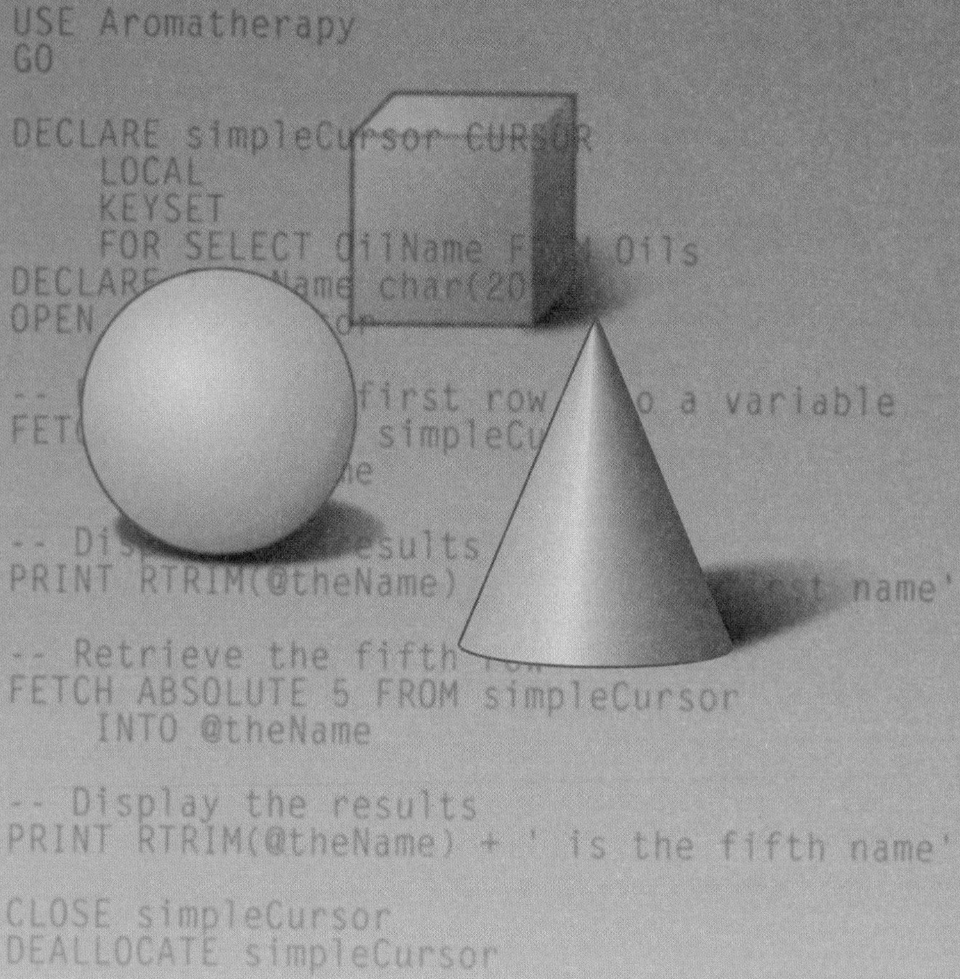

```sql
USE Aromatherapy
GO

DECLARE simpleCursor CURSOR
    LOCAL
    KEYSET
    FOR SELECT OilName FROM Oils
DECLARE       Name char(20
OPEN

--            first row    o a variable
FET                simpleCu
                 e

-- Di        esults
PRINT RTRIM(@theName)                 st name'

-- Retrieve the fifth
FETCH ABSOLUTE 5 FROM simpleCursor
    INTO @theName

-- Display the results
PRINT RTRIM(@theName) + ' is the fifth name'

CLOSE simpleCursor
DEALLOCATE simpleCursor
```

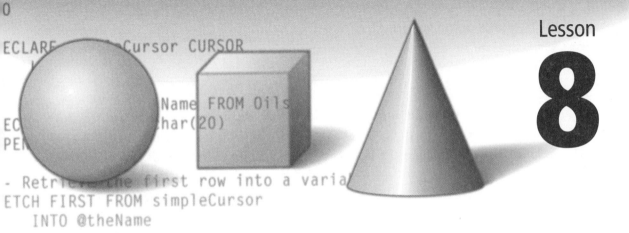

Creating Check Constraints

In this lesson you will learn how to:

- Create a check constraint.
- Change the constraint text.
- Rename a check constraint.
- Delete a check constraint.

Understanding Check Constraints

One of the most important aspects of database design is ensuring *data integrity*. Data integrity rules ensure that the data contained in the database is, if not correct, at least plausible. There are several levels of data integrity. In Lesson 7 we examined relational integrity, which ensures that the associations between tables are created and maintained correctly.

Check constraints, the subject of this lesson, are used to enforce two additional forms of database integrity: *domain integrity* and *entity integrity*. In relational terminology, a *domain* is the range of values that a column can contain. The data type of a column is one of the attributes of a domain, but defining the data type is not always sufficient. For example, a *smallint* column can contain integer values from -32,768 through 32,767, and might be a good data type for a column that contains the year in which an employee received his or her university degree. But the actual range of values of the YearDegreeAwarded column is much more re-stricted—say, between 1900 and the current year. You would use a check constraint to ensure that no one actually entered 1543 or 2075 as the col-umn value.

Entity integrity constraints enforce the integrity of the entity itself. The most important entity integrity constraint is that each entity must be uniquely identifiable. This constraint is implemented by specifying a pri-mary key for the table. Entity integrity can also involve the conditional evaluation of multiple columns in a table, and this type of constraint is most often implemented using check constraints. For example, if a table contains the columns Country and State, you might use a check con-straint to specify that the State column value "AZ" is valid only if the Country column contains the value "USA."

Check constraints are specified as *Boolean expressions*. A Boolean ex-pression evaluates to either TRUE or FALSE. We'll be examining Boolean expressions in Lesson 13. In this lesson, we'll use the expression:

```
LEN(<column>) >= 4
```

LEN is a Transact-SQL function that returns the number of characters in a string, so the expression *LEN(<column>) >= 4* will evaluate to TRUE if *<column>* contains four or more characters or FALSE if it contains fewer than four.

Creating Check Constraints

Like indexes and relationships, you create check constraints using the Properties dialog box of the Table Designer.

Create a check constraint

1. Open the Table Designer for the Oils table by right-clicking the table name in the Details Pane and selecting Design Table.

SQL Server opens the Table Designer.

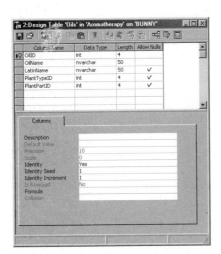

Constraints button

2. Click the Constraints button.

Microsoft SQL Server opens the Table Designer's Properties dialog box with the Check Constraints property page displayed.

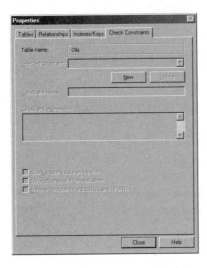

3. Click New.

SQL Server proposes CK_Oils as the constraint name. For this exercise, accept this name.

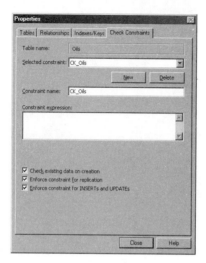

4. Enter *LEN(OilName) >= 4* as the constraint expression.

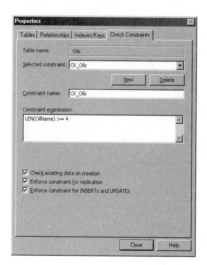

 IP If you are creating a new check constraint and don't care whether existing data complies, you can tell SQL Server to ignore existing data by unchecking Check Existing Data On Creation for the constraint.

5. Click Close.

SQL Server closes the Table Designer's Properties dialog box.

Save button

6. Click the Save button.

SQL Server checks that all the rows in the table meet the check constraint and then saves the constraint.

Managing Check Constraints

As part of the database schema, check constraints shouldn't, under normal circumstances, require a great deal of maintenance. You define them once, when you create the database, and that's pretty much that. However, database schemas will change occasionally, requiring changes to check constraints. The Enterprise Manager makes it easy to maintain constraints.

Altering Check Constraints

The Table Designer provides the mechanism for altering the text of a check constraint via the same Properties dialog box that you used to create it.

Change the constraint text

1. If the Table Designer for the Oils table is not still open from the previous exercise, open it by right-clicking the table name in the Details Pane and selecting Design Table.

SQL Server opens the Table Designer.

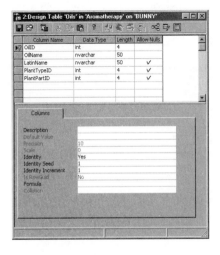

Constraints button

2. Click the Constraints button.

   SQL Server opens the Table Designer's Properties dialog box with the Check Constraints property page displayed.

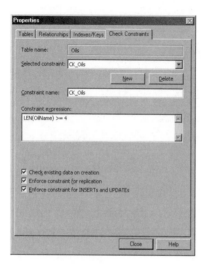

3. Make sure that the CK_Oils constraint is displayed in the Selected Constraint combo box.

4. Change the constraint text to *LEN(OilName) > 2* as the new constraint expression.

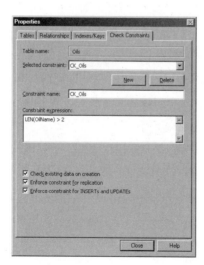

5. Click Close.

   SQL Server closes the Table Designer's Properties dialog box.

6. Click the Save button.

   SQL Server checks that all the rows in the table meet the new check constraint and then saves the constraint.

Maintaining Check Constraints

Like other table properties, check constraints are maintained via the Properties dialog box of the Table Designer.

Rename a check constraint

1. Open the Table Designer for the Oils table by right-clicking the table name in the Details Pane and selecting Design Table.

   SQL Server opens the Table Designer.

Constraints button

2. Click the Constraints button.

   SQL Server opens the Table Designer's Properties dialog box with the Check Constraints property page displayed.

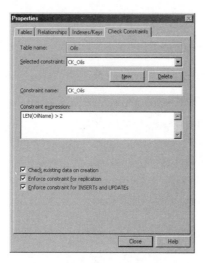

3. Select CK_Oils in the Constraint Name field, and change it to *CK_DeleteMe*.

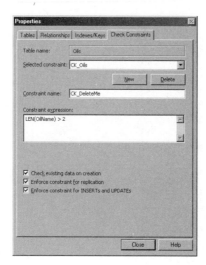

4. Click Close.

   SQL Server closes the Properties dialog box.

5. Click the Save button.

   SQL Server checks that all the rows in the table meet the check constraint and then saves the constraint.

Delete a check constraint

1. Open the Table Designer for the Oils table by right-clicking the table name in the Details Pane and selecting Design Table.

   SQL Server opens the Table Designer.

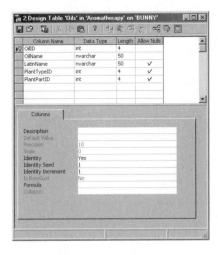

Constraints button

2. Click the Constraints button.

   SQL Server opens the Table Designer's Properties dialog box with the Check Constraints property page displayed.

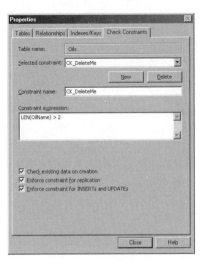

3. Make sure CK_DeleteMe is in the Selected Constraint field, and then click Delete.

   SQL Server removes the constraint.

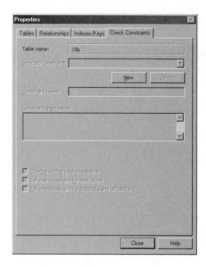

4. Click Close.

   SQL Server closes the Properties dialog box.

5. Click the Save button.

   SQL Server removes the constraint.

6. Close the Table Designer.

Lesson 8 Quick Reference

To	Do this	Button
Create a check constraint	Open the Table Designer for the table, click the Constraints button to open the Table Designer's Properties dialog box, click New, and enter the expression for the check constraint.	
Change the constraint text	Open the Table Designer for the table, click the Constraints button to open the Table Designer's Properties dialog box, select the constraint name in the Constraint Name field, and change the constraint text to a new constraint expression.	
Rename a check constraint	Open the Table Designer for the table, click the Constraints button to open the Properties dialog box, select the constraint name in the Constraint Name field, and type the new name.	
Delete a check constraint	Open the Table Designer for the table, click the Constraints button to open the Properties dialog box, select the check constraint you want to delete, and click the Delete button.	

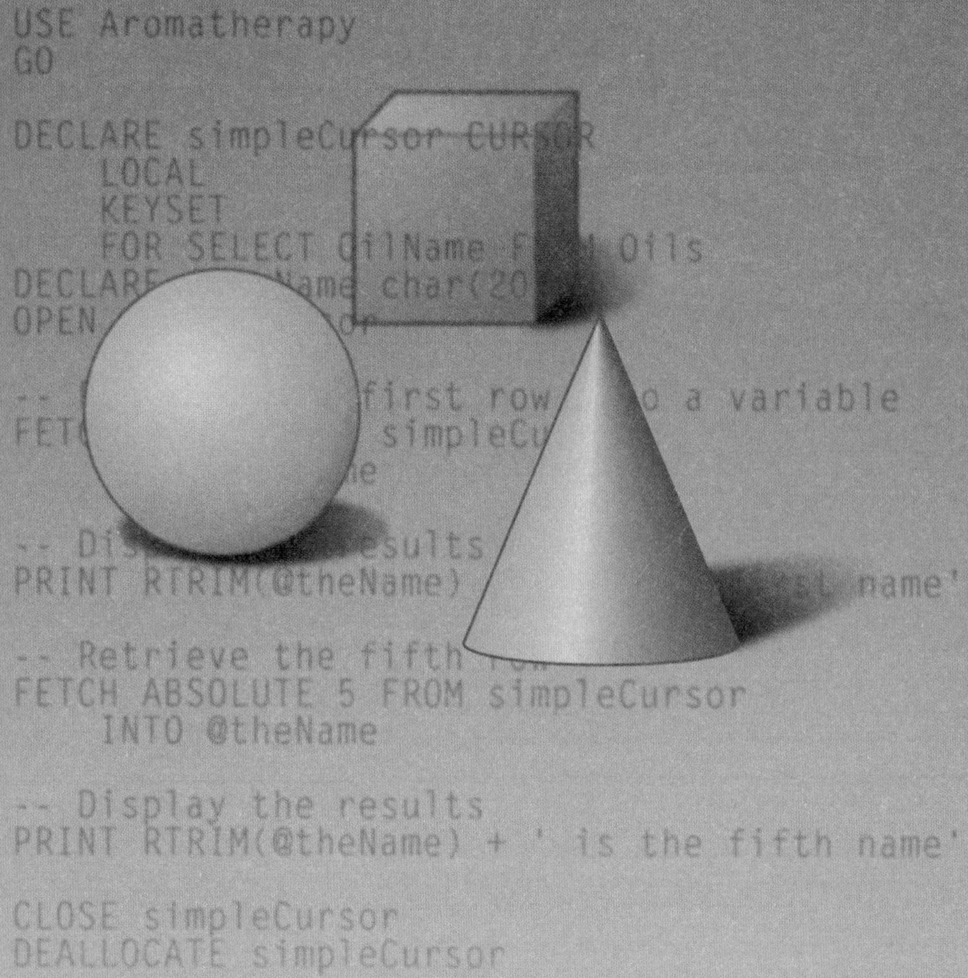

```
USE Aromatherapy
GO

DECLARE simpleCursor CURSOR
    LOCAL
    KEYSET
    FOR SELECT OilName FROM Oils
DECLARE @theName char(20)
OPEN simpleCursor

-- Retrieve first row into a variable
FETCH FIRST FROM simpleCursor
    INTO @theName

-- Display the results
PRINT RTRIM(@theName) + ' is the first name'

-- Retrieve the fifth row
FETCH ABSOLUTE 5 FROM simpleCursor
    INTO @theName

-- Display the results
PRINT RTRIM(@theName) + ' is the fifth name'

CLOSE simpleCursor
DEALLOCATE simpleCursor
```

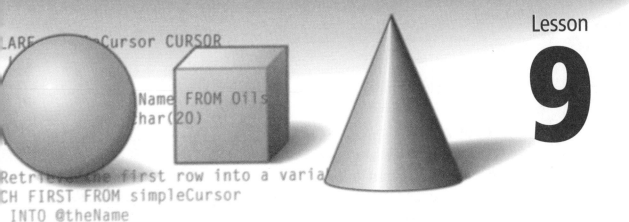

Creating Table Objects

In this lesson you will learn how to:

■ Create a default.

■ Bind a default to a column.

■ Unbind a default.

■ Create a rule.

■ Bind a rule to a column.

■ Create a user-defined data type.

■ Assign a column to a user-defined data type.

In the last few lessons, you've learned how to assign various properties such as default values and check constraints to the individual columns of a table. Sometimes, however, a particular type of column is used in several different tables. In that situation, it is often useful to create those properties in a single place and apply them to every table.

Defaults, rules, and user-defined data types provide mechanisms for creating and maintaining these objects in a single place. Say, for example, that you're building a database to model responses to a customer survey. You initially decide that the default value for any question that wasn't answered should be "Unknown." If you create a default and bind the default to the appropriate columns, you can later change the default to "Unanswered" without changing (and remembering!) every column that uses that default.

Understanding Defaults

Defaults function in the same way as the default property you specify when you create a column in the Table Designer—that is, they are values that are assigned automatically by Microsoft SQL Server if the user doesn't specify a value when creating the row. However, defaults are database-level objects that can be applied to multiple columns.

Creating Defaults

Since defaults are independent objects within the database, you must create the default before you can bind it to a table column.

Create a default

1. Navigate to the Defaults folder of the Aromatherapy database in the Console Tree.

   SQL Server displays a list of defaults in the Details Pane. (There aren't any in the sample database.)

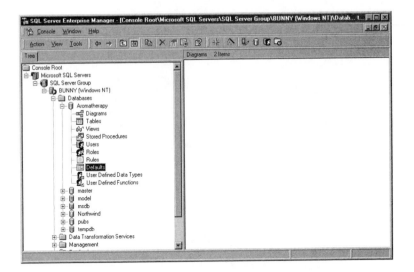

New button

2. Click the New button.

   SQL Server displays the Default Properties dialog box.

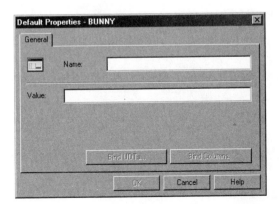

3. Type *DefaultUnknown* in the Name field.

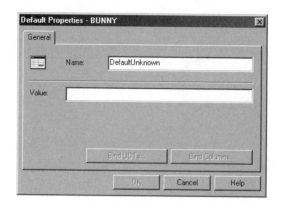

4. Type *'Unknown'* in the Value field.

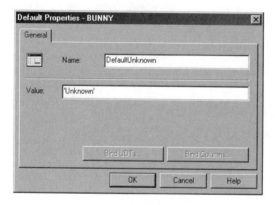

5. Click OK.

   SQL Server creates the default.

Bind a default to a column

1. Navigate to the Tables folder, and open the Table Designer for the Oils table by right-clicking the table name in the Details Pane and selecting Design Table.

   SQL Server opens the Table Designer.

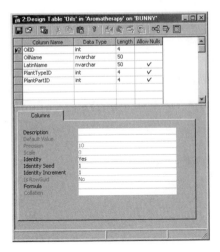

2. Add a new column to the table named *Sample*. Accept the default data type and length proposed by SQL Server.

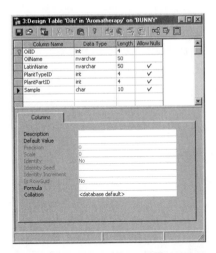

3. Click in the Default Value field for the column, and then select dbo.DefaultUnknown from the list.

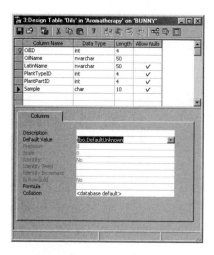

Save button

4. Click the Save button.

SQL Server saves the table.

Unbind a default

1. If the Table Designer for the Oils table is not open from the previous exercise, open it by right-clicking the table name in the Details Pane and selecting Design Table.

SQL Server opens the Table Designer.

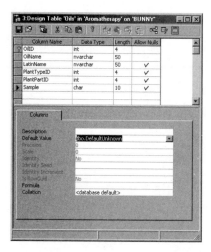

2. Select the Sample column.

   The Table Designer displays the properties of this column.

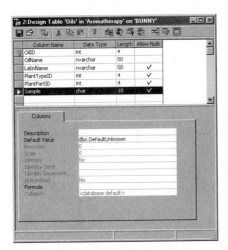

3. Select dbo.DefaultUnknown in the Default Value field, and press the Delete key to remove the value.

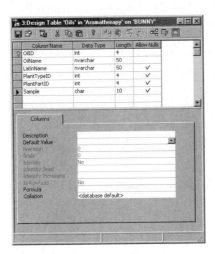

4. Click the Save button.

   SQL Server saves the change to the column definition.

Understanding Rules

Rules, like defaults, are database-level objects that can be applied to columns in multiple tables. A rule is like a check constraint in that it also specifies which data values are acceptable in a column, but its use is more restricted. A column can have multiple check constraints applied to it, but only a single rule, for example.

 IP Microsoft has deprecated rules and recommends that they be replaced by check constraints. However, rules still have their place in SQL Server databases, since only a rule can be applied to a user-defined data type.

Unlike check constraints, a rule can't reference a column name directly. Instead, the value to which the rule is being applied is passed to the rule in a *variable* that takes the format *@variableName*. We'll discuss variables in detail in Lesson 24.

Creating Rules

Since rules, like defaults, are independent database objects, you must create them before you can apply them to a column in a table.

Create a rule

1. Navigate to the Rules folder of the Aromatherapy database in the Console Tree.

   SQL Server displays a list of rules in the database. (The list is empty in the sample database.)

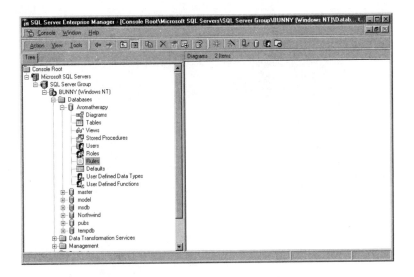

New button

2. Click the New button.

SQL Server opens the Rule Properties dialog box.

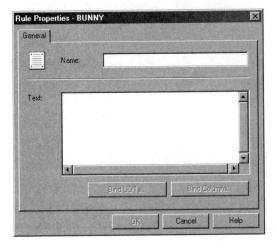

3. Type *SampleRule* as the rule name.

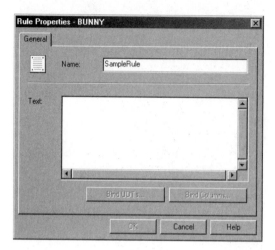

4. Type *LEN(@fldValue) > 3* as the text of the rule.

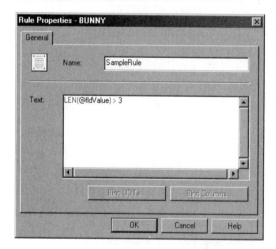

IP Remember that *LEN* is a Transact-SQL function that returns the number of characters in a text string, and that @ before a label in a Transact-SQL statement indicates a variable, a value that will be passed in to the statement. So in this case, the rule will return TRUE only if the length of the column is greater than 3.

5. Click OK.

   SQL Server closes the Rule Properties dialog box and creates the rule.

Bind a rule to a column

1. Open the Rule Properties dialog box for SampleRule by double-clicking the rule name in the Details Pane.

   SQL Server displays the Rule Properties dialog box.

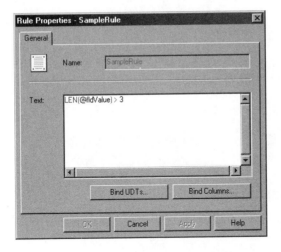

2. Click Bind Columns.

SQL Server displays the Bind Rule To Columns dialog box.

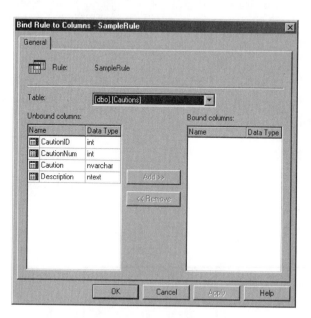

3. Choose [dbo].[Oils] in the Table combo box.

SQL Server displays the fields in the Oils table.

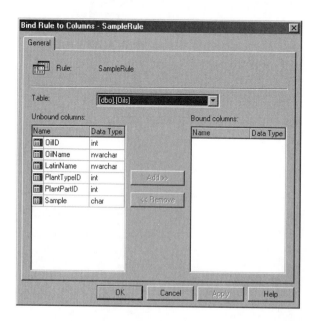

4. Select the Sample column in the Unbound Columns list, and then click Add.

   SQL Server moves the column to the Bound Columns list.

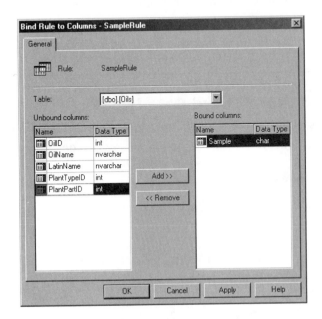

5. Click OK.

   SQL Server closes the Bind Rule To Columns dialog box.

6. Click OK again to close the Rule Properties dialog box.

Understanding User-Defined Data Types

Rules and defaults are useful mechanisms for maintaining database constraints, but SQL Server provides an even more powerful mechanism in user-defined data types. User-defined data types are specified based on any intrinsic SQL Server data type and include the specification of the length of the column. In addition, rules and defaults may optionally be applied to a user-defined data type.

When a column is created based on a user-defined data type, the table column will inherit all the properties specified for that type. When the specification of the user-defined data type changes, the rules for the columns based on that type will also be changed.

> **TIP** If a user-defined data type is created in the model database, all new databases will automatically have access to that type.

Creating User-Defined Data Types

Again, user-defined data types are independent database objects, and must be defined within the database before they can be assigned to columns.

Create a user-defined data type

1. Navigate to the User Defined Data Types folder of the Aromatherapy database.

   SQL Server displays a list of the user-defined data types. (There are none in the sample database.)

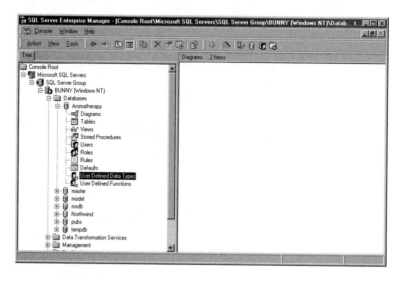

2. Click the New button.

New button

SQL Server displays the User-Defined Data Type Properties dialog box.

3. Type *MySample* as the user-defined data type name.

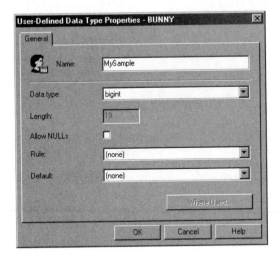

4. Set the base data type to varchar and the length to 20.

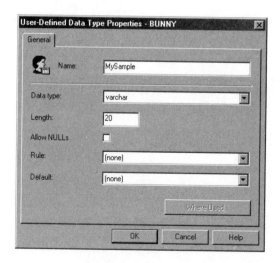

5. Select dbo.SampleRule in the Rule combo box.

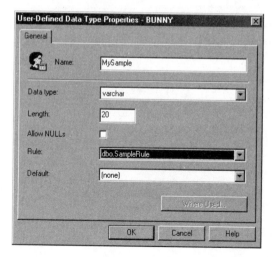

6. Accept the default values for the Allow NULLS and Default options, and click OK.

SQL Server creates the user-defined data type.

Assign a column to a user-defined data type

1. Open the Table Designer for the Oils table by right-clicking the name in the Details Pane, and selecting Design Table.

SQL Server opens the Table Designer.

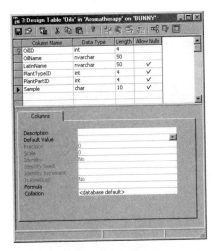

2. Select the Sample column, and choose MySample from the Data Type combo box.

   SQL Server sets the data type to MySample.

 IP User-defined data types are at the bottom of the Data Type list.

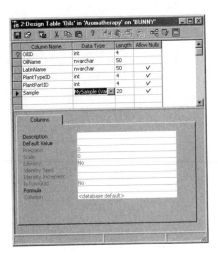

3. Click the Save button.

   SQL Server saves the table with the new definition.

Lesson 9 Quick Reference

To	Do this	Button
Create a default	Navigate to the Defaults folder of the database, click the New button, and fill in the default name and value.	✳
Bind a default to a column	Open the Table Designer for the table, and select the default from the Default Value combo box.	
Unbind a default	Open the Table Designer for the table, select a bound column, and delete the value in the Default Value field.	
Create a rule	Navigate to the Rules folder of the database, click the New button, and set the name and text of the rule.	✳
Bind a rule to a column	Open the Bind Rule To Columns dialog box by clicking Bind Columns in the Rule Properties Dialog box. Select the appropriate field(s) in the Unbound Columns list, and click Add.	
Create a user-defined data type	Navigate to the User Defined Data Types folder for the database, click the New button, and set the properties of the new user-defined data type.	✳
Assign a column to a user-defined data type	Open the Table Designer for the table, and select the user-defined data type from the Data Type list.	

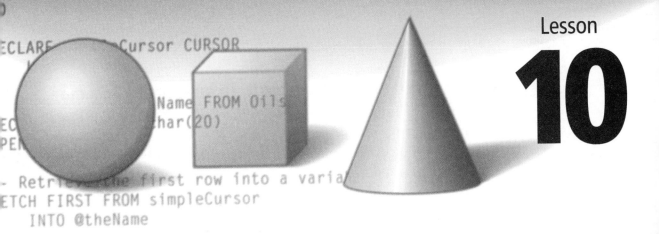

Creating Database Diagrams

In this lesson you will learn how to:

- Create a database diagram.
- Change the detail displayed in a database diagram.
- Add an existing table to a database diagram.
- Remove a table from a database diagram.
- Change a table in the Database Diagram window.
- Create a table in the Database Diagram window.
- Create a relationship in the Database Diagram window.

Understanding Database Diagrams

Database diagrams provide a good way to visualize the structure and relationship of tables in a database (the *database schema*). Including them within the database itself is a handy way of documenting the schema, since the diagrams automatically reflect any changes you make.

Creating a Database Diagram from an Existing Schema

Although it's possible to create an entire database schema from within the Database Diagram window, it's more common to create diagrams from existing tables. The Create Database Diagram Wizard makes that easy—just select the tables you want to include in the diagram, and the Create Database Diagram Wizard does the rest.

Once you have created a database diagram using the Create Database Diagram Wizard, you can add and remove tables and change the amount of detail displayed for each table.

Create a database diagram

1. Navigate to the Diagrams folder of the Aromatherapy database.

   Microsoft SQL Server displays the existing diagrams in the Details Pane.

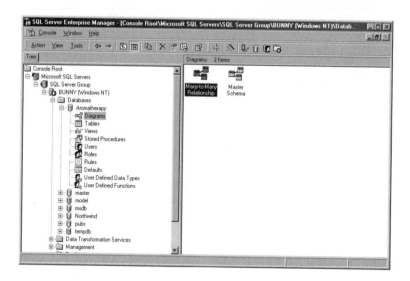

New Button

2. Click the New button.

   SQL Server displays the first page of the Create Database Diagram Wizard.

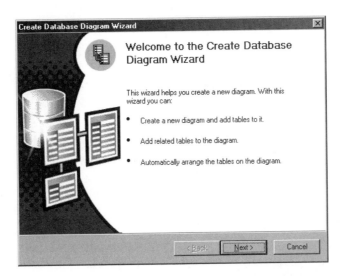

3. Click Next.

The Create Database Diagram Wizard displays a page asking you to select the tables to be included in the database diagram.

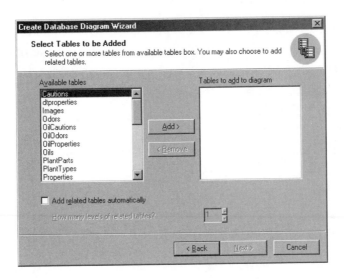

4. Click the Add Related Tables Automatically check box, and set the level of related tables to 2.

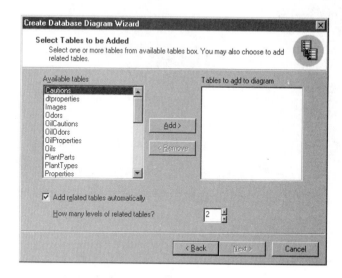

5. Select Oils in the Available Tables list, and then click Add.

The Create Database Diagram Wizard adds the Oils table and all related tables to the list of tables to be added to the diagram.

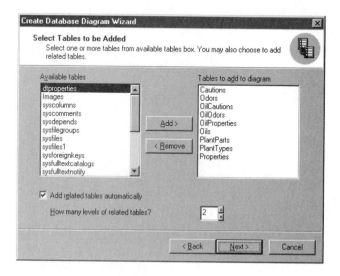

6. Click Next.

   The Create Database Diagram Wizard displays a page asking you to confirm the list of tables to be added to the database diagram.

   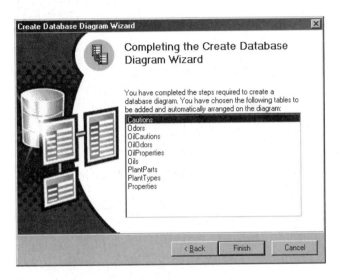

7. Click Finish.

   The Create Database Diagram Wizard creates the diagram.

   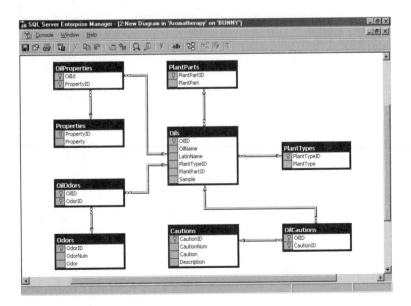

> **TIP** When SQL Server creates a database diagram, it joins the tables by lines indicating the relationships between them. You can rearrange these relationship lines by clicking and dragging. You might, for example, want to rearrange the lines so that they point to the columns involved in the relationship or to make the diagram a bit neater.

Save Button

8. Click the Save button.

   SQL Server displays a dialog box asking for a name for the diagram.

9. Type *Lesson 10* as the name, and then click OK.

   SQL Server saves the diagram.

Change the detail displayed in a database diagram

1. Select the Oils table in the database diagram by clicking its name in the diagram.

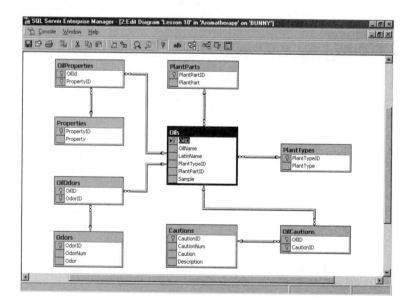

Show Button

2. Select Standard from the dropdown list displayed when you click the Show button on the Database Diagram window toolbar.

SQL Server adds the data type, length, and nullability to the display of the Oils table.

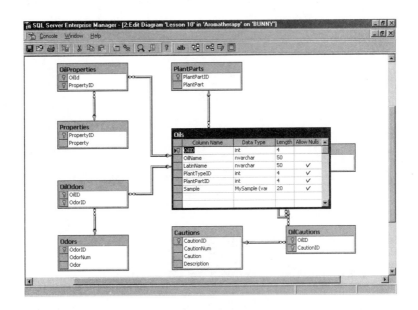

IP   You can change the display for multiple tables in the diagram by selecting them (use Ctrl-Click) in the diagram before selecting the Show button on the toolbar.

*Arrange Tables
Button*

3. Click the Arrange Tables button on the Database Diagram window toolbar.

SQL Server rearranges the database diagram to accommodate the additional space required by the Oils table.

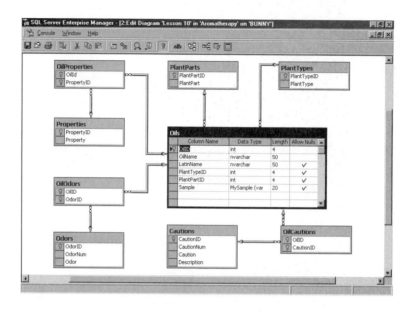

Save Button

4. Click the Save Button.

   SQL Server saves the new diagram layout.

Add an existing table to a database diagram

Add Table Button

1. Click the Add Table button in the database diagram.

   SQL Server displays the Add Table dialog box.

2. Select the table named dtproperties in the list, and then click Add.

SQL Server adds the table to the diagram. Since dtproperties is a system table that isn't related to the data tables in the Aromatherapy database, SQL Server doesn't add any relationship lines to the diagram.

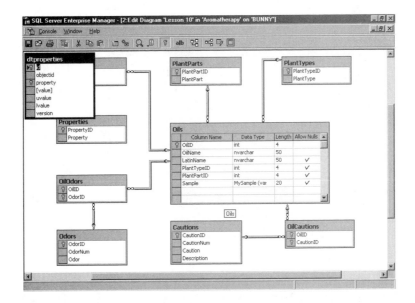

Save Button

3. Click Close to close the Add Table dialog box, and then click the Save button on the Database Diagram window toolbar.

SQL Server saves the diagram with the new table.

Remove a table from a database diagram

1. Right-click the dtproperties table in the database diagram, and select Remove Table From Diagram from the context menu.

SQL Server removes the table from the diagram.

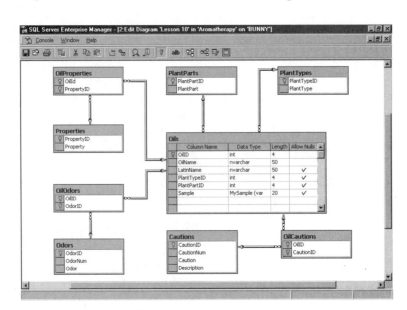

Save Button

2. Click the Save button.

SQL Server saves the diagram.

Using Database Diagrams to Maintain the Database

The SQL Server Enterprise Manager Database Diagram window also allows you to maintain the database schema within its graphical environment. You can add new tables, alter existing ones, and maintain relationships between them.

Changing the Database Schema

One of the most useful capabilities of the Database Diagram window is the ability to modify the database schema from within the diagram itself. The graphical display is an excellent tool for visualizing the tables and relationships in your database, and the ability to modify the schema directly allows you to make minor adjustments easily.

Add a column to a table in the Database Diagram window

1. Enlarge the Oils table in the database diagram by dragging down the lower right corner until an empty row of the column grid is displayed.

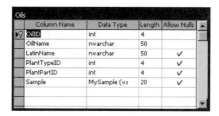

2. Click in the first empty cell in the Column Name field, and add a new column called *Description*. Set its data type to *varchar*, and its length to 50.

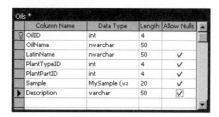

 IP   Notice that the table name for the Oils table has an asterisk (*) following it. SQL Server marks any table that has been changed in the Database Diagram window in this way to indicate that the changes have not yet been saved.

Since SQL Server doesn't change the database schema until you save the diagram, you can use the Database Diagram window to try out changes before committing to them. If you change your mind, just close the window without saving the changes and your database will remain as it was.

Arrange Tables Button

3. Click the Arrange Tables button to get SQL Server to resize the table display.

4. Click the Save button.

SQL Server displays a dialog box asking you to confirm changes to the Oils table.

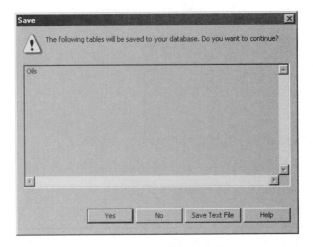

5. Click Yes.

SQL Server updates the Oils table with the new column, and removes the asterisk from the Oils table display.

Creating Database Objects

In addition to changing existing database objects, the Database Diagram window also allows you to add new tables and create relationships.

Create a table in the Database Diagram Window

1. Right-click an empty area of the Database Diagram window, and select New Table from the context menu.

SQL Server displays a dialog box requesting a name for the new table.

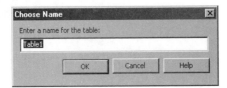

*New Table
Button*

TIP You can also create a new table by clicking the New Table button on the Database Diagram window toolbar.

2. Type *Images* as the new name, and then click OK.

   SQL Server adds the table to the diagram.

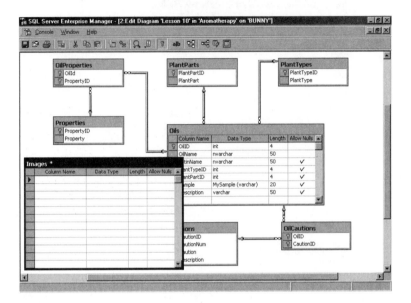

3. Add two columns to the new table:

Column Name	Data Type	Length	Allow Nulls
OilID	*Int*	4	No
Picture	*Image*	16	No

*Primary Key
Button*

4. Select the OilID column by clicking the gray box to the left of the column name, and then click the Primary Key button on the Database Diagram window toolbar.

   SQL Server sets OilID as the primary key of the table.

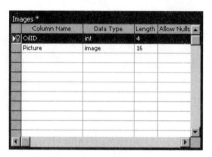

5. Right-click the table, point to the Table View submenu, and select Column Names.

   SQL Server changes the table display.

Save Button

6. Click the Save button.

   SQL Server displays a dialog box asking you to confirm the change to the database schema.

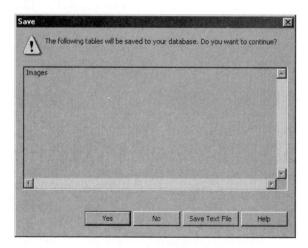

7. Click Yes.

SQL Server adds the new table to the database.

Create a relationship in the Database Diagram Window

1. Select the OilID column in the Oils table in the database diagram, and drag it to the OilID column in the Images table.

SQL Server opens the Create Relationship dialog box.

TIP You can make any changes you need to the relationship in this dialog box.

2. Click OK.

SQL Server closes the dialog box.

TIP Note that the relationship line between the Oils and Images tables has a little key on each end. This indicates that the relationship is one-to-one, since it is between primary keys. The little infinity symbol on the other relationship line indicates that the table on that end is a many-side table in the relationship.

Save Button

3. Click the Save Button.

SQL Server displays a dialog box asking you to confirm the changes to the database schema.

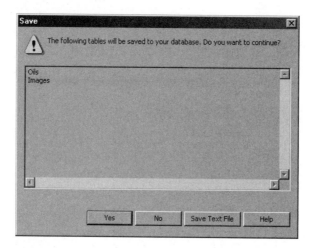

4. Click Yes.

SQL Server saves the diagram and updates the database schema.

Lesson 10 Quick Reference

To	Do this	Button
Create a database diagram	Navigate to the Diagrams folder of the database, click the New button, and follow the instructions in the Create Database Diagram Wizard.	
Change the detail displayed in a database diagram	Select the table or tables you want to change, click the Show button, and select the desired level of detail.	
Add an existing table to a database diagram	Click the Add Table button, select the table name in the list, and click OK.	

(continued)

Lesson 10 Quick Reference *continued*

To	Do this	Button
Remove a table from a database diagram	Right-click the table, and select Remove Table From Diagram from the context menu.	
Add a column to a table in the Database Diagram window	Display the table in standard view, and add the new column specification to the table.	
Create a table in the Database Diagram window	Right-click an empty area of the Database Diagram window and select New Table from the context menu.	
Create a relationship in the Database Diagram window	Drag a field from the primary key table, and drop it on the foreign key table. Complete the Create Relationships dialog box.	

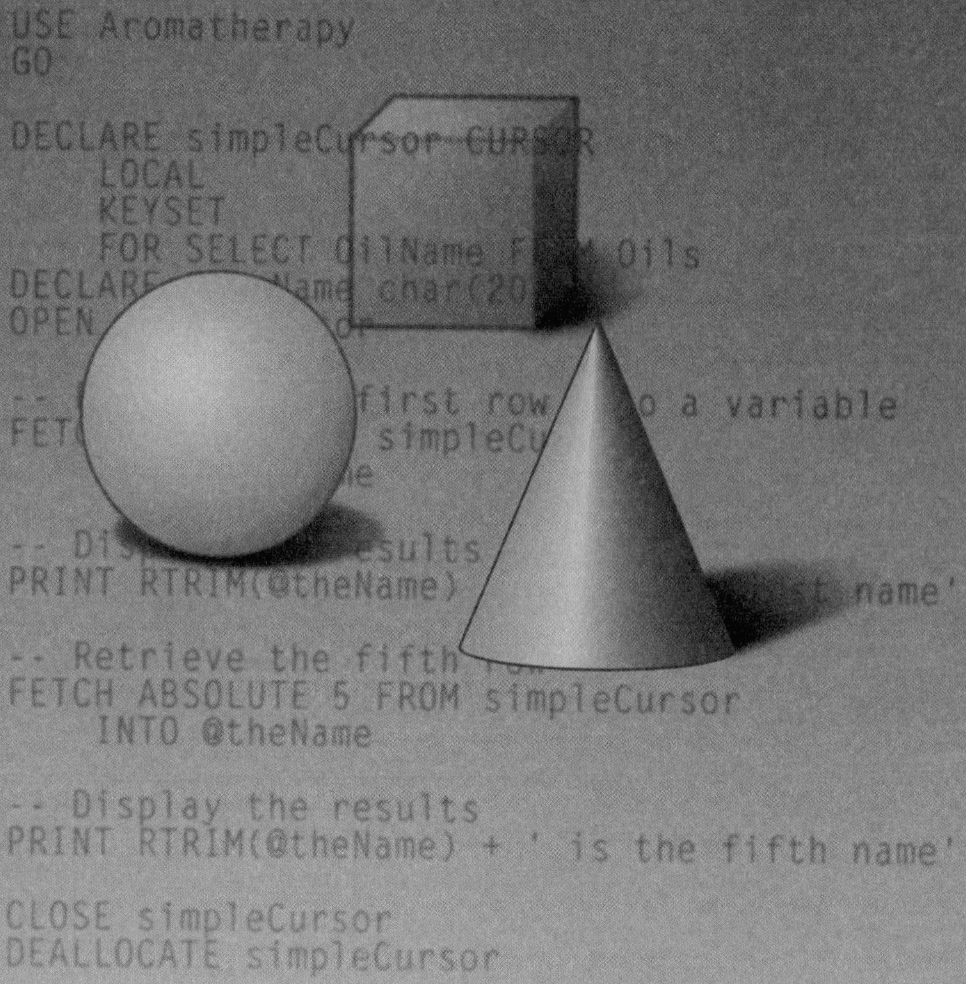

```
USE Aromatherapy
GO

DECLARE simpleCursor CURSOR
    LOCAL
    KEYSET
    FOR SELECT OilName FROM Oils
DECLARE @theName char(20)
OPEN simpleCursor

-- Retrieve the first row into a variable
FETCH FIRST FROM simpleCursor
    INTO @theName

-- Display the results
PRINT RTRIM(@theName) + ' is the first name'

-- Retrieve the fifth row
FETCH ABSOLUTE 5 FROM simpleCursor
    INTO @theName

-- Display the results
PRINT RTRIM(@theName) + ' is the fifth name'

CLOSE simpleCursor
DEALLOCATE simpleCursor
```

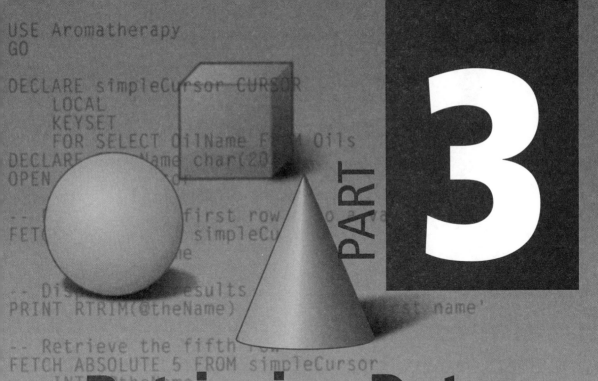

Retrieving Data

Lesson

11 Retrieving Rows   207

12 The SELECT Statement   217

13 Sorting and Selecting Rows   235

14 Joining Tables   257

15 Summarizing Data   281

16 Views   299

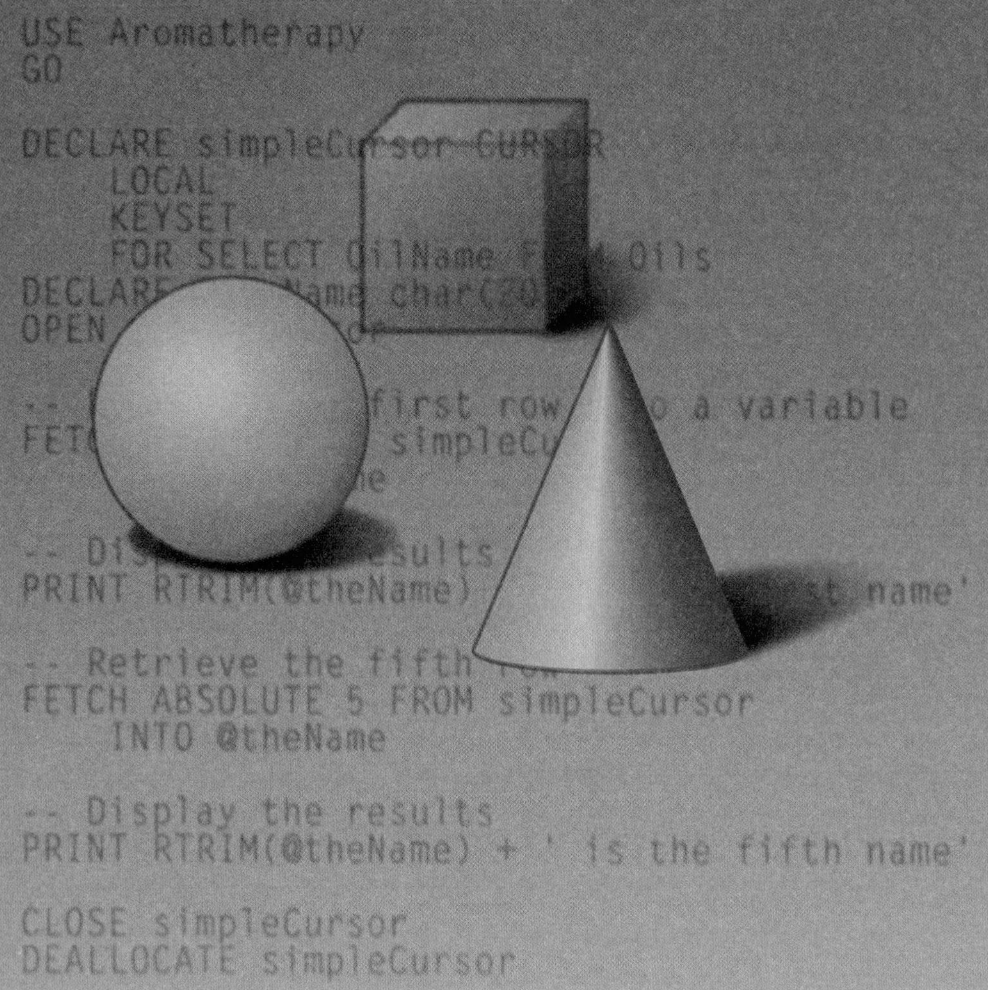

```
USE Aromatherapy
GO

DECLARE simpleCursor CURSOR
    LOCAL
    KEYSET
    FOR SELECT OilName FROM Oils
DECLARE @theName char(20)
OPEN simpleCursor

-- Retrieve the first row into a variable
FETCH FIRST FROM simpleCursor
    INTO @theName

-- Display the results
PRINT RTRIM(@theName) + ' is the first name'

-- Retrieve the fifth row
FETCH ABSOLUTE 5 FROM simpleCursor
    INTO @theName

-- Display the results
PRINT RTRIM(@theName) + ' is the fifth name'

CLOSE simpleCursor
DEALLOCATE simpleCursor
```

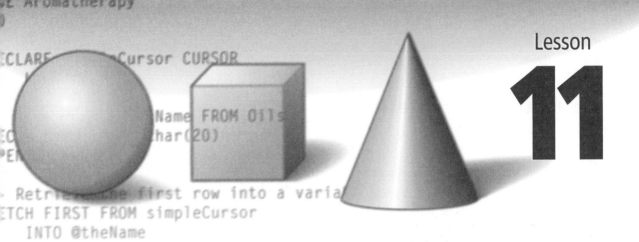

Retrieving Rows

Most database applications will use a programming environment such as Microsoft Access or Microsoft Visual Basic to provide the user interface. However, the Enterprise Manager provides a simple tool, called the Query Designer, to let you easily view the data in one or more tables. In this lesson, we'll examine the Query Designer and use it to display rows from several tables in the Aromatherapy database.

Using the Query Designer

Even though the data stored in a Microsoft SQL Server database is hardly ever used in its "raw" state, without being sorted or filtered in some way, it is sometimes useful to be able to quickly check the contents of a single table. The Enterprise Manager Query Designer makes it easy to view and edit rows, and even to add new ones.

Viewing Rows in a Table

The easiest way to view the rows in a table is to open the Query Designer via a table's context menu.

View all the rows in a table

1. In the Enterprise Manager, navigate to the Tables folder of the Aromatherapy database.

   SQL Server displays a list of tables in the Details Pane.

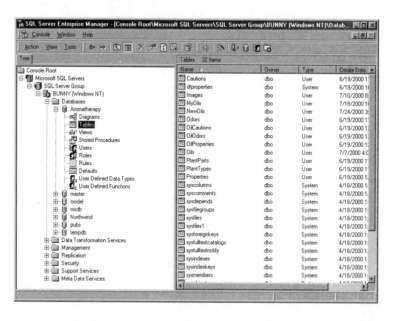

2. Right-click the PlantParts table, point to the Open Table submenu, and select Return All Rows.

SQL Server opens the Query Designer with all the rows in the table displayed.

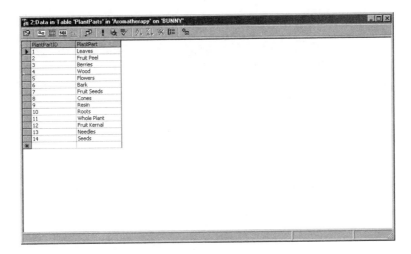

Restrict the number of rows displayed

1. Close the Query Designer if it's still open from the last exercise.

2. Right-click the Odors table in the Details Pane, point to the Open Table submenu, and select Return Top.

   SQL Server displays a dialog box requesting that you specify the number of rows to fetch.

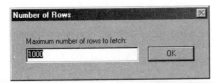

3. Type 5 as the maximum number of rows to fetch.

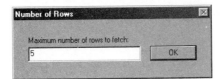

4. Click OK.

The Query Designer opens, displaying the first five rows in the table.

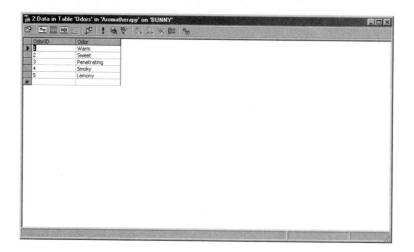

5. Close the Query Designer window.

Updating Rows in a Table

The Query Designer can also be used to change the values of exiting rows in a table or to add new rows.

Edit a row in the Query Designer

1. Right-click the PlantParts table in the Details Pane, point to the Open Table submenu, and then select Return All Rows to open the Query Designer for the PlantParts table.

2. Change the PlantPart column of the row with a PlantPartID of 12 to read *Fruit Kernel* instead of Fruit Kernal.

Edit icon

The Query Designer adds an Edit icon to the row selector to indicate that the record has been edited, but the changes have not yet been saved.

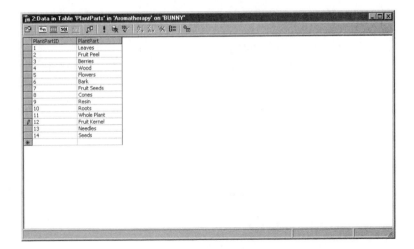

3. Click any other row.

   The Query Designer saves the change and removes the Edit icon.

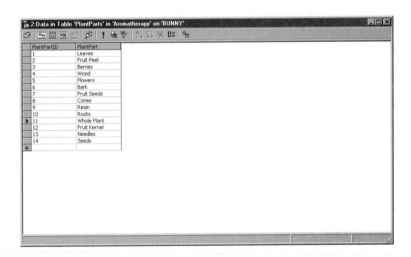

TIP Before you move to another row, you can press the Esc key to undo your changes.

Add a new row in the Query Designer

New icon

1. In the Query Designer, click in the PlantPart column of the last row (marked with the New icon in the row selector).

2. Type *Fruit.*

Edit icon

The Query Designer marks the row with the Edit icon and adds a new row to the bottom of the table.

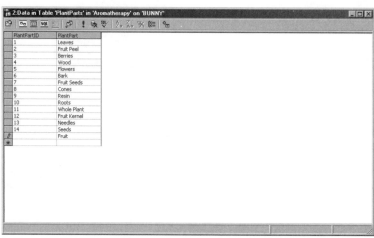

3. Click in any other row in the table.

The Query Designer assigns a PlantPartID to the new row and saves it to the table.

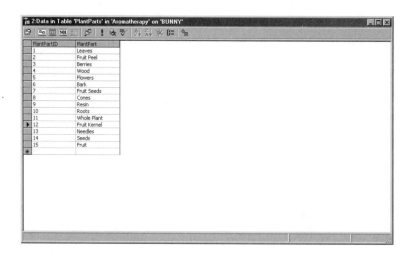

>
>
> **TIP** You can't add a PlantPartID to the new row because it's defined as an identity column. If you try to, the Query Designer will display an error message.

Understanding the SQL Server Query Designer

When you open the Query Designer using the Open Table command, the rows in the table are displayed in a grid similar to the Datasheet view of a table in Microsoft Access. This is the Query Designer's Results Pane. The Query Designer has three additional panes: the Diagram Pane, the Grid Pane, and the SQL Pane.

You control the display of the various panes in the Query Designer using the toolbar buttons. You can display the panes in any combination; the Query Designer will take care of updating each pane's display when you make changes to the query.

The Diagram Pane

*Diagram
Pane button*

Clicking the Diagram Pane button on the Query Designer toolbar displays the Diagram Pane. The Diagram Pane presents a view of the query similar to a database diagram. In addition to all the benefits of a graphic display, the Diagram Pane is useful for specifying the tables and views on which your query will be based and the relationships between them, as well as which columns will be displayed.

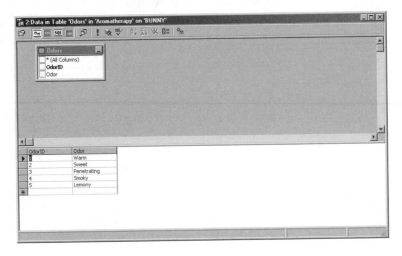

The Grid Pane

*Grid
Pane button*

Clicking the Grid Pane button on the Query Designer toolbar displays the Grid Pane. The Grid Pane is similar to the Query Design Grid in Access. It provides a quick way to change the column heading of a query column, specify the order in which rows will be displayed, and set selection criteria such as "Surname = 'Jones'".

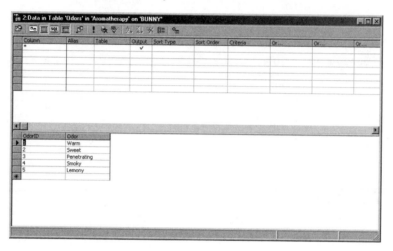

The SQL Pane

SQL Pane button

Clicking the SQL Pane button on the Query Designer toolbar displays the SQL Pane. The SQL Pane displays the actual Transact-SQL statement that will generate the query. You can enter and edit Transact-SQL statements directly using the SQL Pane.

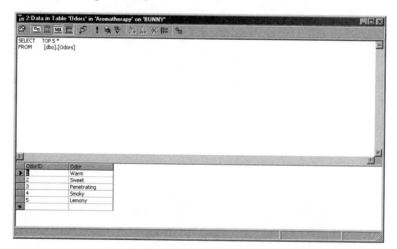

IP When you're first learning Transact-SQL, the SQL Pane is a *great* learning tool. Set up the query using the Diagram and Grid Panes, and the Query Designer will build the Transact-SQL statement for you.

Lesson 11 Quick Reference

To	Do This	Button
View all the rows in a table	Right-click the table name in the Details Pane, point to the Open Table submenu, and select Return All Rows.	
Restrict the number of rows displayed	Right-click the table name in the Details Pane, point to the Open Table sub-menu, and select Return Top. Specify the number of rows to be displayed, and click OK.	
Edit a row in a table	Change the value(s) for the row in the Query Designer, and click on any other row to save the change.	
Add a row to a table	Type the new values in the row marked by the New icon in the Query Designer, and click any other row to save the addition.	✳
View or hide the Diagram Pane	Click the Diagram Pane button on the Query Designer toolbar.	◰
View or hide the Grid Pane	Click the Grid Pane button on the Query Designer toolbar.	▦
View or hide the SQL Pane	Click the SQL Pane button on the Query Designer toolbar.	SQL
View or hide the Results Pane	Click the Results Pane button on the Query Designer toolbar.	▥

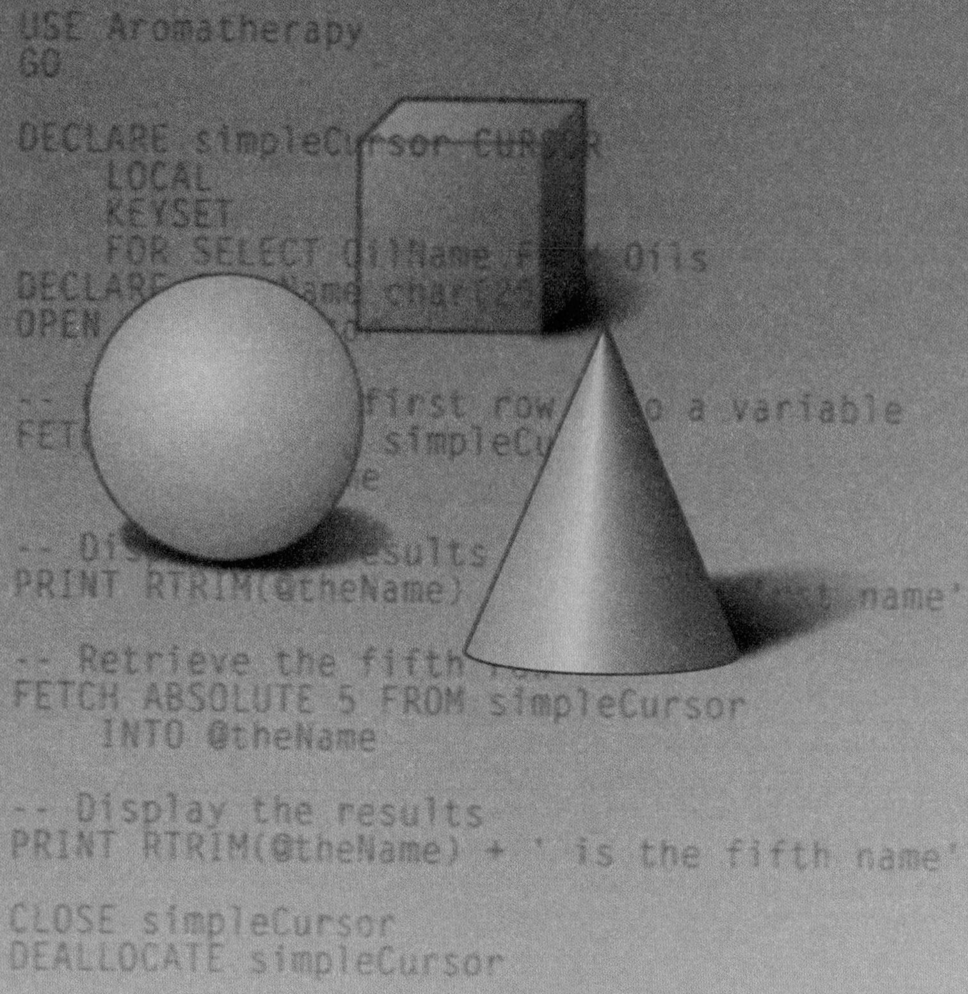

```
USE Aromatherapy
GO

DECLARE simpleCursor CURSOR
    LOCAL
    KEYSET
    FOR SELECT OilName FROM Oils
DECLARE @theName char(25)
OPEN simpleCursor

-- Retrieve the first row into a variable
FETCH NEXT FROM simpleCursor
    INTO @theName

-- Display the results
PRINT RTRIM(@theName) + ' is the first name'

-- Retrieve the fifth row
FETCH ABSOLUTE 5 FROM simpleCursor
    INTO @theName

-- Display the results
PRINT RTRIM(@theName) + ' is the fifth name'

CLOSE simpleCursor
DEALLOCATE simpleCursor
```

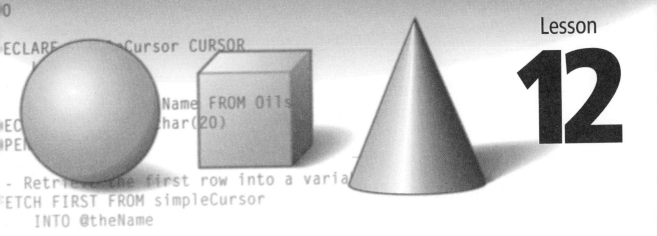

0

ECLARE   Cursor CURSOR

                Name FROM Oils
EC   har(20)
PE

- Retr   first row into a varia
ETCH FIRST FROM simpleCursor
    INTO @theName

- Display the results
RINT RTRIM(@theName) + ' is the first name'

Lesson

12

The SELECT Statement

In this lesson you will learn how to:

- Select all columns in a query.
- Select a subset of columns in a query.
- Rename columns in a query.
- Create calculated columns in a query.
- Return the top *n* rows in a query.
- Return the top *n* percent of rows in a query.

The basis of all data retrieval in the Microsoft SQL Server environment is a single Transact-SQL statement, the SELECT statement. In this lesson, we'll look at the most important components of the SELECT statement, and at ways to use the Query Designer to automatically build the statement for you.

Using the SQL Server Query Designer, you can enter a SELECT statement directly in the SQL Pane, or have the Query Designer build it for you by using the Diagram and Grid Panes. The options aren't mutually exclusive. You can begin a query by adding the tables to the Diagram Pane, rename columns using the Grid Pane, and specify the order in which rows are returned by entering the ORDER BY clause directly in the SQL Pane. The exercises in the lesson will show you a variety of techniques. When working on your own, you can choose the one that seems easiest to you at the time.

Understanding the SELECT Statement

The syntax of the SELECT statement is very complex, with multiple clauses and operators, but the basic structure is actually quite simple:

```
SELECT [TOP n [PERCENT]] column_list
FROM source_list
[WHERE search_condition]
[ORDER BY expression]
```

Only the first and second clauses of the SELECT statement are required. The first clause, SELECT *column_list*, specifies the columns that will be returned by the query. The column list can contain actual columns from the tables and views on which the query is based or can contain calculated columns derived from the original columns. The second clause, FROM *source_list*, specifies the tables and views on which the query is based.

Selecting All Columns

The simplest form of the SELECT statement is one that selects all columns from a single table. As with most versions of the SQL language, Transact-SQL allows you to use the asterisk (*) as a special shorthand for specifying all columns, so this simple form of the statement has the form:

```
SELECT *
FROM table_name
```

Select all columns

1. Open the Query Designer for the Properties table by right-clicking its name in the Enterprise Manager's Details Pane, pointing to the Open Table submenu, and selecting Return All Rows.

SQL Server opens the Query Designer for the table.

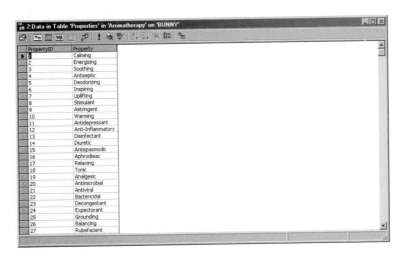

SQL Pane button

2. Turn on the SQL Pane by clicking the SQL Pane button on the Query Designer toolbar.

The Query Designer displays the SQL Pane.

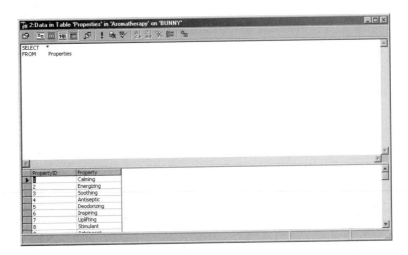

3. Change the SQL statement to show all columns from the Oils table.

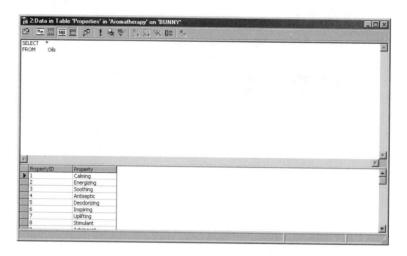

4. Click the Run button on the Query Designer toolbar to execute the query.

Run button

The Query Designer displays all records in the Oils table.

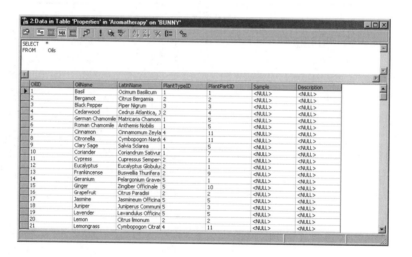

 TIP You can display more rows in the Results Pane by dragging the pane divider between the two panes.

Selecting a Subset of Columns

Although the SELECT * syntax is quick and easy, you'll most often want your query to return only selected columns. This is achieved by specifying the columns in the *column_list* of the SELECT clause.

Select columns using the SQL Pane

1. Replace the * in the SELECT statement by typing the column name *OilName.*

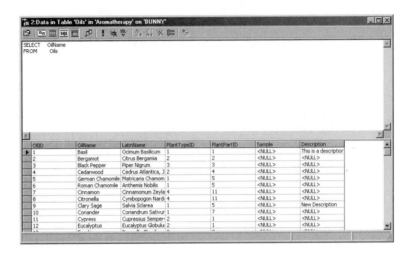

Run Button

2. Click the Run button on the Query Designer toolbar to execute the query.

   The Query Designer displays only the OilName column.

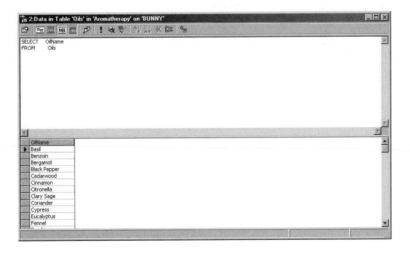

Select columns using the Diagram Pane

SQL Pane button

1. Hide the SQL Pane and display the Diagram Pane by clicking the buttons on the Query Designer toolbar.

Diagram Pane button

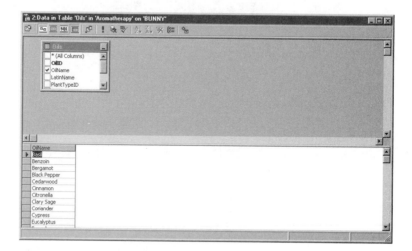

2. Click the LatinName field in the Diagram Pane.

   The Query Designer dims the Results pane to show that the results are no longer valid.

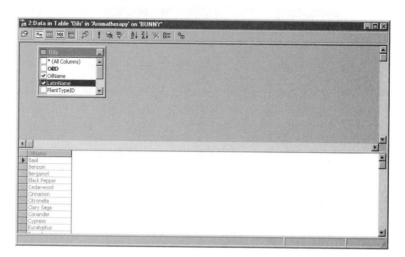

Run button

3. Click the Run button to execute the query.

   The Query Designer displays both the OilName and LatinName columns in the Results Pane.

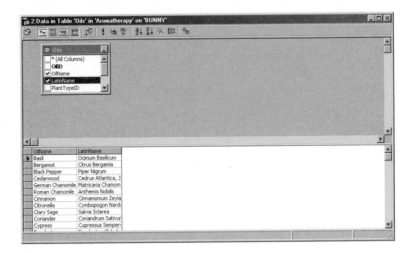

Creating Column Aliases

By default, a column in a query has the same name that it has in the underlying table or view. However, it's often useful to be able to change that name, either because it's awkward ("MyLongColumnNameWithNoSpaces") or simply because it's too ugly to display to a user ("pk_varchar_50_col32713"). The SELECT statement allows you to rename a column in a query by creating an *alias*. An alias changes the name of the column in the query but not in the table.

Create a column alias using the Grid Pane

Diagram Pane button

1. Hide the Diagram Pane and display the Grid Pane by clicking the buttons on the Query Designer toolbar.

Grid Pane button

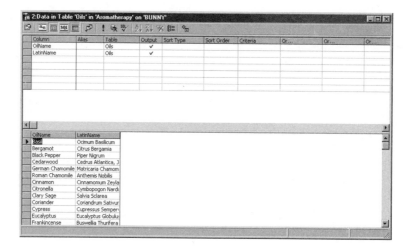

2. Create an alias for the OilName column by typing *Oil Name* in the
   Alias field. The Query Designer automatically adds brackets around
   the alias because the alias contains a space.

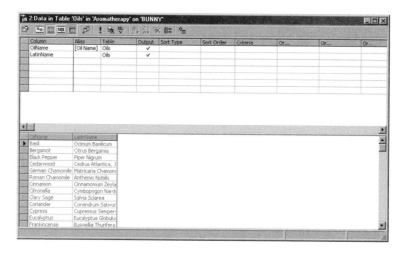

> **TIP** The square brackets won't be displayed in the query output. They simply tell SQL Server to treat the phrase "Oil Name" as a single name. The brackets are only required when the alias contains a space, but they can be used for any column name.

3. Click the Run button on the Query Designer toolbar to reexecute the query.

   SQL Server displays the name in the column header with the space added between the two words.

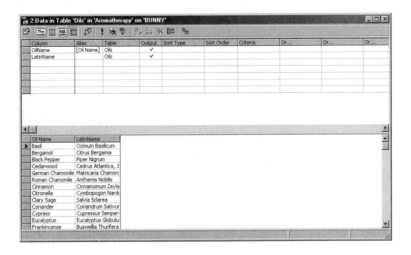

Create a column alias using the SQL Pane

Grid Pane button

1. Hide the Grid Pane and display the SQL Pane by clicking the buttons on the Query Designer toolbar.

SQL Pane button

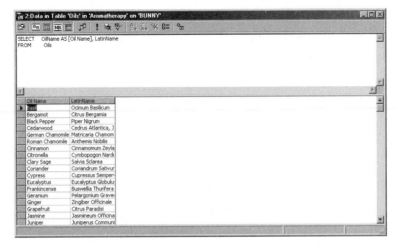

2. Add *[Latin Name]* as the alias for the second column.

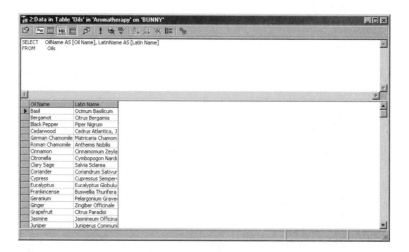

Run button

3. Click the Run button on the Query Designer toolbar to execute the query.

   The Query Designer displays the name in the column header with a space between the two words.

Creating Calculated Columns

In addition to columns that simply display the information in the underlying tables and views, your query can also contain columns that are calculated based on underlying data, SQL Server functions, or any combination of the two. The calculated column is created by specifying an expression as the column. We'll look at Transact-SQL expressions in detail in Lesson 21, "The Transact-SQL Language," so in this exercise we'll just use a pair of simple expressions based on the Transact-SQL string concatenation operator +, which adds two strings, and the function *GETDATE*, which returns the current system date and time.

Create a calculated column using the Grid Pane

SQL Pane button

Grid Pane button

1. Hide the SQL Pane and display the Grid Pane by clicking the buttons on the Query Designer toolbar.

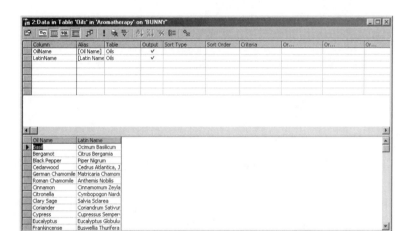

2. Click in an empty column cell in the Grid Pane and type *OilName + ' – ' + LatinName*.

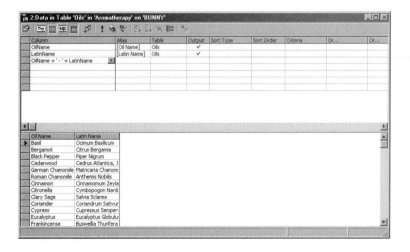

227

IP　You can make cells in the Grid Pane wider by dragging the dividing lines between the column headers.

3. Press the Tab key.

   SQL Server proposes Expr1 as the column alias.

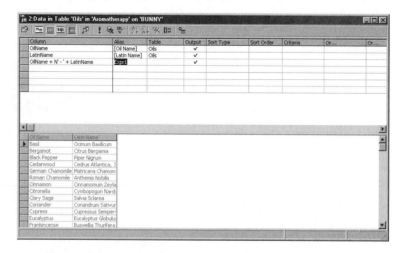

4. Change the alias to *Extended Name*.

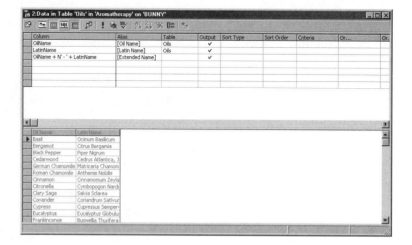

Run button

5. Click the Run button to reexecute the query.

   The Query Designer displays the new column in the Results Pane.

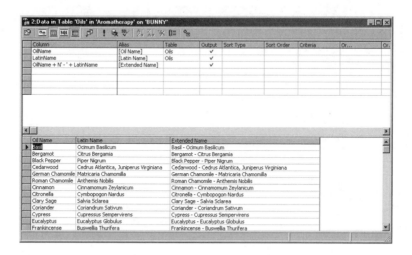

Create a calculated column using the SQL Pane

Grid Pane button

SQL Pane button

1. Hide the Grid Pane and show the SQL Pane by clicking the buttons on the Query Designer toolbar.

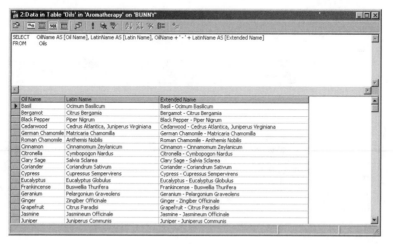

2. Add *GETDATE() AS [Today's Date]* to the column list of the SELECT clause.

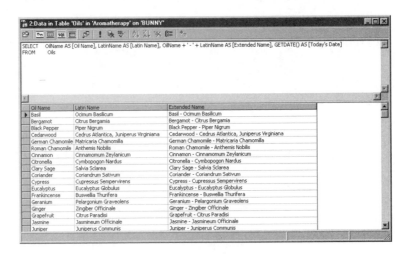

 IP Don't forget the comma before GETDATE!

Run button

3. Click the Run button on the Query Designer toolbar to reexecute the query.

SQL Server displays the current date in each row.

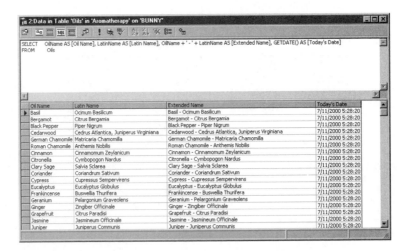

Using the TOP *n* Clause

When you select the Return Top command from the table's context menu, SQL Server is using the TOP *n* clause under the covers to create the display in the Query Designer. In addition to specifying a specific number of rows, you can also display a percentage of rows by using the TOP *n* PERCENT clause, which, as you might expect, returns the specified percentage of rows.

Display the top 5 rows

1. Add *TOP 5* before the first word in the *column_list* of the SELECT clause in the SQL Pane.

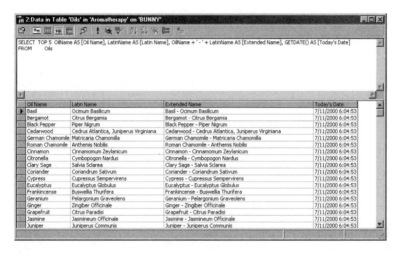

Run button

2. Click the Run button on the Query Designer toolbar to reexecute the query.

SQL Server displays only the first five rows.

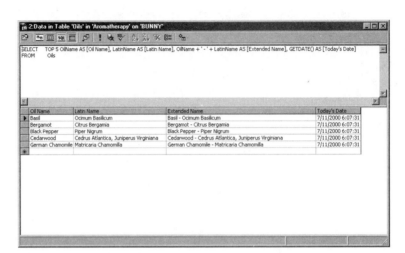

Display the top 5 percent of rows

1. Add the word *PERCENT* after TOP 5 in the SQL Pane.

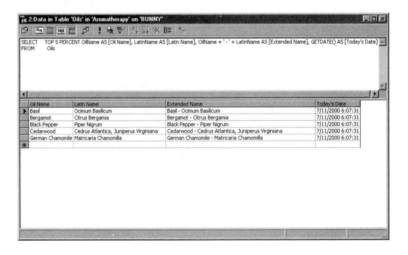

Run button

2. Click the Run button on the Query Designer toolbar to execute the query.

SQL Server displays only the first 5 percent of the rows.

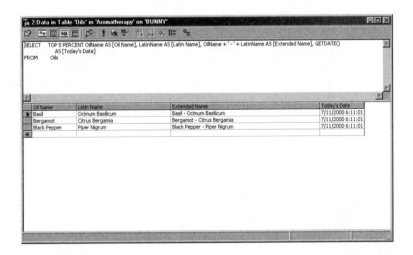

Lesson 12 Quick Reference	
To	**SELECT Statement Syntax**
Select all columns in a query	SELECT * FROM <table>
Select a subset of columns in a query	SELECT <column>, <column>...
Rename columns in a query	SELECT <column> AS <alias>...
Create calculated columns in a query	SELECT <expression> AS <alias>...
Return the top n rows in a query	SELECT TOP <number of rows>...
Return the top n percent of rows in a query	SELECT TOP < percentage of rows> PERCENT ...

```
USE Aromatherapy
GO

DECLARE simpleCursor CURSOR
    LOCAL
    KEYSET
    FOR SELECT OilName FROM Oils
DECLARE        Name char(20
OPEN

--         first row    o a variable
FETC           simpleCu

-- Di    esults
PRINT RTRIM(@theName)              rst name'

-- Retrieve the fifth row
FETCH ABSOLUTE 5 FROM simpleCursor
    INTO @theName

-- Display the results
PRINT RTRIM(@theName) + ' is the fifth name'

CLOSE simpleCursor
DEALLOCATE simpleCursor
```
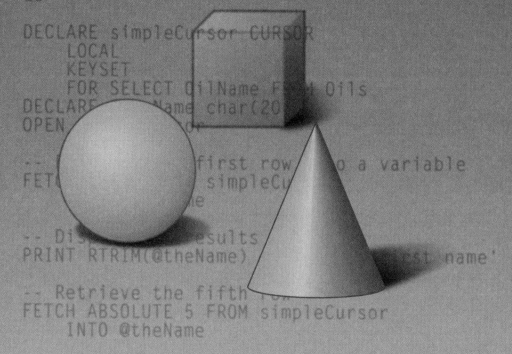

```
 0
 ECLAR         Cursor CURSOR
              Name FROM Oils
             har(20)
 EC
 PE
  - Retrieve the first row into a varia
 ETCH FIRST FROM simpleCursor
      INTO @theName

  - Display the results
 RINT RTRIM(@theName) + ' is the first name'
```

Sorting and Selecting Rows

```
 - Re
 ETCH ABSOLUTE    ROM simpleCursor
      INTO @theName

  - Display the
 RINT RTRIM
```

In this lesson you will learn how to:

- Sort the rows returned by a query.
- Select rows using a basic WHERE condition.
- Select rows using the LIKE operator.
- Select rows using the BETWEEN operator.
- Select rows using the IN operator.
- Combine selection criteria using the OR and AND operators.

In the last lesson, we looked at the most basic form of the SELECT statement and used it to select columns from a single table. But most often you'll want to return the rows in the underlying table or view in a particular order, and you'll want to return only a subset of them. The ORDER BY and WHERE clauses, discussed in this lesson, allow you to do that.

The ORDER BY Clause

The ORDER BY clause is an optional component of the SELECT statement. It allows you to specify the order in which rows will be returned. Multiple columns can be specified, and the rows can be returned in ascending or descending order.

Sorting Rows

The simplest form of the ORDER BY clause provides a single column name that will be used to sort the rows returned by the query.

Sort rows using the Grid Pane

1. Open the Query Designer for the Oils table by right-clicking its name in the Details Pane, pointing to the Open Table submenu, and selecting Return All Rows.

   SQL Server opens the Query Designer for the table.

Grid Pane button

2. Display the Grid Pane by clicking the Grid Pane button on the Query Designer toolbar.

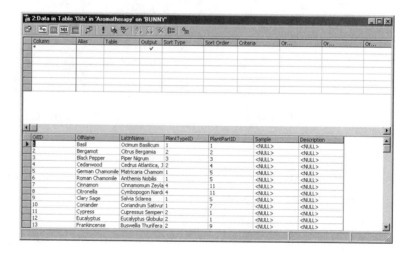

3. Select only the OilID, OilName, and LatinName columns for display.

   The Query Designer dims the contents of the Results Pane to indicate that it no longer matches the query specification.

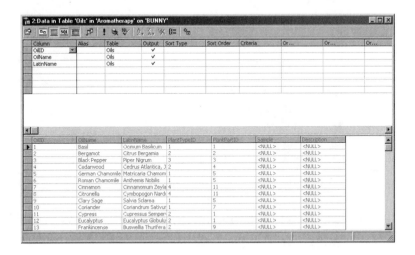

Run button

4. Click the Run button on the Query Designer toolbar to execute the
   query.

   The Query Designer displays only the specified columns.

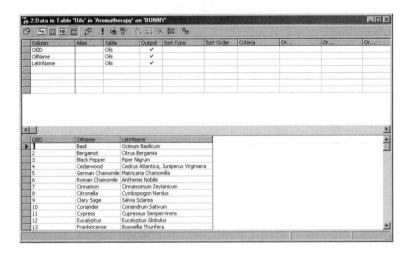

5. Set the Sort Type of the OilName field to Ascending.

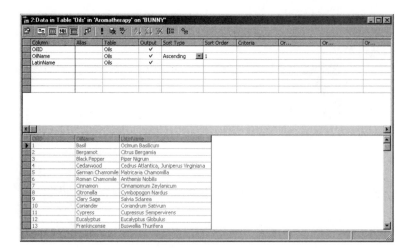

Run button

6. Click the Run button on the Query Designer toolbar to execute the query.

The Query Designer displays the rows sorted by OilName.

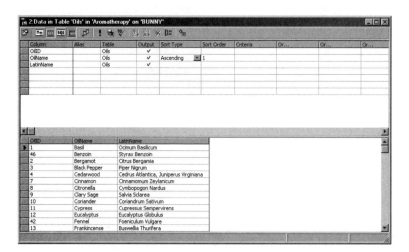

Sort rows using the SQL Pane

Grid Pane button

SQL Pane button

1. Hide the Grid Pane and display the SQL Pane by clicking the buttons on the Query Designer toolbar.

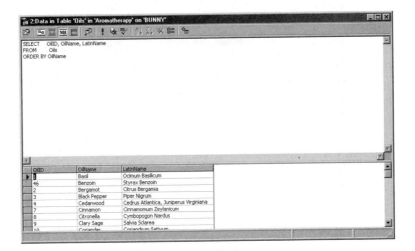

2. Add *DESC* after the ORDER BY OilName clause.

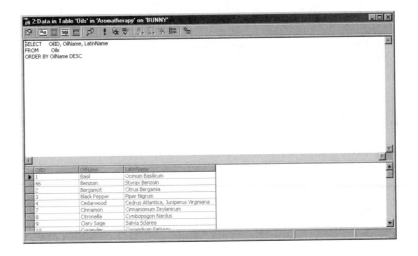

 IP The keyword DESC tells SQL Server to return the rows in descending order. The ASC keyword, which is optional, returns the rows in ascending order.

Run button

3. Click the Run button on the Query Designer toolbar to execute the query.

The Query Designer displays the results sorted by Oil Name, in descending order.

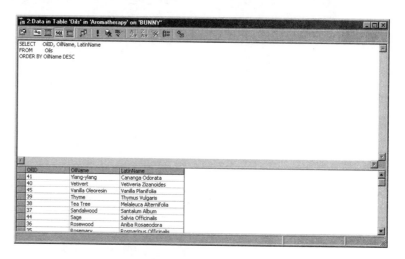

Sorting by Multiple Columns

You can specify multiple columns in the ORDER BY clause. When multiple columns are specified, the order of the columns determines the results—SQL Server will sort the rows by the first column, and then by the second column, and so forth.

> **TIP** The exercises in this section use the OilOdors table, which functions as a junction table that resolves the many-to-many relationship between the Oils and Odors tables. Ordinarily, you would resolve the foreign keys contained in this table using a join. We'll see how to do that in the next lesson, "Joining Tables."

Sort Rows using the Grid Pane

1. Choose window number 1 from the Window menu to return to the console tree.

2. Open the Query Designer for the OilOdors table by right-clicking its name in the Details Pane, pointing to the Open Table submenu, and selecting Return All Rows.

SQL Server opens the Query Designer for the table.

Grid Pane button

3. Display the Grid Pane by clicking the Grid Pane button on the Query Designer toolbar.

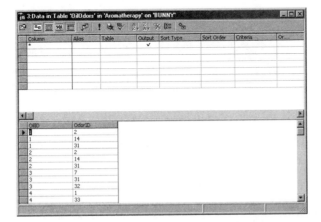

4. Replace the * in the Grid Pane with the two field names.

SQL Server dims the contents of the Results Pane to indicate that it no longer matches the query specification.

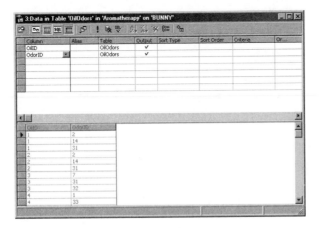

Run button

5. Click the Run button on the Query Designer toolbar to execute the query.

The Query Designer displays only the columns you specified.

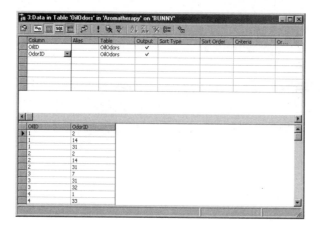

6. Set the Sort Type of both columns to Ascending.

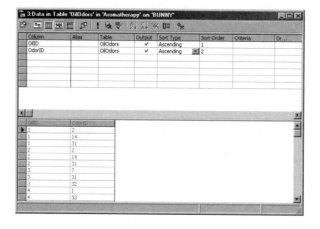

Run button

7. Click the Run button on the Query Designer toolbar to execute the query.

The Query Designer displays the rows sorted by OilID first, and then by OdorID within OilID.

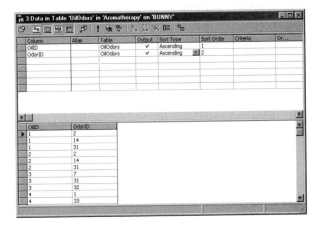

Sort Rows using the SQL Pane

Grid Pane button

1. Hide the Grid Pane and display the SQL Pane by clicking the buttons on the Query Designer toolbar.

SQL Pane button

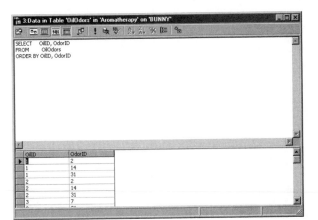

2. Reverse the columns in the ORDER BY clause.

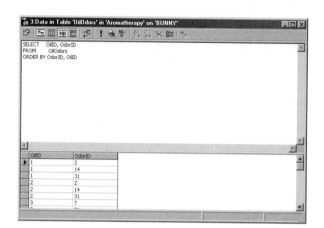

Run button

3. Click the Run button on the Query Designer toolbar to execute the query.

The Query Designer displays the results sorted by OdorID first, then by OilID

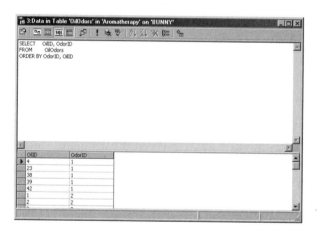

4. Close the Query Designer window.

The WHERE Clause

By using the optional WHERE clause of the SELECT statement, you can specify a subset of rows to be returned. For example, you might want to see only customers who have spent more than $10,000 in the previous twelve months or only oil names beginning with the letter "R". You would specify these criteria using the WHERE clause.

The Basic WHERE Clause

The key to the WHERE clause is the selection criteria that determine which rows will be returned. The basic structure of a WHERE clause is WHERE *<column> <operator> <value>*. SQL Server provides a full range of comparison operators, as shown in Table 13-1.

Operator	Meaning
=	Equal to
>	Greater than
<	Less than
>=	Greater than or equal to
<=	Less than or equal to
<>	Not equal to

Table 13-1.   *Comparison operators*

The *<value>* specified in the WHERE condition can be a constant value such as "Red" or 10000, or it can be an expression that returns a value, such as GETDATE. Similarly, the *<column>* value can be manipulated using Transact-SQL functions such as LEFT, which returns a specified number of characters from the left of a string. We'll look at functions in detail in Lesson 24, "Transact-SQL Language Components."

Specify a WHERE condition using the Grid Pane

1. Choose window number 2 from the Window menu to return to the Query Designer window we used earlier in this lesson.

2. Hide the SQL Pane and display the Grid Pane by clicking the buttons on the Query Designer toolbar.

3. Enter = '*Eucalyptus*' in the Criteria cell of the OilName row of the Grid Pane.

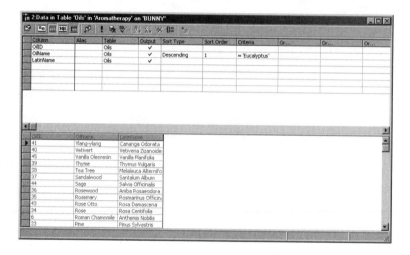

4. Click the Run button on the Query Designer toolbar to execute the query.

The Query Designer displays only a single row.

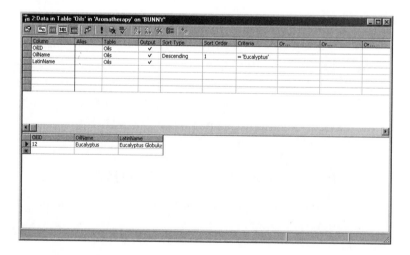

Specify a WHERE condition using the SQL Pane

Grid Pane button

SQL Pane button

1. Hide the Grid Pane and show the SQL Pane by clicking the buttons on the Query Designer toolbar.

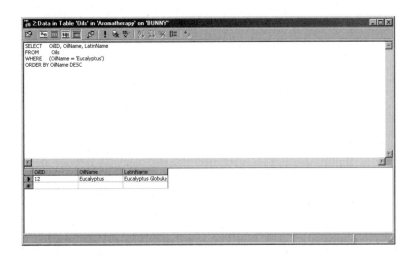

2. Change the WHERE clause to *WHERE (LEFT(OilName,1) = 'R')*.

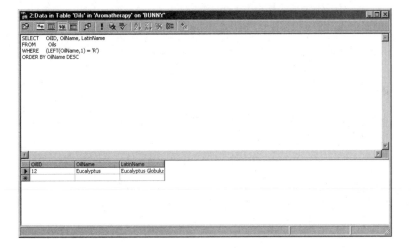

Run button

3. Click the Run button on the Query Designer toolbar to execute the query.

   The Query Designer displays oil names beginning with "R".

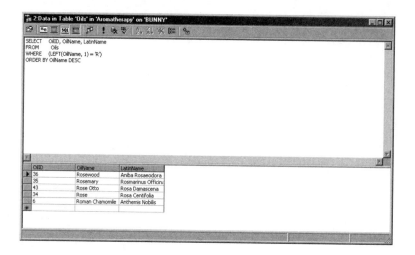

Using Special Operators

In addition to the standard format for a WHERE clause of *<column> <operator> <value>*, SQL Server also supports three special operators: LIKE, which allows you to provide non-specific values using the wildcards shown in Table 13-2; BETWEEN, which allows you to specify a range of values; and IN, which allows you to specify a set of values.

Wildcard	Meaning	Example
_	Any single character	LIKE 'a_' Matches "at" and "as" but not "and"
%	Any string of zero or more characters	LIKE '%t%' Matches "at", "bat", and "together" but not "lucky"

Table 13-2.   *Wildcard characters*

(continued)

continued

Wildcard	Meaning	Example
[]	Any specific character within a range or set	LIKE '[a-c]at' Matches "cat" and "bat" but not "fat"
		LIKE '[ab]at' Matches "bat" but not "cat"
[^]	Any specific character *not* within a range or set	LIKE '[^c]at' Matches "bat" and "fat" but not "cat"

Specify a WHERE condition using LIKE

1. Change the WHERE condition in the SQL Pane to *WHERE (OilName LIKE 'Rose%')*.

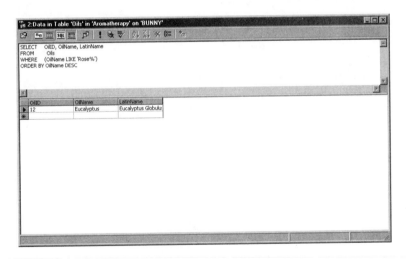

2. Click the Run button on the Query Designer toolbar to execute the query.

Run button

249

The Query Designer displays all the rows beginning with "Rose".

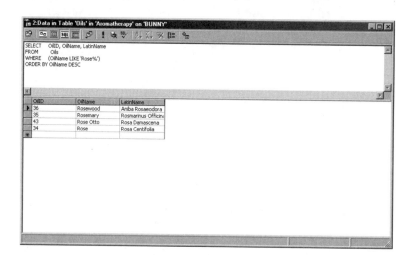

Specify a WHERE condition using BETWEEN

1. Change the WHERE condition in the SQL Pane to *WHERE (LEFT(OilName,1) BETWEEN 'A' AND 'C')*.

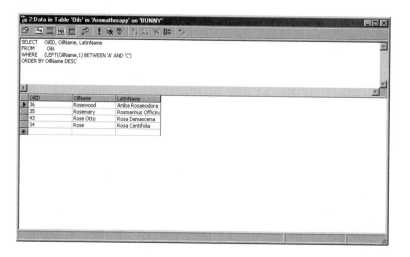

Run button

2. Click the Run button on the Query Designer toolbar to execute the query.

   The Query Designer displays all rows beginning with A, B, or C.

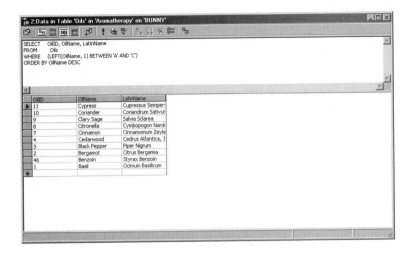

 IP Transact-SQL also supports the NOT BETWEEN operator, which works in exactly the same way, except that it *excludes* a range of values. For example, *Left(OilName,1) NOT BETWEEN 'C' AND 'E'* would return all rows except those whose OilName begins with C, D, or E.

Specify a WHERE condition using IN

1. Change the WHERE condition in the SQL Pane to *WHERE (LEFT(OilName, 1) IN ('G','M','V'))*.

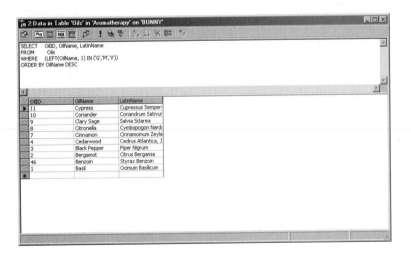

Run button

2. Click the Run button on the Query Designer toolbar to execute the query.

The Query Designer displays 8 rows.

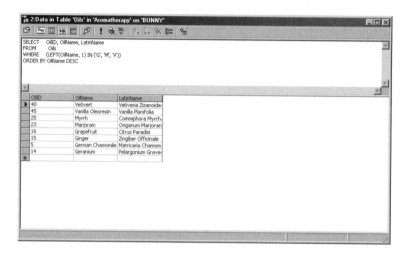

Combining Selection Criteria

In addition to specifying a WHERE clause using a single expression of the format *<column> <operator> <value>*, you can also combine expressions using one of the logical operators OR or AND. A WHERE condition of the format *<expression>* OR *<expression>* will return rows that match *either* criteria, whereas a WHERE condition of the format *<expression>* AND *<expression>* returns rows matching *both* criteria.

Specify complex criteria using OR

1. Change the WHERE condition in the SQL Pane to *WHERE (OilName = 'Rosemary' OR OilName = 'Sage')*.

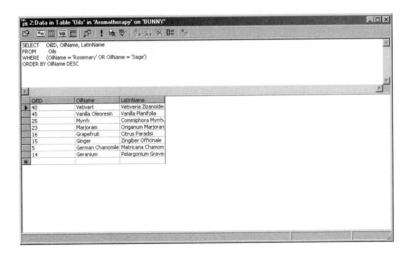

Run button

2. Click the Run button on the Query Designer toolbar to execute the query.

   The Query Designer displays 2 rows.

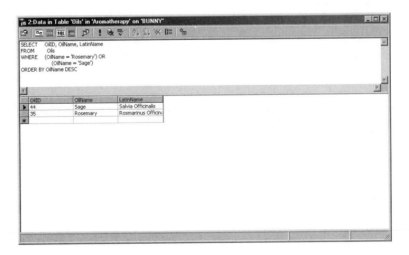

Specify complex criteria using AND

1. Change the WHERE condition in the SQL Pane to *WHERE (OilName LIKE 'Rose%')*.

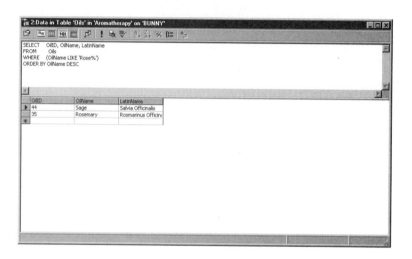

Run button

2. Click the Run button on the Query Designer toolbar to execute the query.

   The Query Designer displays 4 rows.

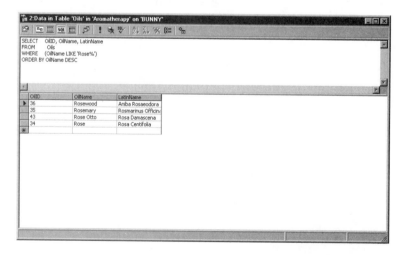

3. Change the WHERE condition in the SQL Pane to *WHERE (OilName LIKE 'Rose%') AND (OilID < 40)*.

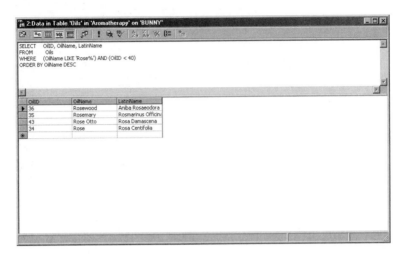

Run button

4. Click the Run button on the Query Designer toolbar to execute the query.

   The Query Designer excludes the row for Rose Otto.

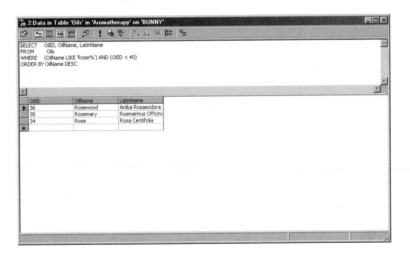

Lesson 13 Quick Reference

To	SELECT Statement Syntax
Select all columns in a query	SELECT * FROM *<table>*
Sort the rows returned by a query	SELECT ... ORDER BY *<column>*
Select rows using a basic WHERE condition	SELECT ... WHERE *<column>* *<operator>* *<value>*
Select rows using LIKE operator	SELECT ... WHERE *<column>* LIKE *<wildcard the value>*
Select rows using the BETWEEN operator	SELECT ... WHERE *<column>* BETWEEN *<value>* AND *<value>*
Select rows using the IN operator	SELECT ... WHERE *<column>* IN (*<value>*, *<value>*...)
Combine selection criteria using OR	SELECT ... WHERE *<criteria>* OR *<criteria>*
Combine selection criteria using AND	SELECT ... WHERE *<criteria>* AND *<criteria>*

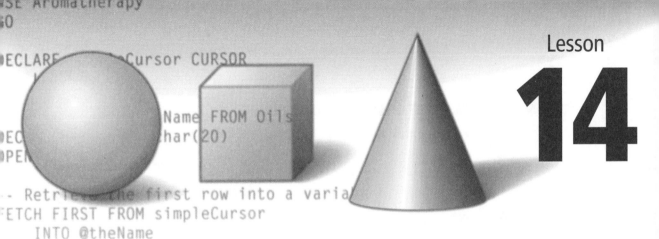

Joining Tables

The queries we have examined so far in Part 3 have drawn their rows from a single table, but queries can be particularly useful for combining columns from multiple tables or views. This is called *joining* tables, and it is done in either the WHERE or the FROM clause of the SELECT statement. In this lesson, we'll concentrate on *joins* created using the FROM clause, which is the recommended method.

Understanding the FROM Clause

As we've seen, the basic structure of the FROM clause simply provides the name of a single table or view. But to gain access to the power of the relational model, we must be able to retrieve columns from multiple tables and views in the same query. The FROM clause provides a mechanism for doing this, using the following syntax:

```
FROM <table_or_view>
<join_operator> <table_or_view> ON <join_condition>
```

The join operator describes the type of join to be performed. Microsoft SQL Server supports inner and outer joins in all their variations, as we'll see in the next section.

The join condition is an expression similar to the selection criteria used in the WHERE clause. It specifies how rows in the two tables will be matched. Most join operations are performed on the basis of expressions of equality such as Column A = Column B. But SQL Server supports any logical operator, and the join condition can be arbitrarily complex, with multiple expressions joined using the logical conjunctions AND or OR in the same way that a WHERE clause can consist of multiple selection criteria.

The join expression can be repeated to add additional tables and views to the query. The syntax for a multi-table join is:

```
FROM <table_or_view>
<join_operator> <table_or_view> ON <join_condition>
<join_operator> <table_or_view> ON <join_condition>
⋮
```

There is a theoretical limitation of 256 tables per query, but it's extremely unlikely that you will ever need more than five or six, and two or three is more usual. In fact, if you find yourself needing to link more than ten tables in a single query, you should look carefully at your database schema to make sure that it's normalized correctly.

Creating Joins

Joins can be created in the Query Designer using either the Grid Pane or the SQL Pane. The Grid Pane is often easier if you are joining tables that are formally related in the database schema, since the Query Designer will create the link between them automatically, but as always, the SQL Pane provides you with the most flexibility.

Naming Objects

When you're working with a single table or view, there can be no ambiguity about the source of a column, since all column names in a table must be unique. Once you begin to work with multiple tables in a query, you must be careful to specify column names precisely.

The full specification for any database object consists of four identifiers: the server name, the database name, the owner name, and the object name. The identifiers are separated by periods. Thus the fully qualified name of the Oils table on my system is:

`BUNNY.Aromatherapy.dbo.Oils`

Some objects, such as tables and views, contain other objects. To reference one of these contained objects (in this case, the columns), you simply append its name to the object name. The fully qualified name of the OilID column of the Oils table is:

`BUNNY.Aromatherapy.dbo.Oils.OilID`

Fortunately, you need only specify enough of the hierarchy to avoid ambiguity. In a query based on a single table, for example, the column name by itself is sufficient identification. If a query joins more than one table, however, and the tables have columns with the same names, you must include the table name in the object name: Oils.OilID and OilProperties.OilID makes the distinction perfectly clear.

Inner Joins

The most common form of join is an *inner join.* An inner join returns only those rows for which the join condition returns TRUE.

Join two tables using the Diagram Pane

1. Open the Query Designer for the Oils table by right-clicking its name in the Details Pane, pointing to Open Table, and selecting Return All Rows.

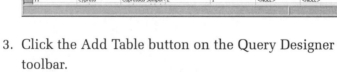

Diagram Pane button

2. Display the Diagram Pane by clicking the Diagram Pane button on the Query Designer toolbar.

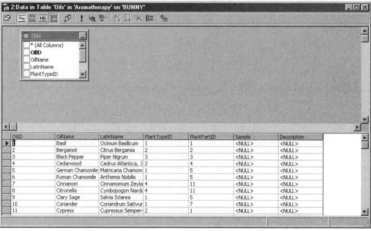

Add Table button

3. Click the Add Table button on the Query Designer toolbar.

   The Query Designer displays the Add Table dialog box.

4. Select the PlantTypes table in the table list and click Add.

   SQL Server adds the table to the query.

5. Click Close to close the Add Table dialog box.

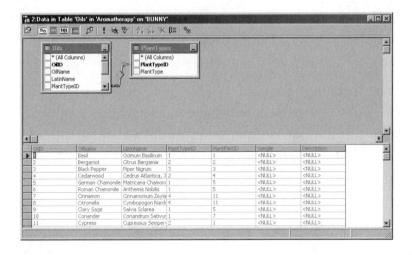

 6. Click the SQL Pane button on the Query Designer toolbar.

SQL Pane button

   The Query Designer displays the SQL Pane.

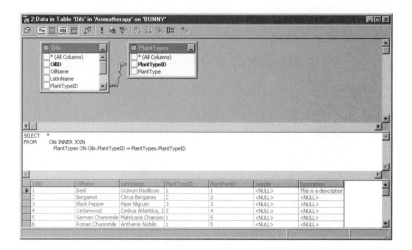

7. Delete the * after the SELECT keyword.

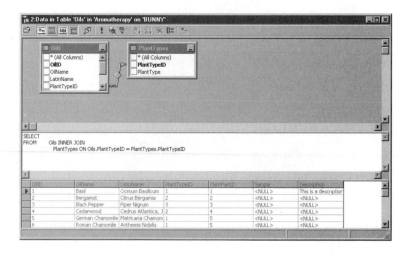

SQL Pane button

8. Click the SQL Pane button on the Query Designer toolbar. (Click OK if the Query Designer displays an error message about the syntax of the SELECT statement.)

The Query Designer hides the SQL Pane.

 MPORTANT When you open the Query Designer, the underlying SQL statement is always SELECT *. Selecting specific columns in the Diagram Pane causes them to be *added* to the column list. Microsoft considers this a feature.

---

9. In the Diagram Pane, click the check boxes next to the OilID and OilName columns in the Oils table and the PlantType column in the PlantTypes table.

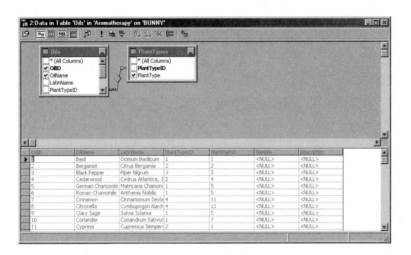

Run button

10. Click the Run button on the Query Designer toolbar to execute the query.

The Query Designer displays the PlantType values for each oil.

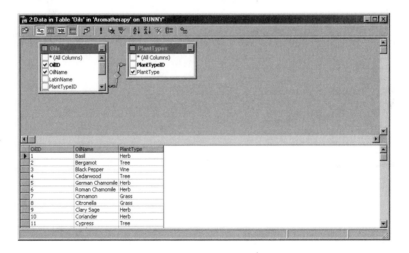

Join two tables using the SQL Pane

Diagram Pane button

SQL Pane button

1. Hide the Diagram Pane and display the SQL Pane by clicking the buttons on the Query Designer toolbar.

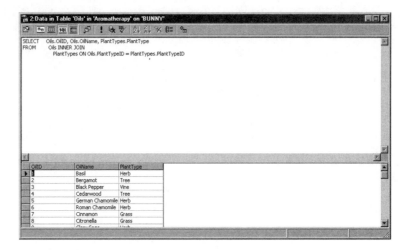

2. Replace the existing SQL statement with:

```
SELECT Oils.OilID, Oils.OilName, PlantParts.PlantPart
FROM   Oils INNER JOIN
         PlantParts ON Oils.PlantPartID = PlantParts.PlantPartID
```

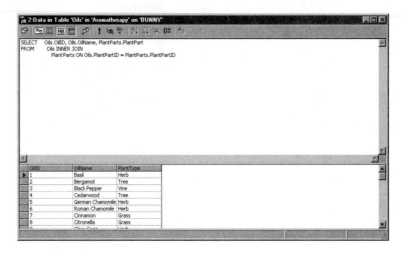

Run button

3. Click the Run button on the Query Designer toolbar to execute the query.

The Query Designer displays the Oils PlantPart values for each row.

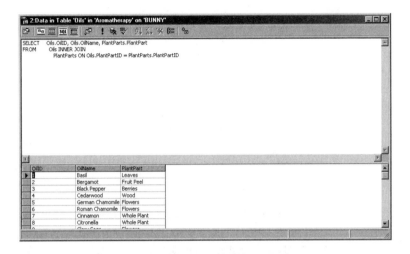

Join multiple tables using the Diagram Pane

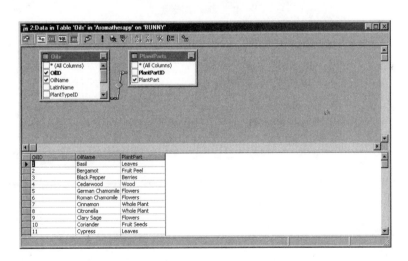

SQL

SQL Pane button

□·□

Diagram Pane button

1. Hide the SQL Pane and display the Diagram Pane.

2. Click the Add Table button on the Query Designer toolbar.

The Query Designer displays the Add Table dialog box.

3. Select the PlantTypes table in the table list, and click Add.

   SQL Server adds the table to the query.

4. Click Close to close the Add Table dialog box.

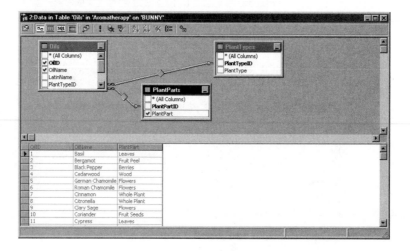

5. In the Diagram Pane, click the PlantType column in the PlantTypes table to add the column to the query.

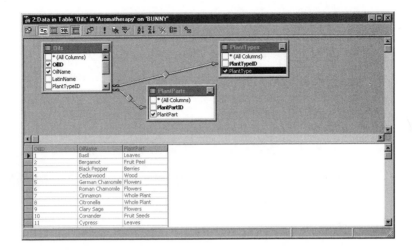

Run button

6. Click the Run button on the Query Designer toolbar to execute the query.

   The Query Designer displays both the PlantPart and PlantType columns for each oil.

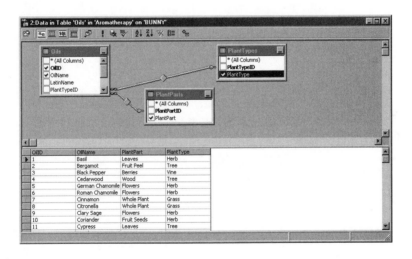

Join multiple tables using the SQL Pane

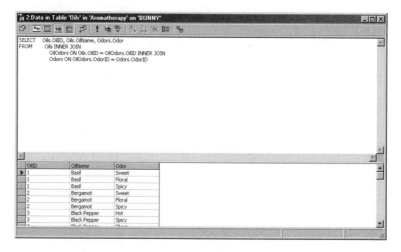

Diagram Pane button

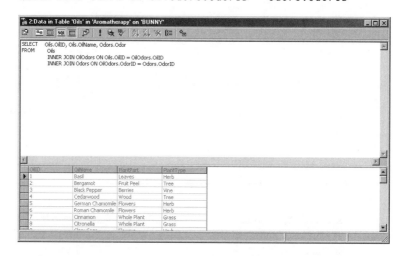

SQL Pane button

1. Hide the Diagram Pane and show the SQL Pane.

2. Replace the existing SELECT statement with:

```
SELECT   Oils.OilID, Oils.OilName, Odors.Odor
FROM     Oils
INNER JOIN OilOdors ON Oils.OilID = OilOdors.OilID
INNER JOIN Odors ON OilOdors.OdorID = Odors.OdorID
```

3. Click the Run button on the Query Designer toolbar to execute the query.

4. Close the Query Designer window.

Outer Joins

Sometimes you want a query to return all the rows from one or more tables, whether or not they have matching rows in the other table. This is accomplished using an *outer join*, which comes in three varieties: left, right, and full.

A left outer join returns all the rows from the left table in the JOIN clause and only those rows from the right table for which the join condition is TRUE. The syntax for a left outer join is:

```
FROM LeftTable LEFT OUTER JOIN RightTable ON <join_condition>
```

For example, the SELECT statement below returns all the rows in the Oils table, matching up the PlantPart values from the PlantParts table where a PlantPartID is specified. Where there is no matching row in the PlantParts table, the query will return NULL as the PlantPart value for that row.

```
SELECT  Oils.OilName, PlantParts.PlantPart
FROM    Oils LEFT OUTER JOIN
        PlantParts ON Oils.PlantPartID = PlantParts.PlantPartID
```

A right outer join is the opposite of a left outer join: it returns all rows from the right table in the JOIN clause and the matching values from the left table, whereas a full outer join returns all rows from both tables, matching them up where possible.

Create a left outer join using the Diagram Pane

1. Open the Query Designer for the Oils table by right-clicking the table name in the Details Pane, pointing to Open Table, and selecting Return All Rows.

2. Display the Diagram Pane.

*Diagram Pane
button*

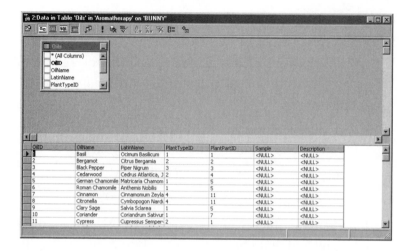

Add Table button

3. Click the Add Table button on the Query Designer toolbar.

   The Query Designer displays the Add Table dialog box.

4. Select Cautions and OilCautions in the table list, and then click Add.

   The Query Designer adds the tables to the query.

 IP You can create a left outer join with two tables. We're using three here, with the OilCautions table acting as a junction table that resolves the many-to-many relationship between Oils and Cautions.

---

5. Click Close to close the dialog box.

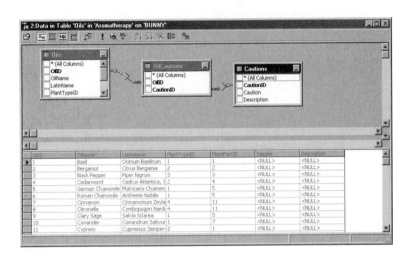

 IP You can drag the tables in the Diagram Pane to clean up the display.

---

6. Click the SQL Pane button on the Query Designer toolbar.

   The Query Designer displays the SQL Pane.

SQL

SQL Pane button

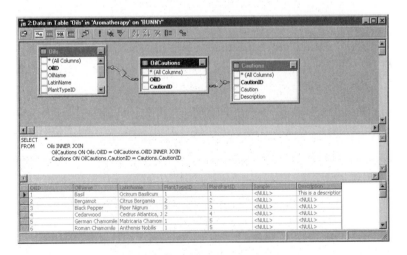

7. Delete the * after the SELECT keyword.

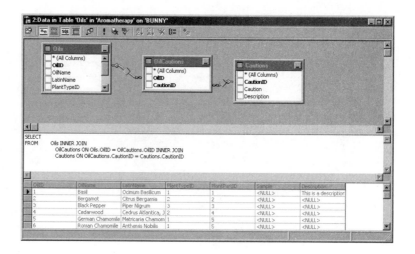

SQL Pane button

8. Click the SQL Pane button on the Query Designer toolbar. (Click OK if the Query Designer displays an error message about the syntax of the SELECT statement.)

The Query Designer hides the SQL Pane.

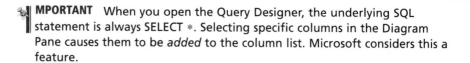

MPORTANT   When you open the Query Designer, the underlying SQL statement is always SELECT ∗. Selecting specific columns in the Diagram Pane causes them to be *added* to the column list. Microsoft considers this a feature.

---

9. In the Diagram Pane, select the OilID and OilName columns of the Oils table and the Caution column from the Cautions table for output.

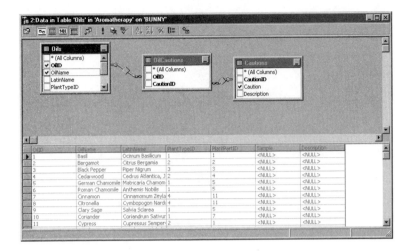

Run button

10. Click the Run button on the Query Designer toolbar to execute the query.

    The Query Designer displays only those oils that have cautions.

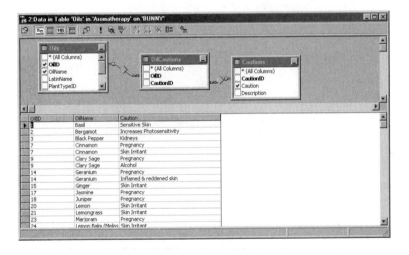

Properties button

11. Select the join line between the Oils and OilCautions tables by clicking it, and then click the Properties button on the Query Designer toolbar.

The Query Designer displays the join Properties dialog box.

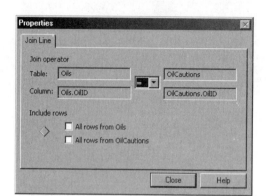

12. Select the All Rows From Oils check box.

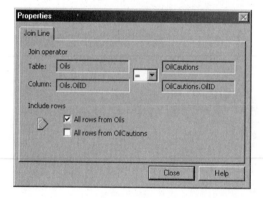

TIP Selecting the All Rows from OilCautions would create a right outer join, and selecting both options would create a full outer join.

---

13. Click Close to close the dialog box.

The Query Designer changes the join line to reflect the new join specification.

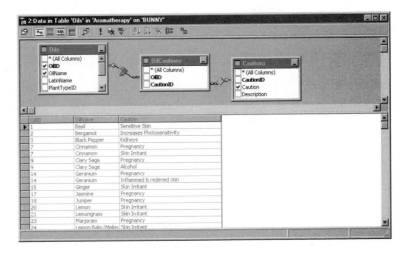

Run button

14. Click the Run button on the Query Designer toolbar to execute the query.

The Query Designer displays all rows in the Oils table and matching values from the Cautions table.

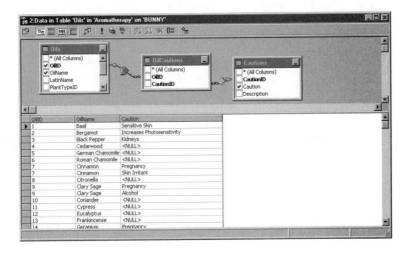

Create a right outer join using the SQL Pane

Diagram Pane button

SQL

SQL Pane button

1. Hide the Diagram Pane and display the SQL Pane in the Query Designer.

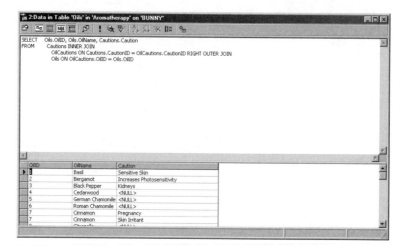

2. Replace the existing SELECT statement with:

```
SELECT  Oils.OilName, Properties.Property
FROM    Oils
        RIGHT OUTER JOIN OilProperties ON
        Oils.OilID = OilProperties.OilID
        INNER JOIN Properties ON
        OilProperties.PropertyID = Properties.PropertyID
```

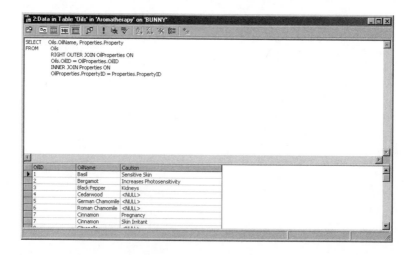

Run button

3. Click the Run button on the Query Designer toolbar to execute the query.

The Query Designer includes all rows from the OilProperties table, with matching values from the Oils table.

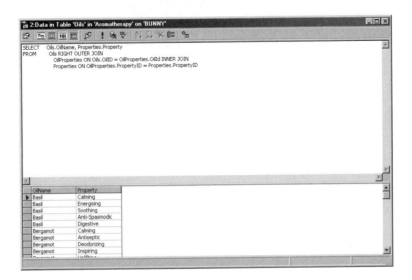

4. Close the Query Designer window.

Unions

The final type of join is known as a *union*. A union combines the results of two distinct SELECT statements into a single set of rows. Inner and outer joins combine columns from the two tables involved in a single row. A union combines rows from the two tables in a single column. You can think of this as taking two sets of rows and returning one on top of the other, although the actual order of the rows returned is determined by the ORDER BY clause.

The syntax of a union is different from joins. A union has the syntax:

```
SELECT <column_list> FROM <table_name>
UNION [ALL]
SELECT <column_list> FROM <table_name>
[ORDER BY <column_list>]
```

You can add as many UNION SELECT statements as you like to a query (subject to the 256-table limitation), but all the SELECT statements must return the same number of columns, of the same or compatible types, in the same order. The first SELECT statement will determine the column names, and the ORDER BY clause of the last SELECT statement will determine the sort order.

By default, SQL Server eliminates duplicate rows from the results of a union query. If you specify UNION ALL, however, duplicate rows will be retained.

Create a union

1. Open the Query Designer by right-clicking the Properties table in the Details Pane, pointing to Open Table, and selecting Return All Rows.

SQL Pane button

2. Display the SQL Pane.

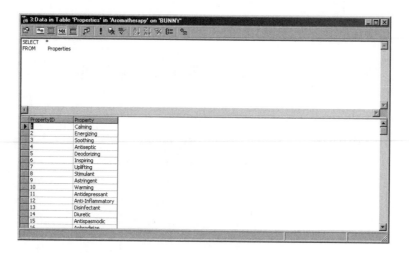

3. Replace the existing SQL statement with:

```
SELECT    'PropertyTable' AS TableName, PropertyID AS ID,
          Property AS Quality FROM Properties
UNION
SELECT    'OdorTable', OdorID, Odor FROM Odors
ORDER BY Quality
```

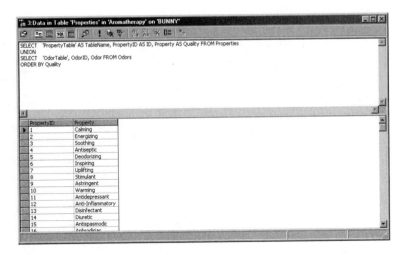

Run button

4. Click the Run button on the Query Designer toolbar to execute the query.

The Query Designer combines the results of the two SELECT statements.

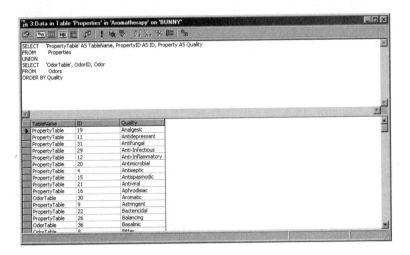

Lesson 14 Quick Reference

To	SELECT statement syntax
Create an inner join	`SELECT … FROM <table>` `INNER JOIN <table> ON <join condition>`

Join multiple tables	`SELECT … FROM <table>`
	`<join operator> <table> ON <join condition>`
	`<join operator> <table> ON <join condition>`

Create a right outer join	`SELECT … FROM <table>` `RIGHT OUTER JOIN <table> ON <join condition>`
Create a left outer join	`SELECT … FROM <table>` `LEFT OUTER JOIN <table> ON <join condition>`
Create a full outer join	`SELECT … FROM <table>` `FULL OUTER JOIN <table> ON <join condition>`

Create a union	`SELECT …`
	`UNION [ALL]`
	`SELECT …`
	`[ORDER BY <column_list>]`

Summarizing Data

In Lesson 14, we saw how to join rows from two or more tables in a query. When two tables are participants in a one-to-many relationship, the query engine repeats the values from the row on the one side for every matching row on the many side.

Sometimes this is exactly what you want, but more often you'll want to group or summarize the repeating rows in some way. In this lesson, we'll look at two methods of doing this, the DISTINCT keyword and the GROUP BY clause.

Understanding SELECT DISTINCT

One of the goals of relational database design is to eliminate repetitive data, but most databases will necessarily contain certain values in multiple rows. A table that contains customer address information, for example, will probably have the same state and country values for many rows. This is neither incorrect nor repetitive, since each state value is the attribute of a different customer. Similarly, a table on the many side of a one-to-many relationship might have any given foreign key value repeated many times. Not only is this not incorrect, it's necessary for the relational integrity of the database.

However, this repetition can sometimes make for awkward query results. Given a Customer table of, say, 10,000 rows, with 90 percent of the customers in California, the following query would return the value CA 9,000 times—not at all a useful result.

```
SELECT State FROM Customer
```

The DISTINCT keyword comes to your rescue in these situations. DISTINCT, which is placed directly after SELECT, instructs SQL Server to eliminate duplicate rows in the result set. Thus the following query returns each State value only once, precisely the list you were looking for.

```
SELECT DISTINCT State FROM Customer
```

 IP The DISTINCT keyword has a counterpart, ALL, that instructs SQL Server to return all rows, whether unique or not. Since this is the default behavior of a SELECT statement, ALL is not normally used, but you might decide to include it if it makes the query syntax more understandable.

Using SELECT DISTINCT

The DISTINCT keyword can be specified in the SQL statement of the Query Designer or by setting the properties of the query.

Create a SELECT DISTINCT query using the Diagram Pane

1. Open the Query Designer for the Oils table by right-clicking the table name in the Details Pane, pointing to Open Table, and selecting Return All Rows.

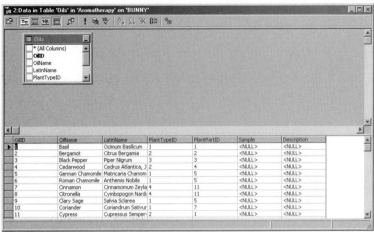

Diagram Pane button

2. Display the Diagram Pane by clicking on the Diagram Pane button on the Query Designer toolbar.

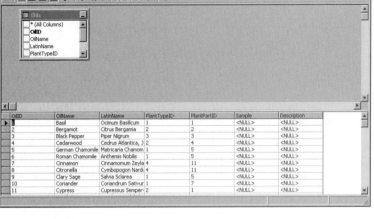

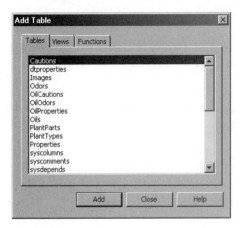

Add Table button

3. Click the Add Table button.

   The Query Designer displays the Add Table dialog box.

4. Select PlantParts in the table list, and then click Add.

   The Query Designer adds the table to the query.

5. Click Close to close the dialog box.

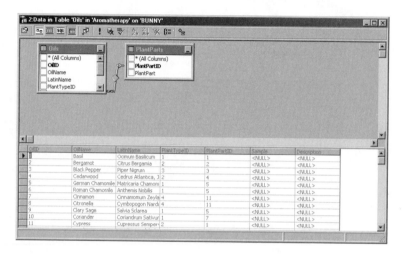

6. Click the SQL Pane button on the Query Designer toolbar.

   The Query Designer displays the SQL Pane.

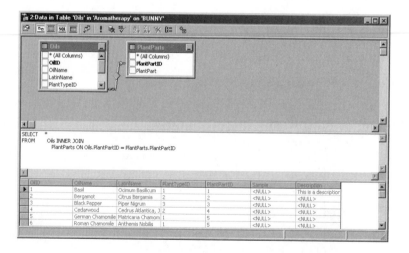

7. Delete the * after the SELECT keyword.

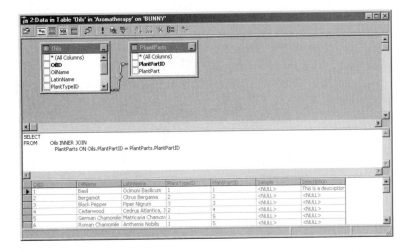

8. Click the SQL Pane button on the Query Designer toolbar. (Click OK if the Query Designer displays an error message about the syntax of the SELECT statement.)

   The Query Designer hides the SQL Pane.

MPORTANT When you open the Query Designer, the underlying SQL statement is always SELECT *. Selecting specific columns in the Diagram Pane causes them to be *added* to the column list. Microsoft considers this a feature.

---

9. In the Diagram Pane, select only the PlantPart column of the PlantParts table for display.

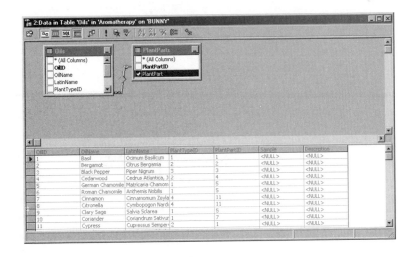

Run button

10. Click the Run button to reexecute the query.

    The Query Designer lists each PlantPart value multiple times.

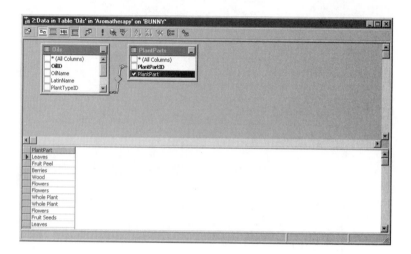

11. Right-click in an empty area of the Diagram Pane, and select Properties.

    The Query Designer displays the Properties dialog box.

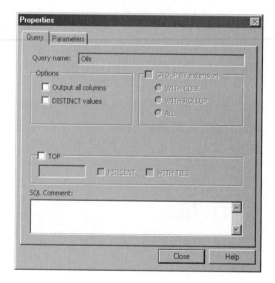

12. Select the DISTINCT Values option.

13. Click Close to close the dialog box.

14. Click the Run button to reexecute the query.

Run button

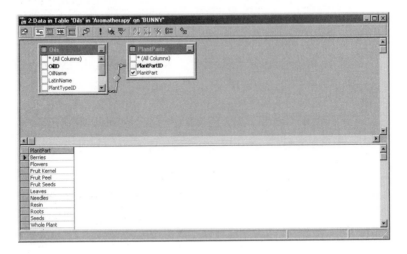

The Query Designer displays each value only once.

Create a SELECT DISTINCT query using the SQL Pane

Diagram Pane button

SQL Pane button

1. Hide the Diagram Pane and display the SQL Pane.

2. Replace the existing SELECT statement with

```
SELECT DISTINCT PlantTypes.PlantType
FROM    Oils INNER JOIN
        PlantTypes ON Oils.PlantTypeID = PlantTypes.PlantTypeID
```

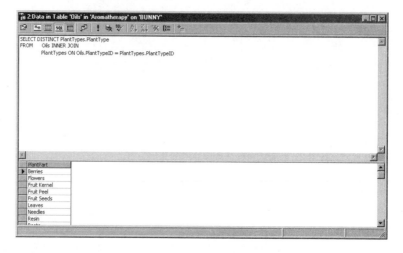

Run button

3. Click the Run button to reexecute the query.

The Query Designer displays distinct PlantType values referenced by the Oils table.

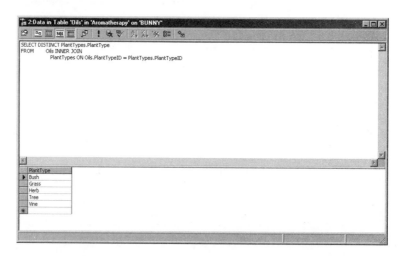

Understanding GROUP BY

The DISTINCT keyword instructs SQL Server to return only unique rows, whereas the GROUP BY clause instructs SQL Server to combine rows with the same values in the column or columns specified in the clause into a single row.

 MPORTANT Any column included in the GROUP BY clause *must* be included in the query output.

The GROUP BY clause is most often used with an *aggregate function.* An aggregate function performs calculations on a set of values and returns a single value result. The most common aggregate functions used in GROUP BY queries are MIN, which returns the smallest value in the set, MAX, which returns the largest value in the set, and COUNT, which returns the number of values in a set.

Using GROUP BY

The GROUP BY clause can be specified using any of the panes in the Query Designer, but the Grid and SQL Panes provide the most control.

Create a GROUP BY query using the Grid Pane

SQL Pane button

1. Hide the SQL Pane and display the Grid Pane.

Grid Pane button

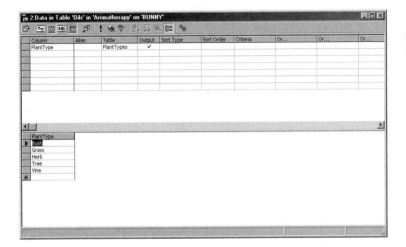

2. Add the OilName column to the query.

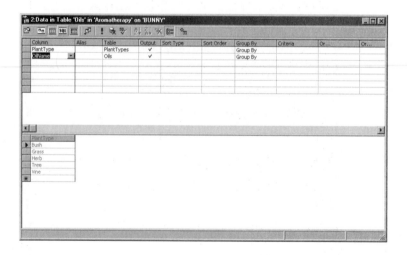

3. Click the Group By button on the Query Designer toolbar.

Group By button

The Query Designer adds a Group By column to the grid and sets both values to Group By.

4. Change the Group By cell for the OilName row to Count.

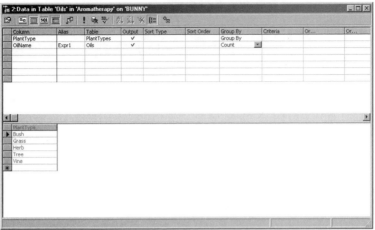

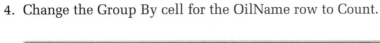

Run button

5. Click the Run button to reexecute the query.

   The Query Designer displays the number of Oils for each PlantType.

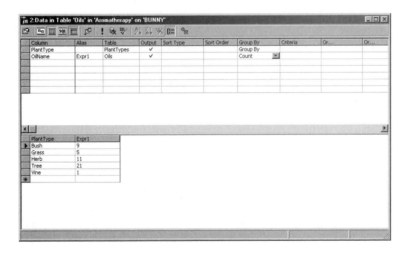

Create a GROUP BY query using the SQL Pane

Grid Pane button

SQL Pane button

1. Hide the Grid Pane and display the SQL Pane.

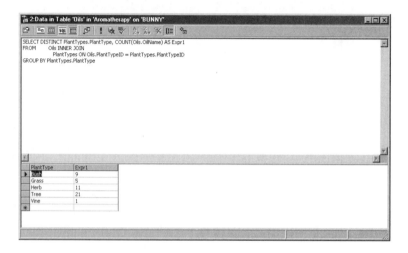

2. Replace the existing SELECT statement with

```
SELECT PlantParts.PlantPart, Count(Oils.OilName) AS NumberOfOils
FROM    Oils INNER JOIN
        PlantParts ON Oils.PlantPartID = PlantParts.PlantPartID
GROUP BY PlantParts.PlantPart
```

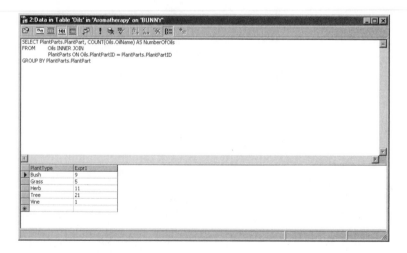

Run button

3. Click the Run Button to reexecute the query.

The Query Designer displays the number of Oils for each PlantPart.

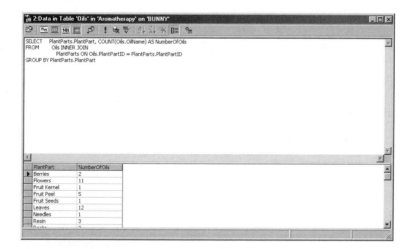

Using the HAVING Clause

The HAVING clause restricts the rows returned by a GROUP BY clause in the same way that a WHERE clause restricts the rows returned by the SELECT clause. Both the WHERE and HAVING clauses can be included in a single SELECT statement—that is, the WHERE clause is applied before the grouping operation, and the HAVING clause is applied after it.

The syntax of the HAVING clause is identical to the WHERE clause with the exception that the HAVING clause can include one of the aggregate functions included in the column list of the SELECT clause. Note, however, that you must repeat the aggregate function. For example, the HAVING clause used in the following statement is correct:

```
SELECT PlantParts.PlantPart, Count(Oils.OilName) as NumberOfOils
FROM   OILS INNER JOIN
       PlantParts ON Oils.PlantPartID = PlantParts.PlantPartID
GROUP BY PlantParts.PlantPart
HAVING Count(Oils.OilName) > 3
```

However, you can't use the alias for the Count function in the HAVING clause. Therefore, the following HAVING clause wouldn't be correct:

```
HAVING NumberOfOils > 3
```

Create a query using HAVING in the Grid Pane

SQL Pane button

Grid Pane button

1. Hide the SQL Pane and display the Grid Pane.

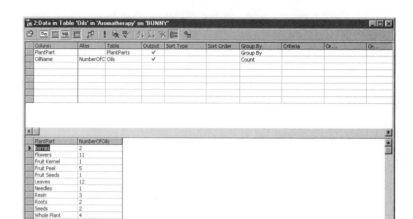

2. Add > 5 to the Criteria cell of the OilName column.

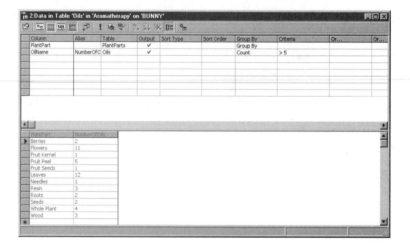

Run button

3. Click the Run button on the Query Designer toolbar to reexecute the query.

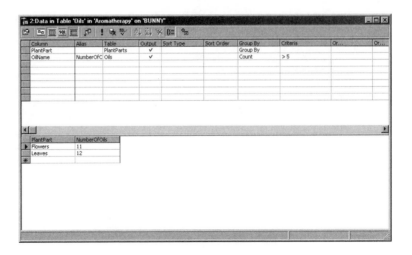

Create a query using HAVING in the SQL Pane

1. Hide the Grid Pane and display the SQL Pane.

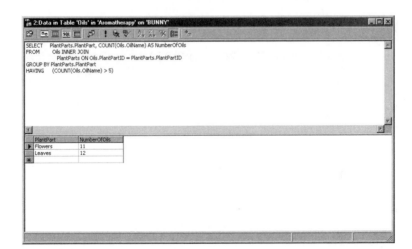

Grid Pane button

SQL Pane button

2. Change the HAVING Clause to *HAVING (Count(Oils.OilName) < 5)*.

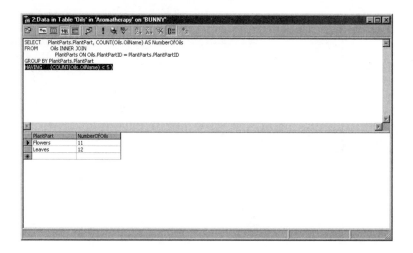

Run button

3. Click the Run button on the Query Designer toolbar to reexecute the query.

   The Query Designer displays only those PlantParts that have fewer than five associated oils.

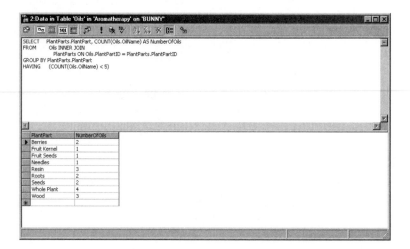

Lesson 15 Quick Reference

To	SQL syntax
Use the SELECT DISTINCT query	SELECT DISTINCT *<column_list>* ...
Create a GROUP BY query	SELECT ... FROM ... GROUP BY *<group_by_column>*
Use the HAVING clause to restrict the rows in a GROUP BY query	SELECT ... FROM ... GROUP BY *<group_by_column>* HAVING *<selection_criteria>*

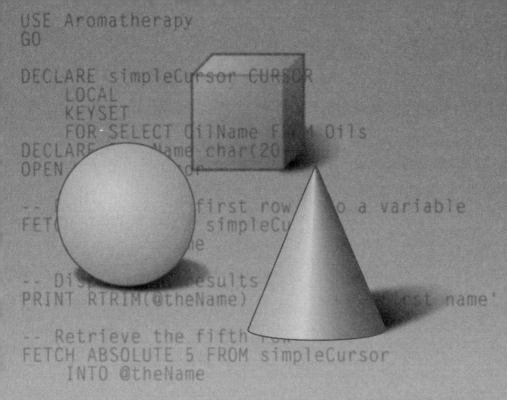

```
USE Aromatherapy
GO

DECLARE simpleCursor CURSOR
    LOCAL
    KEYSET
    FOR SELECT OilName FROM Oils
DECLARE @theName char(20)
OPEN simpleCursor

-- Retrieve the first row into a variable
FETCH FIRST FROM simpleCursor
    INTO @theName

-- Display the results
PRINT RTRIM(@theName) + ' is the first name'

-- Retrieve the fifth row
FETCH ABSOLUTE 5 FROM simpleCursor
    INTO @theName

-- Display the results
PRINT RTRIM(@theName) + ' is the fifth name'

CLOSE simpleCursor
DEALLOCATE simpleCursor
```

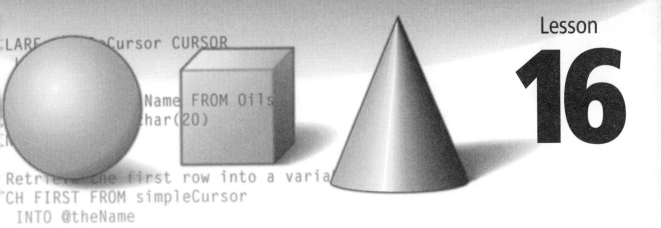

Views

Cursor CURSOR

Name FROM Oils
har(20)

Retrieve the first row into a varia
CH FIRST FROM simpleCursor
    INTO @theName

Display the results
NT RTRIM(@theName) + ' is the first name'

Retr   ifth row
CH A   FROM simpleCursor
 INTO @theName

In this lesson you will learn how to:

- Create a view using the Create View Wizard.
- Create a view using the View Designer.
- Add a view to a query.
- Rename a view.
- Modify a view.
- Remove a view.

Understanding Views

Although the Query Designer makes it easy to query the tables in your database, constantly re-creating a query statement would be tedious. SQL Server provides a means for storing a SELECT statement as a view. Under most circumstances, the data displayed by a view isn't stored in the database—only the SELECT statement is stored.

You can think of a view as a virtual table. It can be used anywhere a table can be used. In fact, the ability to use the results of one SELECT statement as the input to another SELECT statement is one of the fundamental requirements of the relational model, the principle of closure.

Indexed Views

New to SQL Server 2000 is the ability to create an index on a view. When you index a view, the result set of the view is stored in the database and updated whenever the underlying tables and views are updated. Under some circumstances, this can result in significantly better performance, since the result set doesn't need to be recalculated every time it's referenced.

Indexed views work best if the underlying data changes infrequently; otherwise the cost of maintaining an indexed view can be higher than the cost of recalculating the view when necessary. Indexed views work best for the following two types of queries:

- Joins and aggregate queries that process many rows.
- Join and aggregate operations that are frequently performed in other queries.

Creating Views

The Enterprise Manager provides two methods for creating a new view: the Create View Wizard, which walks you through each step in the process of creating a view; and the New View command, which opens the View Designer. The View Designer is identical to the Query Designer except that it allows you to save the SELECT statement you create using it. The Create View Wizard is a useful tool, but sometimes it's easier to create a view using the View Designer.

Create a View using the Create View Wizard

Wizard button

1. Click the Wizard button on the Enterprise Manager toolbar.

The Enterprise Manager displays the Select Wizard dialog box.

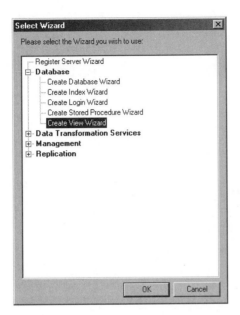

2. Expand the Database section, select Create View Wizard, and click OK.

The Enterprise Manager displays the first page of the Create View Wizard.

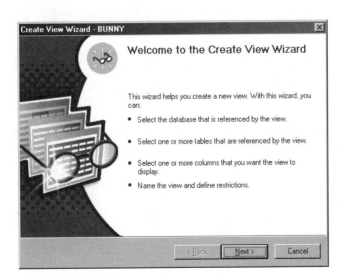

3. Click Next.

The Create View Wizard displays a page requesting the name of the database to contain the view. Select the Aromatherapy database.

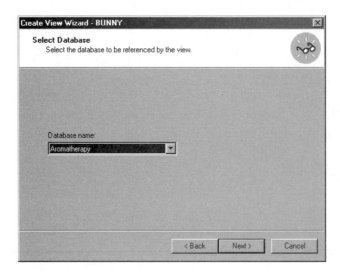

4. Click Next.

The Create View Wizard displays a page requesting that you select the objects to include in the view.

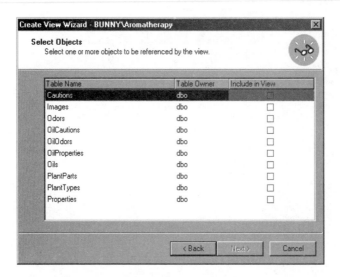

5. Select Cautions, OilCautions, and Oils.

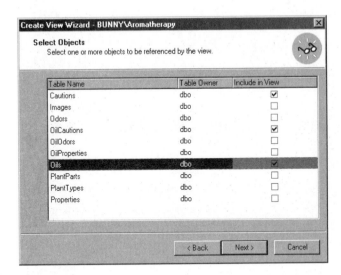

6. Click Next.

The Create View Wizard displays a page requesting that you select the columns to include in the view.

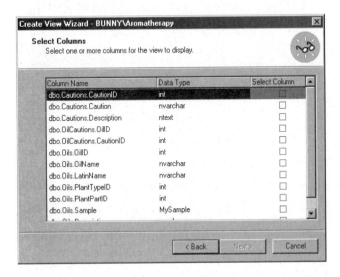

7. Select Cautions.Caution, Cautions.Description, and Oils.OilName.

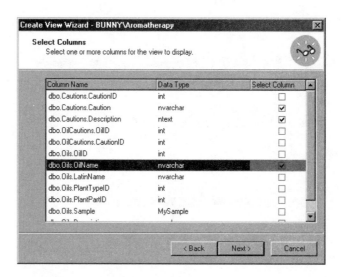

8. Click Next.

   The Create View Wizard displays a page requesting an optional WHERE clause for the view. For this lesson, don't type in a WHERE clause.

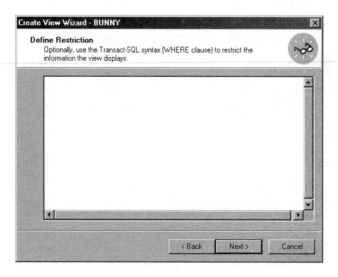

9. Click Next.

The Create View Wizard displays a page requesting the name of the new view.

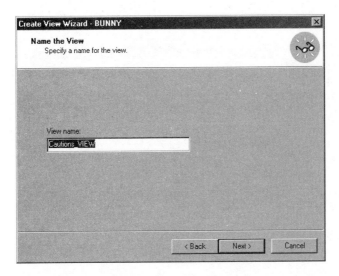

10. Type *OilCautionsExtended* as the name of the view.

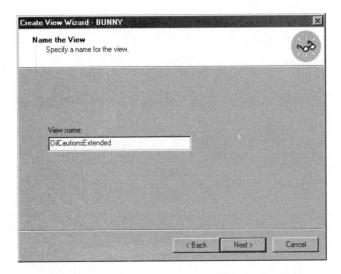

11. Click Next.

    The Create View Wizard displays the SQL statements underlying the new view.

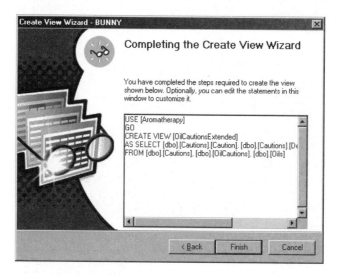

12. Click Finish.

    The Create View Wizard displays a message confirming creation of the view.

Create a view using the View Designer

1. In the Console Tree of the Enterprise Manager, navigate to the Views folder of the Aromatherapy database.

    The Enterprise Manager displays a list of existing views.

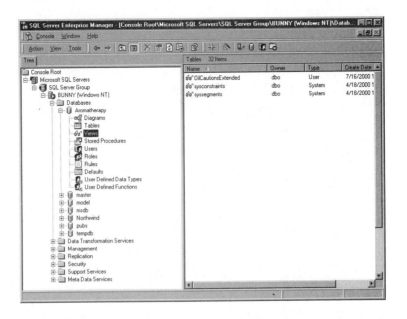

2. Click the New button on the Enterprise Manager toolbar.

New button

The Enterprise Manager opens the View Designer with all four panes displayed.

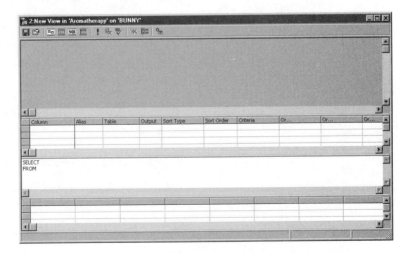

Add Table button

3. Click the Add Table button on the View Designer toolbar.

The View Designer displays the Add Table dialog box.

4. On the Tables tab, add Properties, OilProperties, and Oils to the query, and then click Close to close the dialog box.

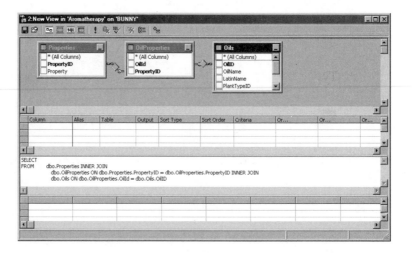

5. In the Grid Pane, select the Oils.OilID, Oils.OilName, and Properties.Property columns for output.

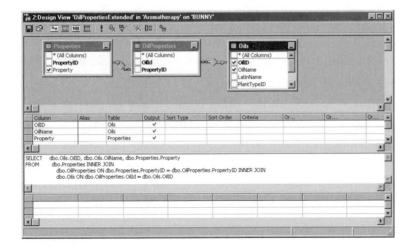

Save button

6. Click the Save Button.

   The Query Designer displays the Save As dialog box.

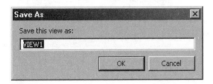

7. Type *OilPropertiesExtended* as the name of the view.

8. Click OK.

   The View Designer creates the view.

9. Close the View Designer.

Using Views

Once you create a view, you can use it just like a table. You can open it in the Enterprise Manager using the View Designer, or you can include it in other queries.

When you open the View Designer for an existing view, the Enterprise Manager treats the view as a virtual table. The underlying SQL statement is either SELECT * FROM <*view name*> or SELECT TOP *n* FROM <*view name*>, rather than the query that creates the view.

Open the View Designer for a View

1. Navigate to the Views folder of the Aromatherapy database in the Console Tree.

   The Enterprise Manager displays a list of views in the database.

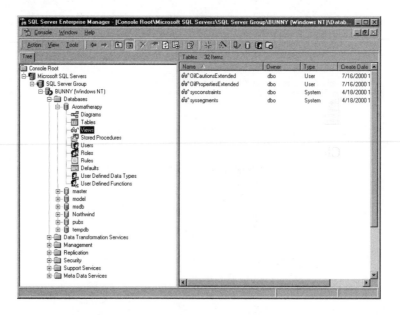

2. Right-click OilPropertiesExtended in the Details Pane, point to Open View, and select Return All Rows.

   The Enterprise Manager opens the View Designer for the view.

SQL Pane button

3. Click the SQL Pane button on the View Designer toolbar.

   The View Designer displays the SQL Pane showing the SELECT statement for the view.

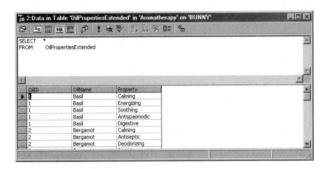

4. Close the View Designer.

Include a view in a query

1. Navigate to the Tables folder of the Aromatherapy database in the Console Tree.

   The Enterprise Manager displays a list of the tables in the Details Pane.

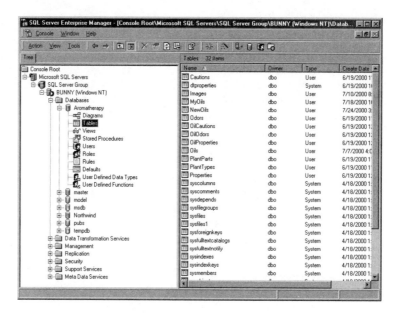

2. Open the Query Designer for the Oils table by right-clicking the table name, pointing to Open Table, and selecting Return All Rows.

The Query Designer opens the Oils table.

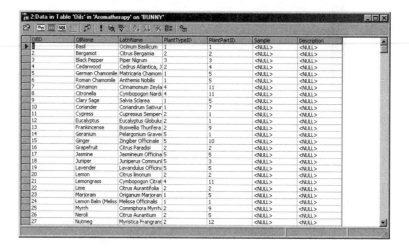

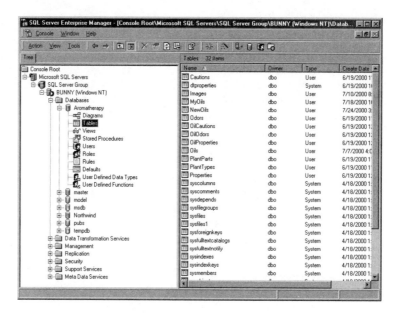

Diagram Pane button

3. Click the Diagram Pane button in the toolbar to display the Diagram Pane.

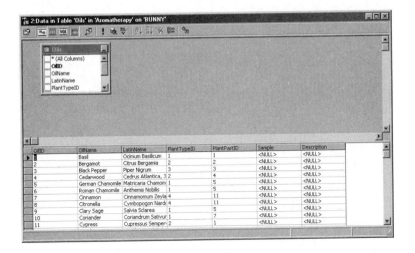

Add Table button

4. Click the Add Table button.

   The Query Designer displays the Add Table dialog box.

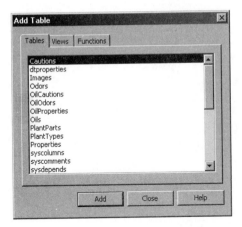

5. Select the Views tab of the Add Table dialog box.

6. Select OilPropertiesExtended in the view list, click Add to add it to the query, and then click Close to close the dialog box.

   The Query Designer adds the view to the query.

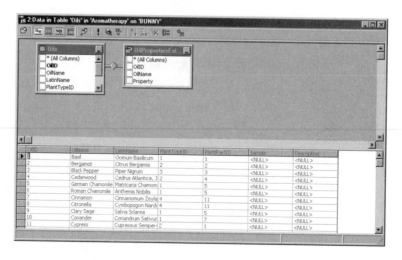

7. Click the SQL Pane Button.

   The Query Designer displays the SELECT statement for the query.

SQL Pane button

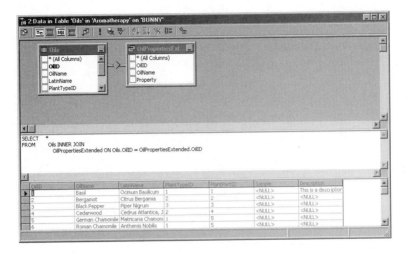

8. In the SQL Pane, replace the * with *Oils.OilName, OilPropertiesExtended.Property.*

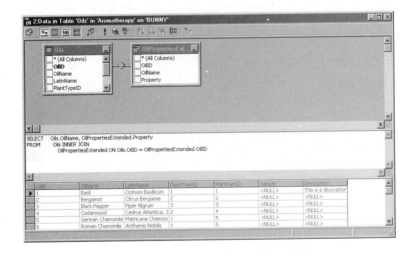

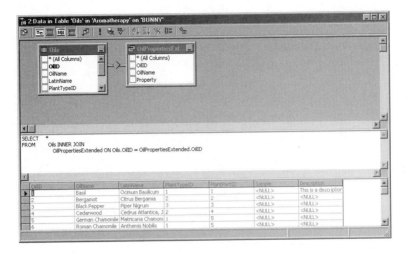

SQL Pane button

9. Click the SQL Pane Button to hide the SQL Pane.

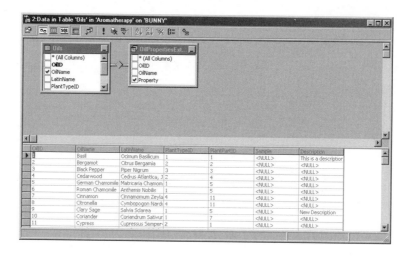

Run button

10. Click the Run button on the Query Designer toolbar to execute the query.

The Query Designer displays the OilName and Property columns.

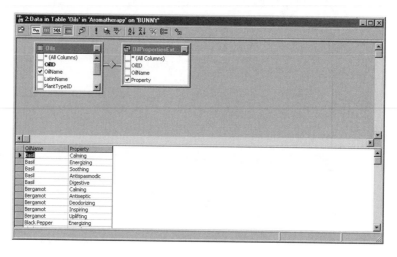

11. Close the Query Designer.

Managing Views

Like other database objects, views might need to be changed. The Enterprise Manager makes it easy for you to do so.

Altering Views

A view can be altered in two ways: you can change its name, or you can change the underlying SQL statement on which it is based.

Rename a view

1. Navigate to the Views folder of the Aromatherapy database in the Console Tree.

   The Enterprise Manager displays a list of the views in the database.

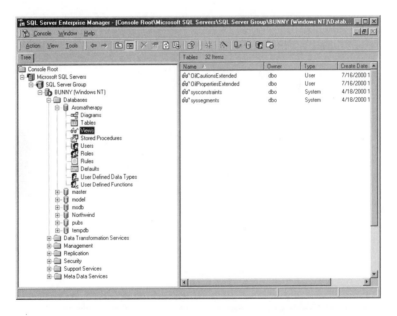

2. Right-click the OilPropertiesExtended view in the Details Pane, and select Rename.

   The Enterprise Manager selects the view name.

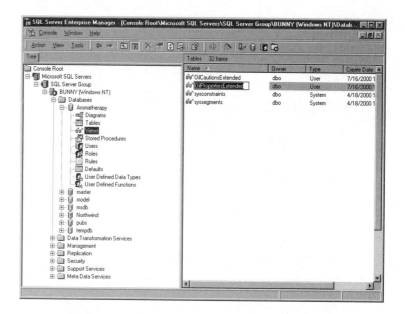

3. Change the name of the view to *OilPropExt,* and press Enter.

The Enterprise Manager displays a dialog box warning that changing the view's name will invalidate any other objects that reference it.

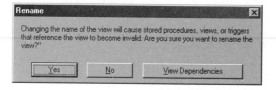

4. Click Yes.

The Enterprise Manager confirms changing the name of the view.

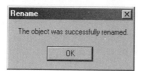

Modify a view

1. Right-click OilCautionsExtended in the Details Pane, and select Design View.

   The Enterprise Manager opens the View Designer for the view.

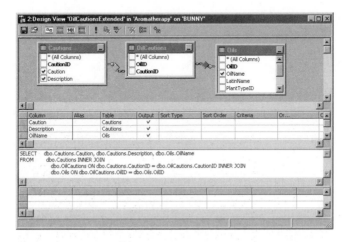

SQL Pane button

2. Hide the SQL Pane by clicking the SQL Pane button, and hide the Results Pane by clicking the Results Pane button.

Results Pane button

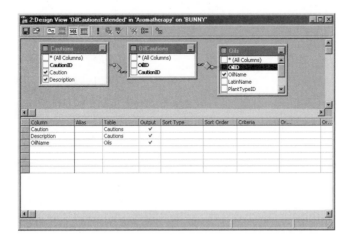

3. Add the OilID column of the Oils table to the view.

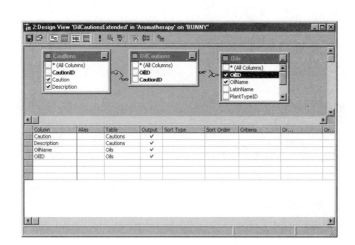

Save button

4. Click the Save button on the View Designer toolbar.

   The View Designer saves the new view definition.

5. Close the View Designer.

Removing Views

You can remove a view from a database in the same way you remove any other database object.

Delete a View

1. Right-click OilPropExt in the Details Pane and select Delete.

   The Enterprise Manager displays a dialog box asking you to confirm the deletion.

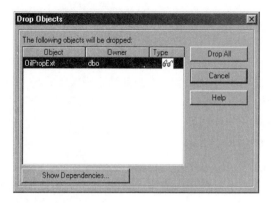

2. Click Drop All.

The Enterprise Manager removes the view from the database.

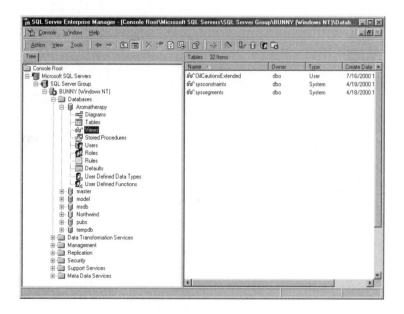

Lesson 16 Quick Reference

To	Do this	Button
Create a view using the Create View Wizard	Start the Create View Wizard by clicking the Wizard button and selecting the Create View Wizard from the Select Wizard dialog box, and follow the instructions.	
Create a view using the View Designer	Navigate to the Views folder, click the New button on the Enterprise Manager toolbar to open the View Designer, and proceed to design the view.	
Add a view to a query	In the Query Designer, click the Add Table button. Select the Views tab, select the view you want, click Add, and click Close.	
Rename a view	Right-click the view in the Details Pane, and select Rename. Type the new name, and press Enter.	
Modify a view	Right-click the view in the Details Pane, select Design View to open the View Designer, and make necessary changes to the view.	
Remove a view	Right-click the view in the Details Pane and select Delete. Confirm the deletion in the Drop Objects dialog box.	

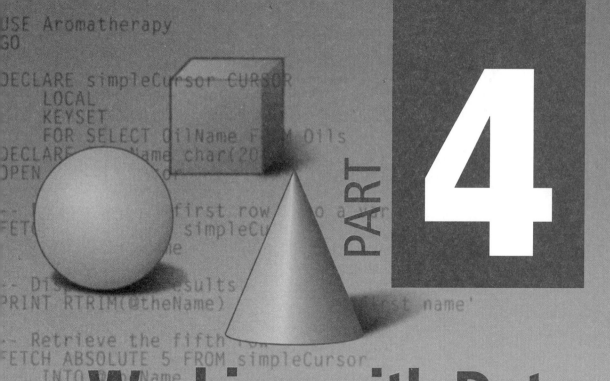

Working with Data

Lesson

17	Adding Rows	325
18	Updating Rows	345
19	Deleting Rows	359
20	Importing and Exporting Data	377

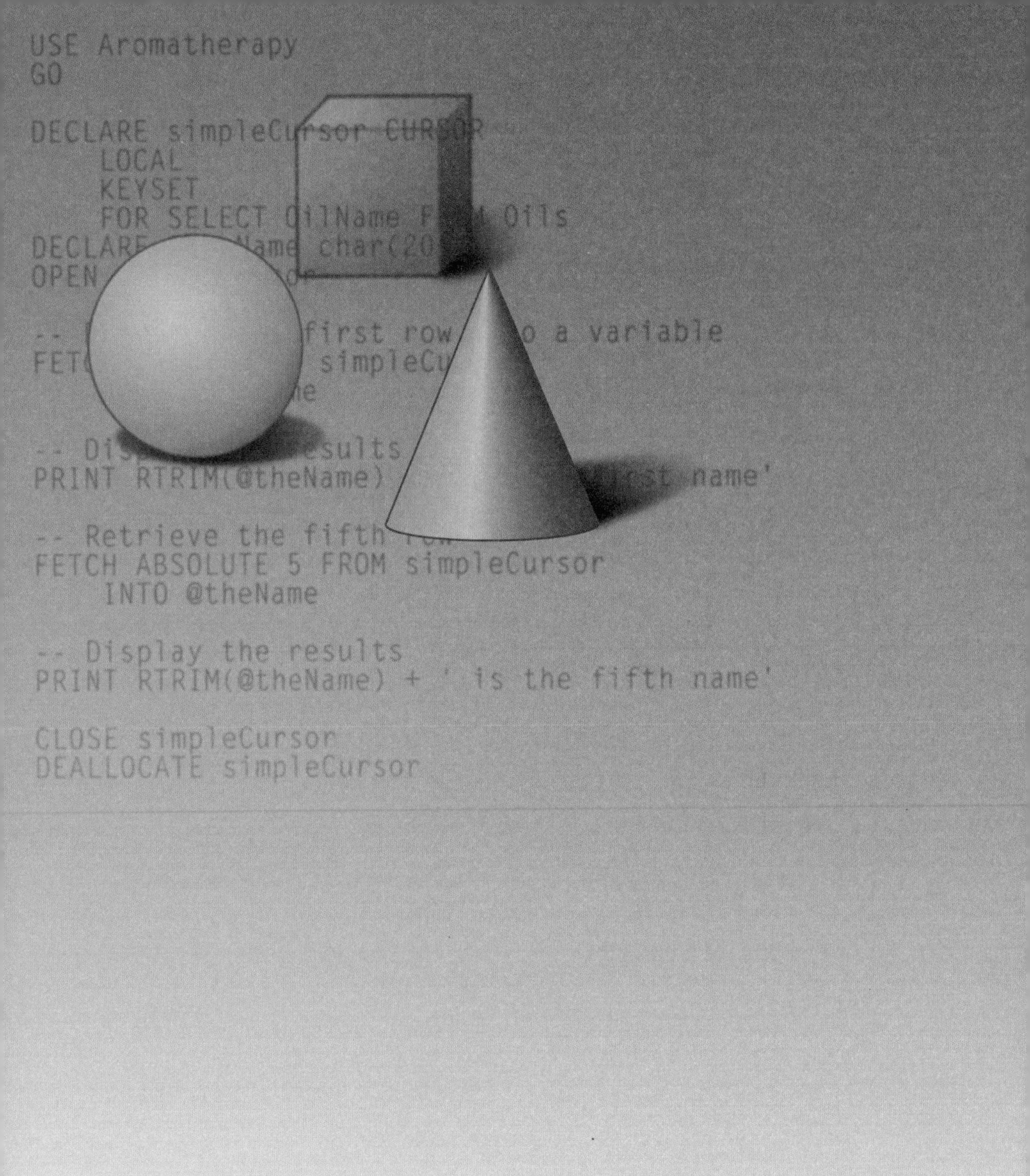

```
USE Aromatherapy
GO

DECLARE simpleCursor CURSOR
    LOCAL
    KEYSET
    FOR SELECT OilName FROM Oils
DECLARE @theName char(20)
OPEN simpleCursor

-- Retrieve the first row into a variable
FETCH FIRST FROM simpleCursor
    INTO @theName

-- Display the results
PRINT RTRIM(@theName) + ' is the first name'

-- Retrieve the fifth row
FETCH ABSOLUTE 5 FROM simpleCursor
    INTO @theName

-- Display the results
PRINT RTRIM(@theName) + ' is the fifth name'

CLOSE simpleCursor
DEALLOCATE simpleCursor
```

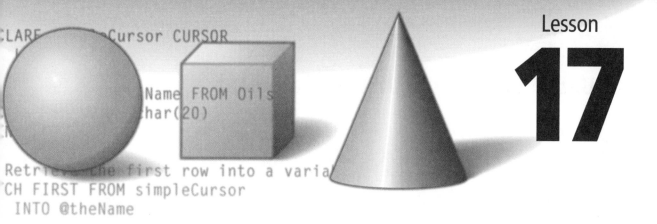

Adding Rows

In Lesson 11, you learned how to use the Query Designer to add rows to a table by typing the values in the Results Pane. In this lesson, you'll learn how to use the Transact-SQL INSERT statement to add rows under program control.

Understanding the INSERT Statement

The syntax of the INSERT statement is similar to that of the SELECT statement. Its most basic form is:

```
INSERT [INTO] table_or_view [(column_list)]
VALUES (value_list)
```

Each INSERT statement can update a single table or view. When you use the INSERT statement to update a view, you must be aware of the following restrictions:

- The view must not contain an aggregate function, such as COUNT or AVG.

- The view must not contain TOP, GROUP BY, UNION, or DISTINCT.

- The view must not contain a calculated column.

- The view must reference a table in the FROM clause.

- The INSERT statement updates columns from only a single table.

The column list in the INSERT statement is optional. If it's not provided, the INSERT statement must include values for all the columns in the table or view, and they must be provided in the same order as the columns in the table or view. You can, however, use the special keyword DEFAULT to specify default values for a row.

When the column list is included, it takes the same format as the column list of a SELECT statement: a comma-separated list of column names. Since the INSERT statement can add a row to only one table, you won't usually need to use the table name identifier for the column name.

Using the INSERT statement

An INSERT statement can be created by using the Grid Pane to specify the columns or by using the SQL Pane to enter the statement directly.

Inserting Rows Using the Grid Pane

The Grid Pane is probably the simplest way to create an INSERT statement since it doesn't require you to remember any of the syntax.

Insert a row using the Grid Pane

1. Navigate to the Tables folder of the Aromatherapy database, right-click the Oils table in the Details Pane, point to the Open Table submenu, and select Query.

   The Query Designer opens with all four panes displayed.

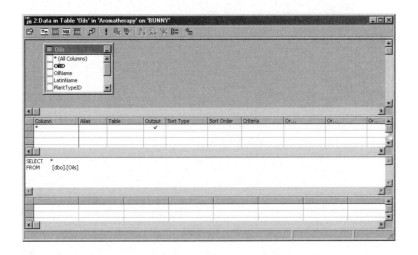

 IP   The Query command on the Open Table or Open View submenu is a quick way to open the Query Designer with all panes displayed. Although the default SQL statement is SELECT * FROM *<table_or_view>*, the query isn't executed, so no rows are returned.

SQL Pane button

Results Pane button

2. Hide the SQL Pane and the Results Pane.

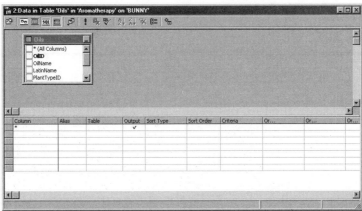

*Change Query
Type button*

3. Click the Change Query Type button on the Query Designer toolbar, and select Insert Into from the list.

The Query Designer changes the Grid Pane so that it shows only Column and New Value cells.

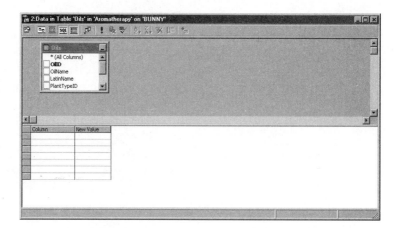

4. Add the OilName column to the Grid Pane, and set its New Value to *'InsertFromGrid'*.

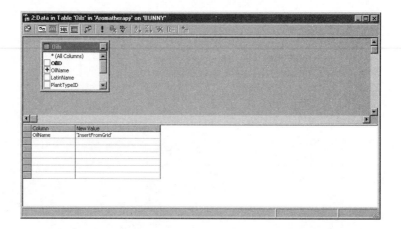

Run button

5. Click the Run button on the Query Designer toolbar to execute the query.

The Query Designer displays a message confirming that one row has been added to the table.

6. Click OK to close the message box. Without closing the Query Designer, open a new view of the Oils table by right-clicking the Oils table in the Details Pane, pointing to Open Table, and selecting Return All Rows.

   A new instance of the Query Designer opens, showing all rows in the Oils table.

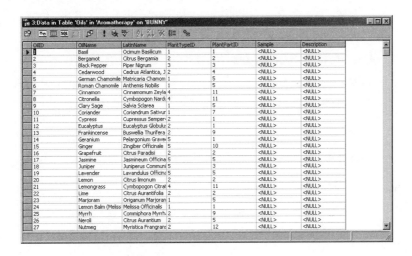

7. Scroll down to the end of the table to confirm that a new row has been added.

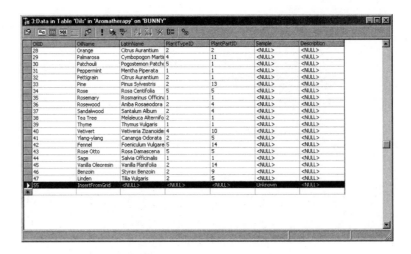

> **MPORTANT** The OilID in your database probably won't match mine. Remember that OilID is defined as an identity column. Identity columns in SQL Server are guaranteed to be unique, but they are not necessarily sequential.

Inserting Rows Using the SQL Pane

Although the Grid Pane provides a simple method of creating an INSERT statement, as always, using the SQL Pane to enter the statement directly provides greater functionality.

Insert a row using the SQL Pane

1. Reselect the Query Designer window containing the INSERT statement.

Grid Pane button

2. Hide the Grid Pane and the Diagram Pane, and display the SQL Pane.

Diagram Pane button

SQL Pane button

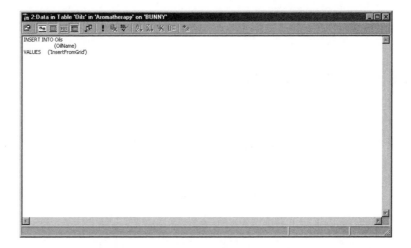

3. Change the SQL statement to

```
INSERT INTO Oils
        (OilName)
VALUES  ('InsertFromSQL')
```

Run button

4. Click the Run button on the Query Designer toolbar to execute the query.

The Query Designer displays a message confirming that the row has been added.

5. Click OK to close the message box. Reselect the Query Designer window showing all rows in the Oils table.

Run button

6. Click the Run button on the Query Designer toolbar to reexecute the SELECT * query, and scroll down to the bottom of the table to confirm that the new row has been added.

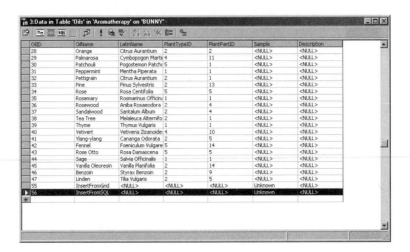

Insert a row specifying all columns

1. Reselect the Query Designer window containing the INSERT statement.

2. Change the SQL statement to read:

```
INSERT INTO Oils
VALUES  ('InsertAllValues','Latin Name',1,1,'Sample',
'Description of the Oil')
```

IMPORTANT The OilID column is *not* included in the SQL statement because it is defined as an identity. SQL Server will provide the value for identity columns and columns that have the (NewID()) default value used to generate a GUID.

Run button

3. Click the Run button on the Query Designer toolbar to execute the query.

   The Query Designer displays a message confirming that the row has been added.

4. Click OK to close the message box. Reselect the Query Designer window showing all rows in the Oils table.

Run button

5. Click the Run button on the Query Designer toolbar to reexecute the SELECT * query, and scroll down to the bottom of the table to confirm that the new row has been added.

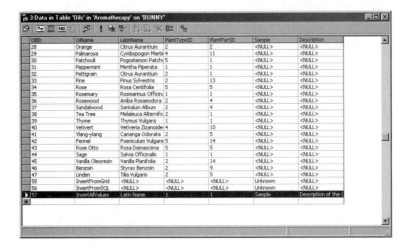

Insert a row with DEFAULT and NULL

1. Reselect the Query Designer window containing the INSERT statement.

2. Change the SQL statement to read:

```
INSERT INTO Oils
          (OilName, LatinName, Sample)
VALUES   ('InsertDefault', NULL, DEFAULT)
```

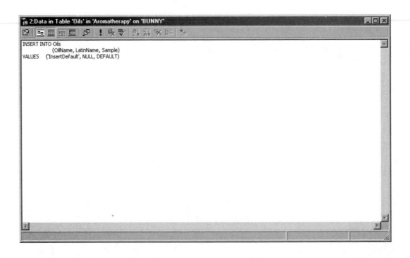

Run button

3. Click the Run button on the Query Designer toolbar to execute the query.

The Query Designer displays a message confirming that the row has been added.

4. Click OK to close the message box. Reselect the Query Designer window showing all rows in the Oils table.

Run button

5. Click the Run button on the Query Designer toolbar to reexecute the SELECT * query, and scroll down to the bottom of the table to confirm that the new row has been added.

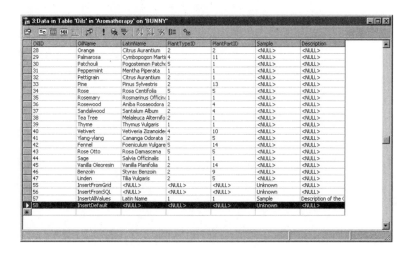

6. Close both Query Designer windows.

Inserting Multiple Rows

The INSERT statement has a second form that uses a SELECT statement rather than a VALUES list to specify the values for the row (or rows) to be added. This form of the INSERT statement has the following format:

```
INSERT INTO table_or_view [(column_list)]
    SELECT (column_list)
    FROM table_or_view
    [WHERE (condition)]
```

The WHERE clause in the statement is optional. If it is not included, all rows from the table or view specified in the FROM clause will be appended to the table or view specified in the INSERT clause.

Insert multiple rows using the Grid Pane

1. Navigate to the Tables folder of the Aromatherapy database, right-click the MyOils table, point to Open Table, and select Return All Rows.

   A new instance of the Query Designer opens.

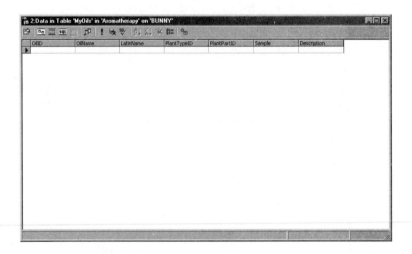

2. Without closing the Query Designer, open a new view of the Oils table by right-clicking the Oils table, pointing to Open Table, and selecting Query.

   A new instance of the Query Designer opens.

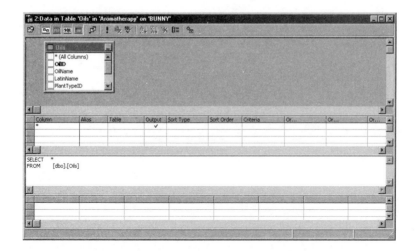

SQL Pane button

3. Hide the SQL Pane and the Results Pane.

Results Pane button

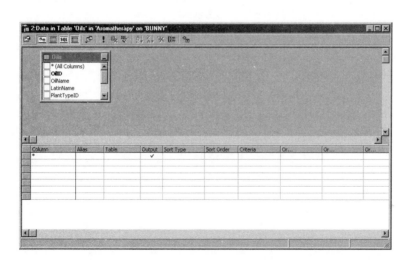

Change Query Type button

4. Click the Change Query Type button on the Query Designer toolbar, and select Insert From from the list.

The Query Designer displays a dialog box requesting that you select the target table.

5. Select MyOils from the list, and click OK.

The Query Designer adds the Append column to the Grid Pane.

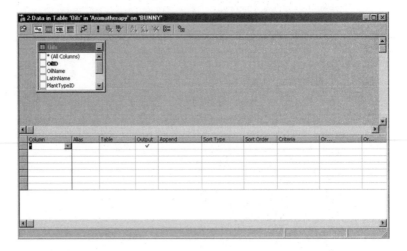

6. Change the Query to insert only the OillD, OilName, and LatinName columns.

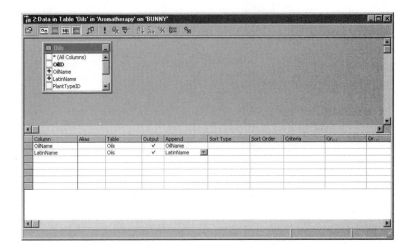

7. Add *Left(OilName, 6)* as a calculated column to the Grid Pane, uncheck the Output cell, and set the Criteria cell to **<>** *'Insert'*.

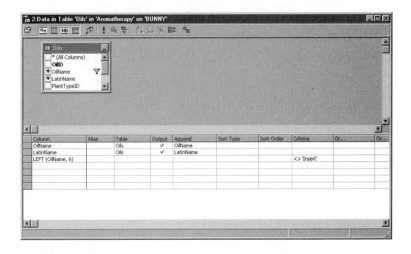

Run button

8. Click the Run Button on the Query Designer toolbar to execute the query.

The Query Designer displays a message confirming that the query has executed.

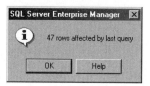

9. Click OK to close the message box. Reselect the Query Designer window showing all rows in the MyOils table.

Run button

10. Click the Run button on the Query Designer toolbar to reexecute the SELECT * query.

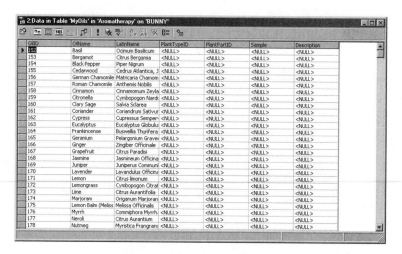

Insert multiple rows using the SQL Pane

1. Reselect the Query Designer window containing the INSERT statement.

Diagram Pane button

Grid Pane button

SQL Pane button

2. Hide the Diagram and Grid Panes, and display the SQL Pane.

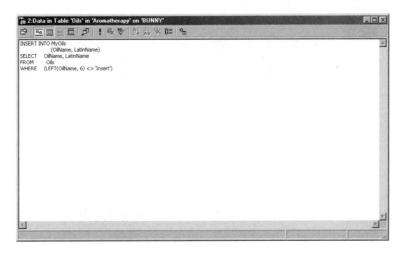

3. Change the SQL statement to

```
INSERT INTO MyOils
            (OilName, LatinName)
SELECT    OilName, LatinName
FROM      Oils
WHERE     (LEFT(OilName, 6) = 'Insert')
```

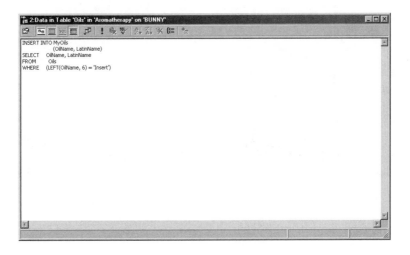

IP The only change here is in the WHERE statement.

Run button

4. Click the Run Button on the Query Designer toolbar to execute the query. The Enterprise Manager displays a message confirming that the query has executed.

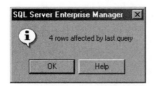

5. Click OK to close the message box. Reselect the Query Designer window showing all rows in the MyOils table.

Run button

6. Click the Run button on the Query Designer toolbar to reexecute the SELECT * query, and scroll down to the bottom of the table to confirm that the new rows have been added.

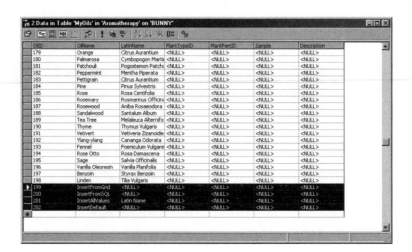

7. Close both Query Designer windows.

Lesson 17 Quick Reference

To	SQL Syntax
Insert a row by specifying columns	INSERT INTO *table_or_view* (*column_list*) VALUES (*value_list*)
Insert a row into all columns	INSERT INTO *table_or_view* VALUES (*value_list*)
Insert multiple rows using a SELECT statement	INSERT INTO *table_or_view* [(*column_list*)] SELECT (*column_list*) FROM *table_or_view* [WHERE (*condition*)]

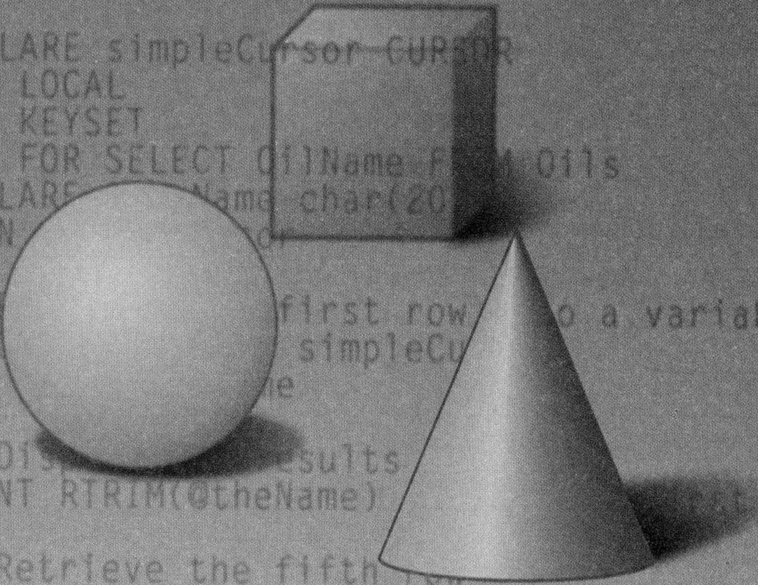

```
USE Aromatherapy
GO

DECLARE simpleCursor CURSOR
    LOCAL
    KEYSET
    FOR SELECT OilName FROM Oils
DECLARE @theName char(20)
OPEN simpleCursor

-- Fetch the first row into a variable
FETCH FIRST FROM simpleCursor
    INTO @theName

-- Display the results
PRINT RTRIM(@theName) + ' is the first name'

-- Retrieve the fifth row
FETCH ABSOLUTE 5 FROM simpleCursor
    INTO @theName

-- Display the results
PRINT RTRIM(@theName) + ' is the fifth name'

CLOSE simpleCursor
DEALLOCATE simpleCursor
```

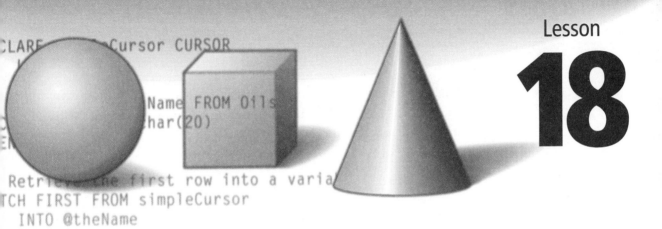

Updating Rows

Understanding the UPDATE Statement

The UPDATE statement allows you to change the values in one or more rows of a table. The basic syntax of the UPDATE statement is:

```
UPDATE table_or_view
SET update_list
[WHERE (condition)]
```

Like the INSERT statement, a single UPDATE statement can update only one table or view. The restrictions on updating a view with the UPDATE statement are the same as those for updating a view with the INSERT statement:

- The view must not contain an aggregate function, such as COUNT or AVG.

- The view must not contain TOP, GROUP BY, UNION, or DISTINCT.

- The view must not contain a calculated column.

- The view must reference a table in the FROM clause.

- The UPDATE statement must update columns from only a single table.

The SET keyword is followed by a comma-separated list of the columns to be updated and their new values, in the form *column_name = new_value*. The new value can be a constant or an expression and can reference the column itself. For example, the expression SalesPrice = SalesPrice * .90 would decrease the values in the SalesPrice column by 10 percent.

The WHERE clause is optional. When it is included, it specifies the rows to be updated. If the WHERE clause is not included in the UPDATE statement, all rows in the table are updated.

Using the UPDATE Statement

As with most other forms of queries, you can create an UPDATE query in the Query Designer by using the Grid Pane or by typing the statement directly into the SQL Pane.

Updating Rows Using the Grid Pane

The Query Designer's Grid Pane provides a simple means for you to create an UPDATE query.

Update all rows using the Grid Pane

1. Navigate to the Tables folder of the Aromatherapy database, right-click the MyOils table in the Details Pane, point to Open Table, and select Query.

   The Query Designer opens.

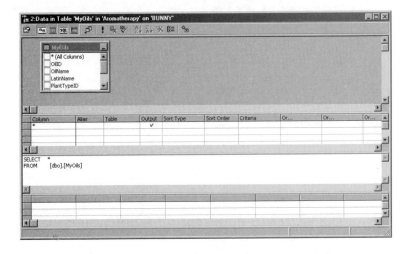

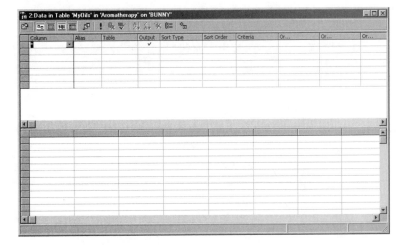

2. Hide the SQL Pane and the Diagram Pane by clicking the SQL and Diagram buttons.

SQL button

Diagram button

347

3. Without closing the Query Designer, open a new view of the MyOils table by right-clicking the MyOils table in the Details Pane, pointing to Open Table, and selecting Return All Rows.

A new instance of the Query Designer opens, showing all rows in the MyOils table.

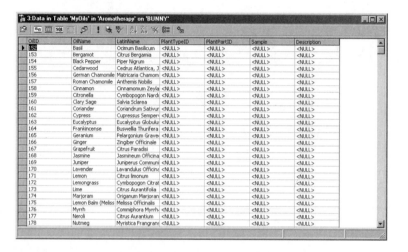

4. Reselect the Query Designer window showing the Grid and Results Panes. Click the Change Query Type button on the Query Designer toolbar, and select Update.

Change Query Type button

The Query Designer adds the New Value column to the Grid.

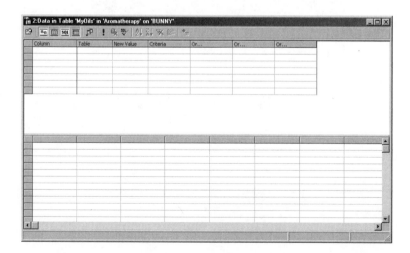

5. Add the Description column to the Grid Pane, and set its New Value cell to *'Description'*.

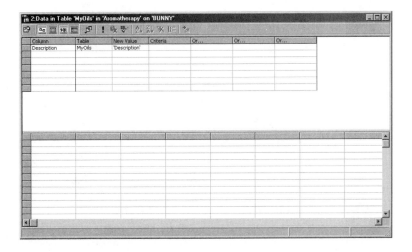

Run button

6. Click the Run button on the Query Designer toolbar to execute the query.

The Query Designer displays a message confirming that the rows have been updated.

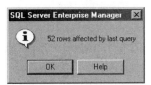

7. Reselect the Query Designer window showing all rows in the MyOils table.

8. Click the Run button on the Query Designer toolbar to reexecute the underlying SELECT * query.

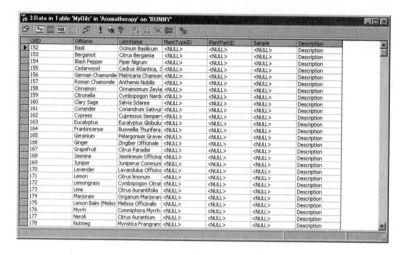

Update a single row using the Grid Pane

1. Reselect the Query Designer window containing the UPDATE statement.

2. Change the New Value cell to *'Description of Basil'*.

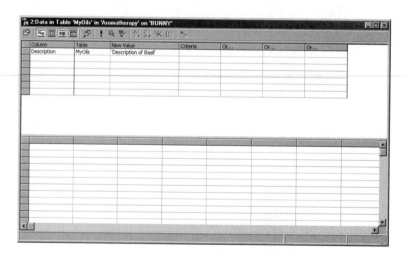

3. Add the OilName column to the Grid, and set its Criteria cell to = *'Basil'*.

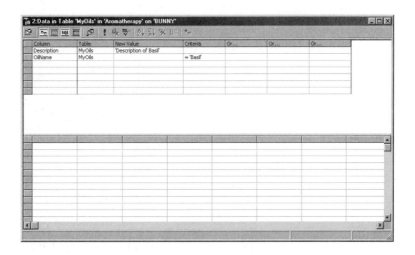

Run button

4. Click the Run button on the Query Designer toolbar to execute the query.

The Query Designer displays a message confirming that one row has been updated.

5. Reselect the Query Designer window showing all rows in the MyOils table.

Run button

6. Click the Run button on the Query Designer toolbar to execute the underlying SELECT * query.

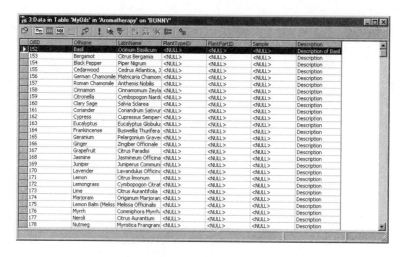

Updating Rows Using the SQL Pane

Just as with other query forms, typing the UPDATE statement directly into the SQL Pane provides more flexibility.

Update all rows using the SQL Pane

1. Reselect the window containing the UPDATE statement.

2. Display the SQL Pane and hide the Grid Pane.

SQL button

Grid button

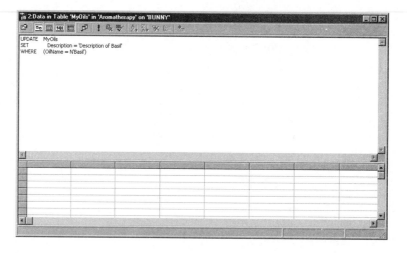

3. Change the SQL statement to

```
UPDATE MyOils
SET     Sample = 'Sample Field'
```

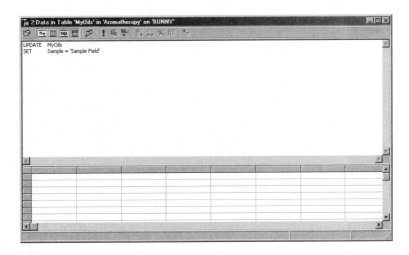

Run button

4. Click the Run button on the Query Designer toolbar to execute the query.

   The Query Designer displays a message confirming the number of rows affected.

5. Reselect the Query Designer window showing all rows in the MyOils table.

Run button

6. Click the Run button on the Query Designer toolbar to reexecute the underlying SELECT * query.

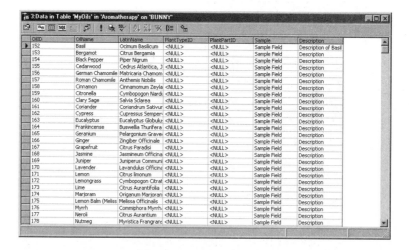

Update rows using a WHERE condition

1. Reselect the Query Designer window containing the UPDATE statement.

2. Change the SQL statement to

```
UPDATE  MyOils
SET     Description = 'Description of Frankincense'
WHERE   OilName = 'Frankincense'
```

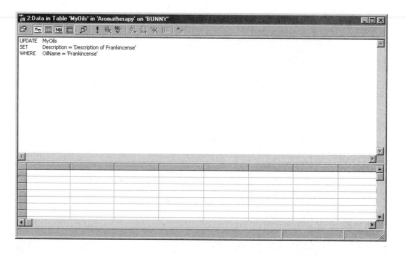

Run button

3. Click the Run button on the Query Designer toolbar to execute the query.

The Query Designer displays a message confirming the number of rows affected.

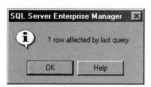

4. Reselect the Query Designer window showing all rows in the MyOils table.

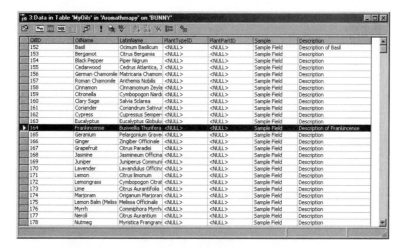

Run button

5. Click the Run button on the Query Designer toolbar to reexecute the underlying SELECT * query.

Updating Rows Using the FROM Clause

As we saw in Lesson 17, you can use a SELECT clause in an INSERT statement to insert values from another table. The UPDATE statement uses a FROM clause to retrieve values from another table:

```
UPDATE table_or_view
SET update_list
FROM table_or_view join_operator join_condition
[WHERE (where_condition)]
```

The FROM clause has exactly the same format as the FROM clause of a SELECT statement, and just as with a SELECT statement, you can specify more than one table or view by adding join statements. The optional WHERE condition can be used to limit which rows are updated.

Update rows using a FROM statement

1. Reselect the Query Designer window containing the UPDATE statement.

2. Change the SQL statement to

```
UPDATE MyOils
SET    MyOils.PlantPartID = Oils.PlantPartID
FROM   MyOils INNER JOIN Oils ON MyOils.OilName = Oils.OilName
```

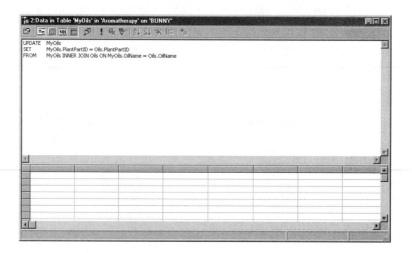

MPORTANT You can't use the OilID columns to link the two tables because the INSERT commands you used to add rows in Lesson 17 created new OilID values for each row in the MyOils table.

Run button

3. Click the Run button on the Query Designer toolbar to execute the query.

The Query Designer displays a message confirming the number of rows updated.

4. Reselect the Query Designer window showing all rows in the MyOils table.

Run button

5. Click the Run button on the Query Designer toolbar to execute the SELECT * query.

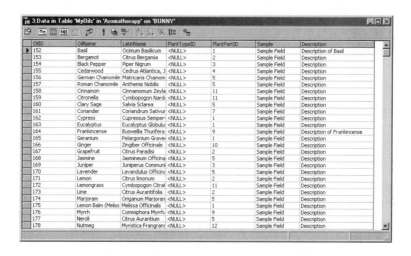

Lesson 18 Quick Reference

To	SQL Syntax
Update all rows in a table	UPDATE *table_or_view* SET *update_list* The *update_list* is a comma-separated list in the form *column = value, column = value, ...*
Update selected rows in a table	UPDATE *table_or_view* SET *update_list* WHERE *condition*
Update rows using a FROM clause	UPDATE *table_or_view* SET *update_list* FROM *table_or_view join_operator join_condition* [WHERE (*where_condition*)]

```
.ARE        Cursor CURSOR

            Name FROM Oils
            har(20)

Retr    e first row into a varia
H FIRST FROM simpleCursor
 INTO @theName

Display the results
NT RTRIM(@theName) + ' is the first name'

Retr
H              simpleCursor
 INTO @theName

Display the r
```

Deleting Rows

In this lesson you will learn how to:

- Delete selected rows from a table using the Grid Pane.
- Delete rows using the DELETE…WHERE statement.
- Delete rows using the DELETE…FROM…WHERE statement.
- Delete rows using a cascade delete.
- Delete all rows using the TRUNCATE TABLE statement.

SQL Server provides two statements for deleting rows from a table or view: the DELETE statement and the TRUNCATE TABLE statement. The TRUNCATE TABLE statement unconditionally deletes all rows in a table. The DELETE statement provides more flexibility, allowing you to delete only selected rows based on a WHERE clause that can include additional tables and views.

Understanding the DELETE Statement

The basic structure of the DELETE statement varies somewhat from the other SQL statements we've looked at. Its syntax is

```
DELETE table_or_view
[FROM table_sources]
[WHERE where_condition]
```

There is no column list in the DELETE statement because all columns are removed when the row is removed. The optional WHERE clause allows you to specify which rows are to be deleted. If you omit the WHERE clause, all the rows in the specified table or view will be removed.

The FROM clause, also optional, allows you to specify additional sources (either tables or views) that will be used in the selection criteria of the WHERE clause. The statement syntax is somewhat misleading here because no rows will be deleted from the tables and views listed in the FROM clause. If you use more than one table or view in the FROM clause, their names should be separated by commas.

 IP The DELETE statement doesn't support the JOIN operator, so you must join the tables or views in the WHERE clause of the statement.

When a table participates in a relationship, it's important to prevent deletions in the primary key table from leaving "orphan" rows. Orphan rows are rows in the foreign key table that have no corresponding row in the primary key table. New to SQL Server 2000 is the ability to implement cascade deletes in the relationship. When a cascade delete is specified for the relationship, SQL Server will automatically delete rows in the foreign key table that would otherwise be left orphans. Figure 19-1 shows the relationship established between the Oils and PlantParts tables.

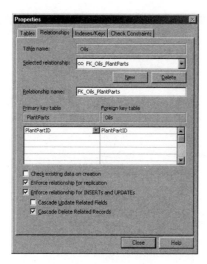

Figure 19-1. *Cascade deletes are implemented on the Relationships tab of the table's Properties dialog box.*

Using the DELETE Statement

Like other SQL statements used in the Query Designer, the DELETE statement can be entered directly into the SQL Pane or created using the graphic panes.

Deleting Rows Using the Grid and Diagram Panes

The Grid and Diagram Panes of the Query Designer provide a graphic means of creating DELETE statements; however, they don't support the FROM clause, which allows you to use additional tables and views in the DELETE statement.

Delete selected rows from a table

1. Navigate to the Tables folder of the Aromatherapy database.

   SQL Server displays a list of tables in the Details Pane.

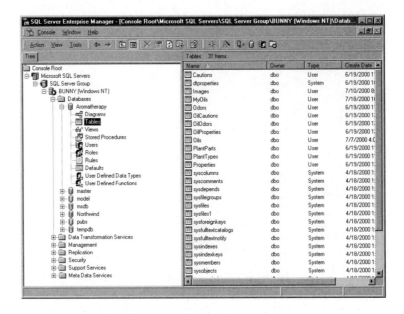

2. Right-click the MyOils table, point to Open Table, and select Query.

   The Query Designer opens.

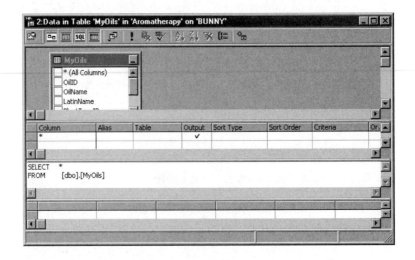

SQL Pane button

3. Hide the SQL Pane and the Results Pane.

Results Pane button

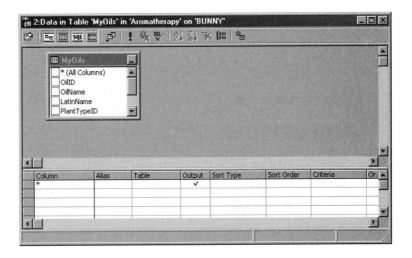

*Change Query
Type button*

4. Click the Change Query Type button on the Query Designer toolbar, and select Delete.

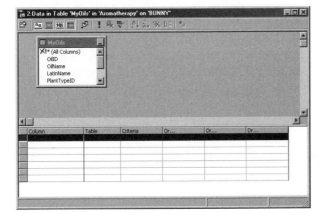

5. Without closing the Query Designer window, open a new view of the MyOils table by right-clicking the table name in the Details Pane, pointing to Open Table, and selecting Return All Rows.

6. Scroll down to the bottom of the table to confirm that there are four rows beginning with "Insert".

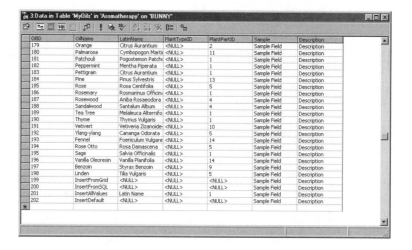

7. Reselect the Query Designer window containing the DELETE statement.

8. Add the expression *Left(OilName, 6)* to the Column cell, and add the criteria = *'Insert'* to the Criteria cell.

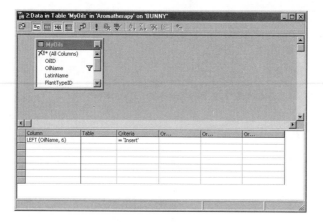

Run button

9. Click the Run button on the Query Designer toolbar to execute the query.

The Enterprise Manager displays a message confirming that four rows have been deleted.

364

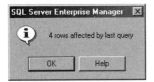

10. Click OK to close the message box. Reselect the Query Designer window showing all rows in the MyOils table.

11. Click the Run button on the Query Designer toolbar to reexecute the underlying SELECT * query.

12. Scroll down to the bottom of the table to confirm that the rows beginning with "Insert" have been removed.

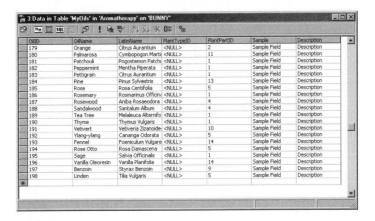

Deleting Rows Using the SQL Pane

As always, entering the DELETE statement directly into the SQL Pane of the Query Designer provides more flexibility, but at the cost of having to remember the syntax of the statement.

Delete rows using the WHERE clause

1. Reselect the Query Designer window containing the DELETE statement.

SQL Pane button

Diagram Pane button

Grid Pane button

2. Display the SQL Pane, and hide the Diagram and Grid Panes.

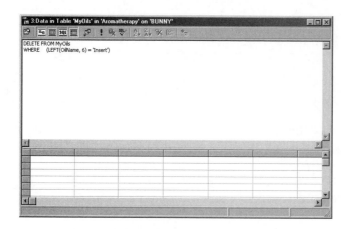

3. Replace the SQL statement with

```
DELETE FROM MyOils
WHERE (OilName = 'Basil')
```

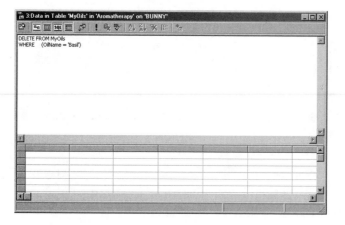

Run button

4. Click the Run button on the Query Designer toolbar to execute the query.

The Enterprise Manager displays a message confirming that the row has been deleted.

5. Reselect the Query Designer window to display all rows in the MyOils table.

Run button

6. Click the Run button on the Query Designer toolbar to reexecute the underlying SELECT * query, and confirm that the row for Basil has been deleted.

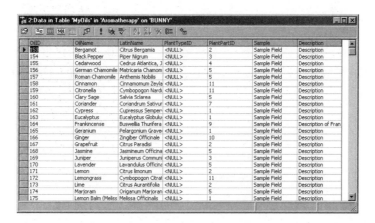

Delete rows using the FROM clause

1. Reselect the Query Designer window containing the DELETE statement.

2. Replace the SQL statement with

```
DELETE  MyOils
FROM    PlantParts
WHERE   (MyOils.PlantPartID = PlantParts.PlantPartID) AND
        (PlantParts.PlantPart = 'Roots')
```

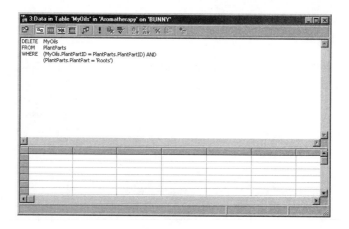

Run button

3. Click the Run button on the Query Designer toolbar to execute the query.

   The Query Designer displays a message confirming that two rows have been deleted.

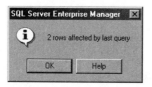

4. Reselect the Query Designer windows showing all rows in the MyOils table.

Run button

5. Click the Run button on the Query Designer toolbar to reexecute the underlying SELECT * query, and confirm that the rows referencing PlantPartID 10 (the ID of the Roots row) have been deleted.

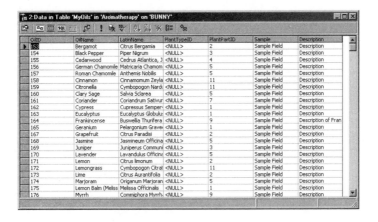

6. Close both Query Designer windows.

Delete rows with a cascade delete

1. Right-click the PlantParts table in the Details Pane, point to Open Table, and select Query.

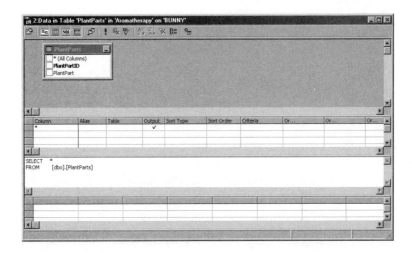

Diagram Pane button

2. Hide the Diagram Pane and the Grid Pane.

Grid Pane button

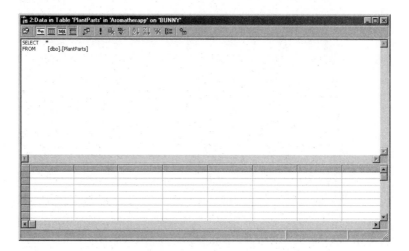

Change Query Type button

3. Click the Change Query Type button on the Query Designer toolbar, and select Delete.

   The Query Designer changes the DELETE statement in the SQL Pane.

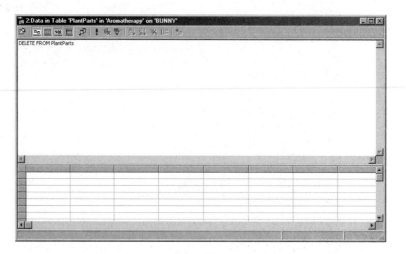

4. Without closing the Query Designer window, open a view of the Oils table by right-clicking the table name in the Details Pane, pointing to Open Table, and selecting Return All Rows.

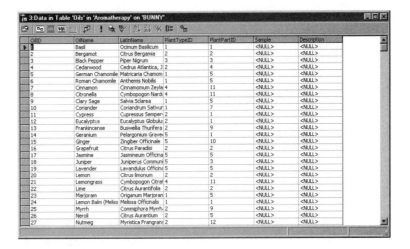

5. Reselect the Query Designer window containing the DELETE statement.

6. Change the SQL statement to

```
DELETE PlantParts
WHERE (PlantPartID = 10)
```

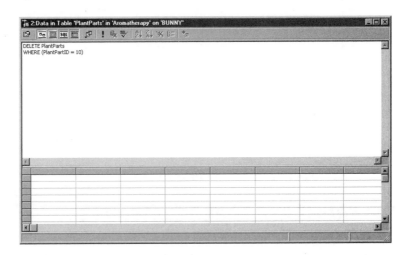

Run button

7. Click the Run button on the Query Designer toolbar to execute the query.

The Enterprise Manager displays a message confirming that the row has been deleted.

8. Reselect the Query Designer window showing all rows in the Oils Table.

Run button

9. Click the Run button on the Query Designer toolbar to reexecute the underlying SELECT * query, and confirm that the rows referencing PlantPartID 10 have been deleted.

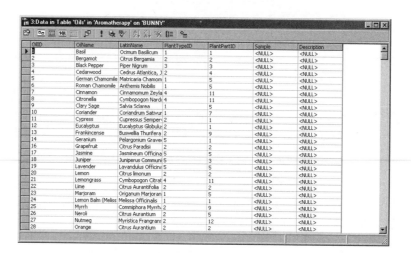

10. Close both Query Designer windows.

Using the TRUNCATE TABLE Statement

The results of the TRUNCATE TABLE statement are identical to those of a DELETE statement with no WHERE clause in that all the rows are removed from the table. The TRUNCATE TABLE statement differs from the DELETE statement, however, in that the TRUNCATE TABLE statement is not recorded in the transaction log, which makes it much faster to execute.

Deleting All Rows Using the TRUNCATE TABLE Statement

The TRUNCATE TABLE statement can be executed only in the SQL Pane of the Query Designer.

Delete all rows using TRUNCATE TABLE

1. Right-click the MyOils table in the Details Pane, point to Open Table, and select Query.

   The Query Designer window opens.

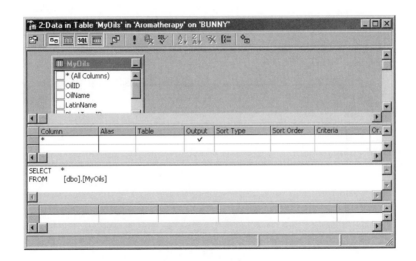

2. Hide the Diagram Pane and the Grid Pane.

Diagram Pane button

Grid Pane button

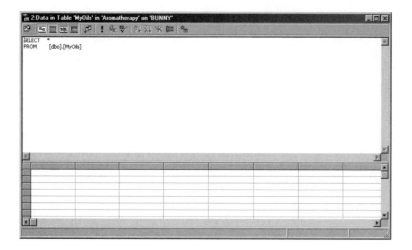

3. Change the existing SQL statement to

```
TRUNCATE TABLE MyOils
```

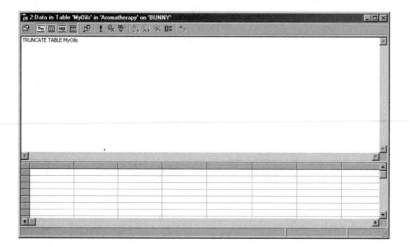

4. Without closing the current Query Designer window, open a new view of the MyOils table by right-clicking the table name in the Details Pane, pointing to Open Table, and selecting Return All Rows.

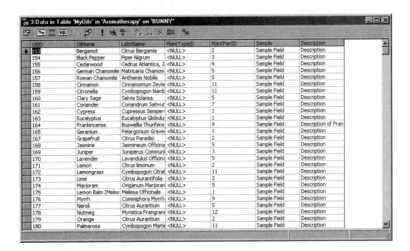

5. Reselect the Query Designer window containing the TRUNCATE TABLE statement.

Run button

6. Click the Run button on the Query Designer toolbar to execute the query.

The Enterprise Manager displays a message confirming the successful execution of the query.

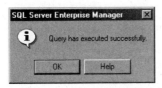

7. Reselect the Query Designer window showing all rows in the MyOils table.

Run button

8. Click the Run button on the Query Designer toolbar to reexecute the underlying SELECT * query, and confirm that all rows have been deleted.

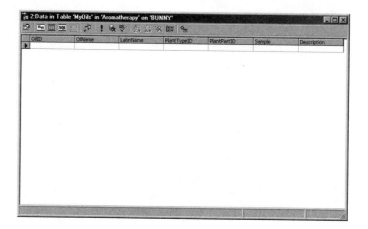

Lesson 19 Quick Reference

To	SQL Syntax
Delete all rows using the DELETE statement	DELETE *table_or_view*
Delete selected rows using the WHERE clause	DELETE *table_or_view* WHERE (*where_condition*)
Delete selected rows using criteria based on another table	DELETE *table_or_view* FROM *table_sources* WHERE (*where_condition*)
Delete all rows using the TRUNCATE TABLE statement	TRUNCATE TABLE *table_or_view*

```
ECLARE        Cursor CURSOR
              Name FROM Oils
EC            har(20)
PE

- Retrieve the first row into a varia
ETCH FIRST FROM simpleCursor
    INTO @theName

- Display the results
RINT RTRIM(@theName) + ' is the first name'

ETCH ABSOLUTE 5 FROM simpleCursor
    INTO @theName
```

Copying and Moving Data

In this lesson you will learn how to:

- Use the DTS Import Wizard.
- Use the DTS Export Wizard.
- Detach a database from a server.
- Attach a database to a server.
- Use the Copy Database Wizard.

In addition to working with data that resides in a SQL Server database, sometimes you need to transfer data from or to another format—such as Microsoft Access or Oracle—or copy data between SQL Server installations. In this lesson, we'll examine three different facilities provided by the Enterprise Manager for performing these tasks.

The Data Transformation Services Wizards

Data Transformation Services (DTS) is an extremely powerful set of graphical tools and programmable objects that allows you to import and export data, transform data structures, and consolidate data from multiple sources for analysis and reporting purposes.

As with any powerful set of tools, using DTS can be complicated. Fortunately, the Enterprise Manager provides wizards to perform the most common tasks: importing and exporting data.

Using the DTS Import Wizard

The DTS Import Wizard allows you to import data from many different types of data sources, including

- OLE DB and ODBC data sources.

- Text files.

- Connections to other instances of Microsoft SQL Server.

- Oracle and Informix databases.

- Microsoft Excel spreadsheets.

- Microsoft Access and Microsoft FoxPro databases.

- dBase and Paradox databases.

Import a table using the DTS Import Wizard

1. Navigate to the Aromatherapy database in the Enterprise Manager.

   SQL Server displays a list of the objects in the database.

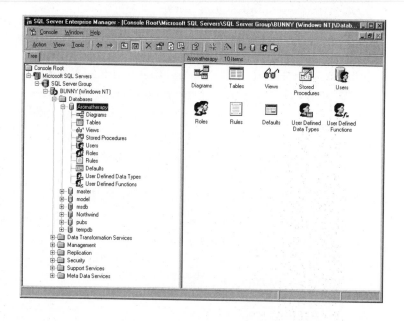

Wizard button

2. Click the Wizard button on the Enterprise Manager toolbar.

   SQL Server displays the Select Wizard dialog box.

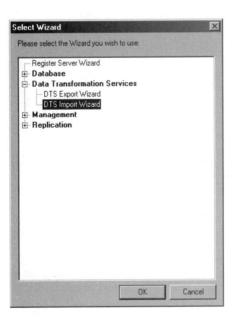

3. Select DTS Import Wizard in the Data Transformation Services category, and click OK.

   SQL Server displays the first page of the DTS Import/Export Wizard.

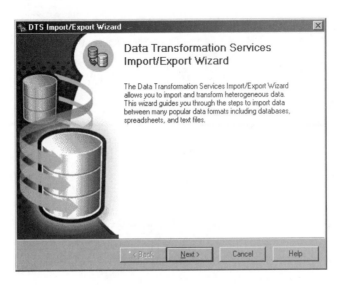

4. Click Next.

The wizard displays a page requesting that you specify the data source.

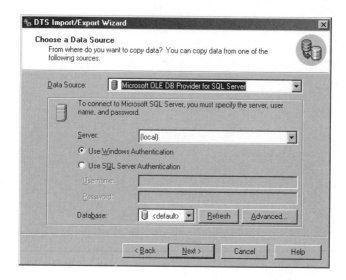

5. Select Microsoft Access as the data source.

The wizard changes the data source details.

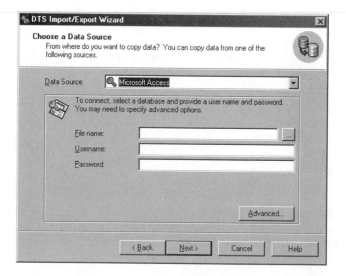

Browse button

6. Click the Browse button to specify the name and location of the source file.

   The wizard displays the Select File dialog box.

7. Navigate to the SQL 2000 Step by Step folder in the root directory, and select the Aromatherapy database.

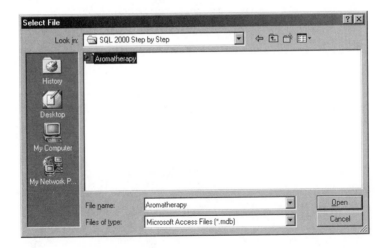

IMPORTANT The companion CD for this book contains two versions of the Aromatherapy database. Here you're importing data from the Microsoft Access version, not the SQL Server version.

8. Click Open.

   The wizard displays the location and name of the selected file in the File Name box.

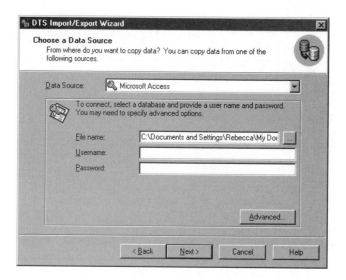

> **TIP** The Advanced button on this page of the DTS Import Wizard allows you to set OLE DB properties. You usually won't need to do this.

9. Click Next.

   The wizard displays a page requesting the data destination details.

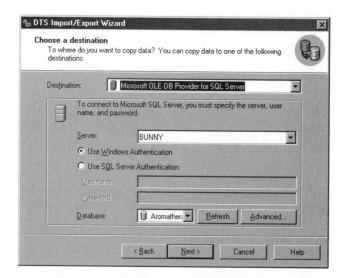

10. The wizard defaults to the SQL Server database that was selected in the Enterprise Manager when you started the wizard. This is the database that we'll use for this exercise, so click Next without changing any of the settings.

The wizard displays a page asking whether to import tables and views or the results of a query.

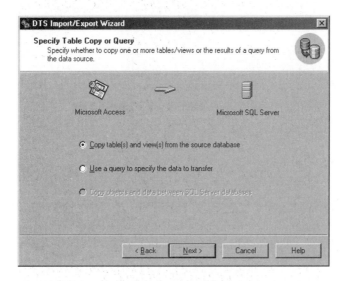

11. Again, we'll accept the default value, which in this case is to copy data from tables, so click Next.

The wizard displays a list of the tables in the database.

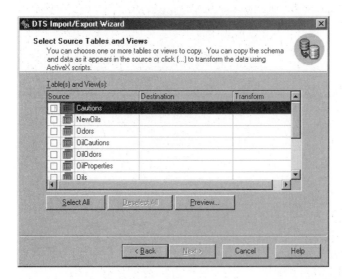

IP The other option on the previous page, Use A Query To Specify The Data To Transfer, presents a dialog box requesting a SQL statement.

12. Select the NewOils table.

The wizard proposes a destination table with the same name.

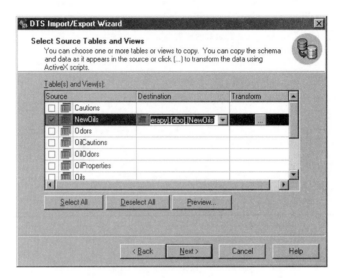

13. Click the Browse button in the Transform column.

Browse button

The wizard displays the Column Mappings And Transformations dialog box.

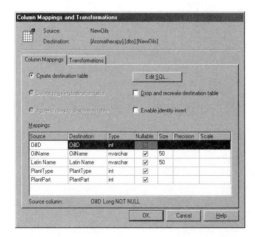

14. Change the size of the OilName column to 25 to import only the beginning of the OilName column.

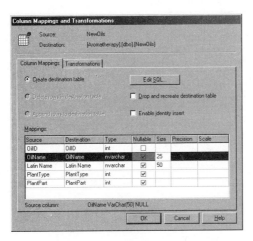

15. Click OK to dismiss the dialog box, and then click Next.

The wizard displays a page asking whether you want to import the data immediately or defer execution until later.

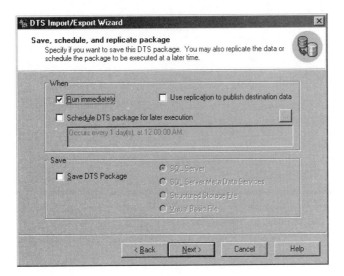

TIP This page of the wizard also gives you the option of saving your import specification as a DTS package. This can be extremely useful if you will need to perform the import task again.

---

16. Accept the default of Run Immediately, and click Next.

   The wizard displays a page confirming your specification.

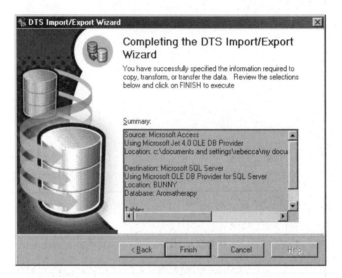

17. Click Finish.

   The wizard displays a progress dialog box while it executes the DTS package, and then it displays a message confirming that the table was imported successfully.

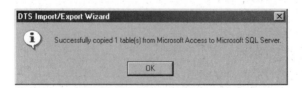

18. Click OK to dismiss the confirmation message.

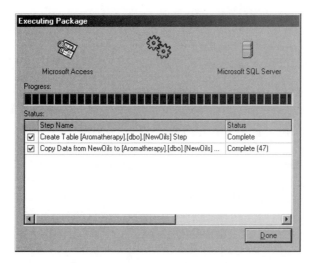

19. Click Done to close the wizard.

20. Navigate to the Tables folder to confirm that the NewOils table has been added to the Aromatherapy database.

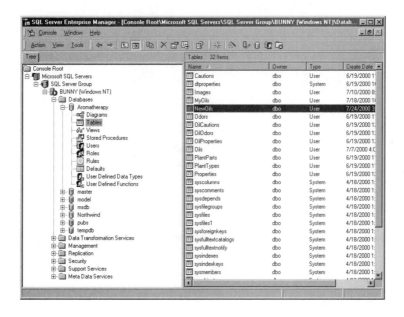

> **TIP** If the table doesn't show up immediately, select Refresh from the Action menu to refresh the list.

Using the DTS Export Wizard

As you would expect, the DTS Export Wizard performs the same function as the DTS Import Wizard, except in reverse.

Export a table using the DTS Export Wizard

Wizard button

1. Navigate to the Aromatherapy database, and click the Wizard button.

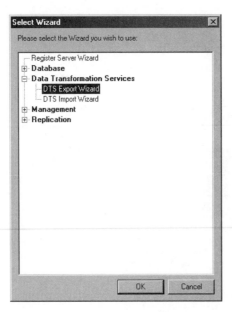

2. Select DTS Export Wizard from the Data Transformation Services category, and click OK.

   SQL Server displays the first page of the DTS Import/Export Wizard.

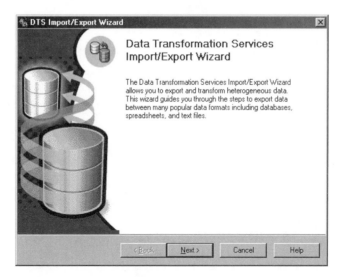

3. Click Next.

The wizard displays a page requesting the data source.

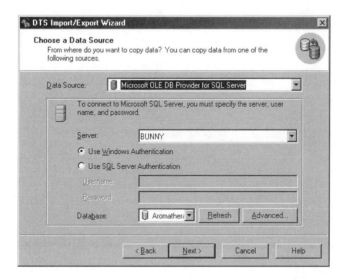

4. Make sure Aromatherapy is selected as the database, and then click Next.

The wizard displays a page requesting the data destination.

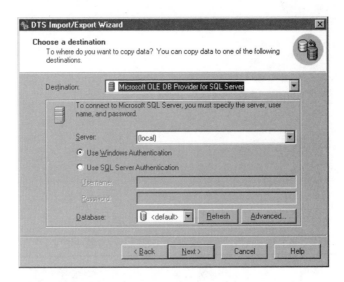

5. Choose Text File as the data destination.

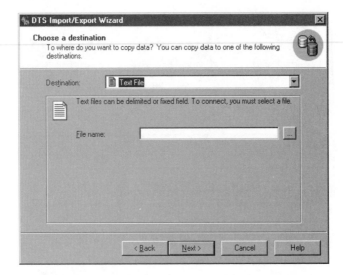

Browse button

6. Click the Browse button to the right of the File Name box.

The wizard displays the Select File dialog box.

7. Navigate to the SQL 2000 Step by Step folder in the root directory, and type *Aromatherapy.txt* as the filename.

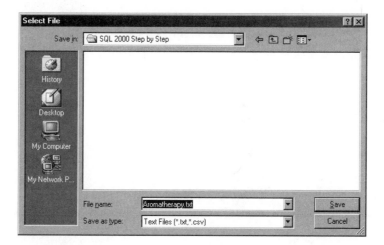

8. Click Save.

The wizard displays the location and name of the text file in the File Name box.

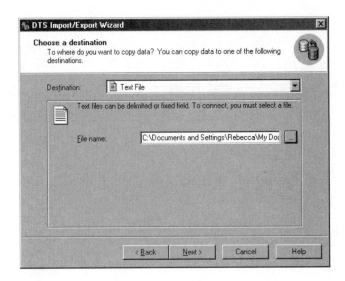

9. Click Next.

   The wizard displays a page asking whether to export tables and views or the results of a query. Copy Tables And Views is selected by default.

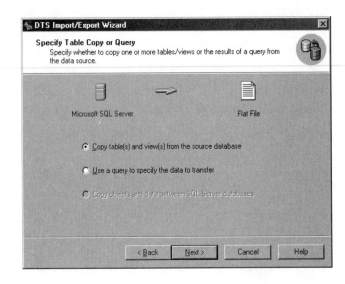

10. Click Next to accept the default.

    The wizard displays a page requesting the destination file format.

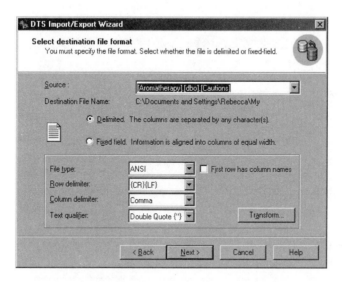

11. Select the PlantParts table in the Source box, and select the First Row Has Column Names option.

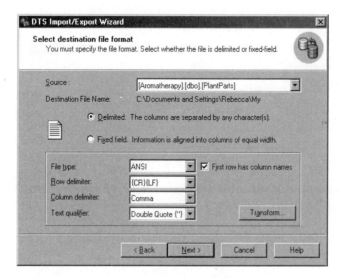

12. Click Next.

The wizard displays a page asking whether you want to export the data immediately or defer execution until later.

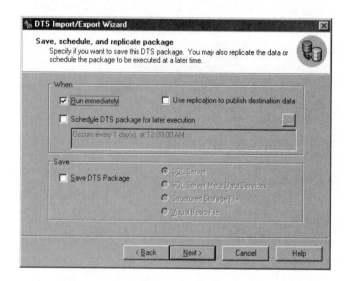

13. Accept the default of Run Immediately, and click Next.

The wizard displays a message confirming your export specifications.

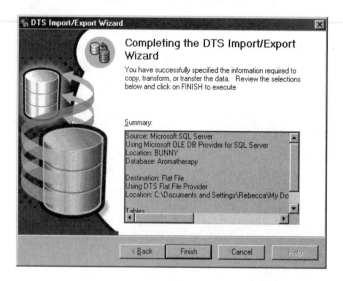

14. Click Finish.

    The wizard displays a progress dialog box while it is executing the DTS package, and then a message confirming that the export was successful.

15. Click OK to dismiss the confirmation message.

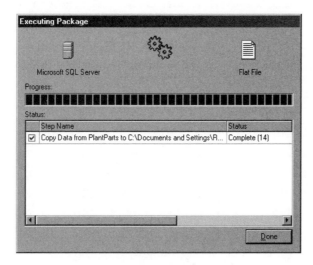

16. Click Done to close the wizard.

17. If you have Microsoft Notepad, open the Aromatherapy text file to confirm that the data has been successfully exported.

```
Aromatherapy - Notepad                    _ □ X
File  Edit  Format  Help
"PlantPartID","PlantPart"
1,"Leaves"
2,"Fruit Peel"
3,"Berries"
4,"wood"
5,"Flowers"
6,"Bark"
7,"Fruit Seeds"
8,"Cones"
9,"Resin"
11,"Whole Plant"
12,"Fruit Kernel"
13,"Needles"
14,"Seeds"
15,"Fruit"
```

Attaching and Detaching Databases

SQL Server stores a database in two or more physical files. Although these files are normal operating system files, you shouldn't simply move or copy them from one place to another because they're linked to the specific instance of the server that contains the database.

However, SQL Server allows you to detach a database from a server, which removes the link between the database and the specific server but otherwise leaves the database and the transaction log intact. Once a database has been detached, you can then move or copy it and reattach it to the same or a different server.

Detaching a Database

The task of detaching the database from the server to which it is linked is a simple process involving only a single dialog box.

Detach the Aromatherapy database

1. Right-click the Aromatherapy database in the Console Tree, point to All Tasks, and then select Detach Database.

   SQL Server displays the Detach Database dialog box.

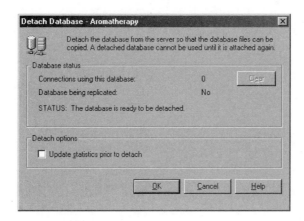

2. Click OK.

   SQL Server displays a message confirming that the database has been detached.

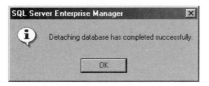

Attaching a Database

Once a database has been detached from a server, you can move or copy the data and transaction log files as you would any other operating system files. You can then reattach the database to the same or a different server.

Reattach the Aromatherapy database

1. Right-click the Databases folder of the server you're using for the exercises, point to All Tasks, and select Attach Database.

   SQL Server displays the Attach Database dialog box.

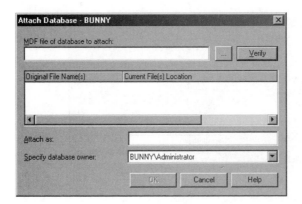

Browse button

2. Click the Browse button.

SQL Server displays the Browse For Existing File dialog box.

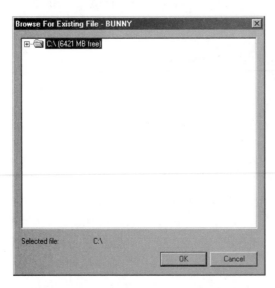

3. Navigate to the SQL 2000 Step by Step folder in the root directory, select Aromatherapy.mdf, and then click OK.

SQL Server fills in the file locations for the data and transaction log files.

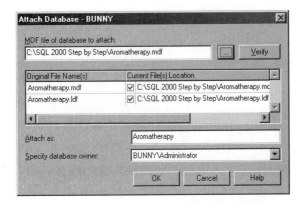

4. Click OK.

SQL Server displays a message confirming that the database has been successfully attached.

The Copy Database Wizard

The Copy Database Wizard provides a simple way to copy or move a database from one instance of SQL Server to another. You can copy a database between different instances of SQL Server 2000, or between SQL Server 2000 and SQL Server 7.0.

Using the Copy Database Wizard

The Copy Database Wizard is available from the Select Wizard dialog box, and also from the All Tasks submenu of both the Server and Databases folder context menus.

Copy a database

> **MPORTANT** You must have access to another server in order to complete this exercise.

Wizard button

1. Navigate to the Aromatherapy database, and then click the Wizard button.

   SQL Server displays the Select Wizard dialog box.

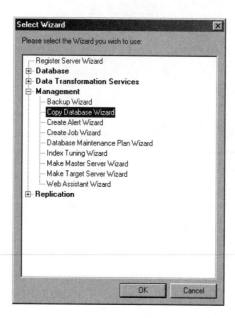

2. Select Copy Database Wizard in the Management category, and click OK.

   SQL Server displays the first page of the Copy Database Wizard.

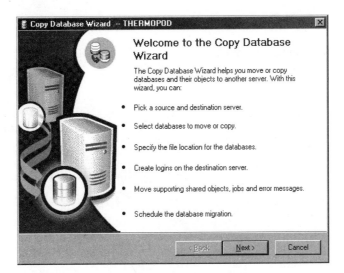

3. Click Next.

   The wizard displays a page requesting the name of the server that contains the database to be copied.

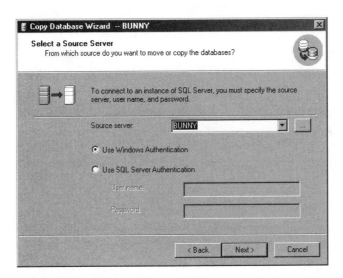

4. Change the authentication method if necessary, and then click Next.

The wizard displays a page requesting the name of the server to contain the new copy.

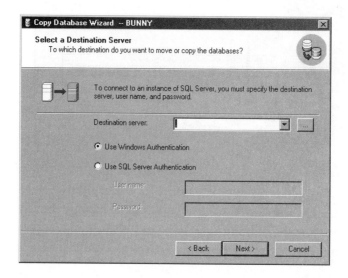

5. Select the destination from the combo box list, and click Next.

The wizard displays a page requesting the name of the database to move or copy.

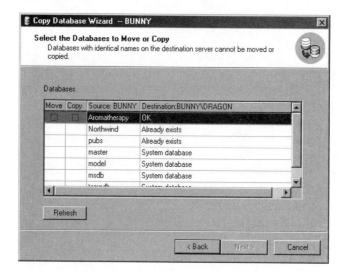

6. Select the Copy check box for the Aromatherapy database.

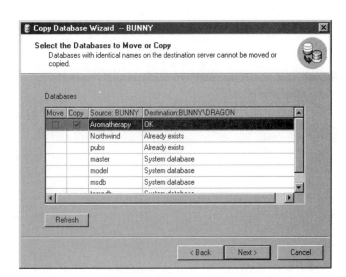

7. Click Next.

   The wizard displays a page showing the target file locations.

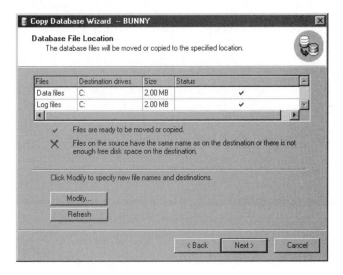

IP   If any of the files have a cross in the Status cell, you can click the
Modify button to correct the problem.

---

8. Click Next.

The wizard displays a page asking which database objects should
be copied along with the database.

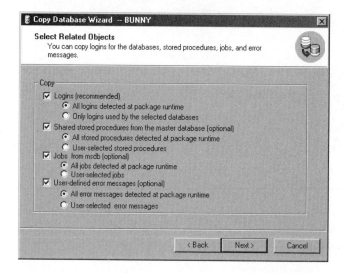

9. Accept the defaults for all objects, and then click Next.

The wizard displays a page asking whether you want to perform the
copy immediately or defer it until later.

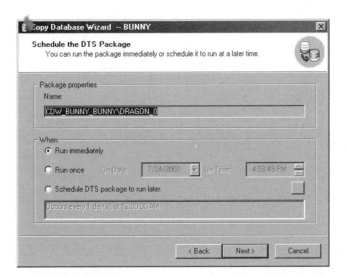

10. Accept the default to run immediately, and click Next.

    The wizard displays a page confirming your selections.

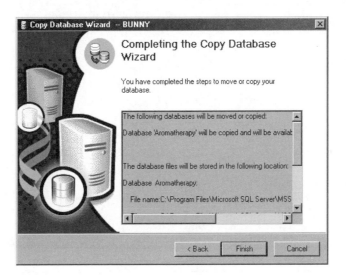

11. Click Finish.

The wizard displays a dialog box showing its progress and then displays a message confirming that the database copy has been completed successfully.

Lesson 20 Quick Reference		
To	**Do this**	**Button**
Import data using the DTS Import Wizard	Open the Select Wizard dialog box, select DTS Import Wizard from the Data Transformation Services category, click OK, and follow the wizard instructions.	
Export data using the DTS Export Wizard	Open the Select Wizard dialog box, select DTS Export Wizard from the Data Transformation Services category, click OK, and follow the wizard instructions.	
Detach a database	Right-click the database in the Console Tree, point to All Tasks, and select Detach database. Complete the dialog box, and click OK.	
Attach a database	Right-click the Databases folder in the Console Tree, point to All Tasks, and select Attach Database. Complete the dialog box, and click OK.	
Use the Copy Database Wizard	Open the Select Wizard dialog box, select Copy Database Wizard in the Management category, click OK, and follow the instructions.	

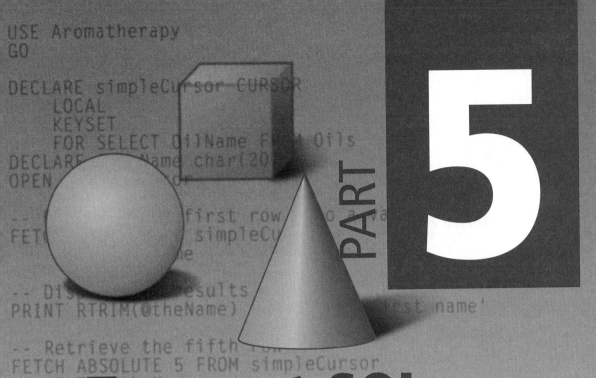

```
USE Aromatherapy
GO

DECLARE simpleCursor CURSOR
    LOCAL
    KEYSET
    FOR SELECT OilName FROM Oils
DECLARE         Name char(20)
OPEN

                first row
FETCH               simpleCu

-- Dis       esults
PRINT RTRIM(@theName)                    st name

-- Retrieve the fifth
FETCH ABSOLUTE 5 FROM simpleCursor
    INT    theName
```

Transact-SQL

```
-- Display      results
PRINT RTRIM(@theName) + ' is the fifth name'

CLOSE simpleCursor
DEALLOC    s
```

Lesson

21	The Query Analyzer	409
22	Data Definition Language	441
23	Analyzing Queries	471
24	Transact-SQL Language Components	491
25	Programming Objects	529
26	Controlling Execution	553
27	Transact-SQL Cursors	571
28	Stored Procedures	597
29	Triggers	623
30	User-Defined Functions	639

```
USE Aromatherapy
GO

DECLARE simpleCursor CURSOR
    LOCAL
    KEYSET
    FOR SELECT OilName FROM Oils
DECLARE        Name char(20)
OPEN

--        first row    o a variable
FETCH                simpleCu
            e

-- Di            sults
PRINT RTRIM(@theName)                     name'

-- Retrieve the fifth
FETCH ABSOLUTE 5 FROM simpleCursor
    INTO @theName

-- Display the results
PRINT RTRIM(@theName) + ' is the fifth name'

CLOSE simpleCursor
DEALLOCATE simpleCursor
```

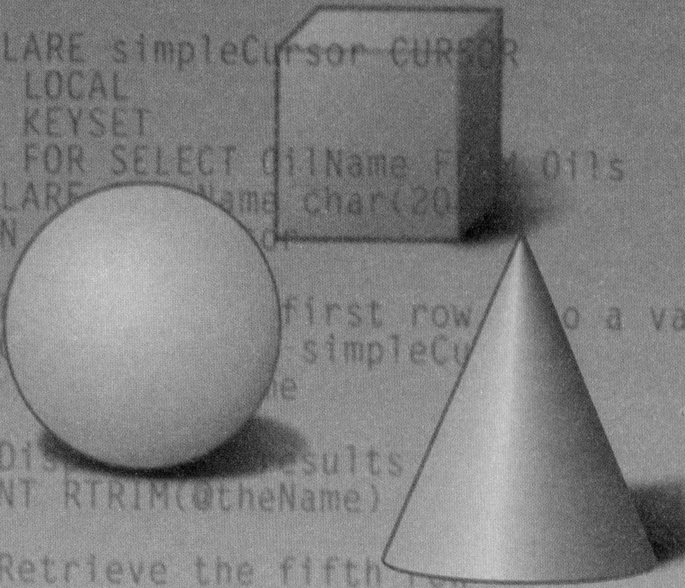

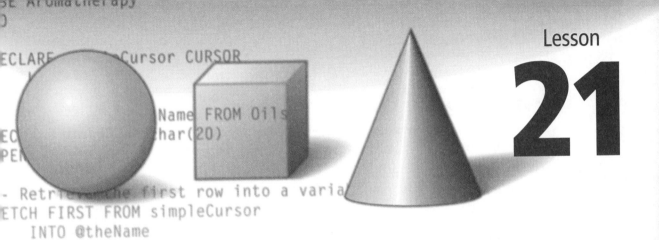

The Query Analyzer

In the previous lessons, we've used the Enterprise Manager to create and maintain database objects and to perform basic data operations. In this lesson, we'll look at another one of Microsoft SQL Server's graphical tools—the Query Analyzer.

Understanding the Query Analyzer

Although it's possible to create and execute queries and other Transact-SQL statements in the Enterprise Manager, its greatest strength is as a tool for database administration. The Query Analyzer, on the other hand, is primarily a programming tool.

The Query Analyzer provides you with powerful tools for writing and debugging complex sets of Transact-SQL statements in various forms. (We'll look at one of these, SQL scripts, in this lesson.) It also provides the means to analyze the performance of queries via execution plans and the Index Tuning Wizard, as we'll see in Lesson 23.

Starting the Query Analyzer

You can start the Query Analyzer from within the Enterprise Manager or from the Windows Start menu. When you start the Query Analyzer from the Enterprise Manager, the Query Analyzer will transfer the connection information from the Enterprise Manager: if you are connected to a server, the Query Analyzer will connect to that server, and if you have a database selected, the Query Analyzer will select that database.

 IP You can use the isqlw command from the command prompt as a third way to start the Query Analyzer.

If you start the Query Analyzer from the Start menu, or if you haven't made a server or database connection in the Enterprise Manager, you must make the connection manually from within the Query Analyzer.

Start the Query Analyzer from the Enterprise Manager

1. Navigate to the Aromatherapy database in the Console Tree in the Enterprise Manager.

   SQL Server displays a list of database objects in the Details Pane.

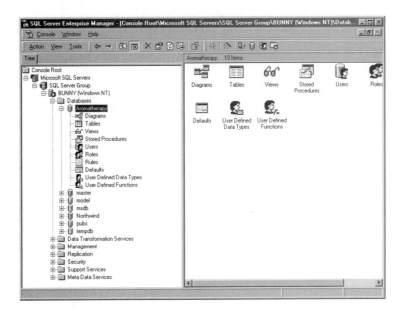

2. Select SQL Query Analyzer from the Tools menu.

   SQL Server opens the Query Analyzer, automatically connecting to the server and the Aromatherapy database.

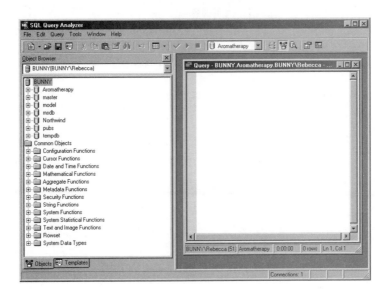

OTE If you don't see the Object Browser in the Query Analyzer, press F8 to display it.

3. Close the Query Analyzer.

Start the Query Analyzer from the Start menu

1. On the taskbar, click the Start button.

2. Point to Programs, and then select the Microsoft SQL Server folder.

   The icons in the Microsoft SQL Server folder appear in a list.

Query Analyzer icon

3. Click the Query Analyzer program icon.

   The Query Analyzer displays the Connect to SQL Server dialog box.

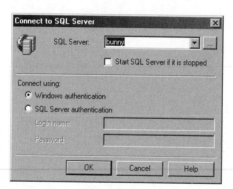

4. Make sure the correct server and authentication mode are selected, and click OK.

   The Query Analyzer connects to the server, and then opens. The Query Analyzer will connect to whichever database has been selected as the default for your login.

IP If your server isn't set to start automatically, you can use the Start SQL Server If It Is Stopped check box to automatically start the server when you connect.

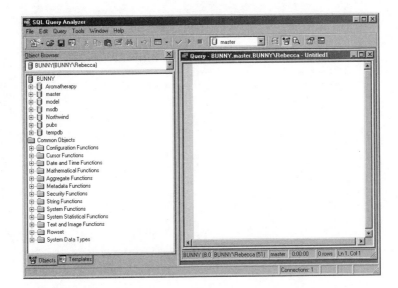

Selecting a Database

The Query Analyzer will use the currently selected database to resolve references in queries and other Transact-SQL statements. Its toolbar, shown in Figure 21-1, contains a combo box showing the database that is currently selected. You can switch to a different database by selecting its name in the toolbar or from the Query menu.

Selected database

Figure 21-1. *The Query Analyzer toolbar displays the currently selected database.*

Selecting a database using the toolbar

1. Select Northwind in the toolbar combo box.

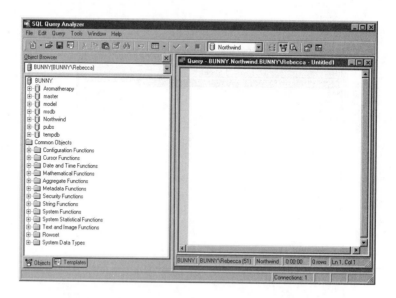

Select a database from the Query menu

1. Select Change Database in the Query menu.

   The Query Analyzer displays the Select Database dialog box.

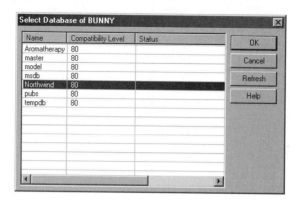

IP   You can also use the shortcut key Ctrl-U to open the Select Database
dialog box.

2. Select the Aromatherapy database by clicking anywhere in that row.

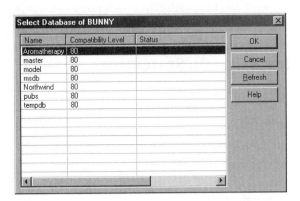

3. Click OK.

The Query Analyzer selects the Aromatherapy database.

Using the Query Window

New Query button

The Query Analyzer initially displays two windows, the Object Browser
and the Query window. When you first open the Query Analyzer, a single
Query window is opened, but you can open a new window at any time by
clicking the New Query button on the Query Analyzer toolbar.

The Query window displays the name of the database server, the current
database, the current login, and the query name in the title bar. The Query
window is similar to the Enterprise Manager's Query Designer but is much
more powerful.

As an editor, the Query window is more flexible and powerful than the
Query Designer's SQL Pane. While the Query Designer can process only a
limited set of SQL statements, the Query window can process any valid
Transact-SQL statement, and you can enter multiple statements for processing in a single batch.

Although the Query window doesn't support the Grid or Diagram views available in the Query Designer, it supports additional views of a query that are used to analyze performance, as we'll see in Lesson 23.

The Query window also gives you the option of displaying each view of the query in a separate tab, rather than as panes. This is often the most convenient way of viewing the query.

Entering Transact-SQL Statements

The simplest way to use the Query window is to type in an SQL statement, just as you would in the SQL Pane of the Query Designer. Unlike the Query Designer, however, the Query Analyzer's Query window provides some extra assistance by color coding the Transact-SQL statements you enter. Table 21-1 shows the colors the Query window uses.

Color	Meaning
Blue	Keyword
Dark Green	Comment
Dark Red	Stored Procedure
Gray	Operator
Green	System Table
Magenta	System Function
Red	Character String

Table 21-1.   *Color coding used in the Query Analyzer's Query window.*

Execute a SELECT query

1. Enter the following SELECT statement in the Query window:

```
SELECT OilID, OilName, LEFT(LatinName, 10)
FROM Oils
```

2. The Query window changes the color of the text as you type.

Execute Query button

3. Click the Execute Query button on the Query Analyzer toolbar.

The Query Analyzer adds a pane to the Query window containing two tabs: the Grids tab, which contains the query results, and the Messages tab.

4. Select the Messages tab.

The Query window displays the messages generated by the query.

Display query results in a separate tab

1. Select Options from the Query Analyzer's Tools menu.

The Query Analyzer displays the Options dialog box.

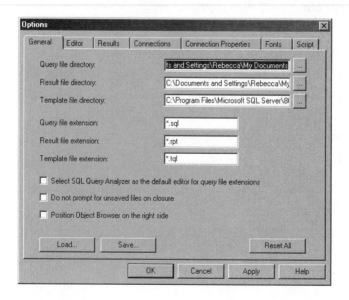

2. Select the Editor tab.

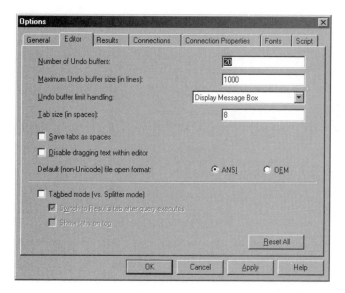

3. Select the check box labeled Tabbed Mode (Vs. Splitter Mode).

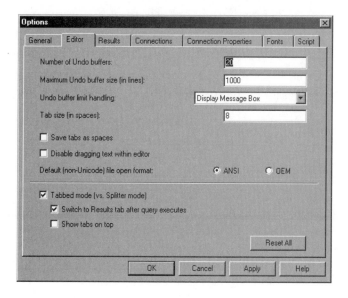

4. Click OK.

The Query Analyzer changes the display of the Query window.

Using SQL Scripts

A *script* is a set of Transact-SQL statements stored in a file. Scripts are most often used to keep a permanent record of the commands used to create and populate database objects. Because the scripts are stored in text files, rather than in the database, they can be used to re-create the database on different servers. (SQL Server actually uses scripts to create the Pubs and Northwind sample databases.)

Although scripts are most often used for creating database objects, they're not limited to this use. Any valid Transact-SQL statement can be included in a script.

The SQL statements in a script are grouped into batches. A script can contain one or more batches, and each batch can contain one or more SQL statements. In a script containing more than one batch, the batches are separated by the GO command. If a script doesn't contain the GO command, all the statements will be executed as a single batch.

Create a script

1. Change the SQL statement in the Query window to read:

```
SELECT OilID, OilName, LEFT(LatinName, 10)
FROM Oils
GO
SELECT PlantPartID, PlantPart
FROM PlantParts
```

 IP   Only the last three lines have been added to the query used in the previous exercise.

2. Click the Execute Query button on the Query Analyzer toolbar.

   The Query Analyzer displays the results in two panes of the Grids tab of the Query window.

Save button

3. Reselect the Editor tab of the Query window, and click the Save button on the Query Analyzer toolbar.

The Query Analyzer displays the Save Query dialog box.

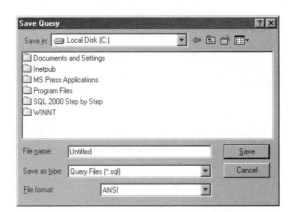

> **IMPORTANT** If you don't select the Editor tab before clicking the Save button, the Query Analyzer will save the *result* of the query, rather than the query itself.

4. Navigate to the SQL 2000 Step by Step folder in the root directory, and name the script *Lesson21*.

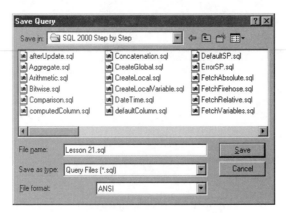

5. Click Save.

The Query Analyzer saves the new script file.

Open a script

New Query button

1. Click the New Query button on the Query Analyzer toolbar.

   The Query Analyzer opens a new, empty Query window.

Open button

2. Click the Open button on the Query Analyzer toolbar.

   The Query Analyzer displays the Open Query File dialog box.

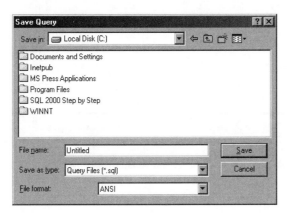

3. Navigate to the SQL 2000 Step by Step folder in the root directory, and select Lesson 21.

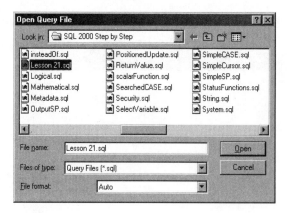

4. Click Open.

The Query Analyzer displays the script in the Query window.

Execute Query button

5. Click the Execute Query button on the Query Analyzer toolbar to run the script.

   The Query Analyzer displays the results in the Grids tab.

6. Close the script window.

Using the Object Browser

The Object Browser is contained in the pane on the left side of the Query Analyzer window. Just as the Console Tree of the Enterprise Manager provides a hierarchical view of the objects in a SQL Server installation, the Objects tab of the Object Browser displays a hierarchical view of the databases in the server to which you're connected, as well as other common objects used in creating Transact-SQL programs.

> **TIP** The Templates tab of the Object Browser contains a hierarchical view of the available programming templates. We'll look at templates in the next lesson.

The Objects tab of the Object Browser is arranged somewhat differently from the Console Tree in the Enterprise Manager. Only database objects are listed, so items such as Logins and Data Transformation Services packages aren't visible. Also, the tables in a database are divided into two folders for convenience: User Tables and System Tables.

Additionally, rather than simply listing the tables in a database the way the Enterprise Manager Console Tree does, the Object Browser displays the columns, indexes, constraints, and triggers that you've defined for the table, as well as the dependencies, the views, and the tables that depend on the table. Figure 21-2 shows the Object Browser display for the Oils table.

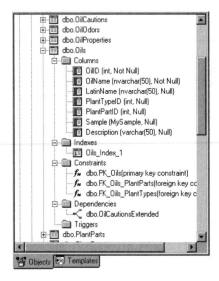

Figure 21-2. *The Object Browser displays information about the tables in your database that's useful from a programming perspective.*

The Common Objects folder of the Object Browser contains, along with the built-in data types, a set of common Transact-SQL functions grouped into categories. For each function, the Parameters folder contains a description of each parameter, including its name and data types. Figure 21-3 shows the LEFT function as it is displayed in the Object Browser window.

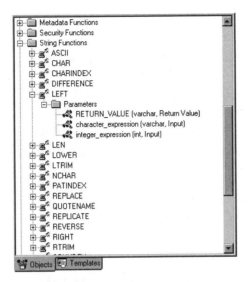

Figure 21-3. *The Object Browser displays functions by categories in the Common Objects folder.*

Using the Object Browser, you can open a table or view, similar to the way you display rows by opening the Query Designer in the Enterprise Manager. Having done so, you can simply view the rows, or you can insert new rows and edit existing ones.

You can also use the Object Browser when you're creating Transact-SQL programs. You can add objects to the Query window using drag-and-drop, and you can create several different kinds of scripts automatically from the context menu.

Opening Objects

When you right-click a table or view in the Object Browser and select Open, the Query Analyzer displays the rows in the table (or the results of the view's SELECT statement) in the Open Table window.

Open a table

1. Expand the User Tables folder of the Aromatherapy database in the Object Browser.

The Query Analyzer displays a list of tables in the database.

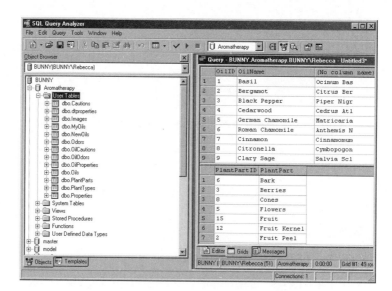

2. Right-click dbo.PlantParts, and select Open.

The Query Analyzer displays the rows in the table in an Open Table window.

3. When you've finished viewing the rows in the table, close the Open Table window.

Open a view

1. Expand the Views folder of the Aromatherapy database in the Object Brower.

   The Query Analyzer displays a list of all views in the database.

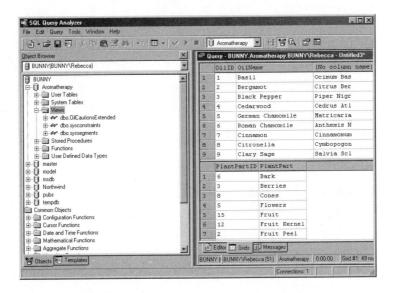

2. Right-click dbo.OilCautionsExtended, and select Open.

   The Query Analyzer displays the rows returned by the query in an Open Table window.

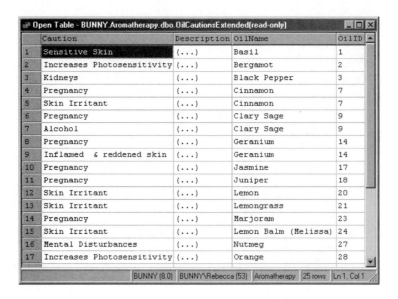

Open Table - BUNNY.Aromatherapy.dbo.OilCautionsExtended(read-only)

	Caution	Description	OilName	OilID
1	Sensitive Skin	(...)	Basil	1
2	Increases Photosensitivity	(...)	Bergamot	2
3	Kidneys	(...)	Black Pepper	3
4	Pregnancy	(...)	Cinnamon	7
5	Skin Irritant	(...)	Cinnamon	7
6	Pregnancy	(...)	Clary Sage	9
7	Alcohol	(...)	Clary Sage	9
8	Pregnancy	(...)	Geranium	14
9	Inflamed & reddened skin	(...)	Geranium	14
10	Pregnancy	(...)	Jasmine	17
11	Pregnancy	(...)	Juniper	18
12	Skin Irritant	(...)	Lemon	20
13	Skin Irritant	(...)	Lemongrass	21
14	Pregnancy	(...)	Marjoram	23
15	Skin Irritant	(...)	Lemon Balm (Melissa)	24
16	Mental Disturbances	(...)	Nutmeg	27
17	Increases Photosensitivity	(...)	Orange	28

BUNNY (8.0) | BUNNY\Rebecca (53) | Aromatherapy | 25 rows | Ln 1, Col 1

3. When you've finished viewing the rows in the table, close the Open Table window.

Adding Objects to the Editor Pane

One of the simplest and most convenient capabilities of the Object Browser is its support for drag-and-drop. Whenever you need to specify an object listed in the Object Browser, simply drag it into position in the Editor Pane of the Query window, and its name will be pasted into the editor window.

 IP If you drag-and-drop one of the functions listed in the Common Objects folders, the Object Browser will paste the function's name, but not its parameters. To paste the function's complete syntax, use the Scripting command described in the next section.

Add a database object

Clear Window button

1. Select the Query window, make sure the Editor tab is selected, and then click the Clear Window button on the Query Analyzer toolbar.

   The Query Analyzer empties the Editor Pane.

2. Type the following SQL statement into the Editor Pane (be sure to put a space after the final FROM):

```
SELECT *
FROM
```

3. Expand the User Tables folder in the Object Browser.

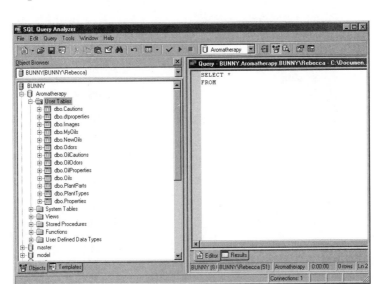

4. Drag the dbo.Properties table from the Object Browser to the Editor Pane and drop it after the word FROM.

The Query Analyzer pastes the table name into the statement.

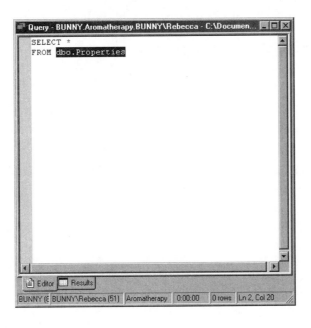

Execute Query button

5. Click the Execute Query button to execute the query.

The Query Analyzer displays the results in the Grids Pane.

Add all objects in a folder

1. Reselect the Editor tab of the Query window.

2. Delete the * from the SELECT statement.

3. Expand the dbo.Properties folder in the Object Browser.

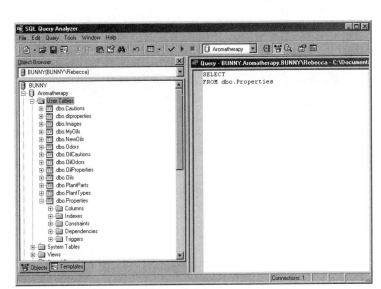

4. Drag the Columns folder from the Object Browser to the Editor Pane and drop it after the word SELECT.

   The Query Analyzer pastes all the column names into the statement.

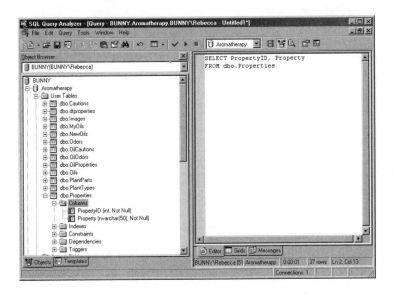

Execute Query button

5. Click the Execute Query button on the Query Analyzer toolbar to execute the query.

The Query Analyzer displays the results in the Grids pane.

Scripting Objects

Scripting is a more sophisticated version of the drag-and-drop functionality of the Object Browser. Scripting creates a complete Transact-SQL statement and is available from the context menus of most objects. Not all script types are applicable to all object types, and some types, such as function parameters or columns, have no scripting available at all.

The available scripts and the objects to which they apply are shown in Table 21-2. We'll be looking at most of these scripts in the next lesson about creating and maintaining database objects.

Script Command	Applicable Objects
Create	Table, Index, Constraint, Trigger, View, Stored Procedure
Alter	Trigger, View
Drop	Table, Index, Constraint, Trigger, View, Stored Procedure
Select	Table, View
Insert	Table, View
Update	Table, View
Delete	Table, View
Execute	Stored Procedure, Function

Table 21-2. *Scripting Options.*

Scripts can be written to a new Query window, a script file, or the clipboard (where they can be pasted into an existing Query window). Some scripts, such as the function execution scripts, use replaceable parameters. The Query Analyzer provides a dialog box to make it easy to replace these parameters with the appropriate values.

Script a SELECT statement

1. Expand the User Tables folder of the Aromatherapy database in the Object Browser.

2. Right-click the dbo.OilProperties table, point to Script Object To New Window As, and choose Select.

   The Query Analyzer opens a new Query window with the SELECT statement.

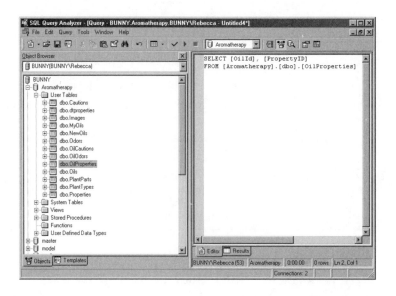

IP The Object Browser creates the SELECT statement on a single line. You
can reformat it to improve readability as shown in the illustration.

▶

Execute Query button

3. Click the Execute Query button on the Query Analyzer toolbar to
execute the query.

The Query Analyzer displays the results in the Grids Pane.

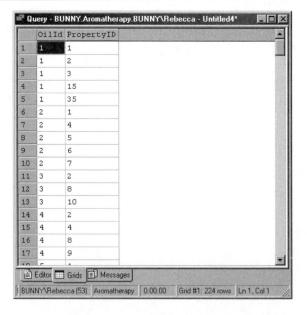

4. When you've finished with the query, close the Query window.

Script a function

1. Expand the String Functions folder within the Common Objects folder.

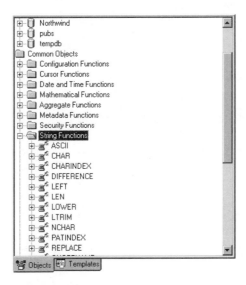

2. Right-click the LEFT function, point to Script Object To New Window As, and choose Execute.

The Query Analyzer opens a new Query window with a SELECT statement, including the function.

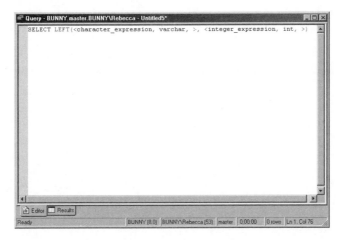

3. Choose Replace Template Parameters from the Edit menu.

   The Query Analyzer opens the Replace Template Parameters dialog box.

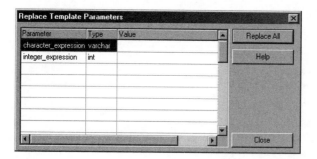

4. Enter *'Test Expression'* as the value for the character_expression parameter, and *4* as the value of the integer_expression parameter.

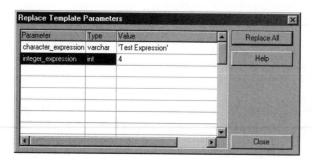

5. Click Replace All.

   The Query Analyzer replaces the parameters in the query.

6. Click the Execute Query button on the Query Analyzer toolbar to execute the query.

Execute Query button

The Query Analyzer displays the results in the Grids Pane.

Lesson 21 Quick Reference

To	Do this	Button
Start the Query Analyzer	Click the Start button on the task bar. Point to Programs and then to Microsoft SQL Server, and click Query Analyzer.	Start
Select a database with which to work	Select the new database from the combo box on the Query Analyzer toolbar.	
Execute a Transact-SQL statement in the Query window	Type the statement in the Editor Pane, and click the Execute Query button on the Query Analyzer toolbar.	▶
Create an SQL script	Enter the Transact-SQL statements in the Query window, and click the Save button on the Query Analyzer toolbar.	💾
Load an SQL script	Click the Open button on the Query Analyzer, and select the script in the Open Script dialog box.	📂
Open a table or view in the Object Browser	Right-click the table or view in the Object Browser, and select Open.	
Add an object to the Editor Pane from the Object Browser	Drag the object from the Object Browser, and drop it in the desired position in the Editor Pane.	
Script an object from the Object Browser	Right-click the object in the Object Browser, point to Script Object to <destination> As, and select the type of script desired.	

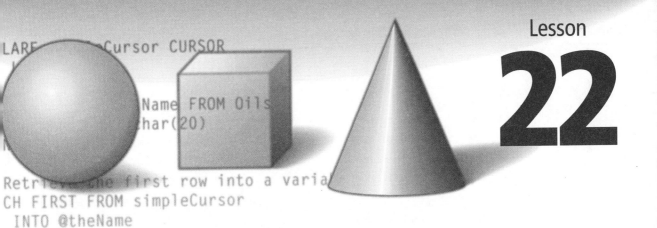

Data Definition Language

LARE   Cursor CURSOR

        Name FROM Oils
        har(20)

Retr   e first row into a varia
CH FIRST FROM simpleCursor
  INTO @theName

Display the results
NT RTRIM(@theName) + ' is the first name'

Ret
CH
  INTO @theName

Display the r
NT RTRIM(@th

In this lesson you'll learn how to:

- Create database objects using the CREATE statement.
- Change database objects using the ALTER statement.
- Remove database objects using the DROP statement.
- Create DDL scripts using the Object Browser.
- Use templates to generate DDL statements.

In Parts II and III, we looked at how to create database objects—the tables, indexes, relationships, and views in your database schema—using the Microsoft Visual Database Tools within the Enterprise Manager. In this lesson, we'll learn how to create, alter, and delete objects using Transact-SQL.

Understanding DDL

The SQL language is divided into two components: Data Manipulation Language (DML) and Data Definition Language (DDL). DML consists of the statements you use to create and retrieve data. DDL consists of the statements you use both to create the objects within the database and to set the property and attribute values of the database itself.

DML vs. DDL

Why are these two sets of statements distinguished? Although DML statements are reasonably similar across SQL implementations (allowing for each vendor's custom extensions), DDL varies widely between products. Every database management system vendor implements the relational model differently at the physical level, and each vendor's DDL inevitably reflects those differences. Most vendors also provide graphic tools for data definition, and many, including Microsoft, don't limit you to SQL DDL. Microsoft provides both ADO and DAO data definition capabilities, for example.

We've already seen the basic DML statements: SELECT, INSERT, UPDATE, and DELETE. The basic statements of SQL DDL are CREATE, ALTER, and DROP, each of which has a number of variations for creating different object types. We'll be looking at several of these statements in this lesson, and others in the lessons to follow.

Creating Objects

Database objects are created programmatically using the CREATE statement. The exact syntax of the CREATE statement for each object varies, of course, but the range of objects that you can create and the basic syntax of the CREATE statement for each object are shown in Table 22-1.

CREATE Statement Syntax	Object Created
CREATE DATABASE <name>	Creates a database
CREATE DEFAULT <name> AS <constant_expression>	Creates a default value
CREATE FUNCTION <name> RETURNS <return_value> AS <tsql_statements>	Creates a user-defined function (See Lesson 30, "User Defined Functions.")
CREATE INDEX <name> ON <table_or_view> (<index_columns>)	Creates an index on a table or view

Table 22-1. *CREATE statements.* *(continued)*

continued

CREATE Statement Syntax	Object Created
CREATE PROCEDURE <name> AS <tsql_statements>	Creates a stored procedure (See Lesson 28, "Stored Procedures.")
CREATE RULE <name> AS <conditional_expression>	Creates a database rule
CREATE SCHEMA AUTHORIZATION <owner> <object_definitions>	Creates tables, views, and permissions as a single object
CREATE STATISTICS <name> ON <table_or_view> (<columns>)	Creates statistics to be used by the query optimizer
CREATE TABLE <name> (<table_definition>)	Creates a table
CREATE TRIGGER <name> {FOR|AFTER|INSTEAD OF} <dml_action> AS <tsql_statements>	Creates a trigger (See Lesson 29, "Triggers.")
CREATE VIEW <name> AS <select_statement>	Creates a view

Of the CREATE statements shown in Table 22-1, only the CREATE TABLE statement is somewhat complex. This is because of the number of different items that comprise a table definition. You must add columns, of course, and each column definition must have at least a column name and a data type. Optionally, you can also specify the nullability of the column, whether it is an identity row or a GUID, its default value, any constraints that apply to the column, and several other properties that we won't be examining here. A simplified version of the syntax for a column definition is:

```
<column_name> <data_type>
[NULL | NOT NULL]
[
[DEFAULT <default_value>] |
[IDENTITY [(<seed_value>, <increment_value>)[NOT FOR REPLICATION]]]
]
[ROWGUIDCOL]
[<column_constraint>[, <column_constraint>…]]
```

Note that default values and identity specifications are mutually exclusive. That is, you can specify a default value for a column, or you can specify that it is an identity column, but not both.

The specification of a <column_constraint> is:

```
[CONSTRAINT <constraint_name>]
[
[PRIMARY KEY | UNIQUE] [CLUSTERED | NONCLUSTERED] |
[[FOREIGN KEY] REFERENCES <referenced_table> (column_name)] |
[CHECK [NOT FOR REPLICATION] (<logical expression>)]
]
```

You can specify more than one <column_constraint> for a column, but you must specify each type of constraint (PRIMARY KEY/UNIQUE, FOREIGN KEY, or CHECK) separately.

All of this looks rather frightening, but it's not as it difficult as it appears if you start with the basic definition (for example, *MyColumn varchar 20*) and simply add clauses as necessary. You'll hardly ever use more than two or three clauses in a single column definition, as in these examples:

```
MyColumn varchar(20)

MyColumn varchar(20) NOT NULL

MyColumn varchar(20)
    PRIMARY KEY CLUSTERED

MyColumn varchar(20)
    IDENTITY (1, 1)
    PRIMARY KEY CLUSTERED

MyColumn varchar(20) NOT NULL FOREIGN KEY REFERENCES Oils (OilName)
```

Create a table with a primary key constraint

1. Make sure that Aromatherapy is the selected database on the Query Analyzer toolbar.

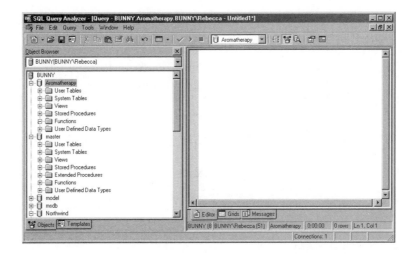

2. Enter the following statement in the Editor Pane of the Query window:

```
CREATE TABLE SimpleTable
(
        SimpleID smallint
                IDENTITY (1,1)
                PRIMARY KEY CLUSTERED,
        SimpleDescription varchar(50)
)
```

*Execute Query
button*

3. Click the Execute Query button on the Query Analyzer toolbar to execute the statement.

   The Query Analyzer creates the SimpleTable table.

4. Expand the User Tables folder of the Aromatherapy database in the Object Browser. (If the folder is already expanded, click on it to make sure the Object Browser is selected.)

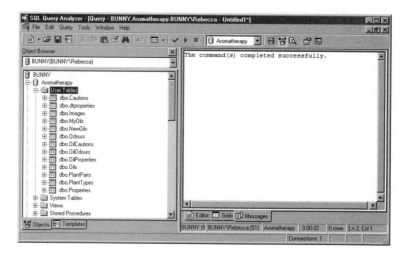

5. Press the F5 key to refresh the display.

   SimpleTable appears in the list.

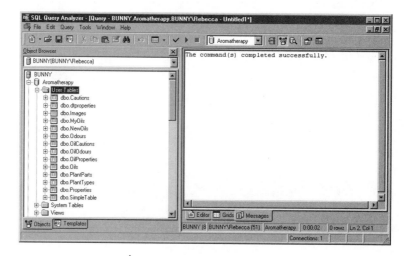

 IP If the query window displays a message saying there is already an object named "SimpleTable," then you didn't click in the Object Browser to select it before pressing F5.

Create a table with a foreign key constraint

Clear Window button

1. Select the Editor tab of the query window, and click the Clear Window button on the Query Analyzer toolbar to clear the Editor Pane contents.

2. Enter the following statement in the Editor Pane:

```
CREATE TABLE RelatedTable
(
        RelatedID smallint
                IDENTITY (1,1)
                PRIMARY KEY CLUSTERED,
        SimpleID smallint
                REFERENCES SimpleTable (SimpleID),
        RelatedDescription varchar(20)
)
```

Execute Query button

3. Click the Execute Query button on the Query Analyzer toolbar to execute the statement.

The Query Analyzer creates the table.

4. Select the Object Browser window by clicking anywhere within it.

5. Press the F5 key to refresh the display.

The Object Browser displays the new RelatedTable table in the User Tables folder.

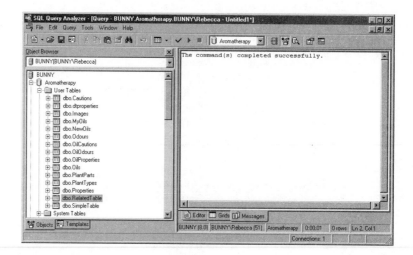

Create a view

Clear Window button

1. Select the Editor tab of the Query window, and click the Clear Window button on the Query Analyzer toolbar to clear the Editor Pane contents.

2. Enter the following statement in the Editor Pane:

```
CREATE VIEW SimpleView
AS
SELECT RelatedID, SimpleDescription, RelatedDescription
FROM RelatedTable
INNER JOIN SimpleTable
ON RelatedTable.SimpleID = SimpleTable.SimpleID
```

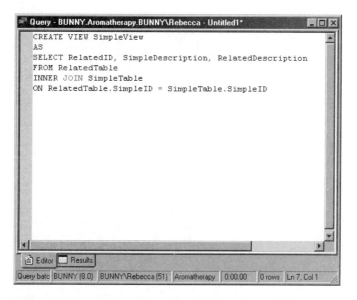

Execute Query button

3. Click the Execute Query button on the Query Analyzer toolbar to execute the statement.

   The Query Analyzer creates the view.

4. Expand the Views folder of the Aromatherapy database in the Object Browser. (If the Views folder is already expanded, click anywhere in the Object Browser to select it.)

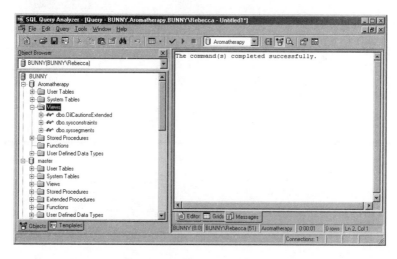

5. Press the F5 key to refresh the display.

   The Object Browser displays the new SimpleView view in the Views folder.

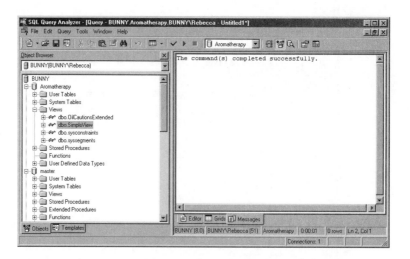

Create an index

*Clear Window
button*

1. Select the Editor Tab of the query window, and click the Clear Window button on the Query Analyzer toolbar to clear the Editor Pane contents.

2. Enter the following statement in the Editor Pane:

```
CREATE INDEX SimpleIndex ON SimpleTable (SimpleDescription)
```

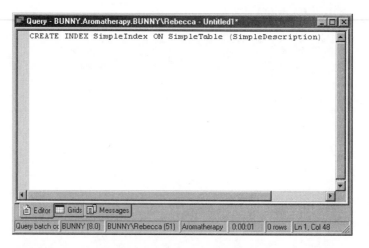

*Execute Query
button*

3. Click the Execute Query button on the Query Analyzer toolbar to execute the statement.

   The Query Analyzer creates the index.

4. Expand the Indexes folder of the SimpleTable table to confirm that the SimpleIndex index has been added.

Altering Objects

Whereas the CREATE statement creates a new object, the ALTER statement provides the mechanism for altering an object definition. Not all of the objects that can be created with a CREATE statement have a corresponding ALTER statement. The syntaxes for objects that can be altered are listed in Table 22-2.

ALTER Statement Syntax	Effect
ALTER DATABASE <name> <file_specification>	Alters the files used to store the database
ALTER FUNCTION <name> RETURNS <return_value> AS <tsql_statements>	Changes the Transact-SQL statements comprising the function
ALTER PROCEDURE <name> AS <tsql_statements>	Changes the Transact-SQL statements comprising the stored procedure (See Lesson 28, "Stored Procedures.")
ALTER TABLE <name> <change_definition>	Changes the definition of a table (We'll examine the <change_definition> in detail in this lesson.)

Table 22-2.   *ALTER statements.*   *(continued)*

Table 22-2. *continued*

ALTER Statement Syntax	Effect
ALTER TRIGGER <name> {FOR | AFTER | INSTEAD OF} <dml_action> AS <tsql_statements>	Changes the Transact-SQL statements comprising the trigger (See Lesson 29, "Triggers.")
ALTER VIEW <name> AS <select_statement>	Changes the SELECT statement that creates the view

The ALTER TABLE statement is complex for the same reasons that the CREATE TABLE statement is complex: there are several different parts to a table definition. The simplified version of the syntax of the ALTER TABLE statement is

```
ALTER TABLE <name>
{
[ALTER COLUMN <column_definition>] |
[ADD <column_definition>] |
[DROP COLUMN <column_name>] |
[ADD [WITH NOCHECK] CONSTRAINT <table_constraint>]
}
```

The (implied) CHECK and NOCHECK keywords before a table constraint tell SQL Server whether to test the existing data in the table against the new constraint. WITH NOCHECK is used only in extremely rare situations.

Altering Columns

There are a number of restrictions on the ALTER COLUMN clause. A column cannot be altered if it is

- Of a datatype *text*, *image*, *ntext*, or *timestamp*.
- Defined as the ROWGUIDCOL of the table.
- A computed column or used in a computed column.
- Replicated.

Altering Columns *continued*

- Used in an index—unless the column has a data type of *varchar*, *nvarchar*, or *varbinary*; the data type is not changed; and the size of the column is not reduced.

- Used in statistics generated by the CREATE STATISTICS statement.

- Used in a PRIMARY KEY constraint.

- Used in a FOREIGN KEY REFERENCES constraint.

- Used in a CHECK constraint.

- Used in a UNIQUE constraint.

- Associated with a DEFAULT.

Alter an view

1. Expand the Columns folder of the SimpleView query in the Object Browser.

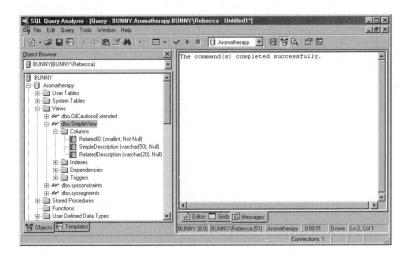

Clear Window button

2. Select the Editor tab of the query window, and click the Clear Window button on the Query Analyzer toolbar to clear the Editor Pane contents.

3. Enter the following statement in the Editor Pane:

```
ALTER VIEW SimpleView
AS
SELECT SimpleDescription, RelatedDescription
FROM RelatedTable
INNER JOIN SimpleTable
ON RelatedTable.SimpleID = SimpleTable.SimpleID
```

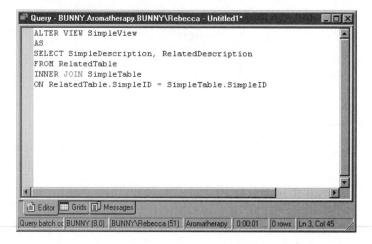

Execute Query button

4. Click the Execute Query button on the Query Analyzer toolbar to execute the statement.

5. Select the Object Browser by clicking anywhere within it, and then press the F5 key to refresh the display.

The Object Browser displays only the SimpleDescription and RelatedDescription columns.

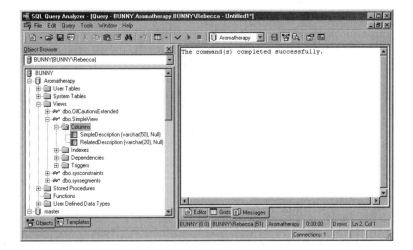

Add a column to a table

1. Expand the Columns folder of the SimpleTable table in the Object Browser.

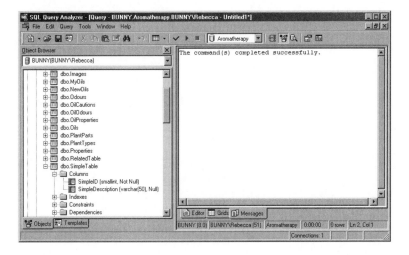

Clear Window button

2. Select the Editor tab of the Query window, and click the Clear Window button on the Query Analyzer toolbar to clear the Editor Pane contents.

3. Enter the following statement in the Editor Pane:

```
ALTER TABLE SimpleTable
ADD NewColumn varchar(20)
```

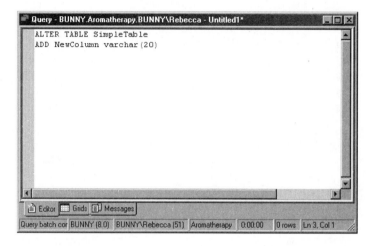

Execute Query button

4. Click the Execute Query button on the Query Analyzer toolbar to execute the statement.

   The Query Analyzer adds the column to the table.

5. Select the Object Browser by clicking anywhere within it, and then press the F5 key to refresh the display.

   The Object Browser displays the new column.

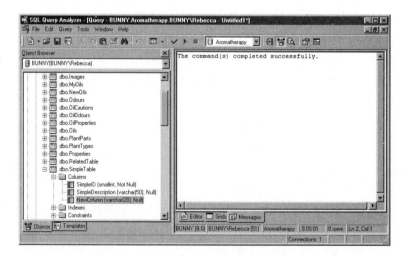

Alter a column in a table

Clear Window button

1. Select the Editor tab of the Query window, and click the Clear Window button on the Query Analyzer toolbar to clear the Editor Pane contents.

2. Enter the following statement in the Editor Pane:

```
ALTER TABLE SimpleTable
ALTER COLUMN NewColumn varchar(10)
```

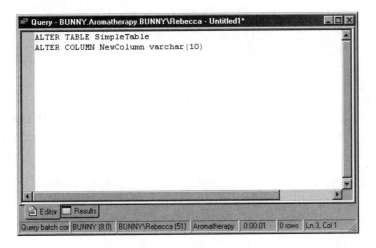

Execute Query button

3. Click the Execute Query button on the Query Analyzer toolbar to execute the statement.

   The Query Analyzer adds the column to the table.

4. Select the Object Browser by clicking anywhere within it, and then press the F5 key to refresh the display.

   The Object Browser displays the new column.

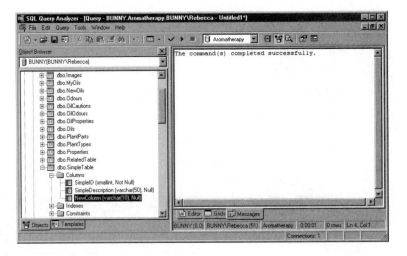

Drop a column from a table

Clear Window button

1. Select the Editor Tab of the Query window, and click the Clear Window button on the Query Analyzer toolbar to clear the Editor Pane contents.

2. Enter the following statement in the Editor Pane:

```
ALTER TABLE SimpleTable
DROP COLUMN NewColumn
```

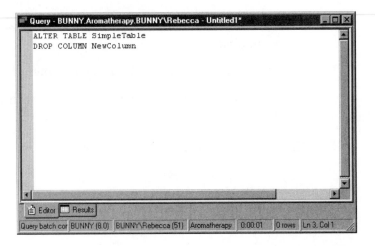

Execute Query button

3. Click the Execute Query button on the Query Analyzer toolbar to execute the statement.

   The Query Analyzer removes the column from the table.

4. Select the Object Browser by clicking anywhere within it, and then press the F5 to refresh the display.

   The Object Browser no longer displays the NewColumn column.

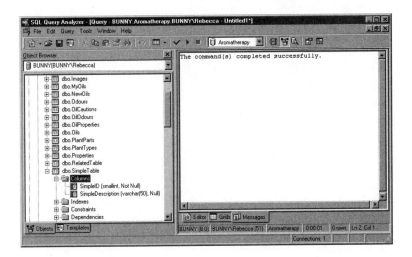

Dropping Objects

The DROP statement removes a database object. Unlike the CREATE and ALTER statements, all the DROP statements have the same simple syntax:

```
DROP <object_type> <name>
```

<object_type> is any of the objects listed in Table 22-1 except a schema.

Drop an index

1. Expand the Indexes folder of the SimpleTable table in the Object Browser.

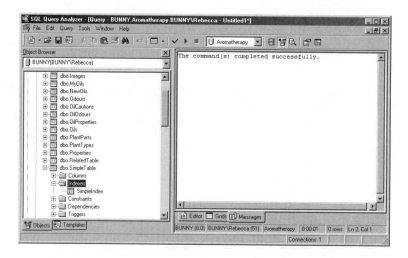

Clear Window button

2. Select the Editor tab of the Query window, and click the Clear Window button on the Query Analyzer toolbar to clear the Editor Pane contents.

3. Enter the following statement in the Editor Pane:

```
DROP INDEX SimpleTable.SimpleIndex
```

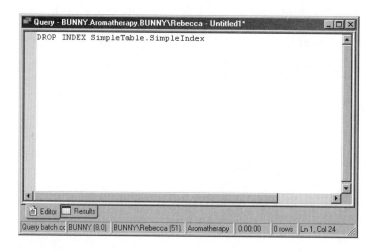

Execute Query button

4. Click the Execute Query button on the Query Analyzer toolbar to execute the statement.

   The Query Analyzer removes the index.

5. Select the Object Browser by clicking anywhere within it, and then press the F5 key to refresh the display.

   The Object Browser displays an empty index folder.

Drop a table

Clear Window button

1. Select the Editor Tab of the Query window, and click the Clear Window button on the Query Analyzer toolbar to clear the Editor Pane contents.

2. Enter the following statement in the Editor Pane:

```
DROP TABLE RelatedTable
```

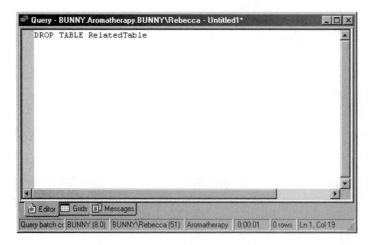

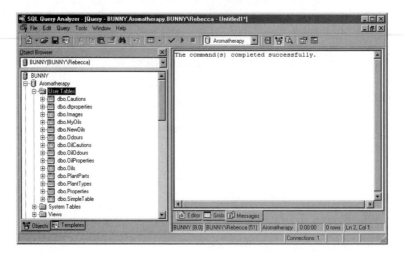

3. Click the Execute Query button on the Query Analyzer toolbar to execute the statement.

Execute Query button

The Query Analyzer removes the table.

4. Expand the User Tables folder of the Aromatherapy database in the Object Browser, and then press the F5 key to refresh the display.

The RelatedTable table is no longer listed.

Using the Object Browser for Data Definition

DDL statements aren't particularly difficult, just occasionally complex, but the Query Analyzer provides two functions through the Object Browser that make DDL even easier to use. As we saw in the previous lesson, the context menu of most objects supports scripting commands that you can use to generate CREATE, ALTER, and DROP statements for those objects.

The Query Analyzer also provides *templates*, which are boilerplate SQL script files with replaceable parameters. You can create your own templates, but SQL Server 2000 provides basic templates for most of the CREATE statements.

Scripting DDL

In the previous lesson, we looked at Object Browser scripting very quickly when we created two SELECT scripts. The Object Browser also supports CREATE, ALTER, and DROP scripts for the majority of database objects. Once the scripts have been generated, you can edit them to suit your requirements.

 IP The CREATE statements generated by scripting can be stored as script files. This is a convenient way to document the structure of the database.

Generate a CREATE TABLE script

1. Right-click the Cautions table in the Object Browser, point to Script Object To New Window As, and select Create.

The Query Analyzer opens a new query window containing a CREATE statement to create the Cautions table.

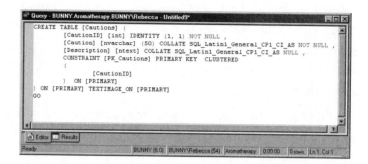

> **IMPORTANT** Because the database can't contain multiple tables with the same name, you must edit the statement if you want to run it now. If you don't want to create the new table, simply close the query window and go on to the next section.

2. Change the table name in the statement to DuplicateCautions and the name of the PRIMARY KEY constraint to PK_DuplicateCautions.

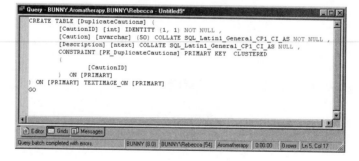

Execute Query button

3. Click the Execute Query button on the Query Analyzer toolbar to execute the query.

   The Query Analyzer creates the new table.

4. Select the Object Browser by clicking anywhere within it, and then press the F5 key to refresh the display.

The Object Browser displays the new DuplicateCautions table in the list.

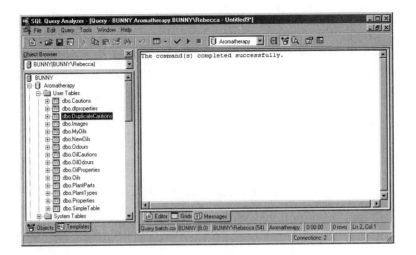

5. Close the query window containing the CREATE statement.

Using Templates

The SQL language differs from many other programming languages—such as C++ or Microsoft Visual Basic, for example—in that it has relatively few statements, but the statement syntax can be complex. In fact, one of the complaints frequently leveled at SQL as a language is that all data retrieval is done with a single statement: the SELECT statement.

Templates are an excellent mechanism for dealing with the complexity of SQL statements. When you use SQL for any length of time, you often find yourself using a few more-or-less standard variations on the basic commands: a SELECT statement from two tables with an INNER JOIN, for example, or a CREATE TABLE statement with an IDENTITY column. Once these statements are implemented as templates, a single command generates all the template text. You can then use a convenient dialog box to customize the statements.

TIP Templates aren't necessarily limited to a single command. They can have all the complexity of any SQL script file, and can contain multiple commands and multiple batches.

Although powerful, templates are easy to use and create. They are simply SQL script files with (by default) a .tql extension. Items to be customized, such as the names of the columns and tables in a CREATE TABLE statement, are defined as parameters. In a template, a parameter has the form <parameter_name, data_type, value>. For example, the following template script contains two parameters, table_name and sort_column:

```
SELECT *
FROM <table_name, sysname, test_view>
ORDER BY <sort_column, sysname, test_column>
```

The script defines both parameters as having the data type *sysname*, which is a special type used to indicate objects' names. The table_name parameter has a default value of "test_view", and the sort_column parameter has a default value of "test_column".

The Query Analyzer provides the Replace Template Parameters dialog box to simplify customizing template text. Simply open the template in a Query window and select Replace Template Parameters from the Edit menu to display the dialog box.

 TIP You can also use the Ctrl-Shift-M keyboard shortcut to open the Replace Template Parameters dialog box.

Generate a CREATE TABLE statement using a template

1. Select the Templates tab in the Object Browser.

   The Query Analyzer displays a list of categories for available templates.

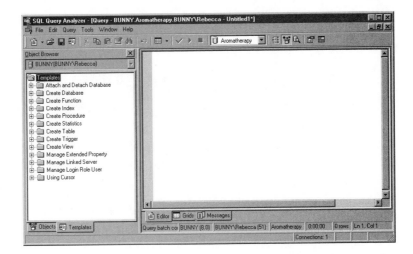

2. Expand the Create Table folder, and double-click Create Table With IDENTITY Column.

   The Query Analyzer opens a new query window and inserts the template text.

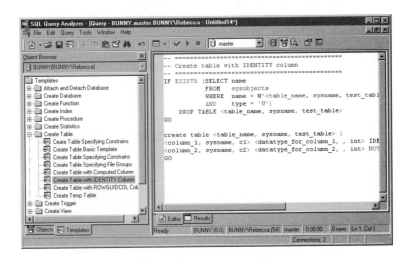

3. Select Replace Template Parameters from the Edit menu.

The Query Analyzer opens the Replace Template Parameters dialog box.

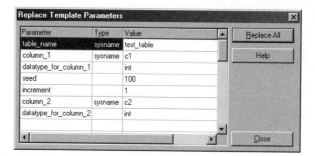

4. Set these parameter values:

Parameter	Value
table_name	TemplateTable
column_1	TemplateID
datatype_for_column_1	smallint
seed	1
increment	1
column_2	Description
datatype_for_column_2	varchar(20)

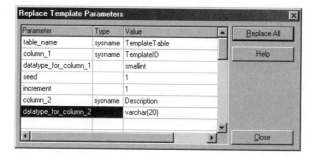

5. Click Replace All.

The Query Analyzer closes the dialog box and substitutes the parameter values for the parameter definitions in the template.

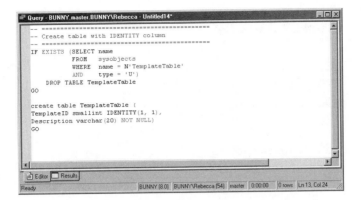

6. Be sure Aromatherapy is selected in the Query Analyzer toolbar.

*Execute Query
button*

7. Click the Execute Query button on the Query Analyzer toolbar to
   execute the statement.

   The Query Analyzer creates the table.

8. Select the Objects tab in the Object Browser, expand the User Tables
   folder, and then press the F5 key to refresh the display.

   The Object Browser displays the new TemplateTable table in the list.

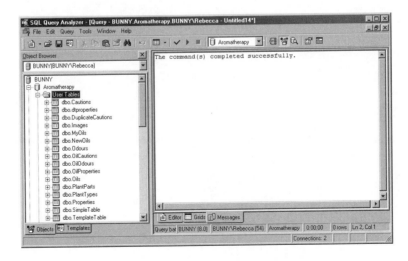

9. Close the Query window containing the CREATE TABLE statement.

Lesson 22 Quick Reference

To	Do this
Create a database object	Use the CREATE statement. (See Table 22-1.)
Change a database object	Use the ALTER statement. (See Table 22-2.)
Remove a database object	Use the DROP statement.
Create a DDL script using the Object Browser	Right-click the object in the Object Browser, point to the Script Object submenu, and select Create.
Use a template	Double-click the template name in the Object Browser. Use the Replace Template Parameters item on the Edit menu to replace template parameters.

Analyzing Queries

DECLARE ... Cursor CURSOR

Name FROM Oils
har(20)

- Retrieve the first row into a varia
FETCH FIRST FROM simpleCursor
    INTO @theName

-- Display the results
PRINT RTRIM(@theName) + " is the first name"

FETCH ... INTO @theName

INTO @theName

In this lesson you'll learn how to:

- Display the execution plan of a SQL script.
- Alter the database schema from the Execution Plan Pane.
- Display a server trace for a SQL script.
- Display client statistics for a SQL script.
- Use the Index Tuning Wizard to optimize the database schema.

When a database application is not performing as well or as quickly as expected, sometimes the most appropriate response is to upgrade the physical infrastructure—that is, add more RAM to the server, add a faster processor or additional processors, or upgrade the communications backbone—but this isn't always the best approach. Sometimes the problem lies within the application itself, and most particularly within the queries the application executes. In this lesson, we'll look at some of the tools Microsoft SQL Server provides for analyzing and optimizing the queries used in your application.

Using the Query Analyzer to Optimize Performance

In addition to the Editor, Grids, and Messages Panes, the SQL Server Query Analyzer's Query window provides three additional displays to help you analyze the performance of specific queries. The Execution Plan Pane shows a graphic representation of the tasks SQL Server will perform in executing the query. The Trace Pane shows detailed information about the server-side execution of a query, including the execution time and the number of reads and writes. Finally, the Client Statistics Pane shows information about the client-side execution of the query, including the number of server roundtrips and the volume of network traffic.

Execution Plans

The Execution Plan Pane of the Query window shows a graphical representation of the steps SQL Server will take when it executes your query. Figure 23-1 shows the execution plan for a simple SELECT statement:

```
SELECT OilName, LatinName
FROM Oils
ORDER BY LatinName
```

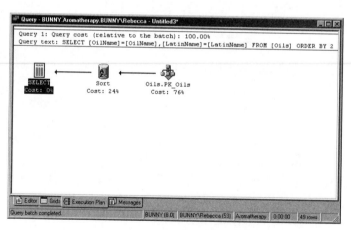

Figure 23-1. *The Execution Plan Pane of the Query window.*

> **TIP** Information displayed in the Execution Plan Pane is identical to the text displayed with the SHOWPLAN database option, which is familiar to many users of earlier versions of SQL Server and is still part of SQL Server 2000. If the statement SET SHOWPLAN_ALL ON is executed as part of the script in the Query window, the SHOWPLAN results will be displayed in the Grids Pane. The Execution Plan Pane, however, displays the information in a format that most people find easier to analyze.

The Execution Plan Pane uses quite a large number of icons to represent the operations the query processor can perform. The icons are documented in SQL Server Books Online, but it isn't necessary to learn them, since holding your mouse cursor over any of the icons displays a ToolTip showing not only the action represented by the icon, but also a number of important statistics, such as the I/O cost, the CPU cost, the number of rows involved in the operation, and the total cost of the operation. Figure 23-2 shows the ToolTip for the Clustered Index Scan operation of the execution plan shown in Figure 23-1.

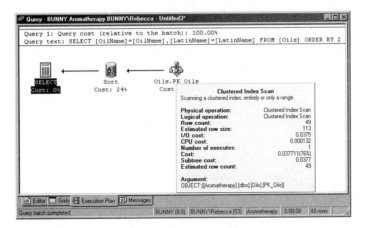

Figure 23-2. *The ToolTip for a Clustered Index Scan.*

The operations in the execution plan are performed from right to left. The ToolTips for the arrows connecting each operation show the number of rows passed from the previous operation and the estimated size of each row, as shown in Figure 23-3.

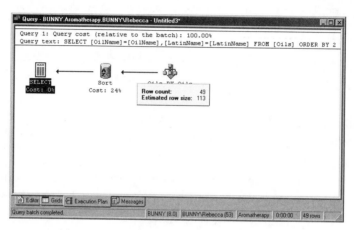

Figure 23-3.   *The ToolTip for a connecting arrow.*

In addition to showing the operations SQL Server will perform when it executes a specified query, the execution plan also provides a mechanism for optimizing the query. Using the context menu of the Execution Plan Pane, you can update the statistics the query optimizer uses to determine its execution strategy, and add indexes to optimize performance.

Display the execution plan of a query

1. Enter the following Transact-SQL statement in the Editor Pane of the Query Analyzer:

```
SELECT PlantParts.PlantPart, Count(Oils.OilName)
    AS NumberOfOils
FROM    Oils
        INNER JOIN PlantParts
            ON Oils.PlantPartID = PlantParts.PlantPartID
GROUP BY PlantParts.PlantPart
```

2. Select Show Execution Plan from the Query menu.

 IP The Execution Plan Pane won't be displayed until the query is executed.

Execute Query button

3. Click the Execute Query button on the Query Analyzer toolbar to execute the query.

   The Query Analyzer executes the query and displays the results in the Grids Pane.

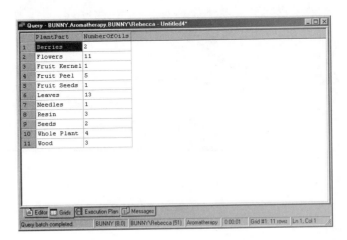

4. Select the Execution Plan tab.

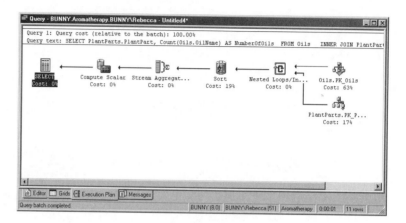

Add an index from the Execution Plan Pane

1. Right-click the icon in the Execution Plan Pane representing a Clustered Index Scan. Since the cost of this operation is 63 percent of the total, we should optimize it if possible.

2. Select Manage Indexes from the context menu.

The Query Analyzer displays the Manage Indexes dialog box.

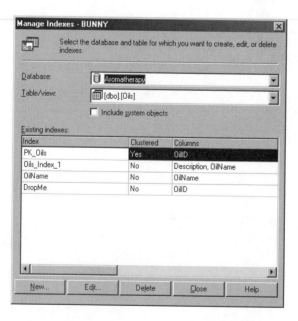

3. Click the New button.

   The Query Analyzer displays the Create New Index dialog box.

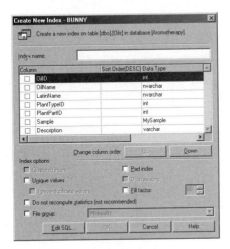

4. Type *Oils_PlantParts* as the index name, and select the PlantPartID column for inclusion.

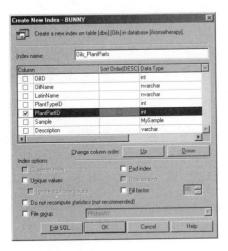

5. Click the OK button.

   The Query Analyzer creates the index and displays it in the Manage Indexes dialog box.

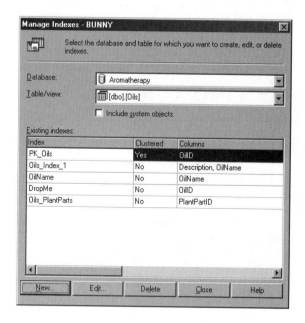

6. Close the Manage Indexes dialog box.

Execute Query button

7. Click the Execute Query button on the Query Analyzer toolbar to reexecute the query.

8. Select the Execution Plan tab of the query window. The Clustered Index Scan of the Oils table has been replaced by an Index Seek, and the cost of this operation has been reduced from 63 percent to only 13 percent of the total.

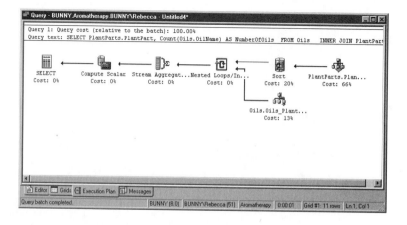

Server Traces

The second tool the Query Analyzer provides for analyzing query performance is the server trace. The Trace Pane shows the commands that are executed by the server when the query is run. The commands don't correspond to the operations in the execution plan—additional commands will be executed, and the actual Transact-SQL commands will not be shown in the same detail.

 TIP SQL Server 2000 provides another tool for performing server traces, the SQL Profiler. We won't be examining the Profiler in this book.

Display a server trace

1. If you closed the Query window after the previous exercise, open a new one and enter the following Transact-SQL statement in the Editor Pane:

   ```
   SELECT PlantParts.PlantPart, Count(Oils.OilName) AS NumberOfOils
   FROM    Oils
           INNER JOIN PlantParts ON Oils.PlantPartID = PlantParts.PlantPartID
   GROUP BY PlantParts.PlantPart
   ```

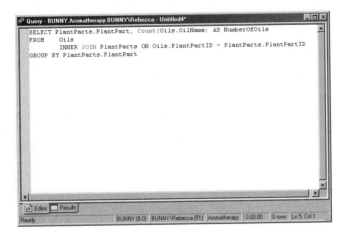

2. Select Show Server Trace from the Query menu.

3. Click the Execute Query button on the Query Analyzer toolbar to execute the query.

Execute Query button

4. Select the Trace tab of the Query window.

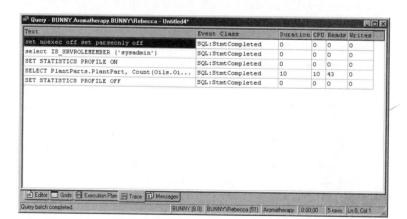

Client Statistics

The final analysis tool provided within the Query Analyzer's Query window is the Client Statistics Pane, which displays the impact that the query has on client-side performance.

The statistics returned in the Client Statistics Pane are divided into three sections: Application Profile Statistics, which returns information about the number of Transact-SQL statements executed and the rows effected; Network Statistics, which provides information about the network traffic generated; and Time Statistics, which helps you determine whether the delay is occurring on the client or the server.

 IP The Network Statistics returned by the Client Statistics Pane will be displayed even if you're connected to a local server.

Display Client Statistics

1. If you closed the Query window after the previous exercise, open a new one and enter the following Transact-SQL statement in the Editor Pane:

```
SELECT PlantParts.PlantPart, Count(Oils.OilName)
    AS NumberOfOils
FROM    Oils
        INNER JOIN PlantParts ON
            Oils.PlantPartID = PlantParts.PlantPartID
GROUP BY PlantParts.PlantPart
```

2. Select Show Client Statistics from the Query menu.

Execute Query button

3. Click the Execute Query button on the Query Analyzer toolbar to reexecute the query.

4. Select the Statistics tab of the Query window.

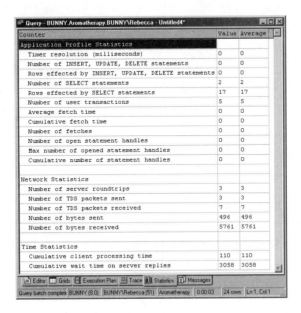

The Index Tuning Wizard

The Query Analyzer provides one more tool for optimizing your database application: the Index Tuning Wizard. By analyzing your database and making suggestions to improve performance, the Index Tuning Wizard can save an enormous amount of time doing trial-and-error performance testing.

Using the Index Tuning Wizard

Database tuning can't be done in a vacuum. It's never a question of a certain schema performing better in absolute terms, but rather of a specific combination of views and indexes performing a specific set of operations better. For this reason, the Index Tuning Wizard requires a specific workload, either a SQL script or a SQL Profiler server trace.

The second page of the wizard requests that you specify the server and database to be analyzed and provides two additional options: Keep All Existing Indexes and Tuning Mode. The Tuning Mode option determines the depth of analysis performed by the wizard. Clearing the Keep All Existing Indexes check box (selected by default) allows the wizard to make recommendations regarding indexes that are not helpful for the selected workload. Be careful about this option because although an index might not be involved in the workload being analyzed, it might be providing significant performance benefits for some other query not under analysis.

Once the wizard has completed the analysis, you have the option of implementing the recommendations immediately, at a scheduled date and time in the future, or writing them out to a SQL script for later implementation.

Use the Index Tuning Wizard to tune a database

1. Expand the Indexes folder of the Oils table of the Aromatherapy database.

2. Select the Oil_PlantParts index, and press the Delete key.

The Query Analyzer requests confirmation of the index delete.

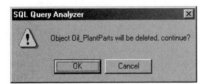

3. Click OK.

The Query Analyzer deletes the index.

4. Select the Query window, and select Index Tuning Wizard from the Query menu.

The Query Analyzer displays the first page of the Index Tuning Wizard.

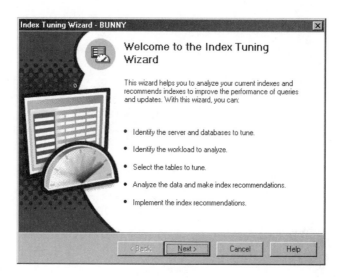

5. Click Next.

The wizard displays a page asking you to specify the database and the tuning mode.

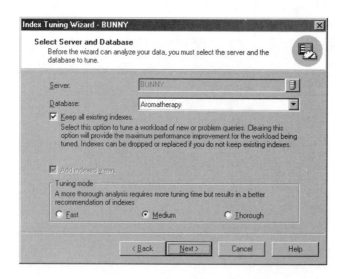

6. Make sure Aromatherapy is the selected database, and select the Thorough tuning mode.

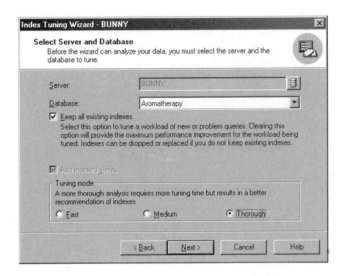

7. Click Next.

The wizard displays a page requesting the workload to be analyzed.

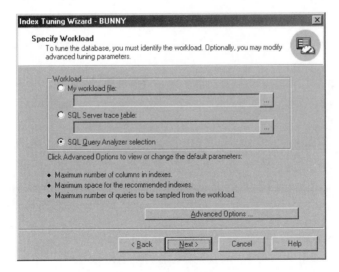

8. Click the Advanced Options button.

The wizard displays a dialog box requesting index tuning parameters.

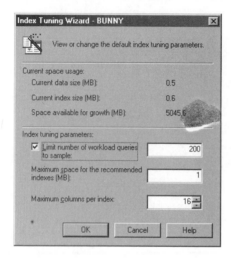

9. Accept the default tuning values by clicking OK.

10. Accept the default value SQL Query Analyzer Selection by clicking Next.

The wizard displays a page requesting you to choose the tables to tune.

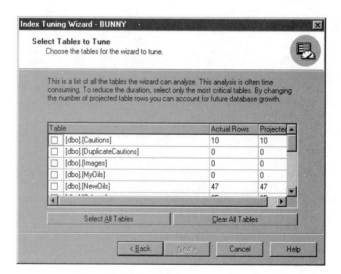

11. Select the Oils table for analysis, and set the Projected Rows value to 1000.

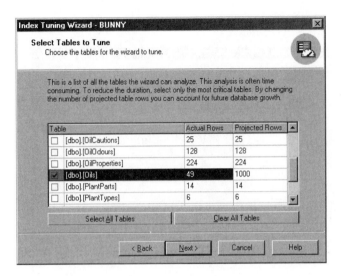

12. Click Next.

    The wizard displays its recommendations.

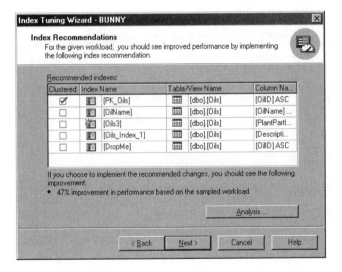

13. Click Next.

The wizard displays a page requesting your choice of execution options.

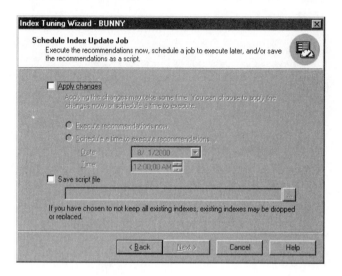

14. Select Apply Changes, and accept the default of Execute Recommendations Now.

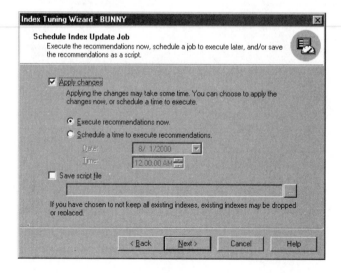

15. Click Next.

The wizard displays a final page allowing you to apply the choices you have made.

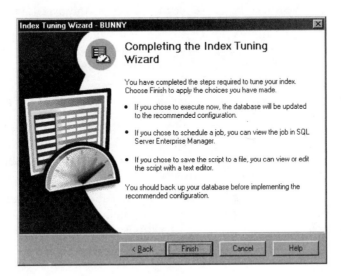

16. Click Finish.

The wizard displays a message confirming its successful completion.

Lesson 23 Quick Reference

To	Do this	Button
Display the execution plan of a SQL script	Select Show Execution Planfrom the Query menu, and execute the query.	▶
Alter a database schema from the Execution Plane Pane	Right-click the execution plan, and select Manage Indexes.	
Display a server trace of a SQL script	Select Show Server Trace from the Query menu, and execute the query.	▶
Display client statistics for a SQL script	Select Show Client Statistics from the Query menu, and execute the query.	
Use the Index Tuning Wizard to optimize the database schema	Select Index Tuning Wizard from the Query menu, and follow the instructions.	▶

```
0
ECLARE      eCursor CURSOR

               Name FROM Oils
EC             har(20)
PE

- Retrie   e first row into a varia
ETCH FIRST FROM simpleCursor
    INTO @theName

- Display the results
RINT RTRIM(@theName) + ' is the first name'
```

Transact-SQL Language Components

```
ETCH           FROM
    INTO @theName
```

In this lesson you'll learn how to:

- Use arithmetic operators in a SELECT statement.
- Use a comparison operator in a WHERE clause.
- Use logical operators in a SELECT statement.
- Use bitwise operators in a SELECT statement.
- Use the concatenation operator in a SELECT statement.
- Use date functions.
- Use mathematical functions.
- Use aggregate functions.
- Use metadata functions.
- Use security functions.
- Use string functions.
- Use system functions.

Like any programming language, Transact-SQL programs are composed of a series of statements. A *statement* is an instruction that describes (in excruciating detail) some action Microsoft SQL Server is to perform.

A statement is composed of some combination of commands, expressions, functions, operators, and symbols. A single statement can be as simple as the GO command—which you use to separate statement batches in a script—or as complex as a statement that combines any or all of these components. In this lesson, we'll examine the components of a Transact-SQL statement.

Transact-SQL Commands

At the heart of the Transact-SQL language are its commands: the core statements that define the fundamental operations the language can perform.

Reserved Words

A *reserved word* is one that is used by the language. If you use a reserved word as an identifier, for example as a column name, you must surround the name with special characters, called *delimiters*. In Microsoft SQL Server, the delimiter characters are [and]. For example, if you use SELECT as a column name, you must reference it in a query as [SELECT], so SQL Server knows it's an identifier. (You should avoid using reserved words as identifiers where possible.)

SQL Server Books Online uses the phrase "reserved keyword" to describe what we're calling "commands." This usage is unfortunate, since there is no way to distinguish between a "reserved keyword" and any other reserved word. For that reason, I'll use the term *command* here to mean the specific set of reserved keywords that represent actions SQL Server is to perform.

Considering the complexity of the applications that can be built with Transact-SQL, the language consists of surprisingly few actual commands, many of which we've already seen.

Understanding the range of Transact-SQL commands is easier if you divide them into groups based on the type of action they perform, such as manipulating the data in a table or view or controlling the SQL Server operating environment.

We've already been using Transact-SQL commands in various ways throughout this book. We've used them directly by typing them in the Editor Pane of the Query Analyzer's query window and the SQL Pane of the Enterprise Manager's Query Designer. We've also used them indirectly by manipulating tools that execute Transact-SQL commands behind the scenes. The Enterprise Manager's Table Designer, for example, issues CREATE and ALTER statements based on the selections you make.

Talking to SQL Server

Many database applications use a conventional programming language, such as Microsoft Visual Basic, to build an interactive interface to SQL Server. Using the interface controls provided by the language, these applications present data to users in a convenient and "friendly" manner. Behind the scenes, however, they issue Transact-SQL commands. Both the Enterprise Manager and the SQL Server Query Analyzer are database applications that do just that.

When you're using a conventional programming language, the language itself will determine how the commands are issued. Some environments, such as Microsoft Access, provide interactive tools similar to the Enterprise Manager and the Query Analyzer. Others, such as Visual Basic or Microsoft Visual C++, use an object model like ADO to communicate with the server.

Data Manipulation Commands

The most important SQL commands belong to the data manipulation language (DML) group that we explored in Parts II and III. DML commands are used to insert, change, remove, and retrieve data.

Table 24-1 shows the DML commands. Most of them will be familiar to you from the lessons in Parts III and IV of this book. The only commands we haven't discussed are BULK INSERT, which allows you to insert multiple rows from a data file, and USE, which specifies a database to be used in a SQL script.

Command	Function
INSERT	Inserts rows into a table or view.
UPDATE	Changes rows in a table or view.
DELETE	Removes rows from a table or view.
SELECT	Retrieves rows from a table or view.
TRUNCATE TABLE	Removes all rows from a table or view.
BULK INSERT	Inserts rows from a data file into a table or view.
USE	Connects to a database.

Table 24-1. *DML commands.*

Data Definition Commands

The data definition language (DDL) commands are shown in Table 24-2. DDL commands are used to create, change, and remove database objects. There are only three primary commands, but as we saw in Lesson 22, each command has a number of variations, depending on the nature of the database object you are creating.

Command	Function
CREATE	Defines a new database object.
ALTER	Changes the definition of a database object.
DROP	Removes a database object from the database.

Table 24-2. *DDL commands.*

Database Administration Commands

Most of the Transact-SQL commands that support database administration tasks are available interactively through the Enterprise Manager. The administration commands themselves provide the ability to perform the same tasks programmatically.

The database administration commands are shown in Table 24-3. The first set, GRANT, DENY, and REVOKE, control database security. The BACKUP, RESTORE, and UPDATE STATISTICS commands duplicate the functionality of the Enterprise Manager's maintenance plans.

The SET command is used with keywords such as DATEFORMAT and LANGUAGE that control the way the current session of SQL Server behaves. In the Enterprise Manager, most of these variables are available from the database properties dialog box.

The final two database administration commands, KILL and SHUTDOWN, are used to control SQL Server execution. KILL ends the processing associated with a specified user connection. SHUTDOWN ends SQL Server unconditionally.

Command	Function
GRANT	Grants a specified permission to a security object.
DENY	Denies a specified permission to a security object, and prevents the object from inheriting permission through its membership in a group or role.
REVOKE	Removes a specified permission to a security object.
BACKUP	Backs up a database or transaction log.
RESTORE	Restores data from a previous backup.
UPDATE STATISTICS	Refreshes the statistics used by the query processor.
SET	Controls the SQL Server environment.
KILL	Terminates a connection and all associated processing.
SHUTDOWN	Unconditionally shuts down SQL Server.

Table 24-3. *Database Administration commands.*

Other Commands

There are three remaining sets of Transact-SQL commands. The first set controls the use of programming variables. We'll examine these commands in Lesson 25.

The set of control-of-flow commands control the execution of statements within a SQL script. We'll examine the control-of-flow commands in the Lesson 26. The set of cursor-handling commands control the behavior of a special kind of object, a cursor, which points to a specific record in a table or view. We'll look at cursors in Lesson 27.

Transact-SQL Operators

An operator is a symbol that specifies an action that SQL Server is to perform. We used the concatenation operator + in Lesson 12, when we created a calculated column in a SELECT statement.

Transact-SQL operators are classified by the number of values on which they operate. This is known as the operator's *cardinality*. Transact-SQL operators have one of two cardinalities: they are either binary or unary.

Most operators are binary. An operator is *binary* if it operates on two values. The + operator in the expression *4 + 3*, and the < operator in the expression *MonthSales < MonthBudget*, are both examples of binary operators. An operator is *unary* if it operates on only a single value. The negative (–) operator in the expression *–10* is a unary operator.

Operator Precedence

When you're building complex Transact-SQL statements, it can be important to understand the order in which operators will be evaluated—their *precedence*. Precedence isn't often a problem, but it can sometimes lead you astray. For example, *3 * (4 + 1)* results in 15, whereas *3 * 4 + 1* results in 13 because the multiplication operator is evaluated before the addition operator. The multiplication operator has higher precedence.

Operators are listed in order of precedence below. Operators that have the same precedence in an expression will be executed from left to right.

1. + (positive), – (negative), and ~ (bitwise NOT)

2. *, /, %

3. + (add), + (concatenate), – (subtract)

4. = (comparison), >, <, >=, <=, <>

5. ^, &, |

6. NOT

7. AND

8. OR

9. = (assignment)

You can always control the order of evaluation using parentheses, as in the previous example.

Like Transact-SQL commands, operators are easiest to understand by grouping them according to the type of operation they perform.

Comment Operators

Transact-SQL supports two special operators which, rather than specifying an operation to be performed, tell SQL Server to ignore specific text in the script. Transact-SQL supports two comment operators. A double-dash (--) tells SQL Server to ignore anything after it on the line. It can be used at the beginning of the line, in which case SQL Server ignores the whole line, or it can be used within the line, in which case SQL Server will ignore everything from the double-dash to the end of the line.

The other comment operator is actually two operators, /* and */, which operate as a pair. SQL Server will ignore everything between the first comment operator /* and the second comment operator */, no matter how many lines are between them.

The use of the comment operators is demonstrated in Figure 24-1.

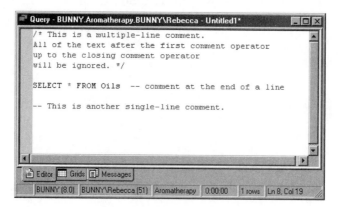

Figure 24-1. *Transact-SQL supports two comment operators.*

> **IP** The /* and */ operators are useful for temporarily disabling a set of Transact-SQL statements when you're debugging.

Arithmetic Operators

Transact-SQL provides operators for performing basic arithmetic, as shown in Table 24-4. These operators perform exactly as expected. The only one that might be unfamiliar to you is *modulo*, which returns the integer remainder of division. For example, the result of the expression *16 % 3* is 1, not $5\frac{1}{3}$.

Operator	Meaning
+	Add.
-	Subtract.
*	Multiply.
/	Divide.
%	Modulo.
+	Numeric value is positive.
-	Numeric value is negative.

Table 24-4. *Arithmetic operators.*

Use arithmetic operators in a SELECT statement

*New Query
button*

1. Click the New Query button on the Query Analyzer toolbar to open a new Query window.

   The Query Analyzer opens a blank Query window.

*Load Script
button*

2. Click the Load Script button on the Query Analyzer toolbar.

   The Query Analyzer displays the Open Query File dialog box.

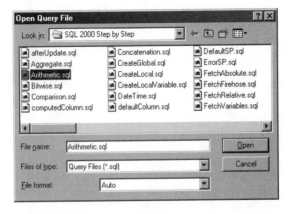

3. Select the file named Arithmetic in the SQL 2000 Step by Step folder in the root directory, and click Open.

The Query Analyzer loads the script into the Query window.

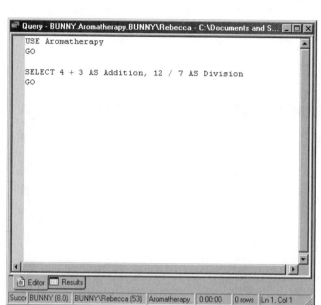

4. Click the Execute Query button on the Query Analyzer toolbar to execute the query.

Execute Query button

The Query Analyzer displays the results in the Grids Pane.

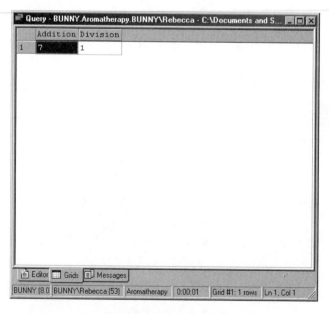

5. Close the Query window.

Comparison Operators

We looked at the use of comparison operators in constructing WHERE clauses in Lesson 13. These operators are repeated in Table 24-5. Comparison operators return a Boolean value of TRUE or FALSE.

Operator	Meaning
=	Equal to.
>	Greater than.
<	Less than.
>=	Greater than or equal to.
<=	Less than or equal to.
<>	Not equal to.

Table 24-5. *Comparison operators.*

Use a comparison operator in a WHERE clause

New Query button

1. Click the New Query button on the Query Analyzer toolbar to open a new Query window.

   The Query Analyzer opens a blank Query window.

Load Script button

2. Click the Load Script button on the Query Analyzer toolbar.

   The Query Analyzer displays the Open Query File dialog box.

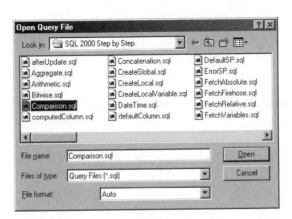

3. Select the file named Comparison, and click Open.

The Query Analyzer loads the script into the Query window.

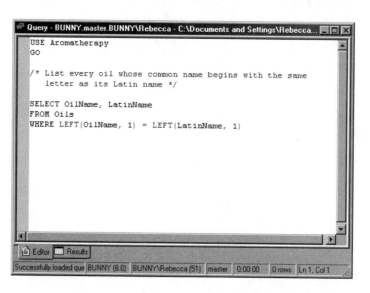

4. Click the Execute Query button on the Query Analyzer toolbar to execute the query.

Execute Query button

The Query Analyzer displays the results in the Grids Pane.

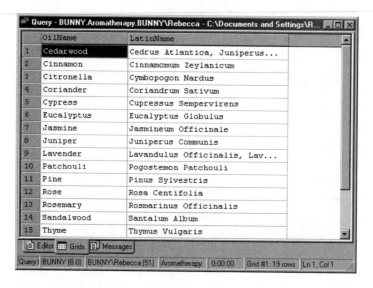

5. Close the Query window.

Logical Operators

Like comparison operators, logical operators return a Boolean value of TRUE or FALSE, but their use is restricted to comparing Boolean values. Table 24-6 shows the three logical operators supported by SQL Server.

Operator	Meaning
AND	TRUE if both of two values are TRUE.
NOT	Reverses the value of a Boolean operator.
OR	TRUE if either of two values is TRUE.

Table 24-6. *Logical operators.*

Use logical operators in a SELECT statement

New Query button

1. Click the New Query button on the Query Analyzer toolbar to open a new Query window.

   The Query Analyzer opens a blank Query window.

Load Script button

2. Click the Load Script button on the Query Analyzer toolbar.

   The Query Analyzer displays the Open Query File dialog box.

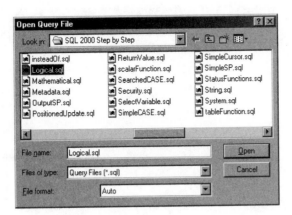

3. Select the file named Logical, and click Open.

The Query Analyzer loads the script into the Query window.

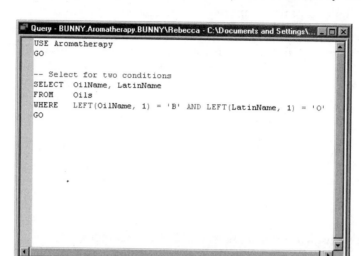

*Execute Query
button*

4. Click the Execute Query button on the Query Analyzer toolbar to execute the query.

   The Query Analyzer displays the results in the Grids Pane.

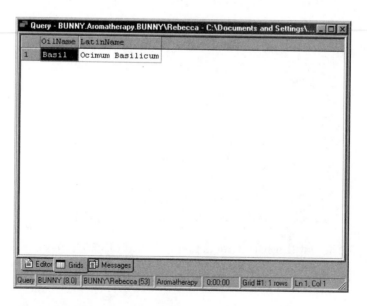

5. Close the Query window.

Bitwise Operators

Bitwise operators perform operations very similar to the logical operators, but whereas logical operators return results based on Boolean values, bitwise operators work at the bit level on integer values. The bitwise operators are shown in Table 24-7.

The bitwise & and | operators function in the same way as their logical counterparts, with the exception that they compare each bit of the two values instead of the two values as a whole.

The ^ operator does not have a corresponding logical operator. In Boolean algebra, a Boolean OR returns TRUE if either or both of the values being compared is TRUE. However, a Boolean exclusive OR returns TRUE if one, but not both, of the values being compared is TRUE. This is exactly what the ^ operator does: it returns TRUE only if one, but not both, of the bits being compared is TRUE.

Operator	Meaning
&	Bitwise AND.
|	Bitwise OR.
^	Bitwise exclusive OR.
~	Bitwise NOT.

Table 24-7.   *Bitwise operators.*

Bit packing

Bitwise operators are required to manipulate integer values that use each bit in the integer to indicate a separate property or attribute, a technique called "bit packing." By definition, if a single integer is being used to store multiple properties, the value is not scalar, and the table is therefore not in normal form.

You should not, under normal circumstances, use bit packing in a relational database. However, bit-packed values are sometimes unavoidable if you're using legacy data, and the bitwise operators are very convenient in those situations.

Use bitwise operators in a SELECT statement

New Query button

1. Click the New Query button on the Query Analyzer toolbar to open a new Query window.

   The Query Analyzer opens a blank Query window.

Load Script button

2. Click the Load Script button on the Query Analyzer toolbar.

   The Query Analyzer displays the Open Query File dialog box.

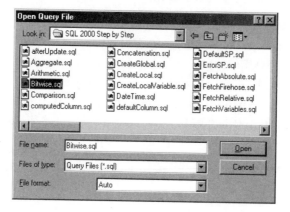

3. Select the file named Bitwise, and click Open.

   The Query Analyzer loads the script into the Query window.

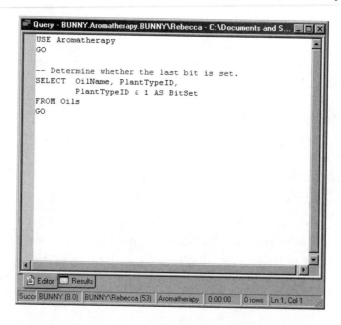

Execute Query button

4. Click the Execute Query button on the Query Analyzer toolbar to execute the query.

The Query Analyzer displays the results in the Grids Pane.

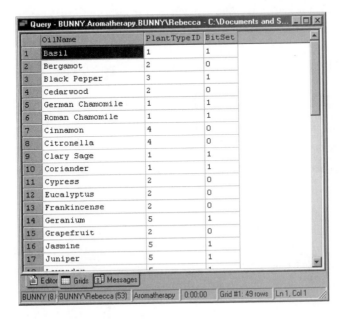

5. Close the Query window.

Other Operators

Transact-SQL provides two other useful operators, shown in Table 24-8. We've already used the string concatenation operator, +, in Lesson 12. The concatenation operator appends the contents of one string to another.

The assignment operator, =, assigns the value on the right side of the operator to the value on the left. Note that this is the reverse of the order you learned in school: not "a + b = c", but "c = a + b". We'll use assignment operator later in this lesson when we look at variables.

Operator	Meaning
+	String concatenation.
=	Assignment.

Table 24-8. *Other operators.*

507

Use the concatenation operator in a SELECT statement

New Query button

1. Click the New Query button on the Query Analyzer toolbar to open a new Query window.

   The Query Analyzer opens a blank Query window.

Load Script button

2. Click the Load Script button on the Query Analyzer toolbar.

   The Query Analyzer displays the Open Query File dialog box.

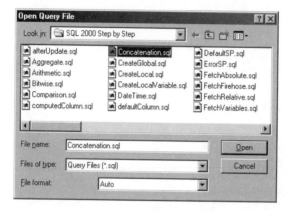

3. Select the file named Concatenation, and click Open.

   The Query Analyzer loads the script into the Query window.

Execute Query button

4. Click the Execute Query button on the Query Analyzer toolbar to execute the query.

The Query Analyzer displays the results in the Grids Pane.

5. Close the Query window.

Transact-SQL Functions

A function is very much like an operator, but instead of a single symbol that results in a single action, a function is composed of multiple statements. A function should perform a single *logical* action, but that logical action can be comprised of any number of physical actions. For example, a function that moves a row from one table to another performs a single logical action (move), but two separate physical actions (an INSERT and a DELETE).

New to SQL Server 2000 is the ability to create your own functions, which are called *user-defined functions*. We'll examine these in Lesson 30. Transact-SQL also provides a number of built-in functions, which we'll discuss here.

IP Not all of the available functions are listed in the tables in this section. The complete list is available in the Common Objects folder of the Object Browser.

Using Functions

Built-in Transact-SQL functions are classified by the nature of the results they return; they are either deterministic or non-deterministic. A *deterministic* function, given the same data values on which to operate, will always return the same result: *SQRT(9)* always returns 3, so the SQRT function is deterministic. A non-deterministic function such as RAND, on the other hand, will return different results each time it's called.

Functions can be used in many places within Transact-SQL. Column defaults, computed columns in tables or views, and the selection criteria in a WHERE clause are only a few examples. However, the determinism of a function establishes whether it can be used in an index. Since index scans must always return consistent results, only deterministic functions can be used in indexes.

Date and Time Functions

Date and time functions accept date and time input values and return either string, numeric, or date and time values. (Remember that time is considered a component of the *datetime* datatype in SQL Server.) The *datepart* parameter specified in many of the functions is actually the unit of measurement, such as "year" or "minute." Table 24-9 shows the Transact-SQL date and time functions.

Function	Parameters	Operation
DATEADD	*datepart, number, date*	Calculates a new date by adding the specified *number* of *datepart* intervals to *date*.
DATEDIFF	*datepart, startdate, enddate*	Returns the number of *dateparts* between the two specified dates.
DATENAME	*datepart, date*	Returns the name of the specified *datepart* in the *date* as a character string.

Table 24-9. *Date and time functions.*

(continued)

continued

Function	Parameters	Operation
DATEPART	*datepart, date*	Returns the specified *datepart* in the *date* as an integer value.
DAY	*date*	Returns the day specified in *date* as an integer value.
GETDATE		Returns the current system date and time.
MONTH	*date*	Returns the month specified in *date* as an integer value.
YEAR	*date*	Returns the year specified in *date* as an integer value.

Use date functions

New Query button

1. Clicking the New Query button on the Query Analyzer toolbar to open a new Query window.

   The Query Analyzer opens a blank Query window.

Load Script button

2. Click the Load Script button on the Query Analyzer toolbar.

   The Query Analyzer displays the Open Query File dialog box.

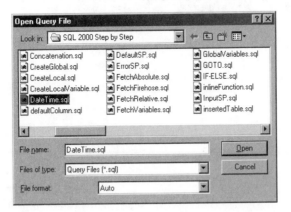

3. Select the file named DateTime, and click Open.

The Query Analyzer loads the script into the Query window.

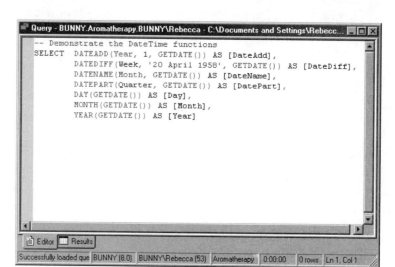

4. Click the Execute Query button on the Query Analyzer toolbar to execute the query.

The Query Analyzer displays the results in the Grids Pane.

Execute Query button

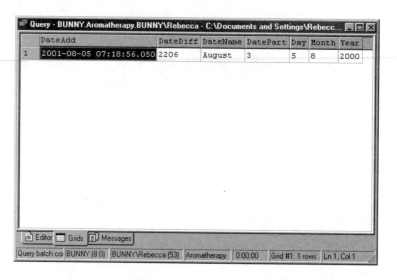

5. Close the Query window.

Mathematical Functions

The mathematical functions, shown in Table 24-10, perform numerical calculations.

Function	Parameters	Operation
ABS	*numeric_expression*	Returns the absolute value of *numeric_expression*.
ACOS	*float_expression*	Returns the arccosine of *float_expression*.
ASIN	*float_expression*	Returns the arcsine of *float_expression*.
ATAN	*float_expression*	Returns the arctangent of *float_expression*.
ATN2	*float_expression, float_expression*	Returns the angle, in radians, whose tangent is between the two *float_expression* values.
CEILING	*numeric_expression*	Returns the smallest integer greater than or equal to *numeric_expression*.
COS	*float_expression*	Returns the trigonometric cosine of *float_expression*.
COT	*float_expression*	Returns the trigonometric cotangent of *float_expression*.
DEGREES	*numeric_expression*	Given an angle in radians, returns the angle in degrees of *numeric_expression*.
EXP	*float_expression*	Returns the exponent value of *float_expression*.
FLOOR	*numeric_expression*	Returns the largest integer less than or equal to *numeric_expression*.

Table 24-10. *Mathematical functions.* (continued)

Table 24-10. *continued*

Function	Parameters	Operation
LOG	*float_expression*	Returns the natural logarithm of *float_expression*.
LOG10	*float_expression*	Returns the base-10 logarithm of *float_expression*.
PI		Returns the constant value of pi.
POWER	*numeric_expression*, *y*	Returns the value of *numeric_expression* raised to the power of *y*.
RADIANS	*numeric_expression*	Given an angle *numeric_expression* in degrees, returns the angle in radians.
RAND	[*seed*]	Returns a random float value between 0 and 1.
ROUND	*numeric_expression*, *length*	Returns *numeric_expression* rounded to length.
SIGN	*numeric_expression*	Returns +1 if *numeric_expression* is positive, 0 if *numeric_expression* is zero, and −1 if *numeric_expression* is negative.
SIN	*float_expression*	Returns the trigonometric sine of the given angle *float_expression* in radians.
SQUARE	*float_expression*	Returns the square of *float_expression*.
SQRT	*float_expression*	Returns the square root of *float_expression*.
TAN	*float_expression*	Returns the tangent of *float_expression*.

Use mathematical functions

New Query button

1. Click the New Query button on the Query Analyzer toolbar to open a new Query window.

   The Query Analyzer opens a blank Query window.

Load Script button

2. Click the Load Script button on the Query Analyzer toolbar.

   The Query Analyzer displays the Open Query File dialog box.

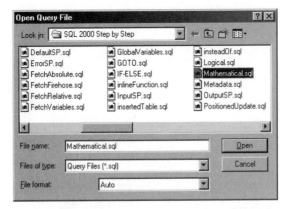

3. Select the file named Mathematical, and click Open.

   The Query Analyzer loads the script into the Query window.

Execute Query button

4. Click the Execute Query button on the Query Analyzer toolbar to execute the query.

The Query Analyzer displays the results in the Grids Pane.

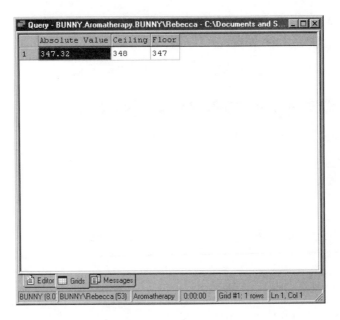

5. Close the Query window.

Aggregate Functions

Aggregate functions, shown in Table 24-11, take a collection of values as a parameter, and return a single value.

Function	Operation
AVG	Returns the average of the values in the collection, ignoring NULL values.
COUNT	Returns the number of values in the collection, including NULL values.
MAX	Returns the largest (maximum) value in the collection.
MIN	Returns the smallest (minimum) value in the collection.

Table 24-11.   *Aggregate functions.*   *(continued)*

continued

Function	Operation
SUM	Returns the sum of the values in the collection, ignoring NULL values.
STDEV	Returns the statistical standard deviation of the values in the collection.
STDEVP	Returns the statistical standard deviation for the population for all values in the collection.
VAR	Returns the statistical variation of the values in the group.
VARP	Returns the statistical variation for the population for all values in the collection.

Use aggregate functions

New Query button

1. Click the New Query button on the Query Analyzer toolbar to open a new Query window.

   The Query Analyzer opens a blank Query window.

Load Script button

2. Click the Load Script button on the Query Analyzer toolbar.

   The Query Analyzer displays the Open Query File dialog box.

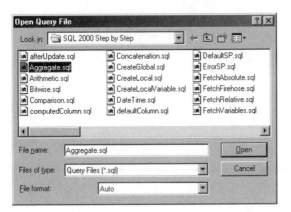

3. Select the file named Aggregate, and click Open.

The Query Analyzer loads the script into the Query window.

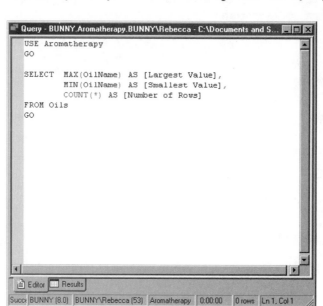

4. Click the Execute Query button on the Query Analyzer toolbar to execute the query.

Execute Query button

The Query Analyzer displays the results in the Grids Pane.

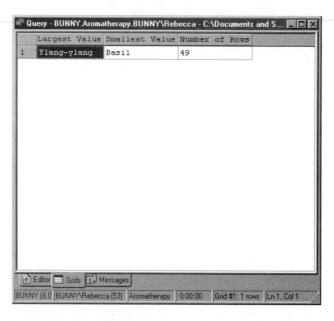

5. Close the Query window.

Metadata Functions

Metadata functions return information *about* the data, rather than the data itself. There are a large number of metadata functions available. Table 24-12 lists the most commonly used metadata functions.

Function	Parameters	Operation
COL_LENGTH	*table*, *column*	Returns the length of *column* in bytes.
COL_NAME	*tableID*, *columnID*	Returns the name of *columnID*.
COLUMNPROPERTY	*ID*, *column*, *property*	Returns *property* information about *column*.
DATABASEPROPERTY	*database*, *property*	Returns the value of *property*.
DB_ID	*database_name*	Returns the database identification number of *database_name*.
DB_NAME	*databaseID*	Returns the database name of *databaseID*.
INDEX_COL	*table*, *indexID*, *keyID*	Returns the indexed column name for *indexID* and *keyID*.
INDEXPROPERTY	*tableID*, *index*, *property*	Returns the value of *property* for *index*.
OBJECT_ID	*object*	Returns the database *object* identification number.
OBJECT_NAME	*objectID*	Returns the object name for *objectID*.
OBJECTPROPERTY	*ID*, *property*	Returns *property* information about the object *ID*.
SQL_VARIANT_PROPERTY	*SQL_variant*, *property*	Returns the specified *property* of the variant.
TYPEPROPERTY	*datatype*, *property*	Returns *property* information about *datatype*.

Table 24-12. *Metadata functions.*

Use metadata functions

New Query button

1. Click the New Query button on the Query Analyzer toolbar to open a new Query window.

   The Query Analyzer opens a blank Query window.

Load Script button

2. Click the Load Script button on the Query Analyzer toolbar.

   The Query Analyzer displays the Open Query File dialog box.

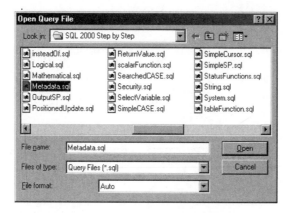

3. Select the file named Metadata, and click Open.

   The Query Analyzer loads the script into the Query window.

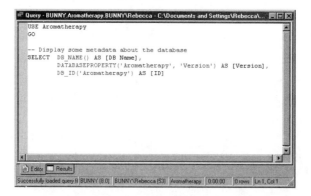

4. Click the Execute Query button on the Query Analyzer toolbar to execute the query.

Execute Query button

The Query Analyzer displays the results in the Grids Pane.

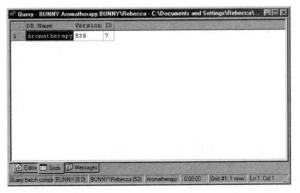

5. Close the Query window.

Security Functions

Security functions, shown in Table 24-13, return information about the security privileges assigned to users and roles.

Function	Parameters	Operation
HAS_DBACCESS	*database_name*	Indicates whether the current user has access to *database_name*.
IS_MEMBER	*group_or_role*	Indicates whether the current user is a member of g*roup_or_role*.
IS_SRVROLEMEMBER	*role* [, *login*]	Indicates whether the current or specified *login* is a member of *role*.
SUSER_SID	[*login*]	Returns the security identification number (SID) of the current or specified *login*.
SUSER_SNAME	[*SID*]	Returns the login name of *SID*.
USER_ID	[*user*]	Returns the identification number of the current or specified *user*.
USER		Returns the current user's database username.

Table 24-13. *Security functions.*

Use security functions

New Query button

1. Click the New Query button on the Query Analyzer toolbar to open a new Query window.

   The Query Analyzer opens a blank Query window.

Load Script button

2. Click the Load Script button on the Query Analyzer toolbar.

   The Query Analyzer displays the Open Query File dialog box.

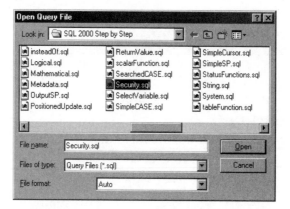

3. Select the file named Security, and click Open.

   The Query Analyzer loads the script into the Query window.

Execute Query button

4. Click the Execute Query button on the Query Analyzer toolbar to execute the query.

   The Query Analyzer displays the results in the Grids Pane.

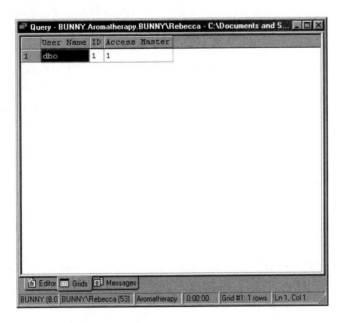

5. Close the Query window.

String Functions

The string functions perform operations on string values, and return either string or numeric values. Table 24-14 lists the most common string functions.

Function	Parameters	Operation
ASCII	*char_expression*	Returns the ASCII code of the leftmost character in *char_expression*.
CHAR	*integer_expression*	Returns the ASCII character with the integer code *integer_expression*.
CHARINDEX	*char_expression,* *char_expression* [*, start_position*]	Returns the position of the first *char_expression* in the second *char_expression*.

Table 24-14. *String functions.* *(continued)*

Table 24-14. *continued*

Function	Parameters	Operation
LEFT	*char_expression, integer_expression*	Returns the leftmost *integer_expression* characters in *char_expression*.
LEN	*char_expression*	Returns the number of characters in *char_expression*.
LOWER	*char_expression*	Returns *char_expression* with all characters converted to lowercase.
LTRIM	*char_expression*	Returns *char_expression* stripped of leading spaces.
NCHAR	*integer_expression*	Returns the Unicode character with the integer code *integer_expression*.
REPLACE	*char_expression, char_expression, char_expression*	Finds all instances of the second *char_expression* in the first *char_expression* and replaces them with the third *char_expression*.
RIGHT	*char_expression, integer_expression*	Returns the rightmost *integer_expression* characters in *char_expression*.
RTRIM	*char_expression*	Returns *char_expression* stripped of trailing spaces.
SOUNDEX	*char_expression*	Returns the four-character SOUNDEX code for *char_expression*.
SPACE	*integer_expression*	Returns *integer_expression* number of spaces.
SUBSTRING	*char_expression, start, length*	Returns *length* characters of *char_expression*, starting at position *start*.
UNICODE	*unicode_expression*	Returns the Unicode integer value of the first character in *unicode_expression*.
UPPER	*char_expression*	Returns *char_expression* with all characters converted to uppercase.

Use string functions

New Query button

1. Click the New Query button on the Query Analyzer toolbar to open a new Query window.

The Query Analyzer opens a blank Query window.

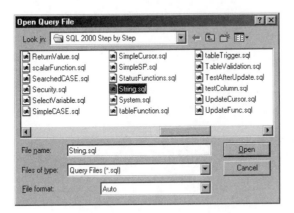

2. Click the Load Script button on the Query Analyzer toolbar.

Load Script button

The Query Analyzer displays the Open Query File dialog box.

3. Select the file named String, and click Open.

The Query Analyzer loads the script into the Query window.

4. Click the Execute Query button on the Query Analyzer toolbar to execute the query.

Execute Query button

The Query Analyzer displays the results in the Grids Pane.

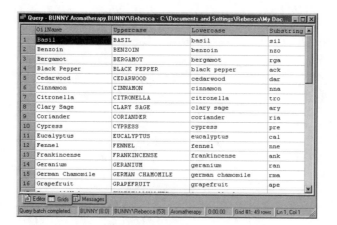

5. Close the Query window.

System Functions

System functions return information about the SQL Server environment. Like metadata functions, there are many system functions, all of them available from the Object Browser. Table 24-15 lists the most common system functions.

Function	Parameters	Operation
APP_NAME		Returns the application name.
DATALENGTH	*expression*	Returns the number of bytes used to represent *expression*.
ISDATE	*expression*	Determines whether *expression* is a valid date.
ISNULL	*expression*	Determines whether *expression* is NULL.
ISNUMERIC	*expression*	Determines whether *expression* is numeric.
NEWID		Creates a new, unique, *uniqueidentifier*.
NULLIF	*expression*, *expression*	Returns NULL if the first and second *expression* are equivalent.
PARSENAME	*object_name*, *name_part*	Returns *name_part* of *object_name*.
SYSTEM_USER		Returns the current system user name.
USER_NAME	[*id*]	Returns the user name of the current or specified user *id*.

Table 24-15. *System functions.*

Use system functions

New Query button

1. Click the New Query button on the Query Analyzer toolbar to open a new Query window.

   The Query Analyzer opens a blank Query window.

Load Script button

2. Click the Load Script button on the Query Analyzer toolbar.

   The Query Analyzer displays the Open Query File dialog box.

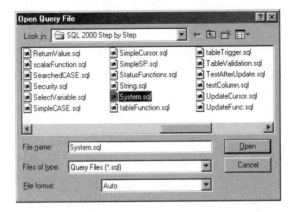

3. Select the file named System, and click Open.

   The Query Analyzer loads the script into the Query window.

*Execute Query
button*

4. Click the Execute Query button on the Query Analyzer toolbar to execute the query.

The Query Analyzer displays the results in the Grids Pane.

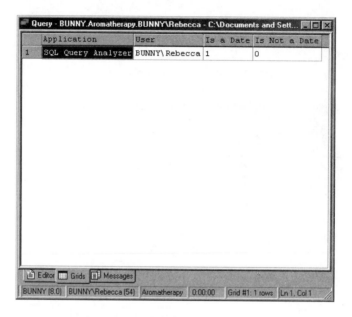

5. Close the Query window.

```
ECLARE        Cursor CURSOR

              Name FROM Oils
EC            har(20)
PE

- Retr     the first row into a varia
ETCH FIRST FROM simpleCursor
    INTO @theName

- Display the results
RINT RTRIM(@theName) + ' is the first name'

- Re
ETCH                          ur
   INTO @theName
```

Programming Objects

In this lesson you'll learn how to:

- Create a local temporary table.
- Create a global temporary table.
- Create a local variable.
- Use a global variable.
- Set the value of a variable using the SET command.
- Set the value of a variable using the SELECT command.

Like any programming language, Transact-SQL provides mechanisms for creating generic, reusable procedures. Two of the most important of these procedures are the ability to create temporary objects and the ability to pass specific values to and from generic procedures.

Temporary objects are supported in Transact-SQL through the creation of temporary tables and the use of variables. Passing specific values to functions and stored procedures is supported using parameters. We'll examine temporary tables and variables in this lesson and parameters in Lesson 28.

Temporary Tables

Temporary tables are like normal tables except that they exist only while they are being used. They are automatically dropped by Microsoft SQL Server when all users are finished with them.

 TIP Creating a temporary table is a fairly expensive procedure in terms of server resources and CPU cycles. Many of the traditional uses of temporary tables can now be replaced with the use of table variables.

Understanding Temporary Tables

Temporary tables are created using the same commands that Transact-SQL uses to create a normal table—either CREATE or SELECT INTO. The difference is that temporary table names begin with either # or ##. Thus the first statement below creates a normal table, and the second statement creates a temporary table.

```
CREATE TABLE NormalTable (theKey INT PRIMARY KEY, theValue CHAR(20))

CREATE TABLE #TemporaryTable (theKey INT PRIMARY KEY, theValue CHAR(20))
```

The only restriction on the creation of temporary tables is that they cannot have FOREIGN KEY constraints. All the other functionality of the CREATE TABLE statement is available—temporary tables can have CHECK constraints, default values, whatever structure you need.

Temporary tables are always created in the tempdb system database. Since tempdb is always re-created whenever SQL Server starts, temporary tables cannot persist between sessions. But temporary tables will always be destroyed when they go out of scope—that is, when no one is using them.

The scope of a temporary table is determined by its name. Temporary tables named with a single hash, like #MyTable, have *local* scope. Temporary tables named with two hashes, like ##MyTable, have *global* scope.

Local temporary tables (sometimes called private temporary tables) are visible only to the connection that creates them. No other connection (even one made by the same user) can see or access them. The connection that creates the temporary table can drop it at any time, but if it's still in existence when the user logs off, SQL Server will drop the table automatically.

Global temporary tables created with a double hash are accessible to all users. There's no need to specifically grant privileges to a global temporary table; any user has privileges automatically.

Global temporary tables can be explicitly dropped, or SQL Server will drop them when the creating connection logs off and all current use of the table is completed. For example, if User A creates the temporary table ##MyTable, User B can execute commands against it. If User A logs off while User B is using ##MyTable, any commands SQL Server is currently executing will complete, but User B will not be able to issue any further commands using that table.

Using Temporary Tables

Temporary tables are created using the same CREATE and SELECT INTO commands as normal tables. Provided the table in question is available to the connection (that is, it isn't a local table created by a different connection), it can also be used exactly like normal tables.

Create a local temporary table

New Query button

1. Click the New Query button on the Query Analyzer toolbar to open a new Query window.

2. Click the Load Script button on the Query Analyzer toolbar.

Load Script button

The Query Analyzer displays the Open Query File dialog box.

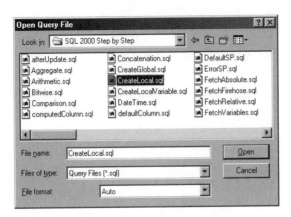

3. Select the CreateLocal script, and click Open.

   The Query Analyzer loads the script.

Execute Query button

4. Click the Execute Query button on the Query Analyzer toolbar.

   The Query Analyzer creates the temporary table.

5. Select the User Tables folder of the tempdb database in the Object Browser.

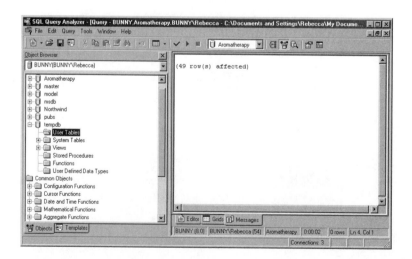

6. Press F5 to refresh the Object Browser display, and expand the User Tables folder.

The Query Analyzer displays dbo.#LocalTable in the list.

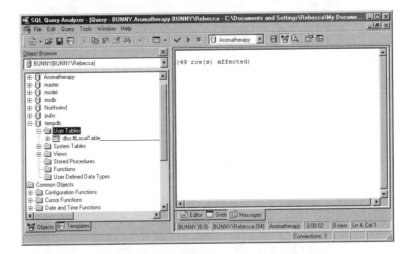

Create a global temporary table

New Query button

1. Without closing the window containing the CreateLocal script, click the New Query button on the Query Analyzer toolbar to open a new Query window.

Load Script button

2. Click the Load Script button on the Query Analyzer toolbar.

The Query Analyzer displays the Open Query File dialog box.

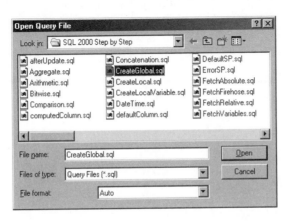

3. Select the CreateGlobal script, and click Open.

The Query Analyzer loads the script.

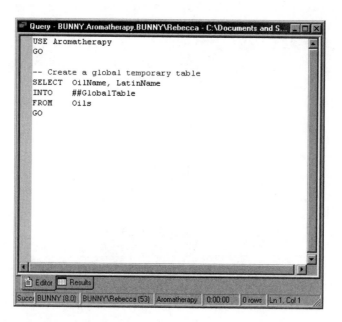

*Execute Query
button*

4. Click the Execute Query button on the Query Analyzer toolbar.

The Query Analyzer creates the temporary table.

5. Select the User Tables folder of the tempdb database in the Object Browser.

6. Press F5 to refresh the Object Browser display.

The Query Analyzer displays dbo.##GlobalTable in the list.

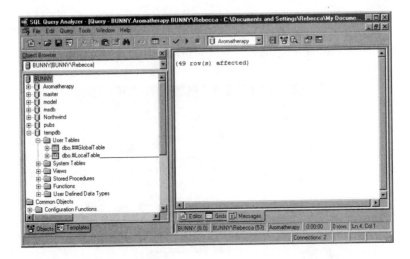

Use a local temporary table from the current session

1. Select the Query window containing the CreateLocal script.

Load Script button

2. Click the Load Script button in the Query Analyzer toolbar.

   The Query Analyzer displays the Open Query File dialog box.

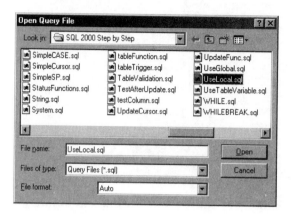

3. Select the UseLocal script, and click Open.

   The Query Analyzer opens the script.

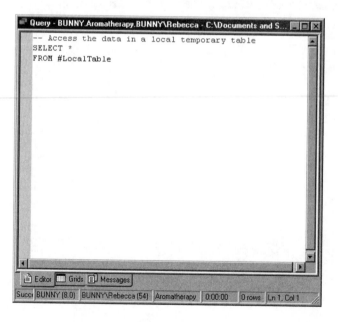

Execute Query button

4. Click the Execute Query button on the Query Analyzer toolbar.

The Query Analyzer executes the SELECT statement.

Use a global temporary table from the current session

1. Select the window containing the CreateGlobal script.

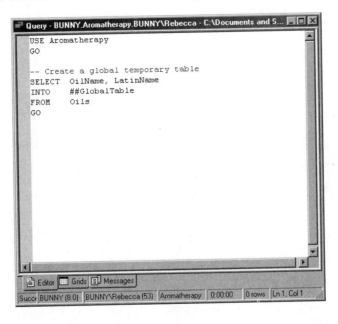

Load Script button

2. Click the Load Script button on the Query Analyzer toolbar.

The Query Analyzer displays the Open Query File dialog box.

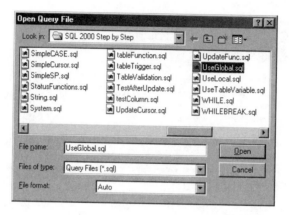

3. Select the UseGlobal script, and click Open.

The Query Analyzer loads the script.

Execute Query button

4. Click the Execute Query button on the Query Analyzer toolbar.

The Query Analyzer executes the SELECT statement.

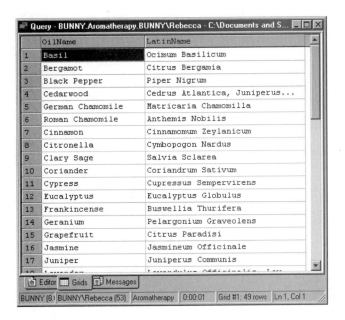

Attempt to use a local temporary table from another session

New Query button

1. Click the New Query button on the Query Analyzer toolbar.

   The Query Analyzer opens a new Query window.

Load Script button

2. Click the Load Script button on the Query Analyzer toolbar.

   The Query Analyzer displays the Open Query File dialog box.

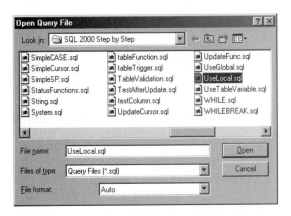

3. Select the UseLocal script, and click Open.

   The Query Analyzer loads the script into the Query window.

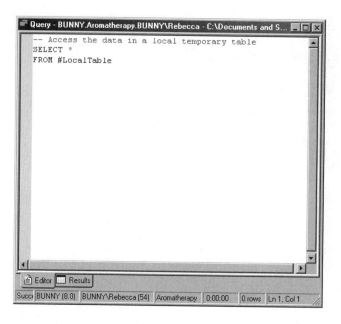

*Execute Query
button*

4. Click the Execute Query button on the Query Analyzer toolbar.

Because the local temporary table is not visible to the new query session, the Query Analyzer displays an error message.

Use a global temporary table from another session

Load SQL Script button

1. Click the Load SQL Script button on the Query Analyzer toolbar.

   The Query Analyzer displays the Open Query File dialog box.

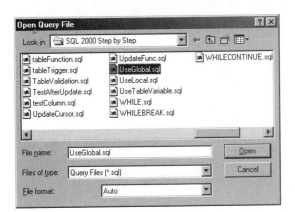

2. Select the UseGlobal script, and click Open.

   The Query Analyzer loads the script into the Query window.

Execute Query button

3. Click the Execute Query button on the Query Analyzer toolbar.

Because the global temporary table is visible to the new session, the Query Analyzer displays the results.

4. Close two of the open Query windows, leaving one open to maintain the connection to the server. If prompted to save changes, click No.

Variables

Although temporary tables are very useful in certain situations, any sort of programming would be all but impossible without variables, which are programming objects that are used to temporarily store values.

Understanding Variables

Variables are identified by the prefix @; for example, @myVariable. Like temporary tables, variables have two levels of scope: local and global, with global variables being identified with a double @: @@VERSION.

There are a couple of differences between variables and temporary tables. All global variables are defined by SQL Server; it isn't possible to define your own. Also, the scope of a local variable is even narrower than that of a local table: it is available only within the batch or procedure in which it is declared.

Local variables

Local variables are created using the DECLARE statement, which has the following syntax.

```
DECLARE @local_variable data_type
```

The *local_variable* identifier must comply with the normal rules for database identifiers; *data_type* can be any of the system data types except *text, ntext,* or *image.* Multiple local variables can be created with a single DECLARE statement by separating them with commas:

```
DECLARE @var1 int, @var2 int
```

The majority of data types are *scalar;* that is, they contain a single value such as a number or a string. The ability to declare variables with a table data type is new in SQL Server 2000. The syntax for creating a table-type variable is shown below.

```
DECLARE @local_variable TABLE ({table_definition})
```

In this example, *table_definition* is identical to a normal CREATE TABLE definition except that the only constraints allowed are PRIMARY KEY, UNIQUE KEY, NULL, and CHECK.

 IP Another useful data type for a variable is *sql_variant.* Variants can hold any type of data. This allows you to assign different types of data to a single local variable over the course of a procedure.

When a local variable is initially created it has a value of NULL. You can assign a value to a variable in the following ways:

- Using the SET command with a constant or expression:

  ```
  SET @myCharVariable = 'Hello, World'
  ```

- Using the SELECT command with a constant or expression:

  ```
  SELECT @myCharVariable = 'Hello, World'
  ```

- Using the SELECT command with another SELECT statement:

  ```
  SELECT @myCharVariable = MAX(OilName) FROM Oils
  ```

- Using the INSERT INTO command with a table-type variable:

  ```
  INSERT INTO @myTableVariable
      SELECT * FROM Oils
  ```

Notice in the third form (the SELECT with another SELECT), the assignment operator (=) replaces the second SELECT keyword; it is not repeated. The last example shows the INSERT INTO...SELECT syntax of the INSERT INTO command. You can also use the INSERT INTO...VALUES syntax:

```
INSERT INTO @myTableVariable
    VALUES ('The Value')
```

Global variables

Global variables, identified with a double @ sign (@@VERSION) are provided by SQL Server and cannot be created by the user. Dozens of global variables are available. Most global variables provide information about the current status of SQL Server. All of them are listed in the Common Functions folder of the Object Browser.

Configuration variables

The most commonly used configuration variables are shown in Table 25-1. They provide information about the current settings of various SQL Server properties and parameters.

Variable	Value
@@CONNECTIONS	The number of connections or attempted connections since the server was last started
@@DATEFIRST	Returns a number indicating the day of the week defined as the first day of the week (Monday = 1, Sunday = 7)
@@DBTS	The last value for a timestamp column inserted into the database
@@LANGID	The local language identifier of the language currently in use
@@LANGUAGE	The name of the language currently in use
@@OPTIONS	Returns the value of a current SET option
@@SERVERNAME	The name of the local server
@@VERSION	The date, version, and processor type of the current installation

Table 25-1.   *Configuration Variables.*

Statistical variables

Statistical variables provide information about what SQL Server has done since it was last started. The most common variables are shown in Table 25-2.

Variable	Value
@@CPU_BUSY	The time that the CPU has spent working since the server was last started
@@IDLE	The time that SQL Server has been idle since the server was last started
@@IO_BUSY	The time that SQL Server has spent performing input and output since the server was last started
@@TOTAL_ERRORS	The number of disk read/write errors encountered since the server was last started
@@TOTAL_READ	The number of disk reads performed by the server since it was last started
@@TOTAL_WRITE	The number of disk writes performed by the server since it was last started

Table 25-2. *Statistical Variables.*

System variables

The system variables are shown in Table 25-3. They provide information about the most recent table actions performed by the server.

Variable	Value
@@IDENTITY	The last value for an identity column inserted into the database
@@ROWCOUNT	The number of rows affected by the last statement

Table 25-3. *System Variables.*

Using Variables

Variables can be used in expressions throughout the Transact-SQL language. However, they cannot be used in place of object names or keywords. Thus the following statements are correct:

```
DECLARE @theOil char(20)
SET @theOil = 'Basil'

-- This command will execute
SELECT OilName, Description
FROM Oils
WHERE OilName = @theOil
```

However, both of the following SELECT statements will fail:

```
DECLARE @theCommand char(10), @theField char(10)
SET @theCommand = 'SELECT'
SET @theField = 'OilName'

-- This command will fail
@theCommand * FROM Oils

-- So will this one
SELECT @theField from Oils
```

Declare a local variable

New Query button

Load Script

1. Click the New Query button on the Query Analyzer toolbar to open a new Query window.

2. Click the Load Script button on the Query Analyzer toolbar.

   The Query Analyzer displays the Open Query File dialog box.

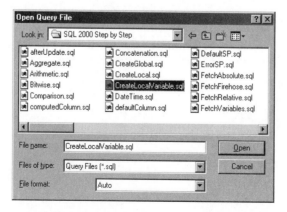

3. Select the CreateLocalVariable script, and click Open.

The Query Analyzer loads the script into the Query window.

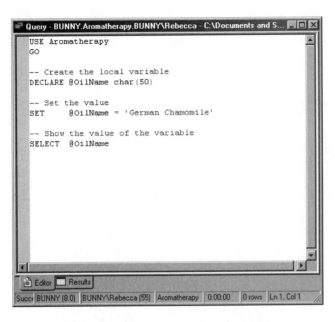

4. Click the Execute Query button on the Query Analyzer toolbar.

The Query Analyzer executes the script and displays the results.

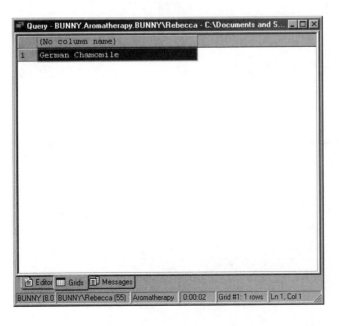

Execute Query button

Use SELECT to assign a value

New Query button

Load Script button

1. Select the Editor Pane in the query window, or open a new Query window if you closed the window used in the previous exercise.

2. Click the Load Script button on the Query Analyzer toolbar.

   The Query Analyzer displays the Open Query File dialog box.

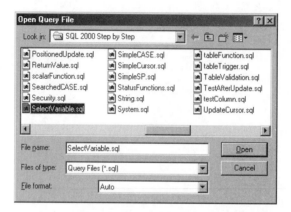

3. Select the SelectVariable script, and click Open.

   The Query Analyzer loads the script into the Query window.

Execute Query button

4. Click the Execute Query button on the Query Analyzer toolbar.

The Query Analyzer executes the script and displays the results.

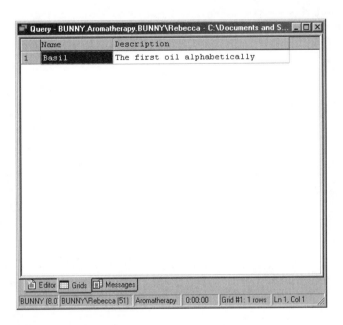

Use a table variable

New Query button

Load Script button

1. Select the Editor Pane in the Query window, or open a new Query window if you closed the window used in the previous exercise.

2. Click the Load Script button on the Query Analyzer toolbar.

The Query Analyzer displays the Open Query File dialog box.

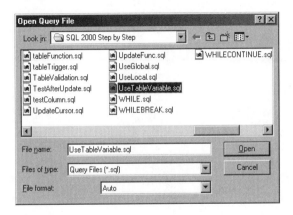

549

3. Select the UseTableVariable script, and click Open.

The Query Analyzer loads the script into the Query window.

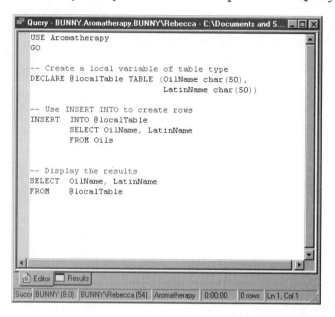

4. Click the Execute Query button on the Query Analyzer toolbar.

Execute Query button

The Query Analyzer executes the script and displays the results.

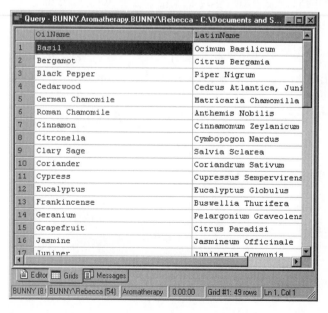

Use global variables to display information about the server

New Query button

Load Script button

1. Select the Editor Pane in the Query window, or open a new Query window if you closed the window used in the previous exercise.

2. Click the Load Script button on the Query Analyzer toolbar.

   The Query Analyzer displays the Open Query File dialog box.

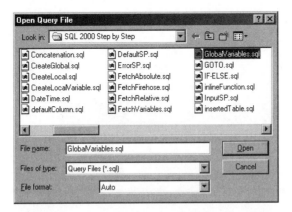

3. Select the GlobalVariables script, and click Open.

   The Query Analyzer loads the script into the Query window.

Execute Query button

4. Click the Execute Query button on the Query Analyzer toolbar.

The Query Analyzer executes the script and displays the results.

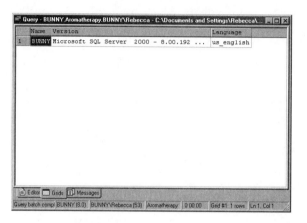

Lesson 25 Quick Reference

To	SQL Syntax
Create a local temporary table	CREATE TABLE @table_name (table_definition)
Create a global temporary table	CREATE TABLE @@table_name (table_definition)
Declare a scalar local variable	DECLARE @variable_name
Declare a table-valued local variable	DECLARE @variable_name TABLE (table_definition)
Set the value of a scalar variable command	SET @variable_name = using the SET constant_or_expression
Set the value of a scalar variable using the SELECT command and a constant	SELECT @variable_name = constant_or_expression
Set the value of a variable using SELECT	SELECT @variable_name = an implicit column_expression FROM table_name
Append rows to a table-valued variable	INSERT INTO @variable_name select_statement

```
CLARE        Cursor CURSOR

             Name FROM Oils
             har(20)
PE

- Retr    the first row into a varia
TCH FIRST FROM simpleCursor
    INTO @theName

- Display the results
RINT RTRIM(@theName) + ' is the first name'
```

Controlling Execution

```
- Re
TCH ABSOLUTE 3 FROM simpleCursor
   INTO @theName

- Display the
RINT RTRIM(@th
```

In this lesson you'll learn how to:

- Use the IF ...ELSE command to control processing.

- Use a simple CASE function to return results based on the equivalency of a single value.

- Use a searched CASE function to return results based on a Boolean expression.

- Use the GOTO command to transfer execution to a statement.

- Use a WHILE loop to execute a statement or statement block multiple times.

- Use the BREAK clause to exit a WHILE loop.

- Use the CONTINUE clause to return execution to the top of a WHILE loop.

Unless you specify otherwise, Transact-SQL processes statements from the top of your script to the bottom, including every statement. This isn't always what you need. Sometimes you want a statement to execute only if certain conditions are true. Sometimes you want a statement to execute a specified number of times, or to repeat until some condition is true.

Transact-SQL control-of-flow commands provide you with the ability to control execution in these ways, and we'll look at control-of-flow commands in this lesson.

Statement Blocks

When you begin to manipulate the way Transact-SQL executes statements, it's convenient to treat a set of statements as a block. Transact-SQL allows you to do this by providing the BEGIN...END command pair.

Following any control-of-flow command with BEGIN causes Transact-SQL to apply the command to all the statements between BEGIN and the matching END.

You can include any Transact-SQL statement in the block, including other BEGIN...END blocks, but there are a few constraints. You cannot combine CREATE DEFAULT, CREATE PROCEDURE, CREATE RULE, CREATE TRIGGER, and CREATE VIEW statements with any other statement. Also, you cannot alter a table structure and then reference the new columns in the same block.

Conditional Processing

The first group of control-of-flow statements we'll look at determine statement execution based on a Boolean expression. (Remember that a Boolean expression evaluates to TRUE or FALSE.)

IF...ELSE

The IF statement is the simplest of the conditional control-of-flow commands. If the Boolean expression following the IF command evaluates to TRUE, the statement or statement block following it will be executed. If the Boolean expression evaluates to FALSE, the statement or statement block following it will be skipped.

The optional ELSE command allows you to specify that a statement or statement block will execute only if the Boolean expression evaluates to FALSE. For example, the Transact-SQL commands below return 'It's true' if @test is true, or 'It's false' if it is not.

```
IF @test
  SELECT 'It's true'
ELSE
  SELECT 'It's false'
```

 IP IF...ELSE statements can be nested within one another, giving a logical structure similar to the IF...ELSEIF...ELSE construct provided in other languages. But beware of using this technique for any but the simplest logic. The CASE statement described below can usually do the same thing and is *much* easier to understand when you need to change it later.

Use IF...ELSE to control execution

New Query button

1. Click the New Query button on the Query Analyzer toolbar to open a new Query window.

Load Script button

2. Click the Load Script button.

   The Query Analyzer displays the Open Query File dialog box.

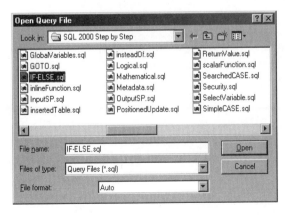

3. Navigate to the SQL 2000 Step by Step folder in the root directory, select the script named IF-ELSE, and click Open.

The Query Analyzer loads the script.

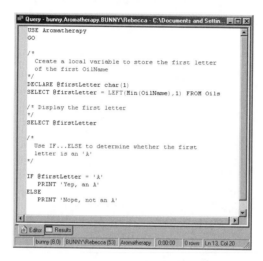

```
USE Aromatherapy
GO

/*
   Create a local variable to store the first letter
   of the first OilName
*/
DECLARE @firstLetter char(1)
SELECT @firstLetter = LEFT(Min(OilName),1) FROM Oils

/* Display the first letter
*/
SELECT @firstLetter

/*
   Use IF...ELSE to determine whether the first
   letter is an 'A'
*/

IF @firstLetter = 'A'
   PRINT 'Yep, an A'
ELSE
   PRINT 'Nope, not an A'
```

 TIP This script uses the PRINT command to display a message in the Messages tab of the Query window. PRINT is useful when you're first developing scripts, but you will rarely use it in real applications.

Execute Query button

4. Click the Execute Query button on the Query Analyzer toolbar.

The Query Analyzer executes the query and displays the Grids tab.

5. Select the Messages tab.

The Query Analyzer displays the result of the IF...ELSE statement.

CASE

In most programming languages, CASE is a sophisticated form of the IF statement that allows you to specify multiple Boolean expressions in a single statement. In SQL Server, CASE is a *function*, not a command. It isn't used by itself the way IF is; it's instead used as part of a SELECT or UPDATE statement.

Statements including CASE can take one of two syntactic forms, depending on whether the expression being evaluated changes. The simplest form assumes that the Boolean expression being evaluated always has the following form:

value = expression

The *value* can be of arbitrary complexity. You can use a constant, a column name, or a complex expression, whatever you require. The comparison operator is always equality. The simple CASE syntax is

```
CASE value
  WHEN expression_one THEN result_expression_one
  WHEN expression_two THEN result_expression_two
  ⋮
  WHEN expression_n THEN result_expression_n
  [ELSE else_result_expression]
END
```

In this form of CASE, *result_expression* is returned only if the expression following the WHEN keyword is logically equal to the value specified. You can have any number of WHEN clauses in the expression. The ELSE clause is optional and acts as a "fall-through" result—it executes only if all the WHEN clauses evaluate to FALSE.

Comparing one value against a number of different values is extremely common, but sometimes you need more flexibility. In this case, you can use what Transact-SQL calls the searched CASE syntax, which has this form:

```
CASE
 WHEN Boolean_expression_one THEN result_expression_one
 WHEN Boolean_expression_two THEN result_expression_two
 ⋮
 WHEN Boolean_expression_n THEN result_expression_n
 [ELSE else_result_expression]
END
```

In this form of CASE, you specify the entire Boolean expression in each WHEN clause, rather than relying on the implicit equality expression of the simple form. Note that it's possible for more than one *Boolean_expression* to evaluate as true. Transact-SQL will return only the first *result_expression* and then skip to the statement following END.

Use a simple CASE

Clear Window button

1. Select the Editor tab of the Query window, and then click the Clear Window button.

   The Query Analyzer clears the window.

Load Script button

2. Click the Load Script button.

   The Query Analyzer displays the Open Query File dialog box.

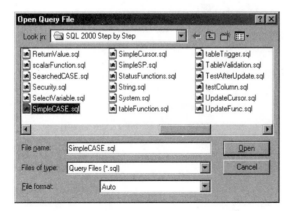

3. Select the script named SimpleCASE, and click Open.

The Query Analyzer loads the script.

4. Click the Execute Query button on the Query Analyzer toolbar to execute the query.

Execute Query button

The Query Analyzer displays the query results.

Use a searched CASE

Clear Window button

1. Select the Editor tab of the Query window, and then click the Clear Window button.

   The Query Analyzer clears the window.

Load Script button

2. Click the Load Script button.

   The Query Analyzer displays the Open Query File dialog box.

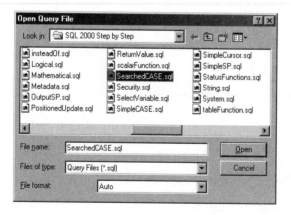

3. Select the script named SearchedCASE, and click Open.

   The Query Analyzer loads the script.

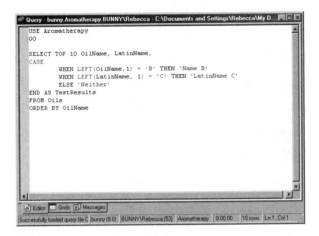

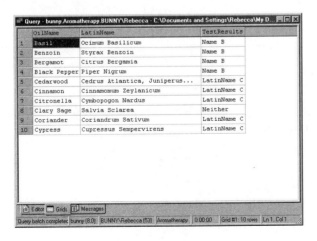

Execute Query button

4. Click the Execute Query button on the Query Analyzer toolbar to execute the query.

   The Query Analyzer displays the query results. Note that even though the third record, containing the OilName value 'Bergamot', meets the criteria for the second WHEN clause (*LEFT(LatinName, 1) = 'C'*), it returns the TestResults value 'Name B' because it matched the *first* Boolean expression.

The GOTO Command

IF...ELSE and CASE control the execution of statements based on the results of a Boolean expression. The GOTO command is unconditional. It transfers execution directly to the statement following the label referenced by the command.

In SQL Server, labels are nonexecuting statements that have the following syntax:

```
label_name:
```

The label name must follow the rules for identifiers. The GOTO command itself has a very simple syntax:

```
GOTO label_name
```

Spaghetti Code

GOTO is a much-maligned command in the programming community. This is largely for historical reasons: early languages provided very few mechanisms for controlling execution—usually only IF and GOTO—and that encouraged complex, difficult-to-read code called *spaghetti code.*

GOTO has its place, however, particularly in handling errors. If you use it carefully, it can actually make code easier to understand. Just make sure you don't use GOTO to perform tasks that other control-of-flow commands or functions can perform more cleanly.

Use GOTO for unconditional control

Clear Window button

1. Select the Editor tab of the Query window, and then click the Clear Window button.

   The Query Analyzer clears the window.

Load Script button

2. Click the Load Script button.

   The Query Analyzer displays the Open Query File dialog box.

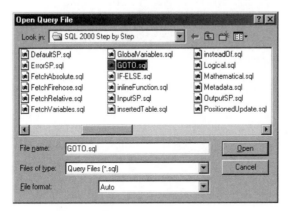

3. Select the script named GOTO, and click Open.

   The Query Analyzer loads the script.

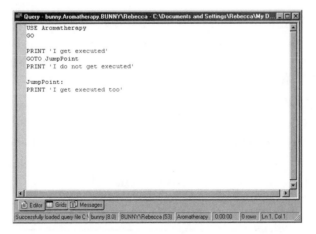

Execute Query button

4. Click the Execute Query button on the Query Analyzer toolbar to execute the query.

The Query Analyzer displays the query results.

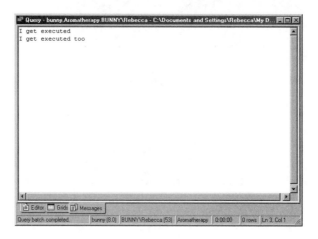

Looping

The final control-of-flow command allows you to specify that a statement or statement block execute until a specified condition is met.

Simple WHILE loop

The simplest form of a WHILE loop specifies a Boolean expression and a statement or statement block. The statements are repeated until the Boolean expression evaluates to FALSE. If the Boolean expression is FALSE when the WHILE statement is first evaluated, the statement or statement block does not execute at all.

Use a simple WHILE loop

Clear Window button

1. Select the Editor tab of the Query window, and then click the Clear Window button.

The Query Analyzer clears the window.

Load Script button

2. Click the Load Script button.

The Query Analyzer displays the Open Query File dialog box.

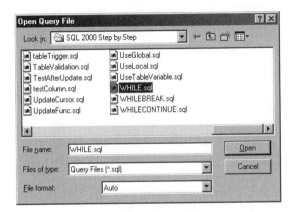

3. Select the script named WHILE, and click Open.

The Query Analyzer loads the script.

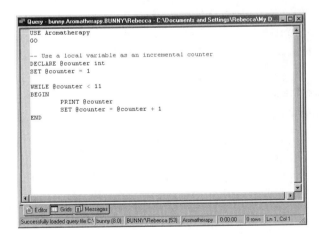

Execute Query button

4. Click the Execute Query button on the Query Analyzer toolbar to execute the query.

The Query Analyzer displays the query results.

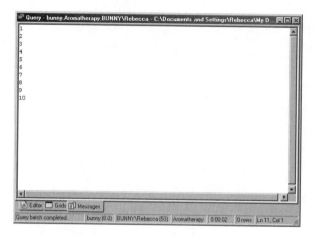

Complex WHILE Loops

The WHILE statement syntax also provides for more complex processing than shown in the previous example. The BREAK clause exits the loop; execution continues with the statement following the END clause of the WHILE statement block. The CONTINUE clause returns execution to the top of the loop, causing the statements following it within the statement block to be skipped. Both BREAK and CONTINUE are usually performed conditionally, within IF statements.

You can use BREAK and CONTINUE in the same WHILE statement if your logic calls for it. You can also use each clause multiple times within a statement block, although only a single instance will ever execute.

Use WHILE...BREAK

Clear Window button

1. Select the Editor tab of the Query window, and then click the Clear Window button.

The Query Analyzer clears the window.

Load Script button

2. Click the Load Script button.

The Query Analyzer displays the Open Query File dialog box.

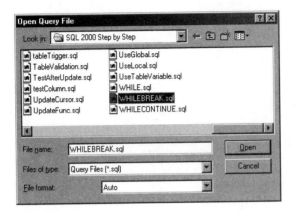

3. Select the script named WHILEBREAK, and click Open.

The Query Analyzer loads the script.

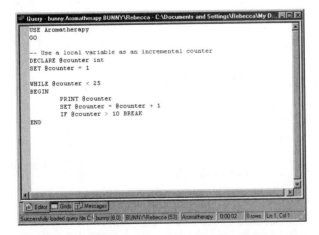

Execute Query button

4. Click the Execute Query button on the Query Analyzer toolbar to execute the query.

The Query Analyzer displays the query results.

Use WHILE...CONTINUE

Clear Window button

1. Select the Editor tab of the Query window, and then click the Clear Window button.

   The Query Analyzer clears the window.

Load Script button

2. Click the Load Script button.

   The Query Analyzer displays the Open Query File dialog box.

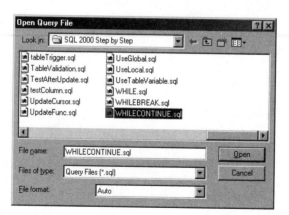

3. Select the script named WHILECONTINUE, and click Open.

The Query Analyzer loads the script.

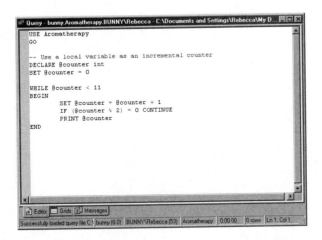

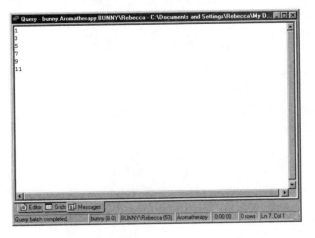

Execute Query button

4. Click the Execute Query button on the Query Analyzer toolbar to execute the query.

The Query Analyzer displays the query results.

Lesson 26 Quick Reference

To	SQL Syntax
| Execute a statement conditionally | ```
IF Boolean_expr
   statement_or_block
[ELSE
   statement_or_block]
``` |
| Return conditional results in a SELECT or UPDATE statement based on the equivalency of a single value | ```
CASE value
  WHEN expr_one THEN result_expr_one
  WHEN expr_two THEN result_expr_two
  :
  WHEN expr_n THEN result_expr_n
  [ELSE else_result_expr]
END
``` |
| Return conditional results in a SELECT or UPDATE statement based on a Boolean expression | ```
CASE
  WHEN Boolean_expr_one THEN result_expr_one
  WHEN Boolean_expr_two THEN result_expr_two
  :
  WHEN Boolean_expr_n THEN result_expr_n
  [ELSE else_result_expr]
END
``` |
| Transfer execution unconditionally | ```
GOTO label_name
label_name:
``` |
| Repeat a statement or statement block as long as a condition is TRUE | ```
WHILE Boolean_expr
   statement_or_block
``` |
| Exit a WHILE loop | ```
WHILE Boolean_expr
BEGIN
   :
   BREAK
   :
END
``` |
| Return processing to the top of a WHILE loop | ```
WHILE Boolean_expr
BEGIN
   :
   CONTINUE
   :
END
``` |
```

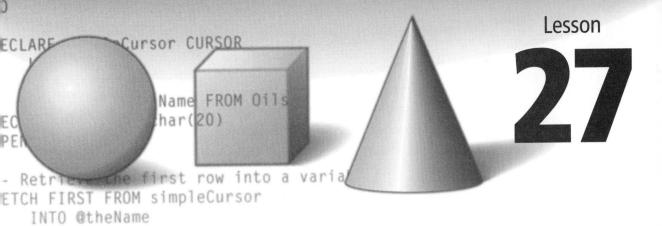

Transact-SQL Cursors

In this lesson you'll learn how to:
■ Declare a cursor.
■ Open a cursor.
■ Close a cursor.
■ Deallocate a cursor.
■ Use a simple FETCH command.
■ Fetch a row into variables.
■ Fetch a row by its absolute position.
■ Fetch a row by its relative position.
■ Perform a positioned update.
■ Perform a positioned delete.
■ Use @@CURSOR_ROWS to determine the number of rows in a cursor set.
■ Use @@FETCH_STATUS to determine the result of a FETCH statement.
■ Use CURSOR_STATUS to query the status of a cursor.

One of the defining characteristics of relational databases is that operations are performed on sets of rows. A set might be empty, or it might contain only a single row, but it is still considered a set. This is necessary and useful for relational operations, but it can sometimes be inconvenient for applications.

For example, since there is no way to point to a specific row in a set, displaying rows to users one at a time can be difficult. And even though the extensions to the SQL standard provided by Transact-SQL make SQL much more programmable, there are still operations that are difficult, expensive, or just plain impossible to perform on a set basis.

To handle these situations, SQL supports *cursors*. A cursor is an object that points to a specific row within a set. Depending on the nature of the cursor you create, you can move the cursor around in the set and update or delete data.

Understanding Cursors

Microsoft SQL Server actually supports two different types of cursors: Transact-SQL cursors and API (application programming interface) cursors. API cursors are created within an application using Microsoft ActiveX Data Objects (ADO), OLE DB, Open Database Connectivity (ODBC), or DB-Library. Each of these APIs supports a slightly different functionality and uses a different syntax. We won't be discussing API cursors in any detail here; if you'll be using them, consult the appropriate documentation for the API and the programming language you'll be using.

Transact-SQL cursors are created using the DECLARE CURSOR command. Both the cursor object and the set of rows it points to exist on the server. This is called a *server-side* cursor. When you use a server-side cursor from an application connected to SQL Server over a network, each operation on the cursor requires a round-trip across the network. API cursor libraries, while they support server-side cursors, also support a *client-side* cursor that exists on the client system and caches the rows it manipulates there.

The set of rows to which a cursor points is defined by a SELECT command. There are a few constraints on the SELECT statement when creating a Transact-SQL cursor:

- It cannot return multiple result sets.

- It cannot contain the INTO clause to create a new table.

- It cannot contain the COMPUTE or COMPUTE BY clauses used to aggregate results. (It can, however, contain aggregate functions such as AVG.)

Cursor Characteristics

Transact-SQL supports several different types of cursors. Sorting out the various characteristics of each type can be confusing, but it gets easier if you think of each type in terms of three more-or-less independent cursor characteristics: its ability to reflect changes to the underlying data, its ability to scroll through the row set, and its ability to update the row set.

Reflecting changes

Whether a cursor reflects changes made to the underlying data is referred to as its *sensitivity*. For example, suppose you create a cursor for the statement:

```
SELECT * FROM Oils
WHERE Left(OilName, 1) = 'B'
```

The Aromatherapy database will return four rows, as shown in Figure 27-1. If, during the time you're using the cursor, someone adds a Description value for Bergamot oil, or adds a row for Bayberry, what happens to the set of rows pointed to by your cursor?

Figure 27-1. *The Aromatherapy sample database contains four rows beginning with the letter B.*

Two types of sensitivity can be determined separately when you create your cursor: changes to which rows are included in the set (the set's *membership*) and changes to the values in the underlying rows.

Scrolling

The second cursor characteristic is whether you can use the cursor to scroll forward and backward, or only forward. The proverbial programming dilemma of speed versus flexibility applies here. Forward-only cursors are significantly faster but are obviously less flexible.

Updating

The final characteristic used to classify cursors is whether the rows can be updated through the cursor. Once again, read-only cursors are generally more efficient but less flexible.

Cursor Types

Transact-SQL supports four different types of cursors: static, keyset, dynamic, and firehose. Each type of cursor stores different data about the rows to which it points, and each supports different combinations of the cursor characteristics described in the previous section.

Static

A static cursor takes a snapshot of the data specified by its SELECT statement and stores it in the tempdb database. It is not sensitive to changes in membership or data values, and because any updates would be reflected in the copy only, it is always read-only. Static cursors can, however, be declared as forward-only or scrollable.

Keyset

A keyset cursor copies into tempdb only the columns required to uniquely identify each row. In order to declare a keyset cursor, each table involved in the defining SELECT statement must have a unique index that defines the keyset to be copied.

Keyset cursors can be updatable or read-only, and they can be scrollable or forward-only.

Membership in a keyset cursor is fixed when you declare the cursor. If a row that would have satisfied the select criteria is added while the cursor is open, it won't be added to the set. In our earlier example, where the selection criteria was *LEFT(OilName, 1) = 'B'*, a new row with the OilName of 'Bayberry' would not be added to the rows affected by the cursor.

Similarly, if a change is made to a row that means it no longer qualifies for membership in the set, like changing 'Basil' to 'Kumquat', the row remains a member of the set. Even if a row is deleted, it is still a member of the set, but SQL Server returns NULL for the column values.

Although membership in the cursor set is fixed when you open the cursor, changes to the data values in the underlying tables are usually reflected. For example, changes to the Description value of the Bergamot row would be returned by the cursor. Changes to keyset values, however, are reflected in the cursor only if they're made through the cursor. To continue the previous example, if the OilName value were changed from 'Basil' to 'Kumquat' through the cursor, the cursor would return 'Kumquat'. If the change were made by another user, however, the cursor would continue to return 'Basil'.

 IP As we'll see in the next section, creating a cursor and opening it are different operations. It's possible to refresh the contents of a keyset cursor by closing and reopening it.

Dynamic

Conceptually, a dynamic cursor behaves as though the SELECT statement were reissued each time a row is referenced. (What actually happens is quite different, but this is a good way to think about dynamic cursors.) Dynamic cursors reflect changes to both membership and underlying data values, whether those changes were made through the cursor or by another user.

There is one constraint on a dynamic cursor: the SELECT statement used to define it can contain an ORDER BY clause only if there is an index containing the columns used in the ORDER BY clause. If you declare a keyset cursor with an ORDER BY clause that isn't supported by an index, SQL Server will convert the cursor to a keyset cursor.

Firehose

SQL Server supports a specially optimized form of a read-only, non-scrollable cursor. This kind of cursor is declared using FAST_FORWARD, but is more commonly known as a *firehose* cursor.

Firehose cursors are very efficient, but there are two important constraints on using them. First, if the SELECT statement you use to define the cursor references *text, ntext,* or *image* columns and it contains a TOP clause, SQL Server converts the firehose cursor into a keyset cursor.

Second, if the SELECT statement you use to define the cursor combines tables that have triggers with tables that don't have triggers, the cursor is converted to a static cursor. Triggers are Transact-SQL scripts that are executed automatically by the server when Data Manipulation Language (DML) statements are executed against a table. We'll examine triggers in detail in Lesson 29, but this is an important issue: if someone adds a trigger to one of the tables used by your cursor, your application can suddenly grind to a halt because SQL Server is converting one of the most efficient cursors into one of the slowest.

Using Cursors

Using a cursor is rather like using a local variable—you declare it, set its value, and then use it. Unlike local variables, however, which are automatically destroyed when they go out of scope, you must explicitly release the rows used by a cursor, and then destroy it.

Creating Cursors

The first step in using a cursor is to create it. You create Transact-SQL cursors by using the DECLARE CURSOR statement.

> **MPORTANT** SQL Server supports two different methods of creating a cursor: SQL-92 syntax and Transact-SQL syntax. The SQL-92 syntax is an ANSI standard, but it is far less powerful than the Transact-SQL syntax that is discussed here.

The syntax of the DECLARE CURSOR statement is:

```
DECLARE cursor_name CURSOR
[visibility]
[scroll]
[type]
[lock]
[TYPE_WARNING]
FOR select_statement
[FOR UPDATE [OF column_names]]
```

Notice that all the parameters that define the characteristics of the cursor—*visibility*, *type*, and so on—are optional. The defaults for these values are complex, with specified and non-specified parameters interacting with the underlying records or views and with the database options. For the sake of readability, it's usually best to explicitly specify any parameter you care about. That way you'll know exactly what you're getting.

The *visibility* of a cursor is defined with the keyword LOCAL or GLOBAL. This has the same effect as using @local_table or @@global_table to declare temporary tables.

 TIP SQL Server will close and deallocate a local cursor when it goes out of scope, but it's always better to do this explicitly, as described later in this section.

The *scroll* parameter accepts the keywords FORWARD_ONLY and SCROLL, which do exactly what you'd expect them to do.

The *type* parameter determines the type of cursor to create. The keywords are STATIC, KEYSET, DYNAMIC, and FAST_FORWARD. The FAST_FORWARD type parameter and the FORWARD_ONLY scroll parameter are mutually exclusive.

The *lock* parameter determines whether rows can be updated through the cursor, and if so whether other users can also update them. If you use the keyword READ_ONLY, no changes can be made to the underlying data through the cursor. It's still possible for other users to update the data, or for you to update the data using a standard UPDATE statement. If you specify SCROLL_LOCKS as the *lock* parameter, updates can be made *only* through the cursor. Any other UPDATE statement, whether made within the same batch or by another user, will fail.

The final lock option, OPTIMISTIC, allows updates to the rows both through and outside the cursor. This is the most flexible option, but there is always the possibility that an update made through the cursor will fail if the row has been changed since the row was read for the cursor.

The TYPE_WARNING parameter instructs SQL Server to send a warning message to the client if a cursor has been converted from the type specified to another type. This will happen whenever you declare a cursor type that doesn't support the specified SELECT statement.

The *select_statement* specified in the FOR clause is required. It specifies the rows to be included in the cursor set.

The FOR UPDATE clause is optional. By default, cursors are updatable unless the READ_ONLY lock parameter is specified, but again, it's safer to include this clause just to be sure you get the results you want. You can use OF *column_names* to identify specific rows that allow updating. If you omit OF *column_names*, all the columns in the SELECT statement will be updatable.

Cursor variables

Transact-SQL allows you to declare variables of type CURSOR. In this case, the standard DECLARE syntax doesn't create the cursor; you must explicitly SET the variable to the cursor:

```
DECLARE myCursor CURSOR
    LOCAL
    FAST_FORWARD
    FOR SELECT OilName FROM Oils

DECLARE @myCursorVariable CURSOR

SET @myCursorVariable = myCursor
```

This syntax is useful when you want to create variables that can be assigned to different cursors, which you might do if you create a generic procedure that operates on multiple result sets.

You can declare a cursor variable, and then use it to create a cursor directly:

```
DECLARE @myCursorVariable CURSOR
SET @myCursorVariable CURSOR
    LOCAL FAST_FORWARD FOR SELECT OilName FROM Oils
```

Using this syntax, the cursor has no identifier and can be referenced only through the variable. This syntax is most useful in stored procedures, which we'll examine in Lesson 28.

Open a cursor

Declaring a cursor creates the cursor object, but it doesn't create the set of records the cursor will manipulate (the cursor set). The cursor set isn't created until you open the cursor. After all the complexity of the DECLARE CURSOR statement, it will no doubt be a relief to see the syntax of the OPEN statement:

```
OPEN [GLOBAL] cursor_or_variable
```

The GLOBAL keyword helps avoid name conflicts: if a cursor declared with the LOCAL keyword and a cursor declared with the GLOBAL keyword have the same identifier, references to the cursor will default to the local cursor unless you use the GLOBAL keyword. As always, it's safest to be explicit if you're opening a global cursor.

Close a cursor

Once you've finished using a cursor, you should close it. The CLOSE statement releases the resources used for maintaining the cursor set, and also releases any locks placed on rows if you've used the SCROLLOCKS parameter of the DECLARE statement. The syntax of the CLOSE command is almost identical to the OPEN statement—only the command keyword changes:

```
CLOSE [GLOBAL] cursor_or_variable
```

Deallocate a cursor

The last statement in the cursor-creation sequence is DEALLOCATE. Again, its syntax is straightforward:

```
DEALLOCATE [GLOBAL] cursor_or_variable
```

But there's a gotcha here: the DEALLOCATE statement removes the cursor identifier or cursor variable, but it doesn't necessarily remove the cursor. The cursor itself won't be removed until all the identifiers referencing it are either deallocated or go out of scope. Consider the following example:

```
-- Create the cursor
DECLARE myCursor CURSOR
    KEYSET
    READ_ONLY
    FOR SELECT * FROM Oils

-- Create a cursor variable
DECLARE @cursorVariable CURSOR

-- Create the cursor set
OPEN myCursor

-- Assign the variable to the cursor
SET @cursorVariable = myCursor

-- Deallocate the cursor
DEALLOCATE myCursor
```

After you deallocate the cursor, the identifier myCursor is no longer associated with the cursor set, but because the cursor set is still referenced by the variable @cursorVariable, the cursor and cursor set aren't released. Unless you explicitly deallocate the cursor variable as well, the cursor and cursor set will remain in existence until the variable goes out of scope.

Manipulating Rows with a Cursor

Cursors wouldn't be very interesting if you couldn't do anything with them. Transact-SQL supports three different commands for working with cursors: FETCH, UPDATE, and DELETE.

The FETCH command retrieves a specific row from the cursor set. At it's simplest, the FETCH command has the syntax:

```
FETCH cursor_or_variable
```

This format returns the row at which the cursor is positioned (the current row).

Use a simple FETCH command

New Query button

Load Script button

1. Click the New Query button on the Query Analyzer toolbar.

   The Query Analyzer opens a new Query window.

2. Click the Load Script button on the Query Analyzer toolbar.

   The Query Analyzer displays the Open Query File dialog box.

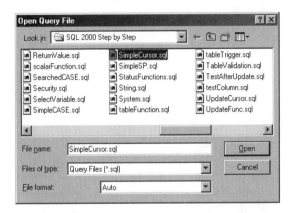

3. Navigate to the SQL 2000 Step by Step folder in the root directory, select the script named SimpleCursor, and click Open.

4. The Query Analyzer loads the script into the Query window.

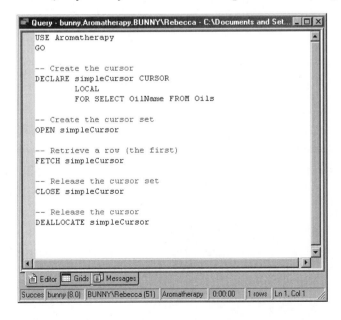

Execute Query button

5. Click the Execute Query button on the Query Analyzer toolbar.

   The Query Analyzer executes the query.

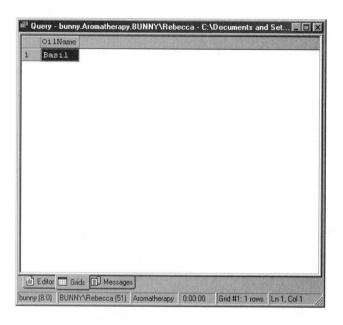

 IP   You'll probably notice that this script takes longer to execute than a corresponding SELECT statement would. That's because of the overhead involved in creating and opening the cursor. Take that as a warning: never use a cursor if a SELECT statement will do.

Rather than returning a row directly, the FETCH command also allows you to store the returned column values into variables. To store the results of a FETCH into a variable, you use the following syntax:

```
FETCH cursor_or_variable
    INTO variable_list
```

The *variable_list* is a comma-separated list of variable identifiers. You must declare the variables before executing the FETCH command. The *variable_list* must include a variable for every column in the SELECT statement that defined the cursor, and the variable data types must be either the same as or compatible with the column data types.

Fetch a row into variables

Load Script button

1. Click the Load Script button on the Query Analyzer toolbar.

   The Query Analyzer displays the Open Query File dialog box.

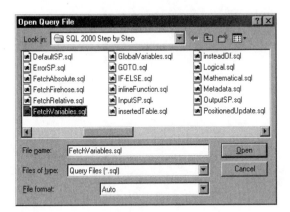

2. Select the script named FetchVariables, and click Open.

   The Query Analyzer loads the script into the Query window.

3. Click the Execute Query button on the Query Analyzer toolbar.

Execute Query button

The Query Analyzer executes the query.

The previous examples have all used the FETCH statement to return the current row. The FETCH statement syntax also provides a number of keywords to specify a different row. When you use one of these keywords, the FETCH statement will return the row specified and make that row the current row.

Three keywords allow you to specify an absolute position in the cursor set. The FIRST and LAST keywords return the first and last rows, respectively, while ABSOLUTE n specifies a row n rows away from the front (if n is positive) or end (if n is negative) of the cursor set. You can express the value of n as either a constant (3) or a variable (@theRow).

Fetch rows by their absolute position

Load Script button

1. Click the Load Script button on the Query Analyzer toolbar.

   The Query Analyzer displays the Open Query File dialog box.

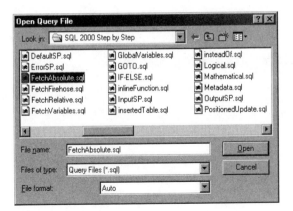

2. Select the script named FetchAbsolute, and click Open.

The Query Analyzer loads the script into the Query window.

 3. Click the Execute Query button on the Query Analyzer toolbar.

Execute Query button

The Query Analyzer executes the query.

In addition to the keywords that allow you to retrieve a row based on its absolute position, the FETCH statement provides three keywords that allow you to retrieve a row based on its position relative to the current row. FETCH NEXT returns the next row, FETCH PRIOR returns the previous row, and FETCH RELATIVE n returns a row n rows from the current row. Like FETCH ABSOLUTE n, FETCH RELATIVE n can specify rows before the current row, if n is negative, or after the current row, if n is positive.

Fetch rows by their relative position

Load Script button

1. Click the Load Script button on the Query Analyzer toolbar.

The Query Analyzer displays the Open Query File dialog box.

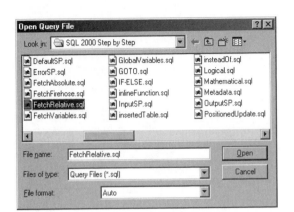

2. Select the script named FetchRelative, and click Open.

The Query Analyzer loads the script into the Query window.

3. Click the Execute Query button on the Query Analyzer toolbar.

Execute Query button

The Query Analyzer executes the query.

If your cursor is FORWARD_ONLY or FAST_FORWARD, the only positioning keyword you can use is NEXT. In fact, if your cursor is of either of these types, the NEXT is unnecessary. SQL Server assumes that every FETCH is a FETCH NEXT.

Use FETCH NEXT with a firehose cursor

Load Script button

1. Click the Load Script button on the Query Analyzer toolbar.

   The Query Analyzer displays the Open Query File dialog box.

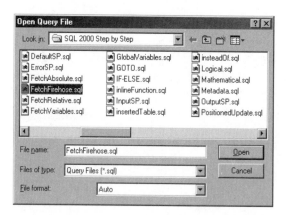

2. Select the script named FetchFirehose, and click Open.

   The Query Analyzer loads the script into the Query window.

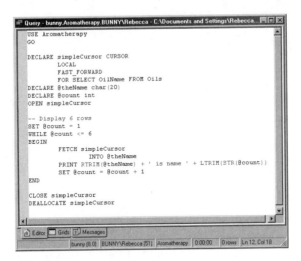

3. Click the Run Query button on the Query Analyzer toolbar.

   The Query Analyzer executes the query.

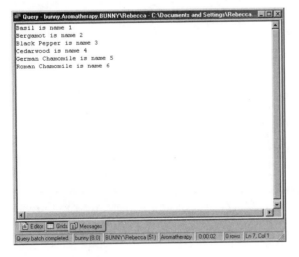

Run Query button

Updating and Deleting Rows with a Cursor

Provided your cursor is updatable, changing the underlying values in a cursor set is quite simple. There is a special form of the WHERE clause that supports updating through a cursor:

```
UPDATE table_or_view
SET update_list
WHERE CURRENT OF cursor_or_variable
```

This is called a *positioned update*. Transact-SQL also supports a *positioned delete* that has the form:

```
DELETE table_or_view
WHERE CURRENT OF cursor_or_variable
```

Perform a positioned update

Load Script button

1. Click the Load Script button on the Query Analyzer toolbar.

   The Query Analyzer displays the Open Query File dialog box.

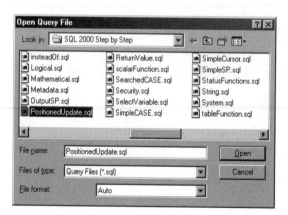

2. Select the script named PositionedUpdate, and click Open.

   The Query Analyzer loads the script into the Query window.

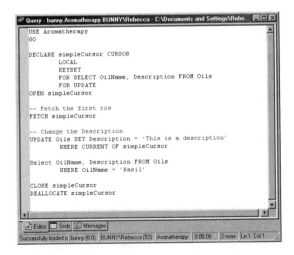

3. Click the Execute Query button on the Query Analyzer toolbar.

Execute Query button

The Query Analyzer executes the query. Note that two grids are displayed. The first is created by the FETCH and shows the initial contents of the columns. The second is the result of the SELECT statement, and shows the Description value after the update.

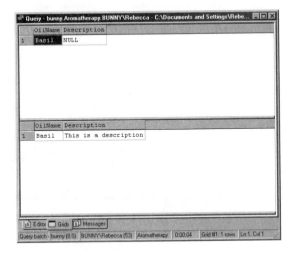

Monitoring Transact-SQL Cursors

Transact-SQL provides two global variables and a function to help you understand what's going on with your cursors. @@CURSOR_ROWS returns the number of rows in the most recent cursor opened on the connection. Table 27-1 shows the values returned by @@CURSOR_ROWS.

Return Value	Meaning
$-m$	The cursor has not yet been fully populated; m rows are currently in the cursor set.
-1	The cursor is dynamic, and the number of rows can vary.
0	Either no cursor has been opened, the most recent cursor has been closed and deallocated, or the cursor contains zero rows.
n	The number of rows in the cursor is n.

Table 27-1.   *@@CURSOR_ROWS return values.*

@@FETCH_STATUS returns information about the last FETCH command issued. Table 27-2 shows the return values from @@FETCH_STATUS.

Return Value	Meaning
0	The FETCH was successful.
-1	The FETCH failed.
-2	The row fetched is missing.

Table 27-2.   *@@FETCH_STATUS return values.*

Finally, Transact-SQL provides the CURSOR_STATUS function. The CURSOR_STATUS function has the syntax:

```
CURSOR_STATUS(type, cursor_or_variable)
```

The value of *type* is 'local', 'global', or 'variable', and *cursor_or_variable* is the identifier of the cursor or cursor variable about which information is required. The results of the CURSOR_STATUS function are shown in Table 27-3.

Return Value	Meaning
1	If the function is called for a dynamic cursor, the cursor set has zero, one, or many rows. If the function is called for another type of cursor, it has at least one row.
0	The cursor set is empty.
−1	The cursor is closed.
−2	Returned only for cursor variables. Either the cursor assigned to the specified variable is closed, or no cursor has yet been assigned to the variable.
−3	The specified cursor or cursor variable does not exist.

Table 27-3. *CURSOR_STATUS return values.*

Use the cursor monitoring functions

Load Script button

1. Click the Load Script button on the Query Analyzer toolbar.

   The Query Analyzer displays the Open Query File dialog box.

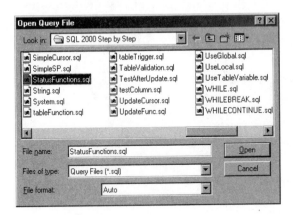

2. Select the StatusFunctions script and click the Open button.

   The Query Analyzer loads the script into the Query window.

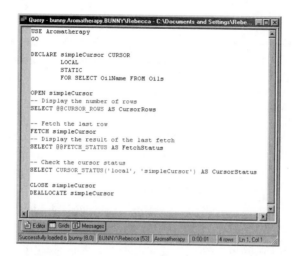

Execute Query button

3. Click the Execute Query button on the Query Analyzer toolbar.

The Query Analyzer executes the query. Four grids are displayed. The first is created by the SELECT @@CURSOR_ROWS statement and the second by the FETCH statement. The third grid is the result of the SELECT @@FETCH_STATUS statement, and the fourth the result of the SELECT CURSOR_STATUS('local', 'simpleCursor') statement.

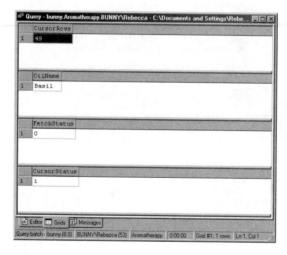

Lesson 27 Quick Reference

To	SQL Syntax
Create a cursor.	DECLARE *cursor_name* CURSOR [*visibility*] [*scroll*] [*type*] [*lock*] [TYPE_WARNING] FOR *select_statement* [FOR UPDATE [OF *column_names*]]
Open a cursor.	OPEN [GLOBAL] *cursor_or_variable*
Close a cursor.	CLOSE [GLOBAL] *cursor_or_variable*
Deallocate a cursor.	DEALLOCATE [GLOBAL] *cursor_or_variable*
Use a simple FETCH command.	FETCH *cursor_or_variable*
Fetch a row into variables.	FETCH *cursor_or_variable* INTO *variable_list*
Fetch a row by its absolute position.	FETCH {FIRST | LAST | ABSOLUTE *n*) FROM *cursor_or_variable*
Fetch a row by its relative position.	FETCH {NEXT | PRIOR | RELATIVE *n*) FROM *cursor_or_variable*
Perform a positioned update.	UPDATE *table_or_view* SET *update_list* WHERE CURRENT OF *cursor_or_variable*
Perform a positioned delete.	DELETE *table_or_view* WHERE CURRENT OF *cursor_or_variable*
Use CURSOR_STATUS to query the status of a cursor.	CURSOR_STATUS ('local', '*local_cursor*') Or CURSOR_STATUS ('global', '*global_cursor*') Or CURSOR_STATUS ('variable', '*cursor_variable*')

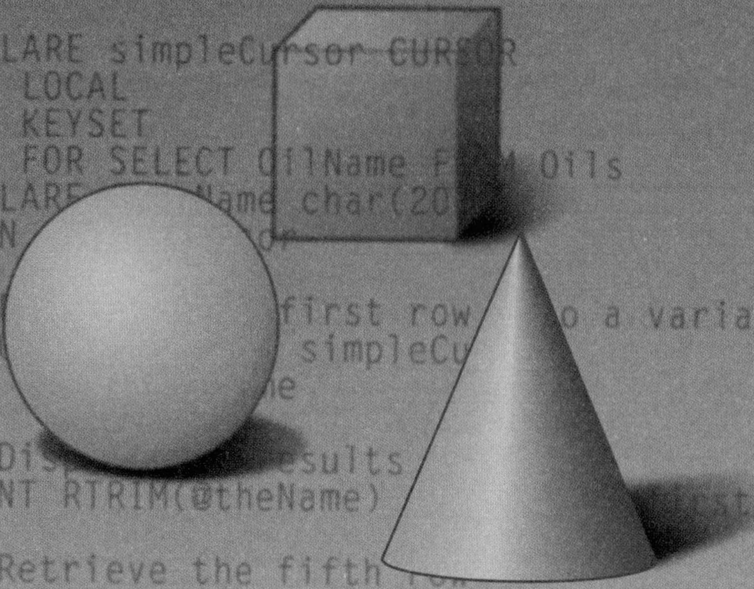

```
USE Aromatherapy
GO

DECLARE simpleCursor CURSOR
    LOCAL
    KEYSET
    FOR SELECT OilName FROM Oils
DECLARE @theName char(20)
OPEN simpleCursor

-- Retrieve the first row into a variable
FETCH NEXT FROM simpleCursor
    INTO @theName

-- Display the results
PRINT RTRIM(@theName) + ' is the first name'

-- Retrieve the fifth row
FETCH ABSOLUTE 5 FROM simpleCursor
    INTO @theName

-- Display the results
PRINT RTRIM(@theName) + ' is the fifth name'

CLOSE simpleCursor
DEALLOCATE simpleCursor
```

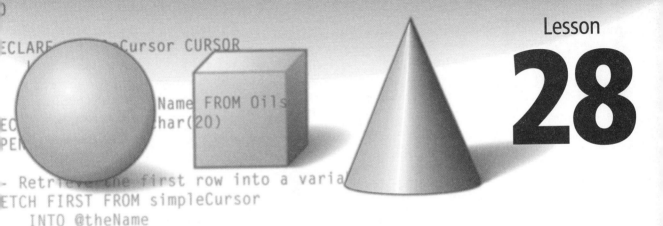

Stored Procedures

> ### In this lesson you will learn how to:
>
> - Execute a simple stored procedure.
> - Execute a stored procedure with input parameters.
> - Execute a stored procedure with named parameters.
> - Execute a stored procedure using the DEFAULT parameter keyword.
> - Execute a stored procedure with output parameters.
> - Execute a stored procedure with a return value.
> - Create a simple stored procedure.
> - Create a stored procedure with an input parameter.
> - Create a stored procedure with a default parameter value.
> - Create a stored procedure with an output parameter.
> - Create a stored procedure with a return value.

In the last few lessons we've been using SQL scripts, which are batches of Transact-SQL statements stored in a text file. SQL Server also provides *stored procedures*, which are batches of Transact-SQL statements stored by the server. We'll look at using and creating stored procedures in this lesson.

Understanding Stored Procedures

Stored procedures are not the only way to execute Transact-SQL statements. We've looked at Transact-SQL scripts, and it's also possible to send commands directly from an application. But stored procedures do have advantages:

- Stored procedures are database objects; they reside in a database file and are moved with the file if you detach or replicate the database.

- Stored procedures allow you to pass data to the procedure for handling and receive both data and a result code back from the procedure.

- Stored procedures are stored in an optimized form, allowing them to execute faster.

Exchanging Data with Stored Procedures

The SQL scripts we worked with in earlier lessons ran independently—there was no way to pass any information into them, and the only information they returned was displayed in the Grids or Messages Pane of the Query window. Stored procedures provide two methods of communicating with external processes: parameters and return values.

Parameters are a special kind of local variable declared as part of the stored procedure. You can use parameters to pass information into the stored procedure (input parameters) or receive data back from the stored procedure (output parameters).

A return value is similar to the result of a function and can be assigned to a local variable in the same way. Return values are always integers. They can theoretically be used to return any result, but by convention they're used to return the execution status of a stored procedure. For example, a stored procedure might return 0 if everything went fine, or −1 if there was an error. More sophisticated stored procedures can return different return values to indicate the nature of the error encountered.

It's important not to confuse parameters and return codes with any result sets that might be returned from a stored procedure. A stored procedure can contain any number of SELECT statements that will return result sets. You don't have to use a parameter to receive them; they will be returned to the application program independently.

System Procedures

Stored procedures come in two "flavors": the system procedures that are created by SQL Server, and user-defined stored procedures that you create yourself. System stored procedures are stored in the master database. All of them begin with the characters *sp_*.

TIP You can create a stored procedure using *sp_* as the first part of the name, but it's not a good idea. Because SQL Server always looks for a stored procedure in the master database first, if a system procedure exists with the same name, your stored procedure will never be executed.

There are literally hundreds of system procedures in the master database. Many of them provide a programmatic way of performing the administrative tasks we examined in Part 1 of this book. For example, sp_addlogin allows you to add a database login id, and sp_add_jobschedule allows you to schedule jobs such as database backups.

TIP SQL Server Books Online has details of all the system stored procedures.

Other system procedures help you manage database objects. For example, sp_rename allows you to rename a database objects, and sp_renamedb provides a means to rename a database.

TIP Using the sp_renamedb system procedure is the only way to rename a database. It can't be done in the Enterprise Manager.

An important group of system procedures provides information about the current system status: sp_who provides information about current users and processes; sp_cursor_list provides a list of the current cursors for an option connection; and sp_helpdb lists the current databases maintained by a server and, for any single database, tells you the physical locations of the data and transaction log files. You can also use sp_help, which provides information about database objects. It can list the name, owner, and type of every database object, the details of system and user-defined data types, and the names and parameters of stored procedures.

User-Defined Stored Procedures

Just like a database table, a user-defined stored procedure is an object that is part of the database in which it is created and will move with it. The difference is that instead of storing data, stored procedure objects store Transact-SQL code.

TIP SQL Server creates a number of stored procedures in each database. The names of these stored procedures all begin with *dt_* and are used for source control and by data transformation services.

Executing a stored procedure is usually faster than submitting a batch of commands from an application. This is because SQL Server can perform some of the steps involved in executing the procedure in advance and store them along with the stored procedure.

Using and Creating Stored Procedures

As you would any other database object, you must first create a user-defined stored procedure before you can use it. To make things a bit easier, we'll look at these two steps in reverse order: First we'll examine using stored procedures, and then you'll create your own.

Using Stored Procedures

The EXECUTE statement is used to invoke user-defined and system stored procedures. If the stored procedure doesn't require parameters or if it doesn't return a result, the syntax is very simple:

```
EXECUTE procedure_name
```

IP   The EXECUTE keyword isn't necessary if the call to the stored procedure is the first statement in a batch. As always, though, better safe than sorry, and getting in the habit of always using EXECUTE or its abbreviation EXEC is likely to save you time down the road when you forget and add a statement above the stored procedure.

Execute a simple stored procedure

New Query button

1. Click the New Query button on the Query Analyzer toolbar.

   The Query Analyzer opens a new Query window.

2. Type the following statement into the Query window:

   ```
   EXECUTE sp_helpdb
   ```

Execute Query button

3. Click the Execute Query button on the Query Analyzer toolbar.

   The Query Analyzer executes the stored procedure and displays the results.

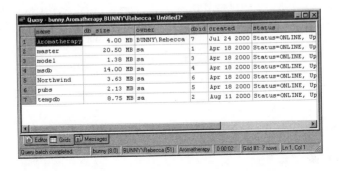

 MPORTANT   Since sp_help displays all the databases in the current server, your installation probably won't match mine. The databases listed in the Grids Pane on your system will be different than those shown in the screen shot.

If the stored procedure accepts input parameters, you can provide them by position or by name. To provide parameters by position, you simply list them after the stored procedure name, separating individual parameters with commas:

```
EXECUTE procedure_name param [, param …]
```

> ## Using the Object Browser with Stored Procedures
>
> The Object Browser contains a Stored Procedures folder for every database, including master. Each stored procedure in the list contains a Parameters folder. The stored procedure parameters are listed in order in the folder, so you can use it as a quick check of parameter names and their positions.
>
> You can also use the scripting commands on the context menu to create an EXECUTE script for the stored procedure. The EXECUTE script the Object Browser creates includes declarations of local variables for return values and output parameters.

Execute a stored procedure with input parameters

Clear Window button

1. Select the Editor Pane of the Query window, and click the Clear Window button on the Query Analyzer toolbar.

2. Type the following statement in the Query window:

```
EXECUTE sp_dboption 'Aromatherapy', 'read only'
```

Execute Query button

3. Click the Execute Query button on the Query Analyzer toolbar.

   The Query Analyzer executes the query and displays the results.

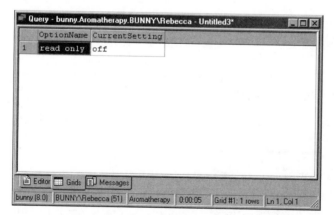

Parameters can also be passed to a stored procedure by explicitly naming them. You need to do more typing with this approach, but it allows you to provide the parameters in any order. The syntax for using named parameters is:

```
EXECUTE stored_procedure @param_name = value [, @param_name = value ...]
```

Execute a stored procedure with named parameters

Clear Window button

1. Select the Editor Pane of the Query window, and click the Clear Window button on the Query Analyzer toolbar.

2. Type the following statement in the Query window:

```
EXECUTE sp_dboption @optname = 'read only',
@dbname = 'Aromatherapy'
```

Execute Query button

3. Click the Execute Query button on the Query Analyzer toolbar.

   The Query Analyzer executes the query and displays the results.

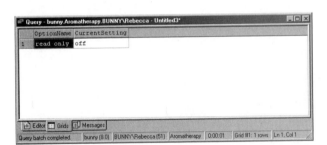

Some stored procedures provide default values for their parameters. Like the default value on a table column, a parameter default is used by the stored procedure if the user doesn't explicitly provide a value. Using the default is easy if you're using named parameters—just don't specify a value for that parameter.

If you're passing the parameters by position, how you access the default parameter depends on where it is in the list. If the parameter is at the end of the list or if it is the only parameter, you can leave it out. We did that when we executed sp_helpdb without specifying a database name. If the parameter isn't at the end of the parameter list, you can use the special keyword DEFAULT to tell the stored procedure to use the default value.

Execute a stored procedure using the DEFAULT parameter keyword

Clear Window button

1. Select the Editor Pane of the Query window, and click the Clear Window button on the Query Analyzer toolbar.

2. Type the following statement in the Query window:

```
EXECUTE sp_dboption DEFAULT, 'read only'
```

Execute Query button

3. Click the Execute Query button on the Query Analyzer toolbar.

The Query Analyzer executes the query and displays the results.

In addition to accepting data passed into them, stored procedures can also pass data back out again using output parameters. Output parameters must be local variables. They can be specified using their names or their positions, but are followed by the keyword OUTPUT.

Execute a stored procedure with output parameters

Clear Window button

1. Select the Editor Pane of the Query window, and click the Clear Window button on the Query Analyzer toolbar.

Load Script button

2. Click the Load Script button on the Query Analyzer toolbar.

The Query Analyzer displays the Open Query File dialog box.

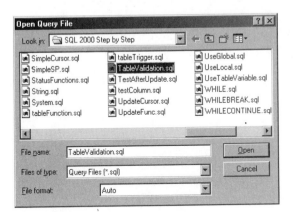

3. Navigate to the SQL 2000 Step by Step folder in the root directory, select the TableValidation script, and click Open.

The Query Analyzer loads the script.

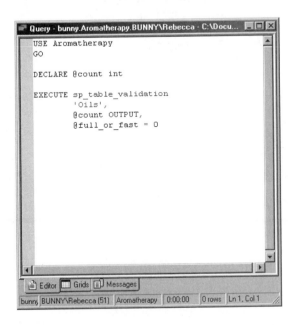

4. Click the Execute Query button on the Query Analyzer toolbar.

Execute Query button

The Query Analyzer executes the script and displays the results.

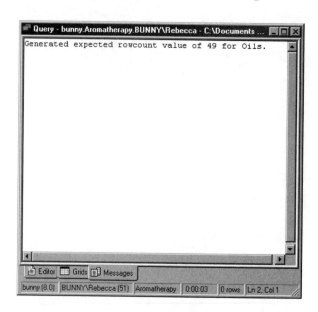

The syntax for stored procedure return values is a hybrid between the EXECUTE statement and the SET statement:

```
EXECUTE @variable_name = stored_procedure [, param [, param … ] ]
```

Most system procedures have return values, but like default parameters, you can ignore them. If you don't specify a local variable to accept the results, SQL Server will simply throw the value away.

Execute a stored procedure with a return value

Load Script button

1. Click the Load Script button on the Query Analyzer toolbar.

   The Query Analyzer displays the Open Query File dialog box.

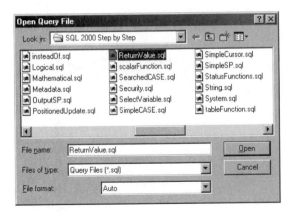

2. Select the ReturnValue script, and click Open.

The Query Analyzer loads the script.

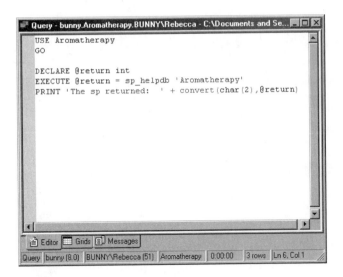

3. Click the Execute Query button on the Query Analyzer toolbar.

Execute Query button

The Query Analyzer executes the query and displays the results.

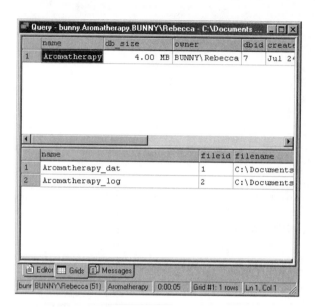

4. Select the Messages tab.

The Query Analyzer displays the results of the PRINT statement, showing the return value.

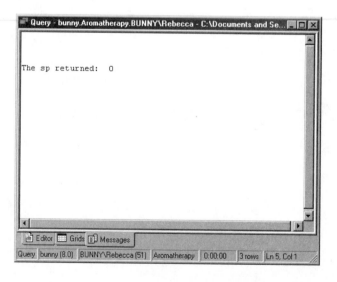

Creating Stored Procedures

As you might have come to expect, stored procedures are created using a variation of the CREATE statement—this time CREATE PROCEDURE. The syntax of the CREATE PROCEDURE statement is:

```
CREATE PROCEDURE procedure_name
[parameter_list]
AS
procedure_statements
```

The *procedure_name* must follow the rules for identifiers.

 IP   You can create temporary local and global stored procedures by prefacing the procedure name with # or ##, respectively.

The *procedure_statements* following AS in the CREATE statement define the actions that will be executed when the stored procedure is invoked. They are exactly the same as the scripts we've been writing. In fact, you can think of everything before the AS keyword as a header to a SQL script.

Stored procedures can call other stored procedures, a process known as *nesting*. In fact, a stored procedure can call a stored procedure that calls a stored procedure, up to a limit of 32 levels deep.

Create a simple stored procedure

Load Script button

1. Click the Load Script button on the Query Analyzer toolbar.

   The Query Analyzer displays the Open Query File dialog box.

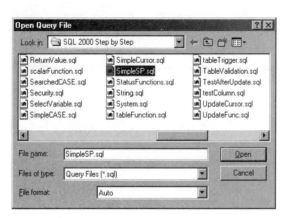

2. Select the SimpleSP script, and click Open.

   The Query Analyzer loads the script.

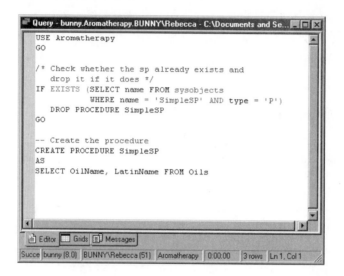

3. Click the Execute Query button on the Query Analyzer toolbar.

   The Query Analyzer creates the stored procedure.

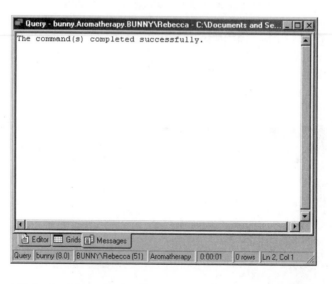

Execute Query button

4. Click the New Query button on the Query Analyzer toolbar.

New Query button

The Query Analyzer displays a new Query window.

5. Type the following statement in the Editor tab:

```
EXECUTE SimpleSP
```

Execute Query button

6. Click the Execute Query button on the Query Analyzer toolbar.

The Query Analyzer executes the stored procedure and displays the results.

7. Close the Query window, discarding changes when prompted.

Each parameter in the *parameter_list* has the structure:

```
@parameter_name data_type [= default_value] [OUTPUT]
```

As always, the *parameter_name* must follow the rules for identifiers. Parameter names always start with @, just like a local variable. Parameters *are* local variables; they are visible only within the stored procedure. You can have a maximum of 2,100 parameters per stored procedure.

The *default_value* is, of course, the value that will be used by the stored procedure if the user doesn't specify the input parameter value in the stored procedure invocation. The OUTPUT keyword, also optional, defines parameters that will be returned to the calling script.

611

Create a stored procedure with an input parameter

1. Select the window containing the SimpleSP script.

Load Script button

2. Click the Load Script button on the Query Analyzer toolbar.

   The Query Analyzer displays the Open Query File dialog box.

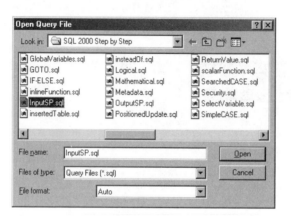

3. Select the InputSP script, and click Open.

   The Query Analyzer loads the script.

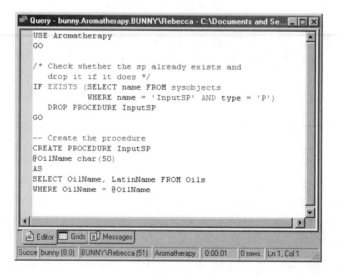

Execute Query button

4. Click the Execute Query button on the Query Analyzer toolbar.

   The Query Analyzer creates the stored procedure.

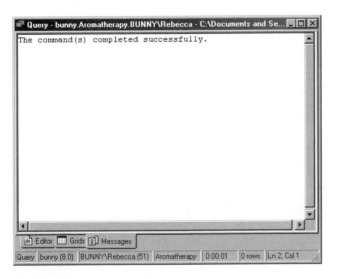

New Query button

5. Click the New Query button on the Query Analyzer toolbar.

   The Query Analyzer displays a new Query window.

6. Type the following statement in the Editor tab:

```
EXECUTE InputSP 'Basil'
```

Execute Query button

7. Click the Execute Query button on the Query Analyzer toolbar.

   The Query Analyzer executes the stored procedure and displays the results.

8. Close the Query window, discarding changes when prompted.

Create a stored procedure with a default value

1. Select the Query window containing the InputSP script.

Load Script button

2. Click the Load Script button on the Query Analyzer toolbar.

The Query Analyzer displays the Open Query File dialog box.

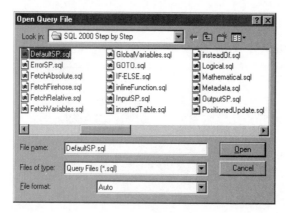

3. Select the DefaultSP script, and click Open.

The Query Analyzer loads the script.

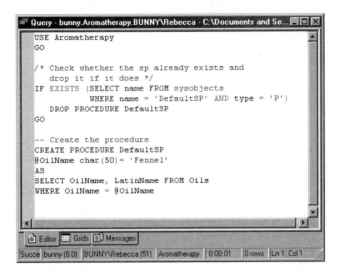

4. Click the Execute Query button on the Query Analyzer toolbar.

Execute Query button

The Query Analyzer creates the stored procedure.

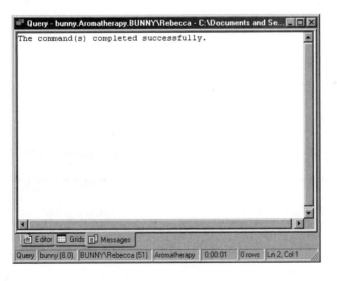

New Query button

5. Click the New Query button on the Query Analyzer toolbar.

   The Query Analyzer displays a new Query window.

6. Type the following statement in the Editor tab:

   ```
   EXECUTE DefaultSP
   ```

Execute Query button

7. Click the Execute Query button on the Query Analyzer toolbar.

   The Query Analyzer executes the stored procedure and displays the results.

8. Close the Query window, discarding changes when prompted.

Create a stored procedure with an output parameter

1. Select the window containing the DefaultSP script.

2. Click the Load Script button on the Query Analyzer toolbar.

Load Script button

The Query Analyzer displays the Open Query File dialog box.

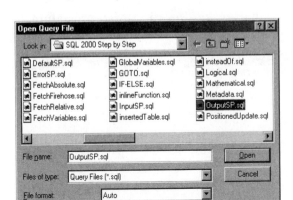

3. Select the OutputSP script, and click Open.

The Query Analyzer loads the script.

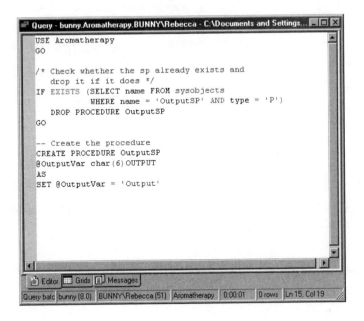

Execute Query button

4. Click the Execute Query button on the Query Analyzer toolbar.

The Query Analyzer creates the stored procedure.

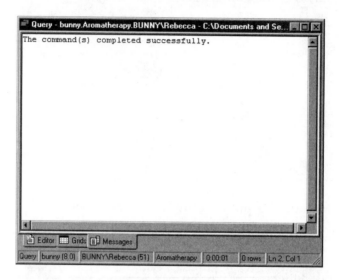

New Query button

5. Click the New Query button on the Query Analyzer toolbar.

The Query Analyzer displays a new Query window.

6. Type the following statements in the Editor tab:

```
DECLARE @myOutput char(6)
EXECUTE OutputSP @myOutput OUTPUT
SELECT @myOutput
```

Execute Query button

7. Click the Execute Query button on the Query Analyzer toolbar.

The Query Analyzer executes the stored procedure and displays the results.

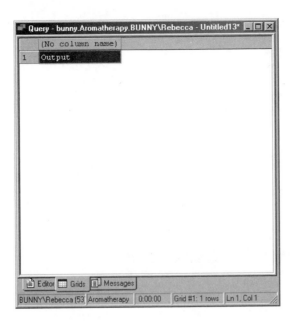

8. Close the Query window, discarding changes when prompted.

Return values are implemented using the RETURN statement, which takes the form:

`RETURN(int)`

In the RETURN statement, *int* is an integer value. As we saw earlier, return values are most often used to return the execution status of a stored procedure, with 0 indicating successful completion, and any other number indicating an error. Errors can be tested using the @@ERROR global variable, which returns the execution status of the most recent Transact-SQL command: 0 for successful completion, or a nonzero number indicating the error that occurred.

> **TIP** SQL Server error message strings are stored in the master database, in the sysmessages table. You can add your own custom error messages to the table using the sp_addmessage system procedure, and then use the RAISERROR function to generate database-specific or even application-specific errors.

Create a stored procedure with a return value

1. Select the window containing the OutputSP script.

2. Click the Load Script button on the Query Analyzer toolbar.

   Load Script button

   The Query Analyzer displays the Open Query File dialog box.

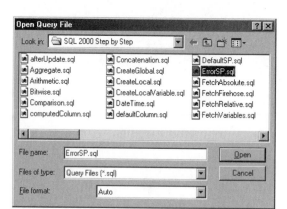

3. Select the ErrorSP script, and click Open.

   The Query Analyzer loads the script.

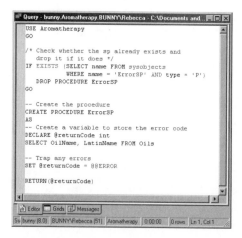

Execute Query button

4. Click the Execute Query button on the Query Analyzer toolbar.

   The Query Analyzer creates the stored procedure.

New Query button

5. Click the New Query button on the Query Analyzer toolbar.

   The Query Analyzer displays a new Query window.

6. Type the following statements in the Editor tab:

```
DECLARE @theError int
EXECUTE @theError = ErrorSP
SELECT @theError AS 'Return Value'
```

Execute Query button

7. Click the Execute Query button on the Query Analyzer toolbar.

   The Query Analyzer executes the stored procedure and displays the results. The second grid shows a 0, indicating that the command executed successfully.

8. Close the Query window, discarding changes when prompted.

Lesson 28 Quick Reference

To	SQL Syntax
Execute a simple stored procedure	EXECUTE *procedure_name*
Execute a stored procedure with input parameters	EXECUTE *procedure_name param* [, *param* ...]
Execute a stored procedure with named parameters	EXECUTE *stored_procedure @param_name = value* [, *@param_name = value* ...]
Execute a stored procedure with output parameters	Follow the *@param_name* in the EXECUTE statement with the keyword OUTPUT
Execute a stored procedure with a return value	EXECUTE *@variable_name = stored_procedure* [, *param* [, *param* ...]]
Create a stored procedure	CREATE PROCEDURE *procedure_name* AS *procedure_statements*
Return a value from a stored procedure	RETURN(*return_value*)

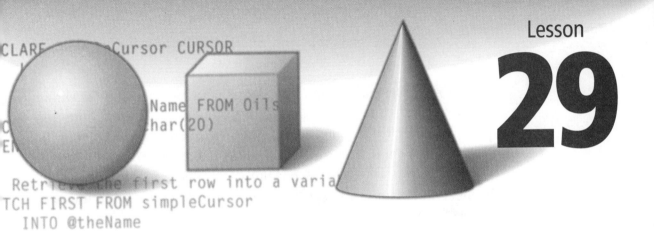

Triggers

> **In this lesson you will learn how to:**
>
> ■ Create an AFTER trigger.
>
> ■ Create an INSTEAD OF trigger.
>
> ■ Use the UPDATE function.
>
> ■ Use the inserted and deleted tables.

A trigger is a special kind of stored procedure that Microsoft SQL Server executes automatically when you modify a row using the INSERT, UP-DATE, or DELETE command. In this lesson, we'll examine the different kinds of triggers, including the powerful INSTEAD OF trigger, which is new to SQL Server 2000.

Understanding Triggers

The advantage of a trigger procedure is that SQL Server invokes it auto-matically whenever the command for which it is defined is issued. This makes the database more robust. You don't need to worry whether the database clients—users or applications—understand and will implement all the subtle data dependencies and business rules.

Say, for example, that a sales organization has a rule that an order with a total value of $10,000 or greater requires a credit check. If CreditApproved is a column in the Customer table but the order is being added to the Order table, you couldn't use a CHECK constraint to implement the rule, but it's worrisome to leave the responsibility for enforcing it to the database clients. A trigger provides a mechanism for enforcing the rule within the database itself.

Triggers can also insulate clients from changes to the database rules. To continue the previous example, if the business rule changes to require credit approval only if the invoice value is $15,000 or more, the new rule can be implemented at the database level, without checking and updating all the client applications.

Triggers are typically used to enforce business rules that can't be enforced with a table constraint. Up until the release of SQL Server 2000, triggers were needed to enforce cascading referential integrity, but this rule can now be enforced at the table level, as we've seen. Most rules that involve multiple tables, however, such as calculating summary values or constraining values based on another table, as in our example, are usually most easily implemented via a trigger.

 IP   Although the performance of triggers isn't normally an issue (as it is with cursors), you should always implement rules at the lowest level possible. Don't use a trigger if a CHECK constraint will do, and don't use a CHECK constraint if you can use a UNIQUE constraint.

AFTER Triggers

SQL Server 2000 supports two different types of triggers: AFTER triggers and INSTEAD OF triggers. The triggers are invoked when you would expect them to be: AFTER triggers are invoked after the command for which it is declared is executed, and INSTEAD OF triggers are invoked instead of the command.

You can create AFTER triggers for the INSERT, UPDATE, and DELETE commands. AFTER triggers can be created only for tables, not views, but you can have multiple triggers for each of these three commands. Conversely, a single trigger can apply to any combination of the three commands.

IP If you create multiple triggers for a single command, you can use the system procedure sp_settriggerorder to specify the first and last trigger to be executed for the command.

An AFTER trigger is invoked after all the lower-level constraint processing is performed and will not be invoked if a constraint violation occurs. For example, if an attempt is made to insert a row that violates the PRIMARY KEY constraint on a table, the INSERT statement will fail *before* the trigger is called.

INSTEAD OF Triggers

INSTEAD OF triggers replace the command for which they're declared. Like AFTER triggers, you can define INSTEAD OF triggers for INSERT, UPDATE, or DELETE commands. A single trigger can be applied to multiple commands.

Unlike AFTER triggers, however, you can create INSTEAD OF triggers for both tables and views, but only a single INSTEAD OF trigger can be created for each action on that table or view.

INSTEAD OF triggers are largely incompatible with cascading referential integrity. You cannot declare an INSTEAD OF DELETE or INSTEAD OF UPDATE trigger on a table that has a foreign key defined with a DELETE or UPDATE action.

Because INSTEAD OF triggers can be declared on views, they're extremely useful for providing view functionality that wouldn't otherwise be available. For example, SQL Server prevents an INSERT statement for a view containing a GROUP BY clause, but allows you to define an INSTEAD OF INSERT trigger for the view. You can use the processing of the trigger to insert records into the tables underlying the view, thereby making it appear to the user that a new row has been inserted into the view.

> ## "BEFORE" Triggers
>
> There isn't a BEFORE trigger, per se, but an INSTEAD OF trigger can issue the command for which it is declared, and the command will be issued as if the INSTEAD OF trigger didn't exist.
>
> For example, if you want to check some condition before an INSERT, you could declare an INSTEAD OF INSERT trigger. The INSTEAD OF trigger would perform the check and then issue an INSERT on the table. The INSERT statement would execute normally, without calling the INSTEAD OF trigger recursively.

Creating Triggers

SQL Server imposes a few constraints on the processing performed by triggers. You cannot CREATE, ALTER, or DROP a database using a trigger; you can't restore a database or log file; and you can't perform certain operations that change the configuration of SQL Server. (Consult SQL Server Books Online for a complete list of prohibited commands.)

If you change database options within the trigger, the change will stay in effect only for the duration of the trigger processing; the option will then revert to its original value.

You can theoretically use the RETURN statement to return a value from a trigger, but you can't rely on a client application knowing that it exists or what to do with it. The RAISERROR command is therefore generally a better technique, since most applications are designed to handle these errors.

Using the CREATE TRIGGER Command

Just as with any other database object, you define a trigger using a form of the CREATE statement. The basic syntax of the CREATE statement is:

```
CREATE TRIGGER trigger_name
ON table_or_view
trigger_type command_list
AS
SQL_statements
```

The *trigger_name* must conform to the rules for identifiers. The *table_or_view* can be a view name only if the *trigger_type* is INSTEAD OF, since you can define only this type of trigger on views. Triggers cannot be created on temporary tables or system tables, but they can reference temporary tables.

The *trigger_type* is one of the keywords AFTER, FOR, or INSTEAD OF, while the *command_list* is any combination of INSERT, UPDATE, or DELETE commands. If you list more than one command, separate them by commas.

 IP Earlier versions of SQL Server supported only AFTER triggers and used the *trigger_type* FOR. This syntax is still supported in SQL Server 2000, but it means precisely the same thing as AFTER.

The *SQL_statements* following the AS keyword define the processing to be performed by the trigger, just as they do for a stored procedure, except that triggers cannot have parameters.

Create an AFTER trigger

New Query button

1. Click the New Query window on the Query Analyzer toolbar.

   The Query Analyzer opens a new Query window.

Load Script button

2. Click the Load Script button on the Query Analyzer toolbar.

   The Query Analyzer displays the Open Query File dialog box.

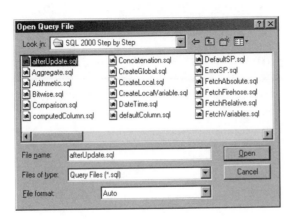

3. Navigate to the SQL 2000 Step by Step folder in the root directory, select the afterUpdate script, and click Open.

The Query Analyzer loads the script into the Query window.

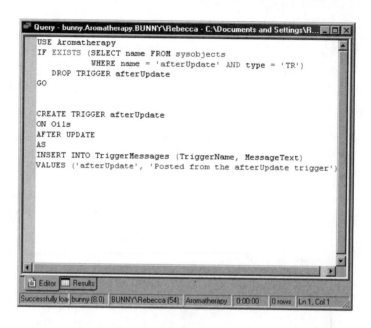

```
Query - bunny.Aromatherapy.BUNNY\Rebecca - C:\Documents and Settings\R...

USE Aromatherapy
IF EXISTS (SELECT name FROM sysobjects
            WHERE name = 'afterUpdate' AND type = 'TR')
    DROP TRIGGER afterUpdate
GO


CREATE TRIGGER afterUpdate
ON Oils
AFTER UPDATE
AS
INSERT INTO TriggerMessages (TriggerName, MessageText)
VALUES ('afterUpdate', 'Posted from the afterUpdate trigger')
```

Editor Results

Successfully loa | bunny (8.0) | BUNNY\Rebecca (54) | Aromatherapy | 0:00:00 | 0 rows | Ln 1, Col 1

4. Click the Execute Query button on the Query Analyzer toolbar.

Execute Query button

The Query Analyzer creates the trigger.

New Query button

5. Click the New Query button on the Query Analyzer toolbar.

The Query Analyzer opens a new Query window.

Load Script button

6. Click the Load Script button on the Query Analyzer toolbar.

The Query Analyzer displays the Open Query File dialog box.

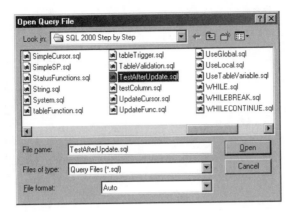

7. Select the TestAfterUpdate script, and click Open.

The Query Analyzer loads the script.

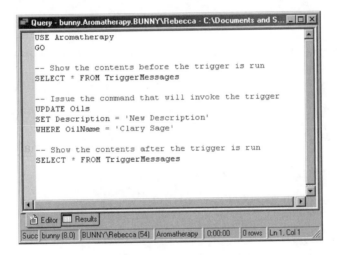

8. Click the Execute Query button on the Query Analyzer toolbar.

The Query Analyzer runs the script and displays the result.

Execute Query button

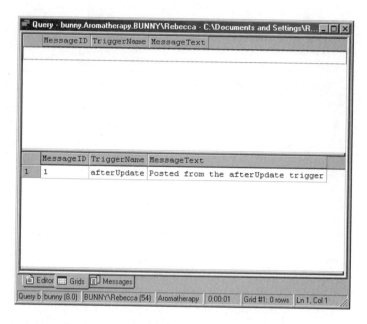

Create an INSTEAD OF trigger

1. Select the Query window containing the afterUpdate script.

Load Script button

2. Click the Load Script button on the Query Analyzer toolbar.

   The Query Analyzer displays the Open Query File dialog box.

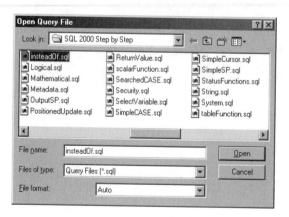

3. Select the insteadOf script, and click Open.

The Query Analyzer loads the script into the Query window.

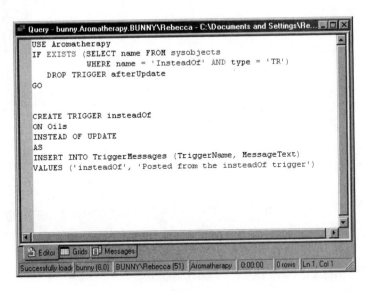

```
Query - bunny.Aromatherapy.BUNNY\Rebecca - C:\Documents and Settings\Re...
USE Aromatherapy
IF EXISTS (SELECT name FROM sysobjects
            WHERE name = 'InsteadOf' AND type = 'TR')
    DROP TRIGGER afterUpdate
GO


CREATE TRIGGER insteadOf
ON Oils
INSTEAD OF UPDATE
AS
INSERT INTO TriggerMessages (TriggerName, MessageText)
VALUES ('insteadOf', 'Posted from the insteadOf trigger')
```

Editor | Grids | Messages
Successfully load | bunny (8.0) | BUNNY\Rebecca (51) | Aromatherapy | 0:00:00 | 0 rows | Ln 1, Col 1

Execute Query button

4. Click the Execute Query button on the Query Analyzer toolbar.

The Query Analyzer creates the trigger.

5. Select the Query window containing the TestAfterUpdate script.

Execute Query button

6. Click the Execute Query button on the Query Analyzer toolbar.

The Query Analyzer runs the script and displays the result.

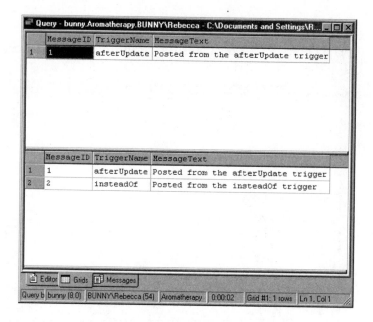

Using the UPDATE Function

SQL Server provides a special function, UPDATE, that can be used within a trigger to determine whether a specific column in the row is being updated. The UPDATE function has the syntax:

```
UPDATE(column_name)
```

UPDATE will return TRUE if the data values for the specified column were changed by either an INSERT or UPDATE command.

 IP Another Transact-SQL function, COLUMNS_UPDATED, returns a bitmask with a bit set for each column updated. COLUMNS_UPDATED can be more efficient than the UPDATE function if you need to check the status of multiple columns.

Use the UPDATE function

1. Select the Query window containing the insteadOf script.

2. Click the Load Script button on the Query Analyzer toolbar.

Load Script button

The Query Analyzer displays the Open Query File dialog box.

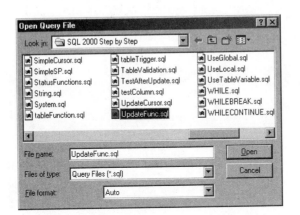

3. Select the UpdateFunc script, and click Open.

   The Query Analyzer loads the script into the Query window.

```
Query - bunny.Aromatherapy.BUNNY\Rebecca - C:\Documents and Settings\Rebecca\...

USE Aromatherapy
IF EXISTS (SELECT name FROM sysobjects
            WHERE name = 'UpdateFunc' AND type = 'TR')
    DROP TRIGGER UpdateFunc
DROP TRIGGER insteadOf
GO


CREATE TRIGGER UpdateFunc
ON Oils
AFTER UPDATE
AS
IF UPDATE(Description)
        INSERT INTO TriggerMessages (TriggerName, MessageText)
        VALUES ('UpdateFunc', 'Description updated')
IF UPDATE(OilName)
        INSERT INTO TriggerMessages (TriggerName, MessageText)
        VALUES ('UpdateFunc', 'OilName updated')
```

Editor | Grids | Messages
Query batch completed. | bunny (8.0) | BUNNY\Rebecca (51) | Aromatherapy | 0:00:00 | 0 rows | Ln 6, Col 3

4. Click the Execute Query button on the Query Analyzer toolbar.

   The Query Analyzer creates the trigger.

Execute Query button

*Execute Query
button*

5. Select the Query window containing the TestAfterUpdate script.

6. Click the Execute Query button on the Query Analyzer toolbar.

   The Query Analyzer runs the script and displays the result.

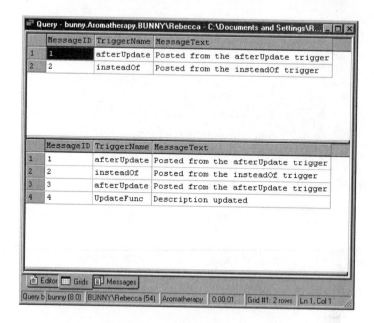

Using the Inserted and Deleted Tables

SQL Server creates two tables to help in manipulating data during triggers. The inserted and deleted tables are temporary, memory-resident tables that contain the contents of the rows affected by the command that invoked the trigger.

When a trigger is called from a DELETE command, the deleted table will contain the rows that were removed from the table. For an INSERT command, the inserted table will contain a copy of the new rows. Physically, an UPDATE statement is a DELETE followed by an INSERT, so the deleted table will contain the old values, and the inserted table the new values. You can reference the contents of these tables from within the trigger, but you cannot alter them.

Remember that AFTER triggers are not called until the modifications to the table have been made, so the rows in the underlying tables will already have been changed. An INSTEAD OF trigger, on the other hand, is called in place of the action for which it is defined, so the table will not yet have been changed. In fact, the table will not be changed at all unless the INSTEAD OF command issues the appropriate commands.

MPORTANT A trigger is called once per *command*, not once per row. You need to be careful to write your triggers to deal with multiple rows, if they exist, in the inserted or deleted tables. The global variable @@ROWCOUNT will return the number of records in these tables if you call it at the beginning of the trigger.

Use the deleted table

1. Select the Query window containing the UpdateFunc script.

Load Script button

2. Click the Load Script button on the Query Analyzer toolbar.

   The Query Analyzer displays the Open Query File dialog box.

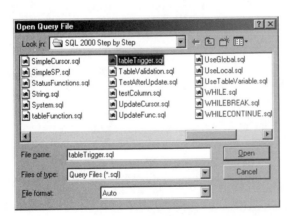

3. Select the tableTrigger script and click Open.

   The Query Analyzer loads the script into the Query window.

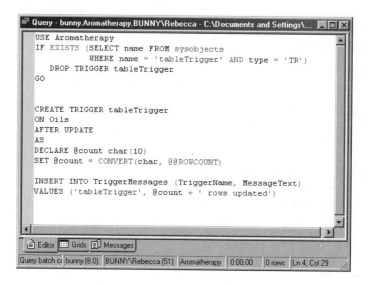

```
USE Aromatherapy
IF EXISTS (SELECT name FROM sysobjects
            WHERE name = 'tableTrigger' AND type = 'TR')
    DROP TRIGGER tableTrigger
GO


CREATE TRIGGER tableTrigger
ON Oils
AFTER UPDATE
AS
DECLARE @count char(10)
SET @count = CONVERT(char, @@ROWCOUNT)

INSERT INTO TriggerMessages (TriggerName, MessageText)
VALUES ('tableTrigger', @count + ' rows updated')
```

Execute Query button

4. Click the Execute Query button on the Query Analyzer toolbar.

   The Query Analyzer creates the trigger.

5. Select the Query window containing the TestAfterUpdate script.

Execute Query button

6. Click the Execute Query button on the Query Analyzer toolbar.

   The Query Analyzer runs the script and displays the result.

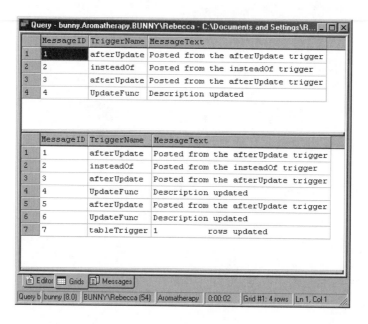

636

Lesson 29 Quick Reference

To	SQL Syntax
Create a trigger	CREATE TRIGGER *trigger_name* ON *table_or_view* *trigger_type command_list* AS *SQL_statements*
Use the UPDATE function	UPDATE(*column_name*)

```
USE Aromatherapy
GO


DECLARE simpleCursor CURSOR
    LOCAL
    KEYSET
    FOR SELECT OilName FROM Oils
DECLARE       Name char(20
OPEN

--           first row     o a variable
FET              simpleCu

-- Di        esults
PRINT RTRIM(@theName)              name'

-- Retrieve the fifth
FETCH ABSOLUTE 5 FROM simpleCursor
    INTO @theName

-- Display the results
PRINT RTRIM(@theName) + ' is the fifth name'

CLOSE simpleCursor
DEALLOCATE simpleCursor
```
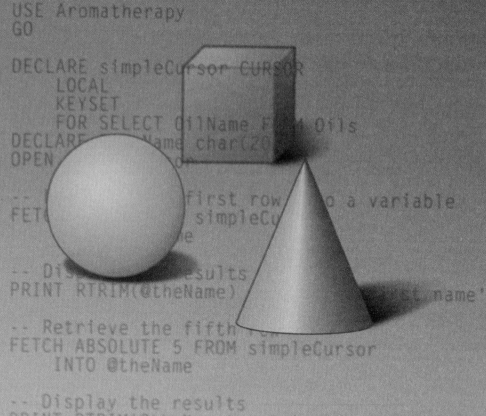

```
DECLARE        Cursor CURSOR

                Name FROM Oils
                har(20)
OPEN

-- Retrieve the first row into a varia
FETCH FIRST FROM simpleCursor
        INTO @theName

-- Display the results
PRINT RTRIM(@theName) + ' is the first name'
```

User-Defined Functions

```
FETCH ABSOLUTE 5 FROM simpleCursor
        INTO @theName
```

In this lesson you will learn how to:

- Create a scalar function.
- Create an inline table-valued function.
- Create a multistatement table-valued function.
- Use a function in a Transact-SQL statement.
- Use a function in a CREATE TABLE statement.

User-defined functions are new to SQL Server 2000. A user-defined function is similar to a stored procedure in that it accepts input parameters and returns a result. However, user-defined functions are more powerful than stored procedures and can be used in places stored procedures cannot, such as table definitions and the FROM clause of a SELECT statement.

Understanding User-Defined Functions

User-defined functions are categorized by the data type of their return values, either scalar or table-valued, and by their *determinism*. The determinism of a function is determined by the constancy of its results.

A function is deterministic if, given the same input values, it always returns the same result. The built-in function DATEADD, for example, is deterministic—adding three days to the 20th of April 1958 will always return the 23rd of April 1958.

A function is non-deterministic if it can return different values given the same input values. The built-in function GETDATE, for example, is non-deterministic. It will return a different value every time it is called.

The determinism of a user-defined function is independent of whether it is scalar or table-valued—both types of functions can be deterministic or non-deterministic. User-defined functions are considered to be deterministic if they reference database objects outside the scope of the function.

Non-deterministic functions cannot be used to create an index on a computed column. Clustered indexes cannot be created on views if the view references any non-deterministic functions (whether or not they're in the index).

Scalar Functions

A scalar user-defined function returns a scalar (single-valued) result, such as a string or a number. There are some restrictions on the data types returned by a scalar function. Non-scalar types such as cursors and tables are obviously prohibited. In addition, scalar functions can't return values with *timestamp, text, ntext,* or *image* data types, nor can the return value be a user-defined data type, even if the base type is scalar.

Scalar functions can be used anywhere a value of the data type returned by the function can be used. This includes the column list and WHERE clause of a SELECT statement, in expressions, and in table definitions as constraint expressions or even as the data type of a table column.

Table-Valued Functions

Not surprisingly, a table-valued user-defined function returns a table. Table-valued functions don't replace stored procedures or views, but in certain situations they can provide functionality that would be awkward, if not impossible, to provide using those objects.

The Oils table in the Aromatherapy sample database, for example, is fully normalized, so the details of PlantParts and Cautions are stored in different tables. None of this makes much sense to the average user, and the SELECT statement to fully denormalize a row in the Oils table would be difficult for most people to put together.

A view could be used to shield clients from this complexity, but views don't support parameters, so there would be no way for the client to specify the oil to be displayed at run time. Stored procedures accept parameters, but they can't be used in the FROM clause of a SELECT statement, which can make handling the results awkward. A table-valued user-defined function overcomes both these problems.

Given a user-defined function called, say, GetOilDetails that accepts an oil name and returns the details for that oil, your client could issue the following simple Transact-SQL statement and receive the fully denormalized oil details as a result.

```
SELECT * FROM GetOilDetails('Basil')
```

This sort of functionality provides obvious benefits for simplifying client software.

Creating User-Defined Functions

Like other database objects, user-defined functions are created using a variation of the CREATE statement. The syntax varies depending on the kind of user-defined function being created.

The Transact-SQL statements within the body of a user-defined function have two restrictions. First, functions cannot have side effects—that is, they cannot make any permanent changes to objects outside the scope of the function.

For example, if a temporary table is created within the function, the statements within the function can add, update, and delete the rows in the temporary table. A user-defined function cannot, however, change any rows in a permanent table.

The second restriction on the statements in a user-defined function is that they cannot invoke any non-deterministic functions (whether built-in or user-defined) or reference non-deterministic global variables such as @@TOTAL_ERRORS, which returns the number of errors encountered by SQL Server since the last time it was started.

Creating Scalar Functions

The CREATE statement for scalar user-defined functions has the simplest syntax of all the function types:

```
CREATE FUNCTION function_name ([parameter_list])
RETURNS data_type
AS
BEGIN
    [tsql_statements]
    RETURN (return_value)
END
```

The *function_name* must conform to the rules for identifiers. Although the *parameter_list* occupies a different place in the CREATE statement, it has the same syntax as the parameter list in a stored procedure:

```
@parameter_name data_type [= default_value]
```

The *parameter_name* must follow the rules for identifiers and must begin with @. User-defined functions can have a maximum of 1024 input parameters. They do not support output parameters—the only value returned from a user-defined function is the result of the function itself. Note that the *parameter_list* is optional, but the parentheses aren't.

The RETURNS clause defines the type of value returned by the function. As described above, scalar functions can return any scalar system data type except *timestamp, text, ntext,* or *image.*

The BEGIN...END statements surrounding the *tsql_statements* that make up the body of the function are required, even if the function body consists only of a single RETURN statement.

Create a scalar function

New Query button

1. Click the New Query button on the Query Analyzer toolbar.

The Query Analyzer opens a new Query window.

Load Script button

2. Click the Load Script button on the Query Analyzer toolbar.

The Query Analyzer displays the Open Query File dialog box.

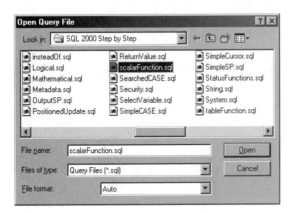

3. Navigate to the SQL 2000 Step by Step folder in the root directory, select the scalarFunction script, and click Open.

The Query Analyzer loads the script.

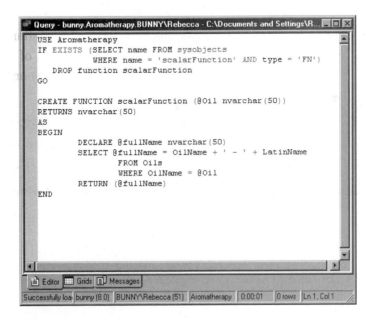

Execute Query button

4. Click the Execute Query button on the Query Analyzer toolbar.

   The Query Analyzer creates the user-defined function.

5. Expand the Functions folder of the Aromatherapy database in the Object Browser, and press F5 to refresh the display.

   The Object Browser displays dbo.scalarFunction in the list.

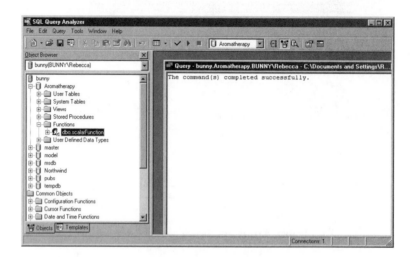

 OTE We'll use the user-defined functions we're creating here in the next section.

Creating Table-Valued Functions

The CREATE FUNCTION statement supports the creation of two different types of table-valued functions: inline and multistatement. The body of an inline table-valued function consists of a single SELECT statement, whereas a multistatement table-valued function can contain any number of Transact-SQL statements.

The syntax for an inline table-valued function is a kind of shorthand version of the CREATE FUNCTION statement. It has no BEGIN...END block and no statements other than the RETURN:

```
CREATE FUNCTION function_name (parameter_list)
RETURNS table
AS
RETURN (select_statement)
```

Create an inline table-valued function

1. Select the Query window containing the scalarFunction script.

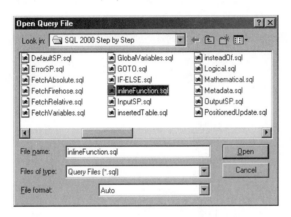

Load Script button

2. Click the Load Script button on the Query Analyzer toolbar.

   The Query Analyzer displays the Open Query File dialog box.

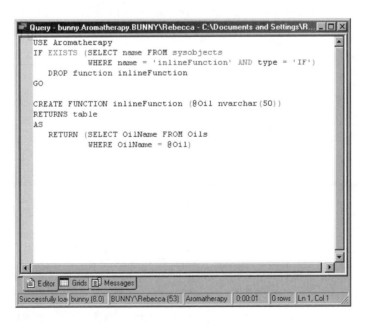

3. Select the inlineFunction script, and click Open.

   The Query Analyzer loads the script.

```
USE Aromatherapy
IF EXISTS (SELECT name FROM sysobjects
          WHERE name = 'inlineFunction' AND type = 'IF')
   DROP function inlineFunction
GO

CREATE FUNCTION inlineFunction (@Oil nvarchar(50))
RETURNS table
AS
   RETURN (SELECT OilName FROM Oils
           WHERE OilName = @Oil)
```

Execute Query button

4. Click the Execute Query button on the Query Analyzer toolbar.

   The Query Analyzer creates the user-defined function.

5. Select the Functions folder in the Object Browser, and press F5 to refresh the display.

   The Query Analyzer lists dbo.inlineFunction in the list.

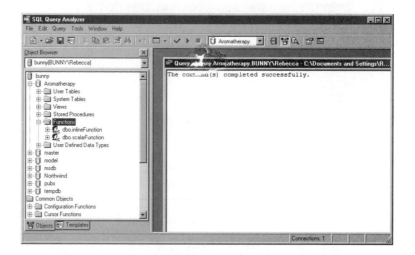

The CREATE FUNCTION syntax for a multistatement table-valued function combines the syntax of the scalar and inline functions:

```
CREATE FUNCTION function_name (parameter_list)
RETURNS @local_table_variable TABLE
    (table_definition)
AS
BEGIN
    tsql_statements
    RETURN
END
```

Like a scalar function, a multistatement table-valued function surrounds the Transact-SQL statements with a BEGIN...END block. Because the block can contain multiple SELECT statements, you must explicitly define the table to be returned in the RETURNS clause.

Since the RETURN statement in a multistatement table-valued function always returns the table defined in the RETURNS clause, it must be executed without arguments—for example, RETURN, not RETURN @myTable.

Create a multistatement table-valued function

1. Select the Query window containing the inlineFunction script.

2. Click the Load Script button on the Query Analyzer toolbar.

   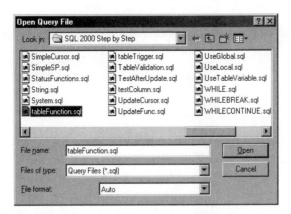

   Load Script button

   The Query Analyzer displays the Open Query File dialog box.

3. Select the tableFunction script, and click Open.

   The Query Analyzer loads the script.

Execute Query button

4. Click the Execute Query button on the Query Analyzer toolbar.

   The Query Analyzer creates the user-defined function.

5. Select the Functions folder in the Object Browser, and press F5 to refresh the display.

   The Query Analyzer lists dbo.tableFunction in the list.

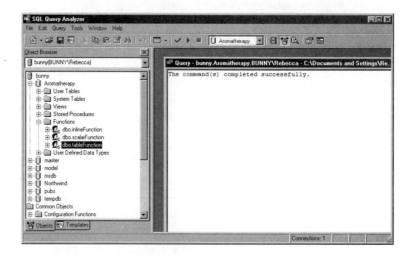

Using User-Defined Functions

Scalar functions are called using the syntax similar to that used by Transact-SQL built-in functions:

```
owner_name.function_name([parameter_list])
```

The *owner_name* of the function is not optional for a scalar function. You cannot use the named parameter syntax (for example, @*parameter_name* = *value*), nor can you omit parameters, but you can use the DEFAULT keyword to specify a default value, just as you can when calling a stored procedure.

 IP   SQL Server provides a few built-in user-defined functions. These aren't the same as the built-in functions. They begin with *fn_* and use the special calling syntax ::*function_name*([*parameter_list*]). The :: replaces the *owner_name* and identifies the function as a built-in user-defined function.

You can also use the EXECUTE statement with a scalar function:

```
EXECUTE @return_variable = function_name(parameter_list)
```

When you use the EXECUTE statement with a user-defined function, you don't need to include the *owner_name*. Using this syntax, you have the option of using named parameters:

```
EXECUTE @return_variable = function_name @parameter = value
                               [, @parameter = value [,...]]
```

If you use named parameters, the parameters do not need to be in the order they're declared in the function, but you must include all of them; you cannot omit parameter references to use the default value.

Table-valued user-defined functions, whether inline or multistatement, must always use the same syntax as built-in functions:

```
function_name([parameter_list])
```

The *owner_name* isn't required here, but you must include all the defined parameters, as you do when calling any user-defined function.

Using User-Defined Functions in Transact-SQL Statements

Scalar user-defined functions can be used anywhere the data type that they return can be used. Table-valued user-defined functions can be used only in the FROM clause of a SELECT statement.

 IP If the SELECT clause is within a DECLARE CURSOR statement, the cursor must be STATIC and READ_ONLY.

Use a scalar function in a PRINT statement

New Query button

1. Click the New Query button on the Query Analyzer toolbar.

   The Query Analyzer opens a new Query window.

2. Enter the following SQL statement in the Query window:

```
PRINT dbo.scalarFunction('German Chamomile')
```

Execute Query button

3. Click the Execute Query button on the Query Analyzer toolbar.

   The Query Analyzer executes the statement and displays the results.

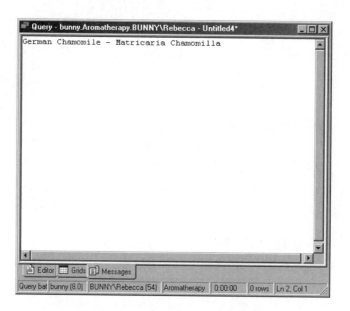

Use a scalar function in a SELECT statement

Clear Window button

1. Select the Editor tab of the Query window, and click the Clear Window button on the Query Analyzer toolbar.

   The Query Analyzer clears the Query window.

2. Enter the following SQL statement in the Query window:

```
SELECT OilID, dbo.scalarFunction(OilName)
FROM Oils
```

Execute Query button

3. Click the Execute Query button on the Query Analyzer toolbar.

The Query Analyzer executes the statement and displays the results.

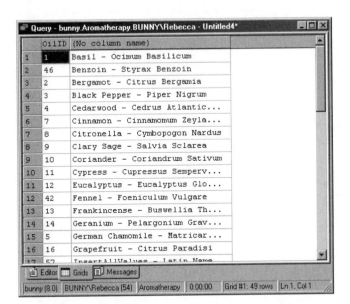

Use a table-valued function in a SELECT statement

Clear Window button

1. Select the Editor tab of the Query window, and click the Clear Window button on the Query Analyzer toolbar.

   The Query Analyzer clears the Query window.

2. Enter the following SQL statement in the Query window:

```
SELECT * FROM tableFunction()
```

Execute Query button

3. Click the Execute Query button on the Query Analyzer toolbar.

   The Query Analyzer executes the statement and displays the results.

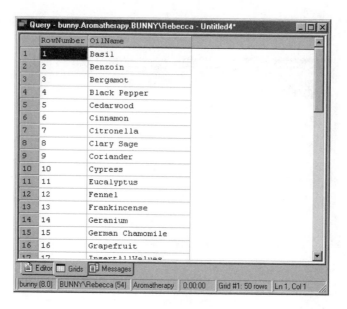

4. Close the Query window, discarding changes when prompted.

Using User-Defined Functions in Table Definitions

User-defined functions can be used in table definitions provided the owner of the table is also the owner of the user-defined function, but the parameters used in the function do have some constraints.

If used as the data type of a computed column, the parameters to the user-defined function must be either other columns in the table or constants. The same is true if the user-defined function is used as a CHECK constraint. If the user-defined function is used as a default value for a column, the parameters must be constants.

Use a user-defined function as a computed column

1. Select the Query window containing the tableFunction script.

2. Click the Load Script button on the Query Analyzer toolbar.

Load Script button

The Query Analyzer displays the Open Query File dialog box.

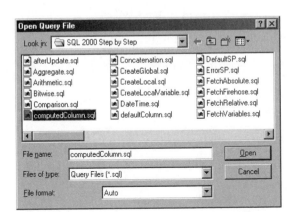

3. Select the computedColumn script, and click Open.

The Query Analyzer loads the script.

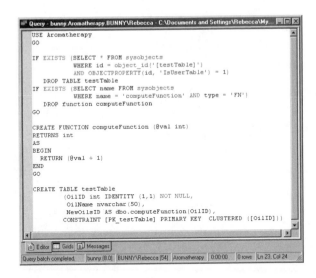

4. Click the Execute Query button on the Query Analyzer toolbar.

Execute Query button

The Query Analyzer creates the function and the table.

New Query button

5. Click the New Query button on the Query Analyzer window.

 The Query Analyzer opens a new Query window.

Load Script button

6. Click the Load Script button on the Query Analyzer toolbar.

 The Query Analyzer displays the Open Query File dialog box.

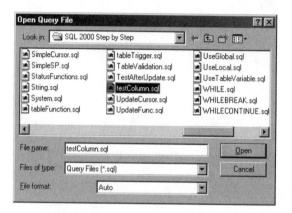

7. Select the testColumn script, and click Open.

 The Query Analyzer loads the script.

Execute Query button

8. Click the Execute Query button on the Query Analyzer toolbar.

The Query Analyzer executes the query and displays the result.

Use a user-defined function in a DEFAULT definition

1. Select the Query window containing the computedColumn script.

Load Script button

2. Click the Load Script button on the Query Analyzer toolbar.

The Query Analyzer displays the Open Query File dialog box.

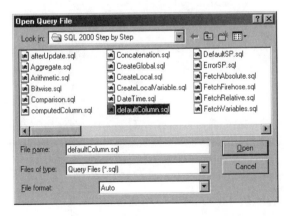

3. Select the defaultColumn script, and click Open.

The Query Analyzer loads the script.

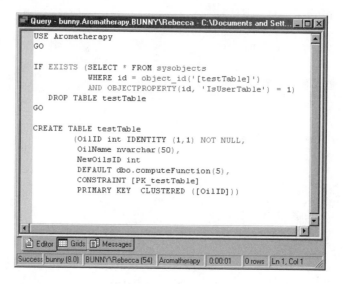

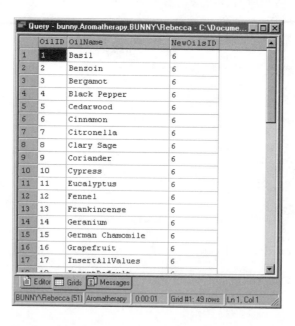

4. Click the Execute Query button on the Query Analyzer toolbar.

Execute Query button

The Query Analyzer creates the table.

5. Select the window containing the testColumn function.

6. Click the Execute Query button on the Query Analyzer toolbar.

Execute Query button

The Query Analyzer executes the query and displays the result.

Lesson 30 Quick Reference

To	SQL Syntax

Create a scalar function	CREATE FUNCTION *function_name*
	([*parameter_list*])
	RETURNS *data_type*
	AS
	BEGIN
	    [*tsql_statements*]
	    RETURN (*return_value*)
	END

Create an inline table-valued function	CREATE FUNCTION *function_name* (*parameter_list*) RETURNS table AS RETURN (*select_statement*)

Create a multistatement table-valued function	CREATE FUNCTION *function_name*
	(*parameter_list*)
	RETURNS @*local_table_variable* TABLE
	    (*table_definition*)
	AS
	BEGIN
	    tsql_statements
	    RETURN
	END

Use a scalar function	*owner_name.function_name*([*parameter_list*])
Use a function in an EXECUTE statement	EXECUTE @*return_variable* = *function_name*(*parameter_list*) or EXECUTE @*return_variable* = *function_name* @*parameter* = *value* [, @*parameter* = *value* [,...]]
Use a function as a computed column	*column_name* AS *function* The parameters must be either other columns or constants
Use a function as a column DEFAULT	*Column_name data_type* = *function* The parameters must be constants

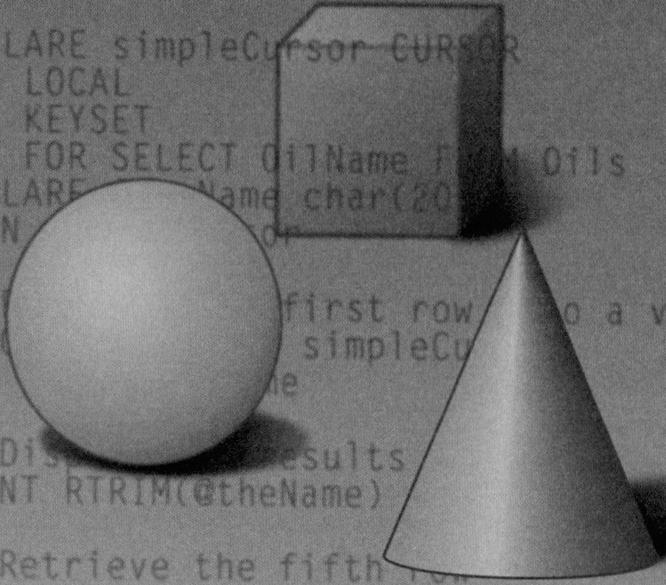

```
USE Aromatherapy
GO

DECLARE simpleCursor CURSOR
    LOCAL
    KEYSET
    FOR SELECT OilName FROM Oils
DECLARE @theName char(20)
OPEN simpleCursor

-- Fetch the first row into a variable
FETCH FIRST FROM simpleCursor
    INTO @theName

-- Display the results
PRINT RTRIM(@theName) + ' is the first name'

-- Retrieve the fifth row
FETCH ABSOLUTE 5 FROM simpleCursor
    INTO @theName

-- Display the results
PRINT RTRIM(@theName) + ' is the fifth name'

CLOSE simpleCursor
DEALLOCATE simpleCursor
```

Glossary

Aggregate function   A function that performs a calculation on a set of values and returns a single value.

Attribute   A specific item of information to be stored about an **entity**.

Authentication   A method of ensuring that only authorized individuals have access to data.

Authentication mode   The method by which Microsoft SQL Server authenticates user logins. *See also* **Windows Authentication.**

Backup   A copy of database objects taken as protection against system failure.

Batch   A group of one or more Transact-SQL statements. A batch is completed by the GO statement.

Binary operator   An operator that requires two values, for example, the + in the expression 4 + 3. *See also* **Unary operator**.

Boolean expression   An expression that evaluates to True or False.

Clustered index   An index that determines the physical ordering of rows within a table.

Composite index   An index that references multiple columns within a table.

Console Tree   The left-hand pane of the Enterprise Manager window, displaying the **Object tree**.

Cursor set   The set of records to which a cursor points.

Data integrity   The rules used by a database to ensure that the data is, if not correct, at least plausible.

Database   A set of tables, views, and other objects stored in a single file.

Default value   A value inserted into a column by SQL Server if the user does not provide it.

Defaults   Values assigned automatically by the system if the user does not provide them.

Determinism   The determinism of a function is determined by whether, given the same input values, it will always return the same result. *See also* **Deterministic** and **Non-deterministic**.

Deterministic   A function is deterministic if, given the same input values, it always returns the same result. *See also* **Determinism** and **Non-deterministic**.

Diagram   A graphic representation of tables in the **Database**.

Differential database backup   A **Backup** that records only the data that has changed since the last database backup.

Domain   The range of values from which a column can be drawn.

Domain integrity   The rules used by a database to determine the range of possible values for a column.

Entity   Something about which the system needs to store information.

Entity   An object in the **Problem space** being modeled by the database.

Firehose cursor   A forward-only, read-only cursor.

Foreign key   The unique identifier from the table on the one-side of a one-to-many or one-to-one relationship that is used to enforce the relationship.

Index   An internal database structure that allows quick access to a **Table**.

Inner join   A join between two tables that returns only those rows for which the **Join condition** returns TRUE.

Join condition   A logical expression used for determining which rows to return in a query.

Junction table   A **Table** used to resolve **Many-to-many** relationships by allowing a **One-to-many** relationship to be established between each entity.

Key constraint   The physical representation of a **Relationship**.

Log shipping   A method of automatically maintaining a backup server by constantly copying the transaction logs to the server.

Login ID   An account identifier that controls access to SQL Server.

Many-to-many relationship   A logical relationship in which many rows of a table are related to many rows in another. Many-to-many relationships are physically implemented using a **Junction table**.

Microsoft Management Console (MMC)   The administrative framework provided by Microsoft Windows that provides a common interface framework for administering server applications by way of **Snap-in**s. The SQL Server Enterprise Manager is the SQL Server MMC snap-in.

Non-deterministic   A function is non-deterministic if, given the same input values, it may return different results each time it is called. *See also* **Determinism** and **Deterministic**.

Object tree   The hierarchical list of objects known to Enterprise Manager that is displayed in the Console Tree.

One-to-many relationship   A logical relationship in which one row of a table is related to zero or more rows in another table.

One-to-one relationship   A logical relationship in which one row of a table is related to zero or one row in another table.

Outer join   A join between two tables that returns all the rows for one table and only those rows where the **Join condition** returns TRUE for the other table. A special case of an Outer Join is the *full outer join*, which returns all rows from both tables.

Parameter   A value passed in to a function, query, or stored procedure.

Positioned update   A special form of the UPDATE statement that uses a cursor to specify the row to be changed.

Precision   The maximum total number of decimal digits that can be stored, both to the left and right of the decimal point.

Primary key table   The controlling table in a **Relationship**.

Problem space   That part of the real world being modeled by a database.

Referential integrity   The integrity constraints that ensure that **Relationships** between entities remain valid.

Reflexive relationship   A **Relationship** in which a table is related to itself.

Relationship   An association between **Entities** in a database.

Roles   Groups of permissions used for security purposes.

Rules   A database object bound to a column or user-defined data type that specifies what data can be entered in that column.

Scale   The maximum number of decimal digits that can be stored to the right of a decimal point.

Schema   The structure and relationship of **Tables** in the **Database**.

Security principal   A User, Computer, or Group assigned an ID for security purposes.

Security role   Groups of users organized to ease security administration.

Sensitivity   An indication of whether a cursor reflects changes to the underlying data.

Server group   One or more servers grouped together to make administration more convenient.

Simple index   An index that references a single column within a table.

Snap-in   A set of administrative tools provided by a server application for use within the **Microsoft Management Console** framework.

SQL Server Authentication   A SQL Server **Authentication Mode** whereby SQL Server handles user authentication. *See also* **Windows Authentication.**

Statement   A combination of commands, functions, operators, and symbols that together comprise an operation to be performed by SQL Server.

Stored procedures   A set of Transact SQL commands that are executed as a batch.

System catalog   The information stored in the master database that controls the users and databases defined within the system.

System databases   Four databases (master, model, msdb, and tempdb) that are used by SQL Server to control the operation of the server and the user databases defined within it.

Table   A set of information organized into rows and columns.

Transaction log   A record of all the transactions that have been performed against the database since the transaction log was last backed up.

Transaction log   A physical file in which SQL Server stores all changes to the **database**.

Trusted connection   A connection to a server that is granted only if the person making the request has been validated by Windows 2000 or Microsoft Windows NT.

Unary operator   An operator that requires a single value, for example, the - in the expression -10. *See also* **Binary operator**.

Unique index   An index that ensures that rows containing duplicate values in the specified column or columns cannot be added to the table.

User-defined data types   A data type defined for the user for custom data storage.

User-defined functions   A set of Transact-SQL commands that accept parameters and return a result.

Users   Individuals identified to the system for security purposes.

Views   A virtual table that provides an alternative method of viewing the information in the database.

Windows Authentication   A SQL Server **Authentication mode** that allows Windows NT and Windows 2000 users to log in to a database transparently using their operating system user name and password. *See also* **SQL Server Authentication**.

Note: Italicized page references indicate figures, tables, or code listings.

Symbols

+ (addition operator), 499–500
= (assignment operator), 507–9
* (asterisk), 218
& (bitwise AND), 505
^ (bitwise exclusive OR), 505
~ (bitwise NOT), 505
| (bitwise OR), 505
[] (brackets, delimiting), 492
[] (brackets, wildcard), 249
/*..*/ (comment operators), 497
+ (concatenation operator), 227, 507–9
/ (division operator), 499–500
-- (double dash), 497
= (equal to operator), 501–2
(hash sign), 530
_ (underline), 248
@ (variable indicator), 611, 622
% (wildcard operator), 248

A

ABSOLUTE, 584–86, 595
absolute values, 513
Access Administrator role, 65
Access databases, importing, 378–88
access rights, 521
ADD, 455–56
adding. *See also* creating; inserting
    columns to tables, 97–107, 455–56
    columns using database diagrams,
        197–99, 203
    columns using Editor Pane, 432–34
    database objects to Editor Pane, 430–34, 440
    indexes from Execution Plan Pane, 476–78
    rows, 212–13, 215, 325–43
    rows to table-valued variables, 549–50, 552
    tables to database diagrams, 189–91,
        194–95, 202
    views to queries, 313, 322
addition operator (+), 499–500
administration, 19
    backing up databases, 20–29
    Database Maintenance Plan Wizard, 30–40

AFTER triggers, 624–25, 627–30, 635
aggregate functions, 289, 293, 516–18
alerts, 15
ALL keyword, 277–80, 282
Alter command, 435
altering. *See also* editing
    columns, 457
    constraints, 453
    objects, 451–59
    schema from Execution Plane Pane, 490
    views, 452–55
ALTER statements, 451–59, 470
    COLUMN, 452, 457–59
    DATABASE, 451
    DROP, 458
    FUNCTION, 451
    PROCEDURE, 451
    syntax, 451–52
    TABLE, 451–52, 455–57
    TRIGGER, 452
    VIEW, 452–55
AND, 254–56, 503–4
application names, function returning, 526
arc functions, 513
arithmetic operators, 498–500
ASC, 239
assignment operator (=), 507–9
asterisk (*), 218
attaching databases, 397–99, 406
attributes, physical implementation, 92
authentication
    login ID checking, 42
    mode selection for logins, 45–46
    SQL Server Authentication, 6–7, 10, 42–46
    Windows 98, 42
    Windows Authentication, 6–7, 10, 42, 45–46
AUTHORIZATION, 443
averages, 226, 346, 516
AVG, 516
    INSERT statement, with, 226
    UPDATE statement, with, 346

B

BACKUP command, 495
Backup Operator role, 65
backups, 20–29
    appending, 26
    BACKUP command, 495
    Backup Database command, 28
    Create Database Backup Wizard, 21–28
    database, choosing a, 23
    Database Maintenance Plan Wizard, 30–40
    destination, choosing a, 25, 36–37
    differential backups, 20
    full backups, 20
    media sets, 28
    operations disabled during, 20
    restoring, 29
    type of, choosing, 24, 34
    verification, 26–28
batches, 420
BEGIN ... END statements, 554
    within user-defined functions, 642, 646, 657
    with WHILE, 564–70
BETWEEN, 248, 250–51, 256
bigint, 93
binary, 94
binary operators, 496
binding defaults to columns, 172–74, 186
binding rules to columns, 179–81, 186
bit, 93
bit packing, 505
bitwise operators, 505–7
blocks, 554
Boolean expressions, 158
brackets, delimiting ([]), 492
brackets, wildcard ([]), 249
BREAK, 566–67, 570
Bulk Insert Administrators role, 49
BULK INSERT command, 494
business rules, using triggers to implement,
        623–24

C

calculated columns, creating, 226–30, 233
calling user-defined functions, 648–52, 657
cardinality, 496
cascading changes, 142
    deletes, 360–61, 369–72, 376
    enabling, 145
case, functions for converting, 524
CASE statements, 557–61, 570
CEILING, 513
changing database objects, 470. *See also* ALTER
        statements
char, 94
character columns, creating, 105–7
character data types, 106
CHECK, 452
check constraints, 157–58
    altering, 453
    Check Existing Data On Creation option, 160
    CREATE TABLE statements, 444–48
    creating, 158–61, 167
    deleting, 165–67
    modifying text, 161–63, 167
    Object Browser display of, 426
    renaming, 163–64, 167
    script commands for, 435
    temporary tables, 530
    triggers as alternatives, 624
clauses, Transact-SQL
    FROM (*see* FROM clause)
    GROUP BY (*see* GROUP BY clause)
    HAVING, 293–97
    TOP *n,* 231–33, 326, 346
    WHERE (*see* WHERE clauses)
Client Statistics Pane, 480–81
closing cursors, 579, 595
closure, 300
CLUSTERED, 444–45
clustered indexes, 116
Codd, E. F., 140
collapsing Console Tree items, 18
color coding in query window, 416
COLUMN, 452, 457–59
column aliases, 223–25, 233

columns
    adding, 97–107, 432–34, 455–56
    aliases, 223–25, 233
    altering, 452–53, 457
    binding defaults to, 172–74, 186
    binding rules to, 179–81, 186
    calculated, creating, 226–30, 233
    changing which are indexed, 133–35
    character, creating, 105–7
    choosing subsets of with SELECT statement,
        220–23, 233
    COLUMNS_UPDATE function, 632
    computed, altering, 452
    computing with user-defined functions,
        652–57
    constraints, altering, 453
    CREATE TABLE statement syntax, 443
    creating with key constraints, 444–48
    Criteria field, 246
    database diagrams, adding with, 197–99, 203
    data types, table of, 93–94
    date, creating, 103–5
    DEFAULT, altering, 453
    default objects, 170–74, 186
    default values, 107
    deleting, 109–10, 458–59
    descriptions, 98
    dropping, 458–59
    fixed-length, 106
    GROUP BY field, 290
    GUID, creating, 101–3
    identity, creating, 99–100
    image data type, 452
    indexed, 133–35, 453
    indexing, 120
    length, returning, 519
    managing, 107–10
    names, returning, 519
    ntext data type, 452
    numeric, creating, 97–99
    Object Browser display of, 426
    precision, 98–99
    PRIMARY KEY, altering, 453
    properties, returning, 519
    renaming, 107–9

columns, *continued*
    renaming for queries, 233
    replicated, altering, 452
    ROWGUIDCOL, 452
    scale, 99
    selecting all from a table, 218–20
    selection for views, 303
    Sort Type field, 238
    specifying, 259
    statistics, altering, 453
    text data type, 452
    timestamp data type, 452
    UPDATE function, 632–34
    user-defined data types, 182, 184–86
    variable-length, 106
COLUMNS_UPDATED function, 632
commands, menu
    Alter, 435
    Backup Database, 28
    Create, 435
    Delete, 435
    Drop, 435
    Execute, 435
    Exit, 18
    Insert, 435
    isqlw, 410
    Manage Index, 476–78, 490
    New Database, 78
    New Login, 43
    Replace Template Parameters, 466–67, 470
    Restore Database, 29
    Return All Rows, 218
    Return Top, 231
    Script, table of, 435
    Script Object To New Window As, 463
    Select, 435–37
    Show Client Statistics, 480–81
    Show Execution Plan, 475
    Show Server Trace, 479–80, 490
    Update, 435
commands, Transact-SQL
    ALTER (*see* ALTER statements)
    BACKUP, 495
    BULK INSERT, 494
    CREATE (*see* CREATE statements)

commands, Transact-SQL, *continued*
  Database Administration, 495
  DDL, table of, 494
  DEALLOCATE, 579–80
  DELETE (*see* DELETE statements)
  DENY, 495
  DML, table of, 494
  DML commands, table of, 494
  DROP (*see* DROP statements)
  FETCH, 580–89
  GO, 420
  GRANT, 495
  INSERT (*see* INSERT statements)
  KILL, 495
  RESTORE, 495
  REVOKE, 495
  SELECT (*see* SELECT statements)
  SET, 495
  SHUTDOWN, 495
  TRUNCATE TABLE, 372–76
  UPDATE (*see* UPDATE statements)
  UPDATE STATISTICS, 495
  USE, 494
comment operators (/*..*/), 497
comments, 497–98
Common Objects folder, 426
comparison operators, 245, 501–2
composite indexes, 116, 128–31
concatenation operator (+), 227
conditional execution, 554–61, 570
configuration variables, 544, 551–52
connections, number of, 544
Console Tree, 4
  collapsing items, 18
  database objects, 16–17
  expanding items in, 18
  system databases, 14–15
constraints. *See* check constraints
CONTINUE, 568–70
controlling execution, 553–70
  CASE statements, 557–61, 570
  conditional execution, 554–61, 570
  GOTO command, 562–64, 570
  IF ... ELSE statements, 554–57, 570
  labels, 562

controlling execution, 553–70, *continued*
  loops, 564–70
  WHILE loops, 564–70
Copy Database Wizard, 399–406
  additional objects to copy, 404
  destination selection, 402–3
  opening, 400
  source selection, 401–2
copying databases. *See* Copy Database Wizard
cosines, 513
cotangents, 513
COUNT, 289, 516
  GROUP BY field, 291
  HAVING clause, 294–97
  INSERT statement, with, 226
  UPDATE statement, with, 346
Create command, 435
Create Database Backup Wizard, 21–28
Create Database Diagram Wizard, 188–92
Create Database Wizard, 78–85
  location, setting, 80–82
  naming the database, 80
  sizing options, 83
  Wizard button, 78
Create Index Wizard
  choosing tables, 118–19
  field order, changing, 122
  including columns in indexes, 120
  naming indexes, 121
  properties of indexes, setting, 121
  starting, 116–18
Create Login Wizard, 43–51
  authentication mode selection, 45–46
  database access permissions, 48, 55
  login ID selection, 46–47
  password selection, 46–47
  role assignment, 47–48, 54
  starting, 44–45
  Windows account ID assignment, 53–54
CREATE statements, 470
  in BEGIN ... END blocks, 554
  columns, 443–48
  constraints, 444
  FUNCTION, 642–48, 657
  INDEX, 450–51

CREATE statements, *continued*
    PROCEDURE, 609–22
    scripting, 463–65
    syntax, 442–43
    TABLE, 443–48, 463–69
    temporary tables, 530, 552
    TRIGGER, 626–31, 637
    VIEW, 306, 443, 448–50
Create View Wizard, 300–306
    column selection, 303
    database selection, 302
    naming views, 305
    object selection, 302–3
    opening, 300–301
    WHERE clause, 304
creating
    character columns, 105–7
    check constraints, 158–61, 167
    column aliases, 223–25, 233
    composite indexes, 128–31
    cursors, 576–79, 595
    database diagrams, 188–92, 202
    database objects, 470
    databases, new, 77–85, 89
    date columns, 103–5
    defaults, 170–72, 186
    foreign key constraints, 447–48
    full outer joins, 280
    GROUP BY queries, 289–97
    GUID columns, 101–3
    identity columns, 99–100
    indexes, 116–31, 138, 450–51, 476–78
    inner joins, 260–68, 280
    joins, 259–80
    left outer joins, 269–75, 280
    logins, 43–51, 74
    numeric columns, 97–99
    objects, 442–51
    outer joins, 269–77, 280
    primary key constraints, 444–46
    primary key indexes, 122–24, 138
    relationships, 142–46, 155
    relationships in database diagrams, 201–3
    right outer joins, 276–77, 280
    rules, 176–79, 186

creating, *continued*
    scripts, 421–22, 440
    simple indexes, 125–28
    stored procedures, 609–22
    tables, 95–96, 463–65
    tables with database diagrams, 198–201, 203
    tables with key constraints, 444–48
    with templates, 466–69
    triggers, 626–31, 637
    unions, 277–80
    user-defined data types, 182–84, 186
    user-defined functions, 641–48, 657
    users, database, 61–62
    variables, 546–47, 552
    views, 300–309, 322, 448–50
criteria
    deleting selected rows with, 364, 376
    HAVING clause, 294–97
    updating rows using, 350–51
cursor, 94
@@CURSOR_ROWS, 592–95
cursors, 572–95
    ABSOLUTE, 584–86, 595
    API, 572
    client-side, 572
    closing, 577, 579, 595
    columns, selecting, 578
    creating, 576–79, 595
    @@CURSOR_ROWS, 592–95
    CURSOR_STATUS function, 592–95
    deallocating, 579–80, 595
    DECLARE CURSOR command, 572, 576–79
    defaults when creating, 577
    defined, 92
    deleting rows, 590, 595
    dynamic, 575–77
    FAST_FORWARD, 576–77
    FETCH command, 580–89, 592, 595
    fetching rows, 580–89
    @@FETCH_STATUS, 592–95
    firehose, 576, 588–89
    FIRST, 584–85
    FOR UPDATE clause, 577–78
    forward-only, 574, 577
    FORWARD_ONLY, 577

GLOBAL, 579
cursors, *continued*
keyset, 574–77
LAST, 584, 595
LOCAL, 579
lock parameter, 577–87
membership, 574–75
monitoring, 592–95
NEXT, 586–89, 595
opening, 579, 595
OPTIMISTIC, 578
overhead from, 582
PRIOR, 586, 595
read-only, 477–78, 574, 577
reflecting changes in data, 573–74
RELATIVE, 586–89, 595
scrolling, 574, 577
SCROLL keyword, 577
SCROLL_LOCKS, 577–78
SELECT command with, 572, 576
sensitivity, 573–74
server-side, 572
SET as variables, 578–79
sp_cursor_list, 600
SQL-92 syntax, 576
static, 574, 577
syntax, 577
with triggers, 576
type selection, 577
types of, 573–76
updating, allowing, 574, 577–78
updating rows, 590–91, 595
user-defined functions, using with, 649
variables, 578–80
visibility, 577
CURSOR_STATUS function, 592–95
CURSOR variables, 578–80, 595

D

DATABASE, 442
Database Administration commands, 495
Database Creators role, 49
database diagrams, 187–203
Arrange Tables button, 193
columns, adding, 197–99, 203

database diagrams, *continued*
creating, 188–92, 202
creating tables, 198–201
deleting tables from, 195–96, 203
detail level, changing, 192–94, 202
naming, 192
primary keys, setting, 200
rearranging, 192
relationships, creating, 201–3
saving changes, 197–98
schema maintenance with, 196–203
tables, adding, 189–91, 194–95. 202
Database folder, 14
Database Maintenance Plan Wizard, 30–40
backup plan, choosing, 34
destination of backups, choosing, 36–37
integrity checks, 30, 34
maintenance history log, 39
optimization information, 33
report generation, 38
schedule, setting, 35
starting, 32
transaction log option, 37–38
database object types, list of, 17
Database Owner role, 65
database roles
assigning, 61–64, 69–71
creating, 65–69, 74
deleting, 73–74
removing users, 71–74
databases
ALTER statement, 451
attaching, 397–99, 406
copying (*see* Copy Database Wizard)
deleting, 88
detaching, 396–97, 406
ID numbers, returning, 519
names, returning, 519
properties, returning, 519
renaming, 599
system, 15
database users. *See* users, database
Data Definition Administrator role, 65
data integrity, entity, 158

Data Reader role, 65
data retrieval. *See* queries
Data Transformation Services. *See* DTS (Data Transformation Services)
Data Transformation Services folder, 14
data types
    character, 106
    properties, returning, 519
    returned by user-defined functions, 640
    scalar, 543
    sql_variant, 543
    table of, 93–94
    user-defined (*see* user-defined data types)
    variables, 543
Data Writer role, 65
date columns, creating, 103–5
date functions, 510–12, 526
dates
    @@DATEFIRST variable, 544
    validity checks, 526
datetime data type, 94, 510
DAY function, 511
dBase databases, importing, 378
DDL (Data Definition Language), 441–42
    commands, table of, 494
    scripting from Object Browser, 463–65
deallocating cursors, 579–80, 595
decimal, 93
DECLARE CURSOR command, 572, 576–79
DECLARE statements, 543, 546–47, 552
default database files location, 80
DEFAULT keyword, 442
    defined by user-defined functions, 655–56
    INSERT statement, 326
    user-defined functions parameters, 648
defaults, 169–70, 186
    binding to columns, 172–74, 186
    creating, 170–72, 186
    unbinding, 174–75, 186
default values, column, 107
degrees, converting radians to, 513
Delete command, 435
deletes, cascading, 360–61, 369–72, 376
DELETE statements, 359–76, 590
    AFTER, 624–25, 627

DELETE statements, *continued*
    cascading deletes, 360–61, 369–72, 376
    creating in Grid Pane, 361–65
    editing in SQL Pane, 365–72
    FROM clause with, 360, 367–69, 376
    INSTEAD OF, 625–27
    JOIN operator, 360
    syntax, 360
    WHERE clause with, 360, 365–67, 371, 376
deleting. *See also* dropping
    check constraints, 165–67
    columns, 109–10, 458–59
    database objects, 470 (*see also* DROP statements)
    database roles, 73
    databases, 88
    indexes, 135–38, 482–83
    logins, 60–61
    relationships, 152–55
    rows, 359–76 (*see also* DELETE statements)
    rows using cursors, 590
    rows using FROM clause, 367–69, 376
    rows using WHERE clause, 365–67, 376
    selected rows, 361–65, 376
    tables, 112–13
    tables from database diagrams, 195–96, 203
    TRUNCATE TABLE statements, 373–76
    users, database, 63–64
    views, 320–22
delimiters, 492
denormalizing, user-defined functions for, 641
DENY, 495
Deny Data Reader role, 65
Deny Data Writer role, 65
dependencies of objects, viewing before deleting tables, 111–12
DESC, 239–40
detaching databases, 396–97, 406
Details Pane, 4
diagrams. *See* database diagrams
differential backups, 20
Disk Administrators role, 49
displaying. *See* viewing
DISTINCT keyword, 281–88, 297
    INSERT statement with, 226
    UPDATE statement with, 346

division operator (/), 499–500
DML (Data Manipulation Language), 441–42, 494
domains, column, 157–58. *See also* check
    constraints
double dash (--), 497
Drop command, 435
dropping
    columns, 458–59
    indexes, 460–61
    tables, 461–62
DROP statements, 458–62, 470
    COLUMN, 458–59
    INDEX, 460–61
    syntax, 459
    TABLE, 461–62
DTS (Data Transformation Services), 377–78
DTS Export Wizard, 388–96, 406
    destinations, choosing for data, 390
    formatting for destination, 393
    opening, 388–89
    selecting data sources, 389–91
DTS Import Wizard, 378–88, 406
    Column Mappings and Transformations
        dialog box, 384
    column size, setting, 385
    data source specification, 380–82
    destination, selecting, 382, 384
    DTS packages, saving as, 386
    OLE DB properties, setting, 382
    opening, 379
    queries within, 384
    tables, importing with, 378–88
    tables, selecting for copying, 383
dynamic cursors, 575–77

E

editing. *See also* altering
    check constraint text, 161–63, 167
    relationships, 146–49, 155
    rows, 210–11, 215
    Transact-SQL statements in Query Designer,
        219, 221
    views, 319–20, 322
ELSE, 554–57, 570

END, 554
    with BEGIN (*see* BEGIN ... END statements)
    with WHILE, 564–70
Enterprise Manager, 3–6
    capabilities, list of, 4
    Console Tree, 5, 6 (*see also* Console Tree)
    deleting tables, 112–13
    Details Pane, 5, 6
    exiting, 17–18
    importing data (*see* DTS Import Wizard)
    login management, 56–61
    Query Analyzer (*see* Query Analyzer)
    registration of SQL Server, 7–12
    renaming tables, 110–12
    renaming views, 318, 322
    starting, 4
    Table Designer (*see* Table Designer)
    views (*see* Create View Wizard; View
        Designer)
    wizards, selecting, 31
entities, implementation as tables, 92
entity integrity, 158
equal to operator (=), 501–2
@@ERROR, 619
error message strings, 620
Excel spreadsheets, importing, 378
exchanging data with stored procedures, 598–99
Execute command, 435
EXECUTE statements, 600–608, 622, 649
executing
    queries, 417–40, 472–78
    scripts, 425
    stored procedures, 600–608
    user-defined functions, 648, 657
execution, controlling. *See* controlling execution
Execution Plan Pane, 472–78, 490
    arrows, 474
    indexes, adding, 476–78
    row counts, 474
    statistics, showing, 473
    viewing plans, 474–76
Exit command, 18
exiting Enterprise Manager, 17–18
expanding items in Console Tree, 18

exponents of floating point values, 513
exporting data, 388–96
extended properties, 98

F

FALSE, 158, 501
FAST_FORWARD cursors, 576–77
FETCH command, 580–89, 592, 595
@@FETCH_STATUS, 592–95
firehose cursors, 576, 588–89
FIRST, 584–85
float, 93
FLOOR, 513
flow, control of. *See* controlling execution
FOREIGN KEY, 444, 447–48
foreign key constraints, 139, 447–48
foreign keys
    modifying fields, 148
    relationships, 142
    selecting fields, 145
    temporary tables with, 530
foreign key tables, 142, 360
FoxPro databases, importing, 378
FROM clause, 257–58
    DELETE statements with, 360, 367–69, 376
    GROUP BY clause, 289–97
    INNER JOIN, 264, 280
    LEFT OUTER JOIN, 269, 280
    RIGHT OUTER JOIN, 276, 280
    with SELECT statement, 218, 256
    syntax, 258
    UNION, 277–80
    UPDATE statement, with, 346, 355–58
full backups, 20
full outer joins, 269, 280
FUNCTION, 442
functions, 509–28
    aggregate, 516–18
    ALTER statement, 451
    CASE statements, 557–61, 570
    COLUMNS_UPDATED, 632
    complete list of, 510
    CURSOR_STATUS, 592–95
    date, 510–12, 526

functions, *continued*
    DAY, 511
    deterministic, 510
    drag-and-drop, 430
    GETDATE, 227, 230, 245, 511
    LEFT, 245, 247–48, 426–27, 437–39
    logical actions, 509
    mathematical, 513–16
    metadata, 519–21
    non-deterministic, 510
    NULL, 526
    Object Browser display of, 426
    parameters, 426–27
    script commands for, 435
    scripting, 437–40
    security, 521–23
    SIGN, 514
    string, 523–26
    system, 526–28
    time, 510–12
    user-defined (*see* user-defined functions)
    using, 510–12

G

GETDATE function, 227, 230, 245, 511
global variables, referencing, 642
GO command, 420
GOTO command, 562–64, 570
GRANT, 495
GROUP BY clause, 281, 289–97
    COUNT with, 289, 291
    creating, 289–92
    HAVING clause, 293–97
    INSERT statement, with, 226
    UPDATE statement, with, 346
groups, 521
growing the file, 86
growth percentage, setting, 86–87
GUID columns, 101–3

H

hash sign (#), 530
HAVING clause, 293–97

I

identity columns, 101–2
    creating, 99–100
    @@IDENTITY, 545
IF ... ELSE statements, 554–57, 570
image data type, 94, 452
importing
    databases, 379, 406 (*see also* DTS Import
        Wizard)
    tables, 378–88, 406
IN, 248, 251–52, 256
INDEX, 442, 460–61
indexes, 116
    adding from Execution Plan Pane, 476–78
    columns, changing, 133–35
    composite, creating, 128–31
    creating, 116–31, 138, 450–51
    creating with user-defined functions, 639
    deleting, 135–38, 482–83
    deterministic functions, 510
    displaying existing, 119
    dropping, 460–61
    DROP statements, 460–61
    field order, changing, 122
    Manage Index command, 476–78, 490
    metadata functions for, 519
    naming, 121
    Object Browser display of, 426
    primary key, creating, 122–24, 128
    renaming, 131–33
    script commands for, 435
    tuning, 482, 485–86
    unique, 127–28
    views, 300
Index Tuning Wizard, 482–90
Informix databases, importing, 378
inline user-defined functions, 644–46, 657
INNER JOIN, 264, 280
inner joins. *See* joins, inner, creating
Insert command, 435
inserting
    rows, 325–43
    rows in tables (*see* INSERT statements)
INSERT INTO statements, 543–44

INSERT statements, 325–43
    AFTER, 624–25, 627–30
    column list, 326
    columns, including all, 332–33
    creating rows in Grid Pane, 326–30
    DEFAULT keyword, 326, 334–35
    editing in SQL pane, 330–35, 341–43
    INSTEAD OF, 625–27, 630–31
    NULL, 334–35
    restrictions, 326
    rows, inserting multiple, 335–43
    rows, inserting specifying columns,
        326–35, 343
    SELECT statement with, 335–43
    syntax, 226
    VALUES, 326, 343
    with views, 326
INSTEAD OF triggers, 625–27, 630–31
int, 93
integrated security. *See* Windows Authentication
integrity checks, 30, 34
isqlw command, 410

J

jobs, 15
joining tables. *See* joins
JOIN operator in DELETE statements, 360
joins, 257
    adding tables to, 260–61, 265–66
    All Row option, 274
    conditions, 258
    creating, 259–80
    FROM clause, 257–58
    indexed views, 300
    inner, creating, 260–68, 280
    left outer, creating, 269–75, 280
    lines, selecting, 273
    multiple table, creating, 265–68, 280
    outer, creating, 269–77, 280
    Properties dialog box, displaying, 273–74
    right outer, creating, 276–77, 280
    specifying objects, 259
    syntax, 258
    unions, 277–80
junction tables, 141

K

keyset cursors, 574–77
keywords, 492. *See also* commands, Transact-SQL; reserved words, Transact-SQL
KILL, 495

L

labels, Transact-SQL, 562
language identifiers, 544
LAST, 584, 595
LEFT function, 245, 247–48, 426–27, 437–39
LEFT OUTER JOIN, 269, 280
left outer joins, 269–75, 280
LEN, 158, 179
length of string function, 524
LIKE, 248–50, 256
loading scripts, 423–25, 440
location of new databases, setting, 80–82
logarithmic functions, 514
logical operators, 503–4
login IDs, 42–43, 46–47
logins
    account ID assignment, 53–54
    Create Login Wizard, 43–56
    database access permissions, 48, 55, 59
    Login ID selection, 46–47
    password selection, 46–47
    properties, changing, 56–61
    removing, 60–61, 74
    role assignment, 47–48, 54, 58
    SQL server, 43–51
    Windows authentication, 51–56
log shipping, 30
loops, 564–70

M

maintaining referential integrity. *See* referential integrity, maintaining
maintenance
    integrity checks, 30, 34
    log shipping, 30, 38
    plans, viewing, 40
    statistics, database, 30, 33

Manage Index command, 476–78, 490
Management folder, 14
managing views, 317–22
many-to-many relationships, 140
master system database, 15
mathematical functions, 513–16
MAX, 516
media sets, 28
messages, displaying, 417–18
Messages tab. *See* Query Analyzer, Messages tab
metadata functions, 519–21
Metadata Services folder, 14
Microsoft Access databases, importing, 378–88
Microsoft Excel spreadsheets, importing, 378
Microsoft FoxPro databases, importing, 378
MIN, 516
MMC (Microsoft Management Console), 4
model system database, 15
modifying. *See* altering; editing
money, 93
MONTH, 511
moving databases. *See* Copy Database Wizard
msdb system database, 15
multistatement user-defined functions, 644, 646–48, 657

N

names, parsing, 526
naming
    database diagrams, 192
    databases, 80
    indexes, 121
    tables, 96
    transaction logs, 84
    variables, 543
    views, 305, 309
Nchar, 94
nesting stored procedures, 609
New button, 62
New Database command, 78
New Login command, 43
NEXT, 586–89, 595
NOCHECK, 452
non-clustered indexes, 116

NOT, 503
NOT BETWEEN, 251
ntext data type, 94, 452
NULL functions, 526
Null values, 101
numeric columns, creating, 97–99
nvarchar, 94

O

Object Browser, 425–34
  adding database objects to Editor Pane,
    430–34, 440
  Common Objects folder, 426–27
  DDL scripts, 470
  displaying objects in, 426
  drag-and-drop, 430
  folders in, 426
  Object tab, 426
  opening objects, 427–30, 440
  opening tables, 427–29, 440
  opening views, 429–30, 440
  scripting a SELECT statement, 435–37
  scripting DDL with, 463–65
  scripting objects from, 434–40
  Script Object To New Window As
    command, 463
  stored procedures, scripting from, 602
  templates, 466–69
objects
  altering, 451–59
  creating, 442–51
  metadata functions for, 519
  opening, 427–30, 440
  scripting from Object Browser, 434–40
  specifying, 259
object types, list of, 17
ODBC, importing data from, 378
OLE DB properties, setting, 382
ON, 258
one-to-many relationships, 140
opening
  cursors, 579, 595
  Enterprise Manager, 4
  objects, 427–30, 440

opening, *continued*
  scripts, 423–25, 440
  SQL Server, 13
  tables, 427–29, 440
  views, 429–30, 440
operators, 496–98
  arithmetic, 498–500
  bitwise, 505–7
  cardinality, 496
  comparison, 245, 501–2
  logical, 503–4
  precedence of, 496–97
  special, 248–52
optimizing. *See* performance
OR, 252–53, 256, 503
Oracle databases, importing, 378
ORDER BY, 236–44, 256
orphan rows, 360
outer joins. *See* joins, outer, creating

P

Paradox databases, importing, 378
parameters
  replacing in queries, 438
  of stored procedures, 598
passwords, 46–47
pausing SQL Server, 13
PERCENT, 231–33
performance
  client-side, 480–81, 490
  cursors, 582
  Index Tuning Wizard, 482–90
  optimization using Query Analyzer, 472–81
  schema, dependence on, 482
  triggers, 624
permissions, 67–69
physical files
  created per database, 77–78
  deleting, 88
  growing, 86
pi, 514
power function, 514
precedence of operators, 496–97
precision, 98–99

@ prefix, 542, 544
PRIMARY KEY, 444–46
primary key constraints, creating, 444–46
primary key fields, selecting, 144
primary key indexes, 116
    creating, 122–24, 138
    uniqueness of, 128
primary keys
    cascading changes, 142
    entity integrity, 158
    junction tables, 141
    reflexive relationships, 141
    relationships, 142
    setting in database diagrams, 200
primary key tables, 142, 144
PRINT statements, 556, 649–50
PRIOR, 586, 595
PROCEDURE, 443
procedures, ALTER statement, 451
Process Administrators role, 49
properties, database, 85–87, 89
Public role, 65

Q

queries. *See also* Query Analyzer; SELECT
    statements
    adding tables to, 260–61, 265–66
    aggregate functions, 289, 293
    comparison operators, 245–52
    editing (*see* Query Analyzer, query window)
    execution plans, 472–78, 490
    GROUP BY clause, 289–97
    indexed views, 300
    logical operators, 252–55
    repetitive data in, 282
    replacing parameters, 438
    row selection, 235
    selection criteria, setting in Query
      Designer, 214
    sorting, 235 (*see also* views)
    summarizing data, 281–97
    updating rows, 346–58
    views, including in, 311–16, 322
    wildcard operators, 248–49

Query Analyzer, 409–10
    adding database objects, 430–34, 440
    Clear Window button, 430
    color coding in, 416
    creating SQL statements, 416–18, 440
    creating tables with foreign key constraints,
      447–48
    creating tables with primary key constraints,
      444–46
    database selection, 413–15, 440
    displaying results in separate tabs, 418–20
    drag-and-drop, 430
    Editor Pane, 430–34, 440
    Editor tab, 422
    Execute Query button, 417, 440
    executing scripts, 425
    Execution Plan Pane, 472–78, 490
    Grids tab, 417
    indexes, creating, 450–51
    Index Tuning Wizard, 482–90
    Manage Index command, 476–78, 490
    Messages tab, 417–18, 608
    New Query button, 415
    Object Browser (*see* Object Browser)
    opening scripts, 423–25, 440
    opening tables, 427–29, 440
    opening views, 429–30, 440
    Options dialog box, 418–20
    performance optimization, 472–81
    query window, 415–18
    Replace Template Parameters command, 438,
      466–67, 470
    Run button, 440
    saving scripts, 421–22
    script commands, 434–40
    scripting a SELECT statement, 435–37
    scripting functions, 437–40
    scripts, creating, 421–22, 440
    Show Client Statistics command, 480–81
    Show Execution Plan command, 475
    Show Server Trace command, 479–80, 490
    starting, 410–13, 440
    tabbed display option, 416, 418–20
    templates, 426, 466–69
    toolbar, 413

Query Analyzer, *continued*
  Trace Pane, 479–80
  views, creating, 448–50
Query Designer, 207, 219, 221
  adding rows, 212–13, 215
  calculated columns, creating, 226–30, 233
  cascading deletes, 369–72
  Change Query Type button, 328, 337
  column aliases, creating, 223–25, 233
  comparison operators, 245–52
  Criteria field, 246
  Delete command, 363, 370
  deleting selected rows, 361–72, 376
  deleting using TRUNCATE TABLE, 373–76
  Diagram Pane, 213, 215
  DISTINCT keyword, 283–88
  editing rows, 210–11, 215
  editing statements, 219, 221
  Grid Pane, 214–15
  GROUP BY clause, 289–97
  HAVING clause, 294–96
  inner joins, creating, 259–68, 280
  Insert From command, 337–38
  inserting multiple rows, 340–43
  inserting rows, 326–40
  joining tables, 259
  logical operators, 252–56
  maximum number of rows, 209–10, 215
  outer joins, creating, 269–77, 280
  Properties dialog box, 286
  Results Pane, 213, 215
  Return All Rows command, 218
  selecting columns, 218–20, 222–23
  selection criteria, setting, 214
  SELECT statements, 217–18
  sorting rows, 214, 236–44
  SQL Pane, 214–15
  TOP *n* clause, 231–33
  Transact-SQL statements, 214
  unions, creating, 277–80
  Update command, 348
  updating rows, 346–58
  viewing rows, 208–10, 215
  views, 311–16, 322 (*see also* View Designer; views)
  WHERE clause, 245–56

R

radians, converting degrees to, 514
random number function, 514
real, 93
referential integrity
  maintaining, 142
  triggers for cascading, 624
reflexive relationships, 141
registering SQL Server, 7–12
Register SQL Server Wizard, 8–12
relations, 140
relationships, 139–42
  cascading changes, enabling, 145
  creating, 142–46, 155, 201–3
  database diagrams for creating, 201–3
  deleting, 152–55
  foreign keys, 139, 142
  junction tables, 141
  key fields, modifying, 148
  many-to-many, 140
  modifying, 146–49, 155
  one-to-many, 140
  one-to-one, 140
  orphan rows, 360
  primary keys, 142
  reflexive, 141
  renaming, 149–51, 155
  selection of key fields, 144–45
RELATIVE, 586–89, 595
removing. *See* deleting; dropping
renaming
  check constraints, 163–64, 167
  columns, 107–9
  databases, 599
  indexes, 131–33
  relationships, 149–51, 155
  tables, 110–12
  views, 317–18, 322
Replace Template Parameters command, 466–67, 470
replacing strings, 524
Replication folder, 14
reserved keywords, 492. *See also* commands, Transact-SQL

reserved words, Transact-SQL, 492
  ABSOLUTE, 584–86, 595
  ADD, 455–56
  AFTER, 624–30, 635
  ALL, 277–80, 282
  ALTER (*see* ALTER statements)
  AND, 254–56, 503–4
  ASC, 239
  AUTHORIZATION, 443
  AVG, 226, 346, 516
  BACKUP, 495
  BEGIN (*see* BEGIN ... END statements)
  BETWEEN, 248, 250–51, 256
  BREAK, 566–67, 570
  BULK, 494
  BY (*see* GROUP BY clause)
  CASE, 557–61, 570
  CEILING, 513
  CHECK, 452
  CLUSTERED, 444–45
  COLUMN, 452, 457–59
  COLUMNS_UPDATED, 632
  CONTINUE, 568–70
  COUNT, 289, 516
  CREATE (*see* CREATE statements)
  CURSOR, 572–95
  CURSOR_STATUS, 592–95
  DATABASE, 442
  DAY, 511
  DECLARE, 543, 546–47, 552
  DEFAULT (*see* DEFAULT keyword)
  DELETE (*see* DELETE statements)
  DENY, 495
  DESC, 239–40
  DISTINCT, 226, 281–88, 297, 346
  DROP, 458–62, 470
  ELSE, 554–57, 570
  END (*see* BEGIN ... END statements)
  FALSE, 158, 501
  FAST_FORWARD, 576–77
  FETCH, 580–89, 592, 595
  FIRST, 584–85
  FOREIGN KEY, 444, 447–48
  FROM (*see* FROM clause)
  FUNCTION, 442

reserved words, Transact-SQL, *continued*
  GETDATE, 227, 230, 245, 511
  GO, 420
  GOTO, 562–64, 570
  GRANT, 495
  GROUP (*see* GROUP BY clause)
  HAVING, 293–97
  IF, 554–57, 570
  IN, 248, 251–52, 256
  INDEX, 442, 460–61
  INNER, 264, 280
  INSERT (*see* INSERT statements)
  INSTEAD OF, 625–27, 630–31
  INTO, 543–44
  JOIN, 360 (*see also* joins)
  KILL, 495
  LAST, 584, 595
  LEFT, 245, 247–48, 426–27, 437–39
  LEN, 158, 179
  LIKE, 248–50, 256
  MAX, 516
  MIN, 516
  MONTH, 511
  NEXT, 586–89, 595
  NOCHECK, 452
  NOT, 503
  ON, 258
  OR, 252–53, 256, 503
  ORDER BY, 236–44, 256
  OUTER, 269, 276, 280
  PERCENT, 231–33
  PRIMARY KEY, 444–46
  PRINT, 556, 649–50
  PROCEDURE, 443
  RELATIVE, 586–89, 595
  RESTORE, 495
  RETURN, 619, 622, 626
  RETURNS, 442, 642, 644, 646, 657
  REVOKE, 495
  RIGHT, 276, 280
  ROWGUIDCOL, 452
  RULE, 443
  SCHEMA, 443
  SCROLL, 577
  SELECT (*see* SELECT statements)
  SET (*see* SET keyword)

reserved words, Transact-SQL, *continued*
    SHOWPLAN, 473
    SHUTDOWN, 495
    SIGN, 514
    STATISTICS, 443
    SUBSTRING, 524–25
    TABLE (*see* TABLE)
    TOP, 231–33, 326, 346
    TRIGGER, 443, 623–37
    TRUE, 158, 501
    TRUNCATE, 372–76
    UNION, 277–80, 326, 346
    UPDATE (*see* UPDATE statements)
    USE, 494
    VALUES, 326, 343
    VIEW, 306, 443, 448–50
    WHEN, 557–61, 570
    WHERE (*see* WHERE clauses)
    WHILE (*see* WHILE loops)
    YEAR, 511
RESTORE, 495
restoring backups, 29
Return All Rows command, 218
RETURNS, 442, 642, 644, 646, 657
RETURN statements
    stored procedures, 619, 622
    triggers, 626
Return Top command, 231
return values, 598–99
REVOKE, 495
RIGHT OUTER JOIN, 276, 280
right outer joins, 269, 276–77, 280
roles
    application, 67
    database (*see* database roles)
    IS_MEMBER, 521
    logins, assigning to, 47–48, 54, 58
    server, 47–49
    standard, 67
rounding function, 514
@@ROWCOUNT, 635
ROWGUIDCOL, 452
rows
    adding, 212–13, 215, 325–43 (*see also* INSERT
      statements)

rows, *continued*
    cascading deletes, 360–61, 369–72, 376
    criteria, updating using, 350–51
    deleting, 359–76 (*see also* DELETE
      statements)
    deleting using cursors, 590, 595
    deleting using TRUNCATE TABLE, 373–76
    duplicated by queries, eliminating, 281–88
    editing in Query Designer, 210–11, 215
    fetching from cursor sets, 580–89, 595
    inserting, 325–43 (*see also* INSERT
      statements)
    as instances of entities, 92
    multiple, inserting, 335–43
    number affected by statement, 545
    ORDER BY, 236–44, 256
    orphan, 360
    sorting, 236–44
    TOP *n* clause, 231–33
    unions of, 277–80
    updating, 346–58, 590–91, 595
    viewing, 208–10, 215
rowversion, 94
RULE, 443
rules
    binding to columns, 179–81, 186
    creating, 176–79, 186
    defined, 176
    in user-defined data types, 184
    variables, 176
running scripts, 425

S

saving
    scripts, 421–22
    table designs, 107
scalar data types, 543
scale, 99
scheduling database maintenance, 35
schema
    altering from Execution Plane Pane, 490
    diagrams (*see* database diagrams)
    maintenance with database diagrams,
      196–203

SCHEMA in CREATE statements, 443
Script Object To New Window As command, 463
scripts, 420–25, 440
    batches, 420
    commands, table of, 435
    CREATE statements, 463–65
    creating, 421–22, 440
    functions, 437–40
    GO command, 420
    LEFT function, 437–39
    object context menus for, 434
    opening, 423–25, 440
    running, 425
    saving, 421–22
    SELECT statements, 435–37
scrolling with cursors, 477, 574
SCROLL keyword, 577
searched CASE syntax, 558, 560–61, 570
security, 41–74
    authentication (*see* authentication)
    database level, 61–73
    functions, 521–23
    login IDs, 42–43, 46–47
    logins (*see* logins)
    permissions, 67–69
    roles (*see* roles)
Security Administrator (Database) role, 65
Security Administrators (Server) role, 49
Security folder, 14
Select command, 435–37
SELECT DISTINCT. *See* DISTINCT keyword
SELECT statements, 217–33
    all columns, 218–20
    ALL keyword, 282
    ASC, 239
    assigning values to variables, 548–49, 552
    * (asterisk), 218, 271–72
    calculated columns, creating, 226–30, 233
    choosing subsets of columns, 220–23, 233
    column aliases, creating, 223–25, 233
    with cursors, 572, 576
    DESC, 239–40
    DISTINCT keyword, 282–88, 297
    FROM (*see* FROM clause)
    GROUP BY clause, 289–97

SELECT statements, *continued*
    HAVING clause, 293–97
    inserting multiple rows with, 335–43
    ORDER BY, 236–44, 256
    PERCENT, 231–33
    Select command, creating with, 435–37
    storing as views (*see* views)
    syntax, 218
    temporary tables, 530, 532, 534
    TOP *n* clause, 231–33
    UNION, 277–80
    user-defined functions with, 649–52
    variables, assigning values to, 543
    views opened in View Designer, 310
    WHERE clause, 245–56
sensitivity of cursors, 573–74
Server Administrators role, 49
Server folder, 14
Server Group folder, 14
server roles. *See* roles, server
servers. *See also* SQL Server
    displaying information about, 551–52
    local, name of, 544, 551–52
    starting automatically, 413
    statistics on, 545
server traces, 479–80, 490
SET keyword, 495
    cursors as variables, 578–79
    @@OPTIONS, 544
    with UPDATE statement, 346, 353, 358
    variables, assigning values to, 543, 552
Setup Administrators role, 49
Show Client Statistics command, 480–81
Show Execution Plan command, 475
SHOWPLAN database option, 473
Show Server Trace command, 479–80, 490
SHUTDOWN, 495
SIDs (security identification numbers), 521
SIGN function, 514
simple indexes, 116, 125–28
sines, 514
smalldatetime, 94
smallint, 93
smallmoney, 93

sorting
    on multiple columns, 240–44
    in Query Designer, 214
    rows, 236–44
special operators, 248–52
specifying objects, 259
sp_ prefix, 599
sp_renamedb, 599
sp_settriggerorder, 625
SQL. *See also* Transact-SQL
    DDL (*see* DDL (Data Definition Language))
    DML (Data Manipulation Language),
        441–42, 494
    templates, 465–66
SQL Pane. *See* Query Designer, SQL Pane
SQL scripts. *See* scripts
SQL Server
    determining whether running, 13
    login security modes, 6
    objects, viewing, 13–14
    pausing, 13
    registering, 7–12
    starting, 13
    stopping, 13
    system databases, 14–15
    traffic light icon for, 13
SQL Server Authentication, 6–7, 10, 42–43,
        45–46
SQL Server Console Tree. *See* Console Tree
SQL statements, 492. *See also* statements,
        Transact-SQL
sql_variant data type, 94, 543
square roots, 514
squaring numbers, 514
standard deviations, 517
standard security. *See* SQL Server
        Authentication
starting
    Enterprise Manager, 4
    SQL Server, 13
statement blocks, 554
statements, Transact-SQL, 492
    ALTER (*see* ALTER statements)
    BEGIN ... END (*see* BEGIN ... END statements)
    + (concatenation operator), 227

statements, Transact-SQL, *continued*
    CREATE (*see* CREATE statements)
    CREATE VIEW, 306
    DELETE (*see* DELETE statements)
    EXECUTE, 600–608, 622, 649
    GETDATE function, 227, 230
    INSERT (*see* INSERT statements)
    PRINT, 556, 649–50
    RETURN, 619, 622, 626
    SELECT (*see* SELECT statements)
static cursors, 574, 577
statistical variables, 545
statistics
    database, 30
    viewing client, 480–81, 490
STATISTICS, 443
stopping SQL Server, 13
stored procedures, 597–622
    advantages, 598
    creating, 609–22
    DEFAULT parameter keyword, 603–4
    default values, 614–16
    dt_, 600
    exchanging data with, 598–99
    EXECUTE statements, 600–608, 622
    executing, 600–608, 622
    input parameters, 602–3, 612–14, 622
    named parameters, 603, 622
    naming parameters, 611
    nesting, 609
    Object Browser for, 602
    output parameters, 604–6, 616–19, 622
    parameters, 598, 601–5, 611–19, 622
    RETURN statements, 619, 622
    return values, 598–99, 606–8, 620–22
    script commands for, 435
    sp_, 599
    sp_cursor_list, 600
    sp_help, 600–601
    sp_helpdb, 600
    sp_settriggerorder, 625
    sp_who, 600
    system, 599–600
    system status, 600
    triggers (*see* triggers)

stored procedures, *continued*
    user-defined, 600, 609–22
    vs. user-defined functions, 639
    @ (variable indicator), 611, 622
storing transaction logs, 78, 82
string functions, 523–26
SUBSTRING, 524–25
summarizing data, 281–97
summing, 517
Support Services folder, 14
sysmessages table, 620
sysname data type, 466
System Administrators role, 49
system catalog, 15
system databases, 15
system functions, 526–28
system procedures, sp_addmessage, 620
system stored procedures, 599–600
System Tables folder, 426
system user names, 526
system variables, 545

T

TABLE, 443
    with ALTER statement, 455–57
    CREATE statements, 463–69
    DROP statements, 461–62
    temporary tables, 530
    variables, table-type, 543, 552
Table Designer
    adding columns to tables, 97–107
    assigning user-defined data types to columns, 184–86
    check constraints, creating, 158–61, 167
    columns, changing which are indexed, 133–35
    composite indexes, creating, 128–31
    Constraints button, 159
    creating tables, 95–96
    defaults, binding to columns, 172–74, 186
    deleting check constraints, 165–67
    deleting indexes, 135–37
    deleting relationships, 152–55
    indexes, creating, 122–31

Table Designer, *continued*
    modifying check constraint text, 161–63, 167
    modifying relationships, 146–49
    naming tables, 96
    primary key indexes, creating, 122–24
    Properties dialog box, 96
    relationships, creating, 142–46
    Relationships button, 143
    removing columns, 109–10
    renaming check constraints, 163–64, 167
    renaming columns, 107–9
    renaming indexes, 131–33
    renaming relationships, 149–51
    saving tables, 107
    simple indexes, creating, 125–28
    unbinding defaults, 174–75, 186
tables
    adding columns to, 97–107, 455–56
    adding rows to (*see* INSERT statements)
    adding to database diagrams, 189–91, 194–95, 202
    ALTER statement, 451–52
    columns (*see* columns)
    creating, 95–96, 463–65
    creating with database diagrams, 198–201, 203
    creating with foreign key constraints, 447–48
    defined, 92
    deleting, 112–13
    deleting from database diagrams, 195–96, 203
    dropping, 461–62
    exporting, 388–96
    foreign key, 142
    importing, 378–88, 406
    indexing (*see* indexes)
    joining (*see* joins)
    junction (*see* junction tables)
    managing, 107–13
    naming, 96
    Object Browser display of, 426
    opening, 427–29, 440
    primary key, 142
    renaming, 110–12
    rows in (*see* rows)
    script commands for, 435

tables, *continued*
  selecting all columns from, 218–20
  specifying, 259
  structure, altering, 554
  System Tables folder, 426
  templates, creating with, 466–69
  temporary (*see* temporary tables)
  user-defined functions for defining, 652–57
  User Tables folder, 426
  viewing rows (*see* rows, viewing)
table-valued user-defined functions, 640–41,
    644–48, 651–52, 657
table variables, 543, 549–50, 552
tangents, 514
tempdb system database, 15, 530
templates, 465–70
  Object Browser, 426
  parameters, 466
  tables, creating, 466–69
temporary tables, 530–42
  CREATE statements, 530, 552
  creating, 531–35
  error messages, 540
  expense of, 530
  foreign keys in, 530
  global, 531, 533–35
  # (hash sign), 530
  local, 530–33
  scope of, 530
  SELECT statements, 530, 532, 534
  using, 537–42
text data type, 94, 452
text files
  exporting data to, 388–96
  importing as data, 378
time functions, 510–12
timestamp data type, 452
tinyint, 93
TOP *n* clause, 231–33
  INSERT statement, with, 326
  UPDATE statement, with, 346
.tql, 466
transaction logs
  attaching, 397–99
  backups, 20–21

transaction logs, *continued*
  log shipping, 30
  naming, 84
  option in Database Maintenance Plan Wizard,
    37–38
  storage, 78, 82
  TRUNCATE TABLE statements, 372–73
Transact-SQL
  clauses (*see* clauses, Transact-SQL)
  commands (*see* commands, Transact-SQL)
  comments, 497–98
  control-of-flow statements (*see* controlling
    execution)
  Database Administration commands, 495
  DDL commands, table of, 494
  delimiters, 492
  DML commands, table of, 494
  editing (*see* Query Analyzer, query window)
  functions (*see* functions)
  labels, 562
  operators, 496–508
  Query Analyzer (*see* Query Analyzer)
  reserved keywords (*see* commands,
    Transact-SQL)
  reserved words (*see* reserved words,
    Transact-SQL)
  statement blocks, 554
  statements (*see* statements, Transact-SQL)
  templates, 465–66
  writing (*see* Query Analyzer)
transferring data. *See* exporting data; importing
TRIGGER, 443
triggers, 623–37
  advantages, 623–24
  AFTER, 624–25, 627–30
  ALTER statements, 452
  business rule implementation, 623–24
  calls, frequency of, 635
  cascading referential integrity with, 624
  CREATE statements, 626–31, 637
  creating, 626–31, 637
  with cursors, 576
  DELETE, 624–27, 634–36
  deleted tables, 634–36
  INSERT, 624–30, 634–35

triggers, *continued*
    inserted tables, 634–35
    INSTEAD OF, 625–27, 630–31, 635
    Object Browser display of, 426
    performance, 624
    restrictions on, 626–27
    RETURN statements with, 626
    @@ROWCOUNT, 635
    script commands for, 435
    syntax, 626
    UPDATE function, 632–34, 637
    views, 624–25
trigonometric functions, 513
TRUE, 158, 501
TRUNCATE TABLE statements, 372–76
trusted connections, 42

U

unbinding defaults, 174–75, 186
underline (_), 248
Unicode, 106, 524
UNION, 277–80
    INSERT statement, with, 326
    UPDATE statement, with, 346
unions, 277–80
uniqueidentifier, 94, 103, 526
unique indexes, 127–28
Update command, 435
UPDATE function, 632–34, 637
UPDATE statements, 345–58, 590–91
    AFTER, 624–25, 627–30
    creating in Grid Pane, 346–51
    editing in SQL Pane, 352–58
    FROM with, 346, 355–58
    INSTEAD OF, 625–27, 630–31
    restrictions on use, 346
    SET keyword with, 346, 353, 358
    STATISTICS, 495
    syntax, 345–46
    WHERE with, 346, 354, 358
updating data optimization information, 33
updating records. *See* UPDATE statements
updating rows, 346–58
USE command, 494

user-defined data types, 181–86
    columns, assigning to, 184–86
    creating, 182–84, 186
    rules, selecting, 184
user-defined functions, 639–57
    BEGIN...END statements, 642, 646, 657
    built–in, 648
    calling, 648–52, 657
    creating, 641–48, 657
    cursors, using with, 649
    data types returned, 640
    DEFAULT parameters, 648
    denormalizing with, 641
    determinism, 639–40
    executing, 648, 657
    inline, 644–46, 657
    limitations, 641–42
    multiple-statement, 644, 646–48, 657
    parameters, 642
    scalar, 640, 642–44, 649–51, 657
    SELECT statements with, 649–52
    side-effects, 641
    syntax, 642, 644, 646, 657
    table definitions with, 652–57
    table-valued, 640–41, 644–48, 651–52, 657
user interfaces, 207
user logins. *See* logins
user names, 63, 521, 526
users, database, 61–64
User Tables folder, 426

V

VALUES, 326, 343
varbinary, 94
varchar, 94
variables, 542–52
    @ prefix, 542, 544
    assigning values to, 543, 548–49, 552
    configuration, 544, 551–52
    CURSOR, 578–80
    data types, 543
    DECLARE statements, 543, 546–47, 552
    declaring, 546–47, 552
    fetching rows into, 582–84

variables, *continued*
  global, 542, 544, 551–52
  indicator (@), 611, 622
  local, 543–44
  naming, 543
  rule, 176
  statistical, 545
  system, 545
  table, 543, 549–50, 552
  table-type, 543
variants, metadata functions for, 519
variation, statistical, 517
versions, 544, 551–52
VIEW, 306, 443, 448–50
View Designer, 306–10, 319–20, 322
viewing
  client statistics, 480–81, 490
  dependencies of objects, 111–12
  execution plans, 474–76, 490
  maintenance plans, 40
  rows, 208–10, 215
  server traces, 479–80, 490
  SQL Server objects, 13–14
views, 299–322
  altering, 452–55
  ALTER statement, 452
  Create View Wizard, 300–306
  creating, 300–309, 322, 448–50
  deleting, 320–22
  editing, 319–20, 322
  including in queries, 311–16, 322
  indexed, 300
  INSERT statement with, 326
  INSTEAD OF triggers, 625
  managing, 317–22
  naming, 305, 309
  Object Browser display of, 426, 440
  opening, 429–30, 440
  renaming, 317–18, 322
  script commands for, 435
  SELECT statements, opened in View
    Designer, 310
  triggers, 624–25
  UPDATE statements with, 346
  using, 310–16
  View Designer, 306–9

W

WHEN, 557–61, 570
WHERE clauses, 245–56
  adding to views, 304
  AND, 254–56
  BETWEEN, 248, 250–51, 256
  comparison operators in, 501–2
  DELETE statements with, 360, 365–67,
    371, 376
  IN, 248, 251–52, 256
  LEFT, 245, 247–48
  LIKE, 248–50, 256
  NOT BETWEEN, 251
  OR, 252–53, 256
  row insertion using, 341, 343
  special operators, 248–52
  with UPDATE statement, 346, 354, 358
  updating using cursors, 590–91
WHILE loops, 564–70
  BREAK, 566–67, 570
  CONTINUE, 568–70
  simple, 564–66, 570
wildcard operator (%), 248–49
Windows 98 authentication, 42
Windows Authentication, 6–7, 10, 42, 45–46
wizards, 31
  Create Database Backup Wizard, 21–28
  Create Database Diagram Wizard, 188–92
  Create Database Wizard, 78–85
  Create Index Wizard, 116–22
  Create Login Wizard, 43–55
  Create View Wizard, 300–306
  Database Maintenance Plan Wizard, 30–40
  DTS Export Wizard, 388–96, 406
  DTS Import Wizard, 378–88, 406
  Index Tuning Wizard, 482–90
  Register SQL Server Wizard, 8–12

Y

YEAR, 511

About the Author

With almost 20 years experience in software design, Rebecca M. Riordan has earned an international reputation as an analyst, systems architect, and designer of database and work-support systems.

She works as an independent consultant, providing systems design and consulting expertise to an international client base. She was awarded MVP status by Microsoft in 1998 for her support in internet newsgroups.

Rebecca currently resides in New Mexico. She can be reached at rebeccar@attglobal.net.

The manuscript for this book was prepared and submitted to Microsoft Press in electronic form. Text files were prepared using Microsoft Word 97 for Windows 95. Pages were composed by Microsoft Press using Adobe PageMaker 6.52 for Windows, with text in Melior and display type in Frutiger Condensed. Composed pages were delivered to the printer as electronic prepress files.

Cover Designer
Girvin | Branding + Design

Cover Illustrator
Daman Studio

Interior Graphic Artist
Joel Panchot

Principal Compositor
Gina Cassill

Principal Proofreader/Copy Editor
Patricia Masserman

Indexer
Bill Meyers

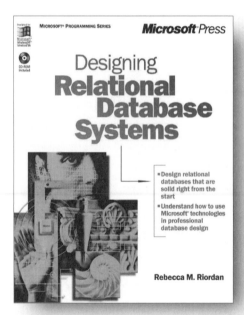

Learn to add a *new dimension* to your data with **analysis services!**

This title shows Microsoft® Excel and Access experts, IS managers, and database developers how to build applications that take advantage of the powerful data-analysis services in Microsoft SQL Server™ 2000. You'll discover why these services make it easier to analyze huge amounts of data quickly, and you'll learn how to develop a wide range of advanced dimensional-data applications—from enterprise reporting tools to advanced decision-support systems. The book's easy-to-follow lessons begin with clear objectives and include real-world business examples, with a companion CD full of sample files that support each lesson.

MICROSOFT LICENSE AGREEMENT

Book Companion CD

IMPORTANT—READ CAREFULLY: This Microsoft End-User License Agreement ("EULA") is a legal agreement between you (either an individual or an entity) and Microsoft Corporation for the Microsoft product identified above, which includes computer software and may include associated media, printed materials, and "online" or electronic documentation ("SOFTWARE PRODUCT"). Any component included within the SOFTWARE PRODUCT that is accompanied by a separate End-User License Agreement shall be governed by such agreement and not the terms set forth below. By installing, copying, or otherwise using the SOFTWARE PRODUCT, you agree to be bound by the terms of this EULA. If you do not agree to the terms of this EULA, you are not authorized to install, copy, or otherwise use the SOFTWARE PRODUCT; you may, however, return the SOFTWARE PRODUCT, along with all printed materials and other items that form a part of the Microsoft product that includes the SOFTWARE PRODUCT, to the place you obtained them for a full refund.

SOFTWARE PRODUCT LICENSE

The SOFTWARE PRODUCT is protected by United States copyright laws and international copyright treaties, as well as other intellectual property laws and treaties. The SOFTWARE PRODUCT is licensed, not sold.

1. GRANT OF LICENSE. This EULA grants you the following rights:

    a. Software Product. You may install and use one copy of the SOFTWARE PRODUCT on a single computer. The primary user of the computer on which the SOFTWARE PRODUCT is installed may make a second copy for his or her exclusive use on a portable computer.

    b. Storage/Network Use. You may also store or install a copy of the SOFTWARE PRODUCT on a storage device, such as a network server, used only to install or run the SOFTWARE PRODUCT on your other computers over an internal network; however, you must acquire and dedicate a license for each separate computer on which the SOFTWARE PRODUCT is installed or run from the storage device. A license for the SOFTWARE PRODUCT may not be shared or used concurrently on different computers.

    c. License Pak. If you have acquired this EULA in a Microsoft License Pak, you may make the number of additional copies of the computer software portion of the SOFTWARE PRODUCT authorized on the printed copy of this EULA, and you may use each copy in the manner specified above. You are also entitled to make a corresponding number of secondary copies for portable computer use as specified above.

    d. Sample Code. Solely with respect to portions, if any, of the SOFTWARE PRODUCT that are identified within the SOFTWARE PRODUCT as sample code (the "SAMPLE CODE"):

        i. Use and Modification. Microsoft grants you the right to use and modify the source code version of the SAMPLE CODE, *provided* you comply with subsection (d)(iii) below. You may not distribute the SAMPLE CODE, or any modified version of the SAMPLE CODE, in source code form.

        ii. Redistributable Files. Provided you comply with subsection (d)(iii) below, Microsoft grants you a nonexclusive, royalty-free right to reproduce and distribute the object code version of the SAMPLE CODE and of any modified SAMPLE CODE, other than SAMPLE CODE, or any modified version thereof, designated as not redistributable in the Readme file that forms a part of the SOFTWARE PRODUCT (the "Non-Redistributable Sample Code"). All SAMPLE CODE other than the Non-Redistributable Sample Code is collectively referred to as the "REDISTRIBUTABLES."

        iii. Redistribution Requirements. If you redistribute the REDISTRIBUTABLES, you agree to: (i) distribute the REDISTRIBUTABLES in object code form only in conjunction with and as a part of your software application product; (ii) not use Microsoft's name, logo, or trademarks to market your software application product; (iii) include a valid copyright notice on your software application product; (iv) indemnify, hold harmless, and defend Microsoft from and against any claims or lawsuits, including attorney's fees, that arise or result from the use or distribution of your software application product; and (v) not permit further distribution of the REDISTRIBUTABLES by your end user. Contact Microsoft for the applicable royalties due and other licensing terms for all other uses and/or distribution of the REDISTRIBUTABLES.

2. DESCRIPTION OF OTHER RIGHTS AND LIMITATIONS.

    • **Limitations on Reverse Engineering, Decompilation, and Disassembly.** You may not reverse engineer, decompile, or disassemble the SOFTWARE PRODUCT, except and only to the extent that such activity is expressly permitted by applicable law notwithstanding this limitation.

    • **Separation of Components.** The SOFTWARE PRODUCT is licensed as a single product. Its component parts may not be separated for use on more than one computer.

    • **Rental.** You may not rent, lease, or lend the SOFTWARE PRODUCT.

    • **Support Services.** Microsoft may, but is not obligated to, provide you with support services related to the SOFTWARE PRODUCT ("Support Services"). Use of Support Services is governed by the Microsoft policies and programs described in the user manual, in "online" documentation, and/or in other Microsoft-provided materials. Any supplemental software code provided to you as part of the Support Services shall be considered part of the SOFTWARE PRODUCT and subject to the terms and conditions of this EULA. With respect to technical information you provide to Microsoft as part of the Support Services, Microsoft may use such information for its business purposes, including for product support and development. Microsoft will not utilize such technical information in a form that personally identifies you.

- **Software Transfer.** You may permanently transfer all of your rights under this EULA, provided you retain no copies, you transfer all of the SOFTWARE PRODUCT (including all component parts, the media and printed materials, any upgrades, this EULA, and, if applicable, the Certificate of Authenticity), **and** the recipient agrees to the terms of this EULA.

- **Termination.** Without prejudice to any other rights, Microsoft may terminate this EULA if you fail to comply with the terms and conditions of this EULA. In such event, you must destroy all copies of the SOFTWARE PRODUCT and all of its component parts.

3. **COPYRIGHT.** All title and copyrights in and to the SOFTWARE PRODUCT (including but not limited to any images, photographs, animations, video, audio, music, text, SAMPLE CODE, REDISTRIBUTABLES, and "applets" incorporated into the SOFTWARE PRODUCT) and any copies of the SOFTWARE PRODUCT are owned by Microsoft or its suppliers. The SOFTWARE PRODUCT is protected by copyright laws and international treaty provisions. Therefore, you must treat the SOFTWARE PRODUCT like any other copyrighted material **except** that you may install the SOFTWARE PRODUCT on a single computer provided you keep the original solely for backup or archival purposes. You may not copy the printed materials accompanying the SOFTWARE PRODUCT.

4. **U.S. GOVERNMENT RESTRICTED RIGHTS.** The SOFTWARE PRODUCT and documentation are provided with RESTRICTED RIGHTS. Use, duplication, or disclosure by the Government is subject to restrictions as set forth in subparagraph (c)(1)(ii) of the Rights in Technical Data and Computer Software clause at DFARS 252.227-7013 or subparagraphs (c)(1) and (2) of the Commercial Computer Software—Restricted Rights at 48 CFR 52.227-19, as applicable. Manufacturer is Microsoft Corporation/One Microsoft Way/Redmond, WA 98052-6399.

5. **EXPORT RESTRICTIONS.** You agree that you will not export or re-export the SOFTWARE PRODUCT, any part thereof, or any process or service that is the direct product of the SOFTWARE PRODUCT (the foregoing collectively referred to as the "Restricted Components"), to any country, person, entity, or end user subject to U.S. export restrictions. You specifically agree not to export or re-export any of the Restricted Components (i) to any country to which the U.S. has embargoed or restricted the export of goods or services, which currently include, but are not necessarily limited to, Cuba, Iran, Iraq, Libya, North Korea, Sudan, and Syria, or to any national of any such country, wherever located, who intends to transmit or transport the Restricted Components back to such country; (ii) to any end user who you know or have reason to know will utilize the Restricted Components in the design, development, or production of nuclear, chemical, or biological weapons; or (iii) to any end user who has been prohibited from participating in U.S. export transactions by any federal agency of the U.S. government. You warrant and represent that neither the BXA nor any other U.S. federal agency has suspended, revoked, or denied your export privileges.

DISCLAIMER OF WARRANTY

NO WARRANTIES OR CONDITIONS. MICROSOFT EXPRESSLY DISCLAIMS ANY WARRANTY OR CONDITION FOR THE SOFTWARE PRODUCT. THE SOFTWARE PRODUCT AND ANY RELATED DOCUMENTATION ARE PROVIDED "AS IS" WITHOUT WARRANTY OR CONDITION OF ANY KIND, EITHER EXPRESS OR IMPLIED, INCLUDING, WITHOUT LIMITATION, THE IMPLIED WARRANTIES OF MERCHANTABILITY, FITNESS FOR A PARTICULAR PURPOSE, OR NONINFRINGEMENT. THE ENTIRE RISK ARISING OUT OF USE OR PERFORMANCE OF THE SOFTWARE PRODUCT REMAINS WITH YOU.

LIMITATION OF LIABILITY. TO THE MAXIMUM EXTENT PERMITTED BY APPLICABLE LAW, IN NO EVENT SHALL MICROSOFT OR ITS SUPPLIERS BE LIABLE FOR ANY SPECIAL, INCIDENTAL, INDIRECT, OR CONSEQUENTIAL DAMAGES WHATSOEVER (INCLUDING, WITHOUT LIMITATION, DAMAGES FOR LOSS OF BUSINESS PROFITS, BUSINESS INTERRUPTION, LOSS OF BUSINESS INFORMATION, OR ANY OTHER PECUNIARY LOSS) ARISING OUT OF THE USE OF OR INABILITY TO USE THE SOFTWARE PRODUCT OR THE PROVISION OF OR FAILURE TO PROVIDE SUPPORT SERVICES, EVEN IF MICROSOFT HAS BEEN ADVISED OF THE POSSIBILITY OF SUCH DAMAGES. IN ANY CASE, MICROSOFT'S ENTIRE LIABILITY UNDER ANY PROVISION OF THIS EULA SHALL BE LIMITED TO THE GREATER OF THE AMOUNT ACTUALLY PAID BY YOU FOR THE SOFTWARE PRODUCT OR US$5.00; PROVIDED, HOWEVER, IF YOU HAVE ENTERED INTO A MICROSOFT SUPPORT SERVICES AGREEMENT, MICROSOFT'S ENTIRE LIABILITY REGARDING SUPPORT SERVICES SHALL BE GOVERNED BY THE TERMS OF THAT AGREEMENT. BECAUSE SOME STATES AND JURISDICTIONS DO NOT ALLOW THE EXCLUSION OR LIMITATION OF LIABILITY, THE ABOVE LIMITATION MAY NOT APPLY TO YOU.

MISCELLANEOUS

This EULA is governed by the laws of the State of Washington USA, except and only to the extent that applicable law mandates governing law of a different jurisdiction.

Should you have any questions concerning this EULA, or if you desire to contact Microsoft for any reason, please contact the Microsoft subsidiary serving your country, or write: Microsoft Sales Information Center/One Microsoft Way/Redmond, WA 98052-6399.